Lecture Notes in Computer Science 8396

Commenced Publication in 1973
Founding and Former Series Editors:
Gerhard Goos, Juris Hartmanis, and Jan van Leeuwen

T0212843

Camille Salinesi   Inge van de Weerd (Eds.)

Requirements Engineering: Foundation for Software Quality

20th International Working Conference, REFSQ 2014
Essen, Germany, April 7-10, 2014
Proceedings

 Springer

Volume Editors

Camille Salinesi
Université Paris 1 Panthéon - Sorbonne, Centre Pierre Mendes France
90, rue de Tolbiac, 75634 Paris Cedex 13, France
E-mail: camille.salinesi@univ-paris1.fr

Inge van de Weerd
VU University Amsterdam, KIN Research Group
De Boelelaan 1105, 1081 HV Amsterdam, The Netherlands
E-mail: i.vande.weerd@vu.nl

ISSN 0302-9743   e-ISSN 1611-3349
ISBN 978-3-319-05842-9   e-ISBN 978-3-319-05843-6
DOI 10.1007/978-3-319-05843-6
Springer Cham Heidelberg New York Dordrecht London

Library of Congress Control Number: 2014933802

LNCS Sublibrary: SL 2 – Programming and Software Engineering

Typesetting: Camera-ready by author, data conversion by Scientific Publishing Services, Chennai, India

Printed on acid-free paper

Springer is part of Springer Science+Business Media (www.springer.com)

Preface

Requirements Engineering is a dominant factor that influences the quality of software, systems, and services. The REFSQ working conference series is well established as one of the leading international forums for discussing RE and its many relations to quality.

This year, 2014, we celebrate REFSQ's 20th anniversary. In 2006, REFSQ became a working conference and since 2010, it has been organized as a stand-alone event. However, REFSQ used to be a workshop associated with the CAiSE Conference. And really, everything started back in 1994, in Utrecht, 20 years ago.

Anyway, enough with history, the bottom line is: we are extremely pleased to present you the REFSQ 2014 proceedings that compiles 23 papers presented during the 8th and 10th of April 2014 in Essen, Germany.

This collection of papers results from a thorough reviewing process. 89 papers were initially submitted. After filtering out the papers that only submitted abstracts, we were left with 64 papers, of which 3 were desk rejected either because they were clearly out of scope or because they did not respect the authoring guidelines and formatting constraints. Three members of the Program Committee reviewed each paper. Then, a discussion was undertaken in order to check consistency of evaluations, enrich reviews, and search for a consensus on the final decision. Last, papers were discussed at the Program Committee meeting. Even though each paper was discussed for its own qualities and issues, the meeting helped reach a homogenous evaluation between all papers. 23 papers were finally selected. Authors of rejected papers were encouraged to submit their papers at the REFSQ workshops, or as a poster.

The REFSQ conference is organized as a three-day symposium with two days devoted to scientific papers presentation with a one-day industry track in-between. Both the industry and scientific presentations concern a variety of topics, which show the liveliness of the requirements engineering domain. These topics are for instance: scalability in RE, communication issues, compliance with law and regulations, RE for self adaptive systems, requirements traceability, new sources of requirements, domain specific RE, natural language issues, and of course games. 'Games for RE and RE for Games' was the special topic of REFSQ 2014. This was materialized by a plenary session at the conference, and by a keynote given by Catherine Rolland, a serious games expert and project manager at KTM Advance, a French company specialized in serious games. As Catherine showed in her keynote, games are a very specific kind of software, whose development involves very specific RE concerns from the special role of art directors in software game projects, to the theoretical foundations of ludicity, probably the most important requirement when it comes to games!

REFSQ is a collaborative effort. As program co-chairs, we would like to thank the Steering Committee, all the members of the Program Committee, and the organizing team, especially Roxana Klippert and Tobias Kaufmann who were invaluable in the organization of this conference. We also want to thank the industry track co-chairs Erik Kamsties and Martin, the poster session co-chairs Krzysztof Wnuk and Vincenzo Gervasi, the workshop co-chairs Birgit Penzenstadler and Anne Persson, the doctoral symposium co-chairs Daniel M. Berry and Roel Wieringa, and the empirical track co-chairs Jolita Ralyte and Xavier Franch. All the publications associated with the satellite events can be found in the REFSQ workshop proceedings published at CEUR.

We hope you will enjoy these proceedings and hope to see you soon at REFSQ where we will have the opportunity to discuss research results, but also ground breaking ideas as well as return on experience!

January 2014   Camille Salinesi
                                                                 Inge van de Weerd

Conference Organization

Programme Co-Chairs

Camille Salinesi   Université Paris 1 Panthéon - Sorbonne, France
Inge van de Weerd   VU University Amsterdam, The Netherlands

Organizing Team

Tobias Kaufmann   University of Duisburg-Essen, Germany
Stella Roxana Klippert   University of Duisburg-Essen, Germany

Secretary of the Organizing Team

Selda Saritas   University of Duisburg-Essen, Germany

Industry Track Co-Chairs

Erik Kamsties   Fachhochschule Dortmund, Germany
Martin Glinz   University of Zurich, Switzerland

Poster Session Co-Chairs

Krzysztof Wnuk   Lund University, Sweden
Vincenzo Gervasi   University of Pisa, Italy

Workshop Chairs

Birgit Penzenstadler   University of California at Irvine, USA
Anne Persson   University of Skövde, Sweden

Doctoral Symposium Co-Chairs

Daniel M. Berry   University of Waterloo, Canada
Roel Wieringa   University of Twente, The Netherlands

Empirical Track Co-Chairs

Jolita Ralyte	University of Geneva, Switzerland
Xavier Franch	Universitat Politècnica de Catalunya, Spain

Steering Committee

Daniel M. Berry	University of Waterloo, Canada
Samuel Fricker	Blekinge Institute of Technology, Sweden
Daniela Damian	University of Victoria, Canada
Joerg Doerr	Fraunhofer IESE, Germany
Andreas L. Opdahl	University of Bergen, Norway
Anne Persson	University of Skövde, Sweden
Klaus Pohl	University of Duisburg-Essen, Germany
Camille Salinesi	Université Paris 1 Panthéon - Sorbonne, France
Kurt Schneider	Leibniz Universität Hannover, Germany
Inge van de Weerd	VU University Amsterdam, The Netherlands
Roel Wieringa	University of Twente, The Netherlands

Program Committee

Benoit Baudry	Inria, France
Richard Berntsson Svensson	Department of Computer Science, Lund University, Sweden
Dan Berry	University of Waterloo, Canada
Travis Breaux	Carnegie Mellon University, USA
Sjaak Brinkkemper	Utrecht University, The Netherlands
David Callele	University of Saskatchewan, Canada
Jane Cleland-Huang	DePaul University, USA
Rolland Colette	Université Paris 1 Panthéon-Sorbonne, France
Daniela Damian	University of Victoria, Canada
Maya Daneva	University of Twente, The Neherlands
Joerg Doerr	Fraunhofer IESE, Germany
Eric Dubois	CRP Henri Tudor, Luxembourg
Sergio España	PROS Research Centre, Canada
Xavier Franch	Universitat Politècnica de Catalunya, Spain
Samuel Fricker	Blekinge Institute of Technology, Sweden
Donald Gause	Binghamton University, USA
Vincenzo Gervasi	University of Pisa, Italy
Martin Glinz	University of Zurich, Switzerland
Tony Gorschek	Blekinge Institute of Technology, Sweden
Olly Gotel	Independent Researcher, USA
Paul Gruenbacher	Johannes Kepler University Linz, Austria

Peter Haumer	IBM Rational, USA
Andrea Herrmann	Free Software Engineering Trainer, Germany
Patrick Heymans	University of Namur (FUNDP)/PReCISE Research Centre, Belgium
Jennifer Horkoff	DISI, University of Trento, Italy
Erik Kamsties	University of Applied Sciences and Arts Dortmund, Germany
Marjo Kauppinen	Aalto University, Finland
Eric Knauss	University of Victoria, Canada
Kim Lauenroth	Adesso AG, Germany
Soren Lauesen	IT University of Copenhagen, Denmark
Pericles Loucopoulos	Loughborough University, UK
Raimundas Matulevicius	University of Tartu, Estonia
Raul Mazo	Université Paris 1 Panthéon-Sorbonne, France
Isabelle Mirbel	I3S, France
John Mylopoulos	University of Toronto, Canada
Cornelius Ncube	Bournemouth University, UK
Andreas L Opdahl	University of Bergen, Norway
Barbara Paech	Universität Heidelberg, Germany
Oscar Pastor Lopez	Valencia, Spain
Anne Persson	University of Skövde, Sweden
Kai Petersen	Blekinge Institute of Technology/Ericsson AB, Sweden
Klaus Pohl	University of Duisburg-Essen, Germany
Jolita Ralyté	University of Geneva, Switzerland
Gil Regev	Ecole Polytechnique Fédérale de Lausanne, Switzerland
Bjorn Regnell	Lund University, Sweden
Kristian Sandahl	Linkoeping University, Sweden
Pete Sawyer	Lancaster University, UK
Kurt Schneider	Leibniz Universität Hannover, Germany
Norbert Seyff	University of Zurich, Switzerland
Guttorm Sindre	NTNU, Norway
Janis Stirna	Stockholm University, Sweden
Thorsten Weyer	University of Duisburg-Essen, Germany
Roel Wieringa	University of Twente, The Netherlands
Krzysztof Wnuk	Lund University, Sweden
Eric Yu	University of Toronto, Canada
Didar Zowghi	University of Technology, Sydney, Australia

Additional Reviewers

Bano, Muneera
Dalpiaz, Fabiano
de La Vara, Jose Luis
Hesse, Tom-Michael
Hübner, Paul
Knauss, Alessia
Maier, Andreas

Riegel, Norman
Sannier, Nicolas
Todoran, Irina
Villela, Karina
Vlaanderen, Kevin
Zorn-Pauli, Gabriele

Sponsors

Platinum Level Sponsors

Gold Level Sponsors

Silver Level Sponsors

Keynotes (Abstract)

Do Not Fear the Plumber

Catherine Rolland, KTM Advance, Serious Game Lab

Paris, France
catherine.rolland@ktm-advance.com

What do Tetris, World of Warcraft, Assasin's Creed and Fold It have in common? And what can they do for Requirements Engineering? They are all games, video games. Either created for fun or for more serious purposes, each of them has marked the history of the video game industry and illustrated the various uses one can have of it. If consumers have quite quickly been attracted by this engaging tool to the point of making it the first cultural good worldwide, its industry is still under development and the width of its potential not yet exploited.

A video game is a complex mix between informatics, graphical arts, technics and game design. Either made by one person or a team of more than 200 experts, the suc-cess of a game is still difficult to predict/determine. Numbers of methods and methodologies for its creation are being conceived, tested, adapted and a huge effort is done in order to industrialize its production. Influences from other areas where indus-trialization has long been proven and optimized can be of key value but challenges have still to be met in order to keep a space for creativity, design and playability in these processes.

With the infatuation of Serious Game and Serious Gaming, more and more illustra-tions of the use of games in very diverse areas are being described. Successful con-ception of adapted games, discovery of adequate use, concrete benefits' evaluation... are among the challenges still ahead for several domains. Nevertheless the game itself has proven its efficiency in enhancing the finding of new solutions. Thanks to the space of freedom the game offers, the player explores, he tries, fails and finally un-leashes his imagination. The conditions created by the game, encourage different thinking, which is key for innovation.

Table of Contents

Is Requirements Engineering Useless in Game Development?

Jussi Kasurinen, Andrey Maglyas, and Kari Smolander

Software Engineering and Information Management
Lappeenranta University of Technology, Finland
{jussi.kasurinen,andrey.maglyas,kari.smolander}@lut.fi

Abstract. **[Context/motivation]** Game development is characterized by a high level of creativity when compared to other fields of software development. Games cover a multitude of themes and genres, and represent a heterogeneous group of different products with varying requirements and business goals. **[Question/problem]** Requirements engineering (RE) should be relevant to game development, but is this true and if it is, how does game industry apply RE in practice? **[Principal ideas/Results]** We interviewed 27 software professionals in seven organizations to understand how requirements engineering is applied in game developing organizations. The results suggest that in game development business practicalities and drive for "fun" dominate the areas associated with requirements engineering. Additionally, game development organizations apply approaches and methods that are comparable to requirements engineering and requirement management, but do not consciously apply common RE practices. **[Contribution]** This paper extends our understanding of requirements engineering in video game development and contributes to the requirements engineering body of knowledge.

Keywords: game development, requirements engineering, requirements management, game design.

1   Introduction

The game industry is characterized by a high level of creativity and uncertainty [1]. Its products are directed at a mass public and they are developed for entertainment rather than for a clearly utilitarian purpose [2]. The game industry products include hits (successful and popular games) and misses (failed and unpopular games) [3] and its products differentiate horizontally, which means the creation of novel products without making them fundamentally different from other products [4]. Due to the creativity-oriented approach to the development and entertainment, the value of games and the role of requirements engineering in the game industry remain unclear. However, computer games have several features distinguishing them from other consumer products. The end products of other creative industries like fashion, music, and movies are unchangeable after the release or production, but games are similar to conventional software products that can evolve incrementally with updates. These updates may add

C. Salinesi and I. van de Weerd (Eds.): REFSQ 2014, LNCS 8396, pp. 1–16, 2014.

new characters, levels, and tools to the existing game and at the same time, extend the time a user spends playing the game. Nevertheless, the game evolution cycle is often based on the game company vision rather than on the requirements collected from the users. This raises a question whether the methods, tools, and practices of requirements engineering can be applied to game development, or are game products results of chaotic creativity.

In this paper, we aim to answer to the following research questions:

(i)   What is the role of requirements engineering in game development?
(ii) How does requirements engineering fit together with a high level of creativity and uncertainty of game development?
(iii) How do game companies develop prototypes of new games?

Our research team interviewed 27 game development professionals in seven game developing organizations to examine their game development processes and to understand how these organizations function. We were especially interested in understanding if requirements engineering methods were applied – or not - in game development processes.

The rest of the paper is structured as follows: Section 2 discusses related research. Section 3 introduces the research process, and Section 4 reports the results of the analysis. Section 5 discusses the results, their validity and applicability. Section 6 concludes the paper.

2   Related Research

Callele at al. studied requirements engineering in the video game industry and concluded that the success of games depends on solving the communication issues between stakeholders with technical and art backgrounds, the impact of previously developed games, integration between media and technology, and the impact of non-functional requirements [5]. The role of non-functional requirements like fun, aesthetic, look and feel is especially important in games but they are difficult to manage and trace [5].

Fun, or enjoyment, has been called as the main aim of computer games [6]. This relates to the intrinsic motivation to play games but other, extrinsic, motivators such as learning can be involved in playing as well [6]. In order to be attractive and played repeatedly, digital games should deal with the emotions of a player and, as a result, games include emotional requirements. These requirements can be managed using emotional terrain maps, emotional intensity maps, and emotion timelines [7].

Another attempt to apply requirements engineering in user experience design, so-called experience requirements, were done in order to provide a mechanism for game developers to predict impressions and experiences of a player. The idea was to allow companies to apply requirements engineering techniques early in the game development, but the complexities of using this technique were greater than anticipated [8].

The creation of games is also tightly coupled with iterations and prototyping. It is usual to create several prototypes in order to meet the requirements for fun and enjoyment [8]. Prototyping takes place in the preproduction stage in order to help the game designers to find the type of game they would like to create. Kanode and Haddad discuss that requirements engineering should take place at the end of the preproduction phase when the final game idea has been identified [9]. Other researchers argue that requirements engineering practices should be introduced to the game project at the earlier stage [7, 8]. In this regard, the place of requirements engineering in the process models of game development has not been confirmed yet.

A process model is defined as *"an abstract representation of a process architecture, design, or definition"* [10]. Its goal is to improve process understanding in order to facilitate human communication, process improvement, and management [10, 11]. There is a number of process models developed for managing requirements changes [12], project management [10], and others, but a process model viewpoint has not been widely studied in the game industry, which is assumed to be dominated by the waterfall model [9].

Overall, requirements engineering in the game industry has been periodically studied by researchers in order to bring "more engineering" into creativity. However, these practices are not widely used in companies mainly because of the creative side in game companies, including designers, artists, and producers who are against bringing strict engineering approaches into their day-to-day work [7]. Therefore, we conducted this study in order to understand the place, if this place exists, of requirements engineering in game development.

3   Research Method

The goal of this study was to understand and clarify how requirements engineering practices are used in game companies. It was designed as an interpretive qualitative study using the Grounded Theory research method. The Grounded Theory was chosen because it is suited well for discovering and analyzing the activities in companies within their social and organizational context [13].

Developed by Glaser and Strauss in 1967 as a pragmatic approach for conducting social science research [14], Grounded Theory is built upon two main concepts: *constant comparison* and *theoretical sampling* [15]. The idea of *constant comparison* is that every new piece of collected data is compared with other data to find similarities and differences. Therefore, data is collected and analyzed simultaneously. The concept of *theoretical sampling* represents an iterative process of theory building in which the next source of data, such as an interviewee, is selected based on the analysis of the previous samples [15].

In this study we follow the Strauss and Corbin version of grounded theory. This method relies on systematic codification and categorization process for observations [16]. It enabled us to study and understand the processes and underlying connections between different activities in a large context such as game development. The interpretation of the field study results was completed in accordance with principles derived from [17] and [18].

Table 1. Organizations participating in the study

Case	Organization size	Development team size	Release platform	Future platforms	Organizational maturity
A	Medium	Large	PC, Consoles	Handheld devices	>10 products
B	Small	Small	Handheld devices	PC	<5 products
C	Medium	Medium	Consoles, PC		>5 products
D	Small	Medium	Handheld devices		<5 products
E	Small	Small	Handheld devices		<5 products
F	Medium	Medium	PC		Making the first product
G	Small	Small	Browser-based		Making the first product

3.1   Data Collection

The initial set of companies for the interviews was selected from our research partners and then supplemented with other volunteering organizations. Our objective was to have a heterogeneous group of different target audiences, development platforms, and organizational histories. In total, we selected seven organizations representing small to medium-sized professional game developers to the sample. We applied the EU SME scale as the size measure for the companies [19]; less than 50 employees for a small organization, less than 200 for a medium and more than 200 for a large. However, since we also observed that the case organizations applied outsourcing and insourcing assets to a significant degree, we graded the development team and project sizes separately from the organizations. As it can be observed in Table 1, several case organizations (A, C and D) had larger projects than what the company size would have indicated. For example, Case A had less than one hundred own employees, but frequently developed products that had approximately three hundred contributors. In contrast, our smallest observed project had three developers and two outsourced artists.

We aimed to cover differences between organizations and therefore used the polar type selection to include cases from different target platforms and different sizes of development. Five of the seven were either recent business startups or new game development companies that have released less than five products. The other two companies were more experienced in product development and had released more than five products. The target release platforms also varied from different handheld devices (smartphones, tablets) to PCs and console systems (PlayStation, Xbox, etc.) and to browser-based games played online. Two of the seven interviewed organizations also reported that they would expand to new platforms in the future, Case A to handheld devices and Case B to PCs. All cases were commercial companies and game development was their main source of income.

The selection of interviewees was guided by our existing contacts in the studied organizations. The companies selected their most representative employees based on our short description of the interviewee roles (see Table 2). Overall, 27 interviews were conducted during the spring, summer, and fall of 2012 by seven researchers from two research laboratories. The interviews were grouped into four rounds. The goal of conducting several rounds was to gain a broader understanding of the game development practice and to identify the general factors affecting design and innovation in game development. The semi-structured interviews [20] were guided by questionnaires developed in advance by our research team. In total we developed four set of questions corresponding to the interview rounds and included questions related to development methods, quality requirements, and design processes. Before the first interview round the first set of questions was peer reviewed internally to check its sanity. Between the interview rounds some follow-up-questions were added to collect a richer data set. All of the sets of questions are available at http://www.it.lut.fi/project/SOCES/.

The interviews lasted approximately one hour and were recorded for further transcription and analysis. They were arranged with one or two participants from the case organizations with one or two researchers present.

The project managers were interviewed first to understand the software development practices in the studied companies. These interviews allowed us also to compare game companies with the observations and experiences we had from conventional software development companies [18]. The more technical second round of interviews was conducted with developers and testers. During these interviews we discussed software development and programming techniques, quality requirements, software development processes and tools. In the third round of interviews with the owners and the upper management representatives, we concentrated on the overall process of game development starting from the idea to its release to the market. During this round additional themes beyond the software development, such as marketing, innovation and financing, were collected to better understand the context in which the game industry operates. The last, fourth, round of interviews investigated the creativity aspects of game development. During this round we discussed the

Table 2. Interview rounds and their descriptions

Interview rounds	Interviewee	Description
Round 1: Qualitative interview with 7 organizations	Team leader or project manager	The interviewee is responsible for the management of the development of one product, or one phase of development for all products.
Round 2: Qualitative interview with 6 (+1*) organizations	Developer or tester	The interviewee was responsible for the development tasks, preferably also with the responsibilities of software testing activities.
Round 3: Qualitative interview with 7 organizations	Upper management or owner	The interviewee was from the upper management, or a business owner with an active role in the organization.
Round 4: Qualitative interview with 7 organizations	Lead designer or Art designer	The interviewee was a game designer, or managerial level person with the ability to affect the product design and selection of the implement features.

* Interview themes discussed during later rounds with other representatives of the organization

importance and impact of the creativity aspects to the final design of the developed product with game designers and managers.

3.2   Data Analysis

In grounded theory the fundamental process to analyze data and generate a theory is coding. The coding consists of three basic steps: open coding, axial coding, and selective coding [16]. Open coding is *"the interpretive process by which data are broken down analytically"* [15]. The goal of open coding is to understand what data really means, compare different pieces of data in order to find differences and similarities, and attach a conceptual label to each observation/phenomena/action. Then, the identified concepts are grouped together to form categories with subcategories, dimensions, and properties that represent a higher level of abstraction than the original data. Often the process starts with *seed categories* [33] that come from the goals of the study, the research questions, and predefined variables of interest. In this study, the selection of seed categories was guided by utilizing the concepts from research questions and included categories like *creativity, requirements engineering, game company,* and *game industry.* Overall, at the end of the open coding, we had 172 codes with 1547 observations, collected from over 1400 minutes of recordings from 27 interview sessions.

In axial coding relationships between the categories are established and tested against data. For example, the identified codes like *Design process: objectives, Test process: effect on product, Marketing: effect on product* formed a chain of evidence on how the organizations design their software, on what their actual objectives are and on what kind of impact different stakeholders and process activities have on the design work. In our data, these categories occurred repeatedly and therefore we were able to establish a connection "is related to" between them as in most organizations testing and marketing had a clear effect on the design process.

Selective coding aims at identification of the core category and relating it systematically to the other categories. The core category can be one of the existing categories or a new category that is broad enough to cover the central phenomenon and explain its relationships to other categories observed [16]. In this study, the core category was formed by abstracting the categories as none of the existing categories was considered influential enough to explain the entire phenomenon. Since the objective was to assess requirements engineering in game organizations, we collected a number of observations from business aspects, testing methods, development processes and general development process models to provide a chain of evidence. As the core category we selected an abstract category *"Requirements and change management in game development"*, which explains how requirements are handled, verified and validated during the game development process. By concentrating on this we were able to discuss the applicability of requirements engineering in game developing organizations.

4 Results

The data analysis uncovered seven categories which had relevance to requirements engineering, which led to four main observations on the applied RE activities. In addition, the analysis of how the organizations functioned gave us more insight into the existence and applicability of RE in the game industry. In the following we will introduce the categorized observations (summarized in Table 3), and then discuss the main findings. After this we introduce two stereotypical process models used in the studied organizations.

4.1 Categories

The category *Design objective* summarizes the objective that the organization has on the first design phase of a new product. We included this category to the analysis to understand the types of requirements needed to achieve these design objectives. *Marketable demo* means that the organization aims to design a version of the product, which can be used as marketing material for publishers or financiers. *Proof-of-concept* means that the organization designs and develops the first version which tests that the core features of the new product work as intended and that the concept is sound from the technological point of view.

The category *Design method* indicates the way the organization does the design work. *Vision* indicates that the organization has one or few people, who design the first version based on their initial idea. In these cases, the role of requirements engineering is limited to the vision of experts who decide what should be done. *Idea pitching* means that the organization has separate design and idea pitching events, from which the most promising candidates are examined further. *Prototypes* means that the organization starts with a very simple idea such as a theme and a genre, and examines with prototypes what sorts of functionality and content would work. *Brainstorming* indicates that the organization has design discussions in a group, trying to come up with new concepts for game products. Finally, *Drawings* means that the designers work by drawing out their ideas and by creating mock screenshots, concept art and such to give an idea on how the new product should look like. In all cases requirements were collected internally or externally through initial prototypes and collecting the feedback from their use.

The category *Changes between the first and published version* indicates roughly the amount of changes that typical game products go through from the first functional version to the final published product. *Large* indicates that there may be shifts in game genre, theme or that several core features might be added, dropped or changed during the development. *Small* indicates that the published games are mostly similar to the design version, with minimum changes on features, themes or game rules.

The category *Level of details in the first design* indicates the amount of details the organizations bring to their initial game design. *Functional prototype* indicates that the organizations design and build entirely functional proof-of-concept prototype with all the core features before starting to develop the actual product. The category *Basic gameplay elements* indicates that the organizations design most of the game content, but may not commit resources to develop anything functional such as a prototype. *Core features and concept art* means that the design consists only of core features, some early forms of rule sets and a decision on the artistic style of the game visuals.

The category *Testing on design* implies the amount of influence the testing activities in the organization have on the product design. *Large* implies that testing results may warrant large changes to the game, even dropping core features or major content or change in the genre or theme of the game. *Medium* indicates that the testing work can cause large changes to the game content and features, such as dropping content or making changes to the story, but that the main features more or less stay the same. *Small* indicates that the testing activities are mostly used to balance rules or game mechanics, and do not affect features or content to a large degree.

Similarly, *Marketing on design* indicates the power the marketing has on the product design. *High* indicates that the marketing team has the ability to dictate what sort of features the products need, change features of existing products and based on the feedback from publishers, what sort of games should be developed in the future. *Medium* indicates that the marketing team can dictate themes and core features of the games or, for example, affect the theme of the game or its visual style. *Low* means that the marketing team mostly suggests the changes that have little to no impact on the final product.

The category *Main testing objective in development* summarizes the objectives that the organization has in testing activities. *User experience* means that the organization tests the usability aspects and how "fun" the game product is to use. In terms of RE, it can be considered as collecting non-functional requirements from a target audience. As part of *usability experience, game mechanics* indicates that the testing is used to balance the internal game rules so that there are no always winning strategies. *Technical aspects* indicate that the company focuses on ensuring that everything functions technically correctly, models load correctly, effects are displayed, and that the game is stable. Minor and major issues identified during testing can lead to new functional requirements in the game engine and/or platform. In organizations where several goals are listed the goals are in the order of priority.

4.2   Findings

Finding 1: Game developers need to manage plans and product requirements, as the product may vary greatly between the first design and release.

In game development the first design may not be close to the final product. Cases A, C and F reported that there is usually a big difference in the product between the first design and the final product. In the other organizations the first design was more simplified and covered only the core features and concept art, which in many cases stayed relatively stable.

"Putting the core ideas in - that does not take that many months, but the final version always seems to take time. We have to change stuff, take things away, put new stuff in and keep doing so until everything works." – Case F, Upper management

Table 3. Categorized observations

	Case A	B	C	D	E	F	G
Design objective	Marketable demo	Proof-of-concept	Proof-of-concept	Marketable demo	Proof-of-concept	Marketable demo	Proof-of-concept
Design method	Idea pitching, prototypes, brainstorming	Vision, brain-storming	Vision, Idea pitch-ing, proto-types	Vision, drawings	Brainstorming, prototypes, drawings	Prototyping, Vision	Vision
Changes between the first and published design	Large	Small	Large	Small	Small	Large	Small
Level of details in the first design	Functional prototype	Basic gameplay elements	Functional prototype	Core features, concept art	Basic game-play elements	Core fea-tures, con-cept art	Basic gameplay elements
Testing on design	Large, able to affect fea-tures	Medium, able to affect features	Large, may cause major changes	Small, some changes possible	Large, may cause major changes	Large, may cause major changes	Large, able to affect features
Marketing on design	Low	High	Low	High	High	Medium	Medium
Main testing objective in development	User experi-ence, tech-nical aspects	User experience, technical aspects	Technical aspects, game mechanics, user expe-rience	Game mechanics, user expe-rience, technical aspects	Technical aspects, user experience	Technical aspects, Game mechanics	Game mechanics, technical aspects

"I'd say that they [first and published version] differ to some degree, but the basic idea stays the same, and the core design, is still the same." – Case B, Designer

"Our first functional prototype was quite close to the designs we had. Of course we had to make some changes during development, mostly from new ideas emerging during development." -Case E, Designer

In the game industry it is not common to collect requirements in advance. Instead, the approach of *test and tune* is widely used. The initial idea is generated and developed inside the game company and then it is tested on the target audience to identify what will be liked and what will not. However, the feedback from users is rarely systematically documented. Brainstorming, pitching, and drawing were the main instruments to get new insights on how the game should be further developed in the studied companies.

Finding 2: Game products can be changed significantly based on the feedback from marketing and testing.

In all case organizations, marketing and testing teams affected the design process to a large degree. In all organizations except in Case D, the testing phase had the possibility to affect the product design and change features in the product.

"No [the testing work] does not affect that much"..."Mostly the bigger things are decided and thought out on the early stages of development." – Case D, Manager

"You can design all for all the things you want, but the only way to know for sure [if the design works] is to test things with users." – Case E, Designer

"It [testing results] does affect and it should affect."..."Even in late stages, if we find out that something is [expletive], we do it again and again until it works." – Case C, Designer

However, the organizations which were doing large productions (Cases A and C) were also the only organizations to say that marketing has only small impact on their products. They were also the only organizations in which the design work was done to the degree of a marketable prototype, meaning that when the product is sold to the financiers or publishers, it is already relatively mature, fully designed package. In other organizations, the marketing had quite a large impact on the product design.

"We try to understand the pros and cons of our design, and assess the design from the financial point of view. After that concept design we make a proof-of-concept prototype to get the overall design"..."after the proof-of-concept prototype comes actual demo. What separates the demo and actual product is the amount of content." – Case C, Designer

"And then there is the business aspect. Obviously, [our games] have to make money." – Case B, Upper management

"The crude fact is that you have to make what sells, not what you necessarily personally like." – Case D, Upper management

"Even if our idea in business is to make great games, we still have to have enough financial perspective to get food on the table." – Case G, Designer

Finding 3: Requirement analysis is conducted mostly with user tests and usability testing.

In all examined cases, the organizations reported that testing had at least some effect on product features. In addition, all organizations except Cases F and G, one of the main test objectives was the user experience.

"Our testing is more like finding out if, for example, the controls feel appropriate. It is more like reacting to feedback [from user testing] than hunting down bugs." – Case E, Project manager

Based on these observations, organizations do requirements analysis in form of usability testing and assessment of their product features. Since the features of game products are usually associated with the user experience – "the fun factor"- analysis of the requirements is usually done with usability testing or user tests since the objective is to understand what the target demographic may want from the product.

"We sometimes make drastic changes because [the result is not considered fun]". –Case F, Designer

Finding 4: Game developers try to minimize the amount of functional requirements that should be implemented.

In Cases A, B, C, D and F the organization was using third party game engines instead of designing and implementing their own. In these organizations the decision was usually made to cut complexity and, from the viewpoint of game development, unnecessary work which could be outsourced. The technical solutions to problems such as physics modeling or 3d object manipulations were left to the third party. In this regard, these companies attempted to minimize efforts in managing functional requirements by using 3rd party components.

[Using engine] helps a lot; a game engine is a huge piece of software."..."People from our company may not have an answer, but somebody from another company may have come across the same problem, and can give the answer [via support service provided by the engine provider]". – Case F, Developer

"If I already have things available in the engine format, I just include them from our repository. Using existing resources leaves people free [to do other things]." – Case A, Developer

However, most of these organizations still had to do technical development. Cases E and G still have their own game engines, and Case B was recently using an own solution. In addition, Case organizations A, C, and F reported that they sometimes do extensive modifications to their third party game engines. In addition, all organizations reported that they test their product for technical aspects.

"I think that most important is that the game functions without crashing. Of course, the game content is also balanced..." Case C, Project manager

"Our leading principle is that nothing leaves the office unless QA lead has accepted it, whatever the reason." – Case A, Project manager

Based on these observations, we conclude that game companies try to minimize technical requirements in favor to non-functional ones, which are mostly related to usability and user experience. However, functional requirements cannot be fully avoided in the development of new games.

4.3　Process Models

The organizations were also asked to describe how their game development processes were organized. We used the models drawn according to these descriptions to assess how requirements engineering could be applied systematically in the game development context.

Based on the models made according to the descriptions, we divided the organizations into two groups. We call these stereotypical process models as development pipelines (cases A, B, C and D, Fig. 1A) and iterative models (cases E, F and G, Fig. 1B). The division between the two models is on the expected amount and role of iteration; in pipelines the expected model is that the product matures from one main phase to another with minimal iterations, whereas in the iterative model the development is expected to return to design and requirements gathering, and the development work is interlaced between multiple phases of design and testing.

The pipeline model is a straightforward waterfall-type approach to game development. The reason why organizations applied this method was that the design was developed to a functional prototype before the contract to develop a full game was sold (Cases A and C), or that the testing work had only a low influence on the product (Case D) or that the organization applied strict phases and deadlines in their development process (Case B). The common denominator in all these organizations was that the process minimized the need for testing requirements or changing features

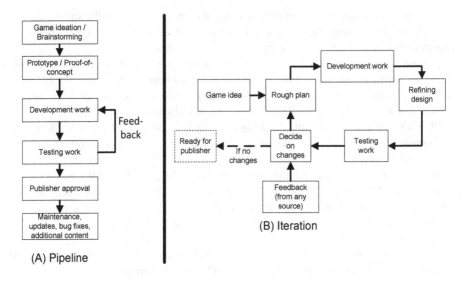

Fig. 1. Different development models adopted by organizations: pipeline approach (cases A, B, C and D) and iteration approach (cases E, F and G)

when the organization committed to the development work. In most cases this behavior was related to the business aspects: "real" development started only when there was a clear demand, at least partial return of investment was ensured and the amount of required effort was relatively well-known. Interestingly, all the pipeline processes, except for Case B, considered themselves to be agile organizations, applying variations of Scrum or a similar method in daily work, but in the bigger picture doing development work with a rather plan-driven approach.

The iterative model used by case organizations E, F and G starts with a less-than-complete plan, where existing features are tested and assessed periodically and if needs arise, are changed in the next iteration. These organizations apply collected feedback extensively during development and are willing to make major changes to their product. The decision to apply iterative approach can be explained with organizational experience: Cases F and G were developing their first commercial product and this approach allowed more control to steer the product towards the intended objectives. In Case E, the organization had good experiences with "user testing"-driven development; one of their earlier products underwent drastic changes after user tests discovered a new, well-received unintended feature from the product.

5   Discussion

The in-depth investigation of development processes and discussions with the professional game developers in the companies lead us to the conclusion that the organizations may not strictly apply requirements engineering principles, but they do have process activities which can be characterized as "requirements analysis" and "requirements identification." In most organizations the development process and applied process models were rather informal (only Cases A and C had assigned roles and documented process model), and the need to do these activities originated from the practical needs related to things like testing objectives or design methods.

The development of games often starts with an idea generated through brainstorming or pitching. In this phase, the elicitation of functional and non-functional requirements is rarely done, but the analysis of fun and enjoyment plays an important role [6, 7]. In the following phases, the role of requirements engineering is important for collecting and analyzing the requirements coming from testing the game design. Callele et. al. call these requirements as experience requirements [8]. In this study, we found that the decision about continuing or stopping the development of a game can be made based on the collected experience requirements. Some designs and ideas for products may simply be rejected after proof-of-concept studies. This was also the reason why game companies develop several prototypes that are not very different from each other, and test different approaches to the same problem with focus groups. They do this in order to find the well-received solutions to components such as user interfaces and internal game mechanics. In contrast to the high attention to non-functional requirements, game companies pay less attention to functional requirements and try to minimize them by using 3rd party engines and platforms. This is especially important for small companies like Cases B, D, E, G, which lack resources to develop, maintain, and support their own game platform. For large game companies the development of an own platform or engine is also a resource-consuming activity that has little chance to provide a competitive advantage to the company because most games differentiate horizontally [4] and therefore a new product platform can rarely be fundamentally different from the existing ones.

Game development is an area where engineering meets creativity [8]. In our study, the game companies generated new game ideas mainly in-house. However, as soon as the idea is identified and the game design documents are created, most of the process deals with engineering rather than with creative activities like brainstorming new characters, levels, or story canvases. In this regard, our results are similar to the viewpoint of Kanode and Haddad who said that RE should be used when the game idea is identified and agreed to be implemented [9]. It seems to be difficult to adopt engineering practices like RE at the earlier stage as suggested by [7, 8], because it is common to generate tens of ideas initially but a few of them will be considered for detailed evaluation and implementation. Overall, in this study we did not observe a conflict between creative and engineering activities. Instead, these activities supported each other at different stages of the development cycle.

As a result of our attempt to get a deep understanding of the game development process, we sketched out two stereotypical process models of game development. We called these two models pipeline-type and iterative-type processes. The pipeline-type process in the game industry, or waterfall model [9], was already identified previously. This process is suitable for mature companies that do not heavily rely on testing their prototypes with end users and mainly produce games in-house without constant collaboration and communication with the market they aim at. This process in the game industry is very similar to the waterfall model used for development of other software products and therefore RE practices can be used in the same way, before starting developing a prototype or a proof-of-concept. The iterative-type process model relies on the feedback from customers and the role of the feedback is critical for making decisions about continuing, releasing, or withdrawing a game. In this type of process there are no predetermined requirements in the beginning, but as the feedback is collected and analyzed, new requirements are introduced into the developed game. However, the feedback is rarely documented systematically and in the form of requirements. More often they are managed informally by changing directly the source code and testing a newer version again. In this regard, we see that there are benefits in a more formal approach to managing requirements in the iterative-type process model as it could help to decrease the number of iterations needed before the game release.

There are several threats to the validity of this study as for any qualitative study [21]. The collected observations, findings, and process models are dynamic rather than static [15] meaning that the collected data could be extended by collecting and analyzing more data. However, already this set of data that includes game companies of different size, working with different game platforms, and aiming at different markets enabled us to identify the variety of approaches to the adoption of RE practices in the game industry. Our purpose was not to describe all possible ways to adopt RE in game companies. Instead, our aim was to understand if RE has its own place in game development or if it is obsolete for the industry that is dominated by insights, ideas, fun, and enjoyment. The study has also a territorial bias as we interviewed game companies in Finland only. However, due to the size of Finnish market, these companies all aim at the international market, which decreases this bias.

6   Conclusion

Game developing organizations do not significantly differ from other organizations that develop software products. However, the focus on non-functional requirements and quality assurance with user testing has an impact on how game organizations operate: the game developers apply mostly informal processes, with two stereotypical approaches which in this paper were identified as waterfall-like pipeline model and iteration approach which basically is a prototype-driven incremental development model. As for findings, the game developers do need requirements management, as the products may have significant differences between the first prototypes and the final product, based on customer and market feedback. Nevertheless, RE practices are not widely adopted by game organizations. In addition, many game developers try to minimize the amount of implemented functional requirements simply by insourcing the technically challenging parts from the development process. This little focus on managing non-functional requirements and outsourcing of functional requirements lead to the situation when RE practices have not been adopted by game organizations consciously but they do apply concepts from requirements engineering, especially requirements identification and requirement management and manage risks caused by the non-functional requirements with constant prototyping and user testing. Overall with this evidence it can be argued that requirements engineering needs to be adopted by game organizations more systematically because RE methods do not contradict with creativity, but support it and provide solutions to dealing with game development in the turbulent market environment.

Acknowledgement. This study was supported by the European Union Regional Development Fund projects A31814, "Kaakon Peliklusteri" and A32139 "Game Cluster". A part of the funding came also from the Academy of Finland grant #259454. We would also like to thank InnoVire research group at LUT Kouvola for their cooperation.

References

1. Tschang, T.: When Does an Idea Become an Innovation? The Role of Individual and Group Creativity in Videogame Design. Presented at the DRUID Conference (2003)
2. Hirsch, P.M.: Processing Fads and Fashions: An Organization-Set Analysis of Cultural Industry Systems. American Journal of Sociology 77, 639–659 (1972)
3. Lampel, J., Shamsie, J.: Critical Push: Strategies for Creating Momentum in the Motion Picture Industry. Journal of Management 26, 233–257 (2000)
4. Lampel, J., Lant, T., Shamsie, J.: Balancing Act: Learning from Organizing Practices in Cultural Industries. Organization Science 11, 263–269 (2000)
5. Callele, D., Neufeld, E., Schneider, K.: Requirements engineering and the creative process in the video game industry. In: 13th IEEE International Conference on Requirements Engineering, pp. 240–250 (2005)
6. Draper, S.W.: Analysing fun as a candidate software requirement. Personal Technologies 3, 117–122 (1999)
7. Callele, D., Neufeld, E., Schneider, K.: Emotional Requirements in Video Games. In: 14th IEEE International Conference on Requirements Engineering, pp. 299–302. IEEE (2006)
8. Callele, D., Neufeld, E., Schneider, K.: An Introduction to Experience Requirements. In: 18th IEEE International Conference on Requirements Engineering, pp. 395–396 (2010)
9. Kanode, C.M., Haddad, H.M.: Software Engineering Challenges in Game Development. In: 6th International Conference on Information Technology: New Generations, pp. 260–265. IEEE Computer Society, Washington, DC (2009)
10. Feiler, P.H., Humphrey, W.S.: Software process development and enactment: concepts and definitions. In: 2nd International Conference on the Continuous Software Process Improvement, pp. 28–40 (1993)
11. Curtis, B., Kellner, M.I., Over, J.: Process modeling. Communications of the ACM 35, 75–90 (1992)
12. Harjani, D.-R., Queille, J.-P.: A process model for the maintenance of large space systems software. Presented at the The International Conference on Software Maintenance (1992)
13. Charmaz, K.: Constructing Grounded Theory: A Practical Guide through Qualitative Analysis. Sage Publications (2010)
14. Suddaby, R.: From the Editors: What Grounded Theory is Not. Academy of Management Journal 49, 633–642 (2006)
15. Corbin, J., Strauss, A.: Grounded Theory Research: Procedures, Canons, and Evaluative Criteria. Qualitative Sociology 13, 3–21 (1990)
16. Strauss, A., Corbin, J.: Basics of Qualitative Research: Techniques and Procedures for Developing Grounded Theory. SAGE Publications (2008)

17. Paré, G., Elam, J.J.: Using case study research to build theories of IT implementation. Presented at the International Conference on Information Systems and Qualitative Research, London, UK (1997)
18. Kasurinen, J., Taipale, O., Vanhanen, J., Smolander, K.: Exploring perceived quality in software organizations. In: 5th International Conference on Research Challenges in Information Science (RCIS), pp. 1–12 (2011)
19. The commission of the European Communities: Commission recommendation concerning the definition of micro, small and medium-sized enterprises (2003)
20. Robson, C.: Real World Research - A Resource for Social Scientists and Practitioner-Researchers. Blackwell Publishing, Malden (2002)
21. Onwuegbuzie, A.J., Leech, N.L.: Validity and Qualitative Research: An Oxymoron? Quality & Quantity 41, 233–249 (2006)

Towards Model-Driven Requirements Engineering for Serious Educational Games: Informal, Semi-formal, and Formal Models

Kendra M.L. Cooper[1,*], Eman S. Nasr[2], C. Shaun Longstreet[3]

[1] The University of Texas at Dallas, Richardson, U.S.A.
kendra.m.cooper@gmail.com
[2] Independent Researcher, Cairo, Egypt
nasr.eman.s@gmail.com
[3] Marquette University, Wisconsin, U.S.A.
christopher.longstreet@marquette.edu

Abstract. Serious educational games (SEGs) are receiving significant attention, as they provide immersive, engaging learning environments with a rigourous pedagogical foundation. SEG engineering requires an interdisciplinary approach involving game developers, educators, and software engineers. The requirements engineering (RE) community has substantial expertise in processes, notations, tools, and techniques. Here, we explore how can we tailor and adopt this expertise for developing SEGs with a three step model-based approach that integrates established techniques: create an informal model of the SEG requirements (narrative captured like a storyboard); transform the narrative into a semi-formal, tailored UML use case model (visual and tabular, using templates); transform the semi-formal model into formal models for testing and verification. A collection of SEGs (test games) has been created using the process; currently the transformations are performed manually. The formal model is represented in XML, which can be loaded, played, and tested in the game engine. In the future, we will explore semi-automatically transforming the models and creating Statechart models, which can be verified using simulations.

Keywords: requirements engineering, serious educational games, model-driven.

1   Introduction

Serious educational games (SEGs) have significant pedagogical potential as they provide immersive, engaging and fun environments that require deep thinking and complex problem solving within a construct of overcoming obstacles and challenges [1]. They create interactive student-centered environments rather than a passive content-centered classroom environment. SEGs are complex applications, requiring expertise from multiple disciplines including game development, education, and software engineering. Established game development approaches are document-centric, often using a pre-production game design document and production game software

C. Salinesi and I. van de Weerd (Eds.): REFSQ 2014, LNCS 8396, pp. 17–22, 2014.
© Springer International Publishing Switzerland 2014

requirements specification [2]. Recently, the potential value using model-driven engineering (MDE) [3] approaches for games [4] and more specifically to SEGs [5] has been presented. UML-based game specifications have also been considered that focus on tailoring Statecharts [6]; they offer a rigorous, state machine foundation, but may be more difficult for some stakeholders (e.g., game designers) to use. Game designers with experience using Storyboards [7], for example, may find a tabular use case (UC) specification format quite familiar, as Storyboards are often presented as a sequence of cells in a tabular format. Tabular specifications are well-established [8]; they are considered straightforward to define, understand, and maintain.

To improve the development of SEGs, our research project, SimSYS, is underway. SimSYS is a MDE approach that uniquely integrates elements of traditional game design, pedagogical content, and software engineering methodologies. Our proposed approach has three main steps: create an informal model of the SEG requirements (captured like a storyboard with textual descriptions of the learning objectives and game play in addition to user interface concepts e.g., graphics, audio); transform the informal model into a semi-formal tailored UML UC model (visual and tabular, template based specifications) [9]; transform the semi-formal model into formal, executable models (Statechart for comprehensive simulation and XML [10], which can be loaded and played in the game engine). Our approach adopts and tailors well-established solutions (e.g., Storyboards, UML UC, XML, Statecharts) as the need for a completely new solution is not evident at this time. Our MDE-based approach can be applied in an agile, iterative development process, for example, by describing a part of the game and allowing earlier assessment and feedback. Learning objectives, for both topic specific subject matter and transferable skills, are thoroughly integrated.

In previous work, we have presented an underlying meta-model for SimSYS [11] and preliminary work on the models, with a focus on the semi-formal, tabular templates [12]. The meta-model facilitates the development of high-quality, engaging, educational games because it explicitly ties knowledge requirements, transferable skills and course outcomes to game production. The templates, which embody the meta-model concepts, help to systematically and efficiently structure SimSYS games into Acts, Scenes, Screens, and Challenges.

Here, we present initial results on our proposed three step approach to create and refine informal, semi-formal, and formal (XML, Statechart) models. The validation uses an internally defined collection of simple test games, which currently has six symbolic games, an algebra game for grade four students, and a software engineering game on design patterns. The approach is illustrated with part of a Challenge from the software engineering test game; we focus on the transformation to an XML representation that can be loaded and tested in a game engine. An overview of the new approach is presented in Section 2. The manual transformations (informal to semi-formal and semi-formal to formal) are introduced in Sections 3 and 4. Conclusions and future work are in Section 5.

2   Overview

The SimSYS approach to engineering games has three main steps (Figure 1). The first step is to create an informal, high level model of the SEG as a narrative. The narrative captures the game like a Storyboard with textual descriptions of the learning objectives and game play in addition to user interface concepts (e.g., graphics, audio). This model is important as it allows the game designers to focus on the creative aspects of the game play, in place of a pre-production game design document.

The second step is to transform the informal model into a semi-formal tailored UML UC model (visual and tabular, template-based specifications). UML UCs have been adopted as they are a well-known notation that can be tailored. The overall game is organized into Acts, Scenes, Screens, and Challenges. Each of these has a tabular template to assist in the game development. Tabular, template-based representations are considered straightforward to develop, review, and maintain; they allow the modularization of a specification into sub-tables to manage complexity. As this semi-formal model is developed and reviewed, errors can be identified and corrected.

The third step is to transform the semi-formal model into formal models (Statechart and XML). The Statechart model can undergo comprehensive simulation/animation to verify its behavior using commercial tool support. The XML model is the game specification, which can be loaded, played, and tested using the SimSYS Game Play Engine. The errors identified using testing or simulation/animation techniques can be rapidly corrected, across the formal and semi-formal models.

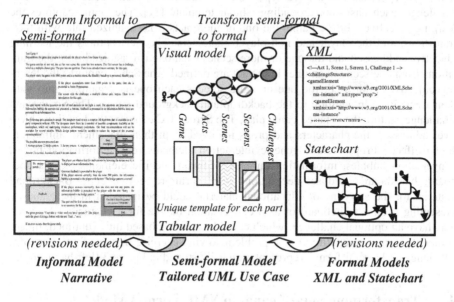

Fig. 1. Overview of Models in the SimSYS Approach (informal, semi-formal, formal)

3   Transforming the Informal to Semi-formal Model

The informal model is organized into a title, overview of the game (number of acts, scenes, screens, challenges), the learning objectives (both topic specific and transferable skills), initial conditions for the game (such as number of points a player starts with, backdrop for the scenes), and rules that need to be applied as the game is played. After this, the game play is described as a sequence of game play interactions over time, followed by the conditions at the end of the game (Figure 2). The game play interactions include Challenges for the player that address specific learning objectives.

Title: Test Game 4 SE Design

Overview: The game consists of one act; the act has one scene; the scene has two screens. The first screen has a challenge, which is a multiple choice quiz. The quiz has one question on design patterns; it is a dialogue question requiring critical thinking, problem solving, and analysis skills in addition to SWEBOK Software Design topics (general, process, context). The Bloom's taxonomy categories are knowledge and application. There is no introduction or summary for this quiz. The second screen provides a summary of the player's progress in the game.

 Initial conditions: The player starts the game with 1000 points and is a student intern; the BlueSky backdrop is presented (BlueSky.png).

Game rule (how to win): If the player accumulates more than 1000 points...

Fig. 2. Informal Model of a (Partial) Test Game

The narrative is manually, iteratively refined into a tailored UC model (visual, textual). The approach has a stereotyped UC for the Game, Act, Scene, Screen, and Challenge; each has a corresponding tabular template [12]. The Game captures the learning objectives for the game, the one or more acts it is organized into with their transitions, and the player and non-player characters. The Act captures the learning objectives addressed and the one or more scenes each one is organized into; the transitions from one scene to another in the act are defined. The Scene captures the learning objectives addressed; the one or more screens each one is organized into with their transitions, in addition to the backdrop and background music. The Screen and Challenge capture the detailed game play. The Screen UC captures the learning objectives addressed, the characters and props involved, with their placement, animation, sound effects. Props include generic interaction elements (e.g., information boxes, conversation bubbles, information bubbles), domain specific elements (e.g., whiteboard, blackboard), and set decorations (e.g., furniture, coffee cup). Background material for the storyline or educational material could be included in the game by presenting it on a whiteboard or as a conversation bubble for a character. A screen may have an optional challenge, which could be a dialog based quiz (untimed, timed, competition, non-competitive) or a problem solving exercise in a sandbox. Part of a Challenge in the semi-formal representation is illustrated in Figure 3 (left-hand side).

4   Transforming Semi-formal to XML Formal Model

The collection of tabular, semi-formal representations of the Game, Acts, Scenes, Screens, and Challenges is transformed into a single XML file that can be loaded into the SimSYS Game Play Engine. The manual transformation is done one part at a time, using tags in a schema definition to organize the content. There are tags, for example, to organize the overall model with respect to the Game, Acts, Scenes, Screens, and Challenges. The tags are nested, to reflect the composition relationships (a Game has one or more Acts, an Act has one or more Scenes, a Scene has one or more Screens, a Screen has an optional Challenge). Part of the XML file is illustrated in Figure 3 (right-hand side), focusing on the Challenge. Within a Challenge, for example, one question in the quiz is related to subject specific topics in SE Design and transferable skills described in the tabular specification (What kind of knowledge is in the challenge?); these are represented in XML using two kinds of tags to define lists of topics (<domainKnowledgeList>, <transferableKnowledgeList>). Following this (not presented in the Figure), the assessment approach (e.g., Bloom taxonomy categories) and one or more quiz question with answer options, evaluation, hints, rewards, and feedback for the player are defined. As the mapping proceeds, errors are detected and corrected in the semi-formal and informal models, making the approach highly iterative. The manual mapping from the semi-formal tabular model to the XML model is time consuming, but not too difficult.

Test Game on SE Design Patterns - Act 1, Scene 1, Screen 1, Challenge 1

Identifier	Challenge 1	

Purpose	Design pattern selection. Challenge type: Multiple choice quiz (dialogue)	`<Challenge>`
		`<id>Challenge 1<\id>`
		`<scope>design pattern selection<\scope>`
		`<type>Multiple choice quiz<\type>`...

Learning Objectives	Domain Specific Skills
	Software Engineering,
	 Software Design
	Standard: SWEBOK 2004
	1. Software Design Fundamentals
	 1.1 General Design Concepts
	 1.2 Context of Software Design
	 1.3 Software Design Process
	 1.3.2 Detailed Design
	3. Software Structure and Architecture
	 3.2 Design Patterns
	
	Transferable Skills
	 Analysis
	 Critical Thinking
	 Problem Solving
	
	Bloom's Taxonomy:
	knowledge, application
	Understand the purpose of established design patterns ...
		`<! What kind of knowledge is in the challenge? -->`
		`<domainKnowledgeList>`
		`  <domainKnowledge>software engineering <\domainKnowledge>`
		`  <standard>SWEEBOK 2004<\standard>`
		`  <area>Software Design</area>`
		`  <subarea>Software Design Fundamentals<\subarea>`
		`  <topic_list>`
		`    <topic>General_Design_Concepts<\topic>`
		`    <topic>Context_of_Software_Design<\topic>`
		`    <topic>Software_Design_Process<\topic>`
		`    <subtopic>Detailed Design<\subtopic>`
		`    <subarea>Software Structure and Architectures<\subarea>`
		`    <topic>Design Patterns<\topic>`
		`  </topic_list>`
		`</domainKnowledgeList>`
		
		`<transferableKnowledgeList>`
		`  <transferableKnowledge>analysis </transferableKnowledge>`
		`  <transferableKnowledge>critical_thinking </transferableKnowledge>`
		`  <transferableKnowledge>problem_solving`
		`</transferableKnowledge>`
		`<\transferableKnowledgeList>`

Fig. 3. Semi-formal Model and Formal Model for a (partial) Test Game

5   Conclusions and Future Work

Initial results on an iterative, three step, model-based RE approach for SEGs is previewed here. The approach begins with an informal narrative, like a Storyboard, which is subsequently transformed into a tailored semi-formal UML UC model (with visual and tabular specifications) and lastly into a formal XML model. Learning objectives, for example, are initially captured in natural language in the informal narrative; transformed into the semi-formal model in a learning objective row, then represented with nested XML tags in the formal model. The XML model can be loaded and tested in the SimSYS Game Play Engine. In applying the three step approach to engineering a collection of test games, we have found it to be straightforward, but labor intensive. In particular, the formal XML model required significant time to create. An Intelligent Semi-Automated Game Generation module is currently being prototyped to alleviate the effort in populating the informal narrative and semi-formal models; a goal is to automatically generate the formal models. Related work is available on automating UC transformations, indicating this is feasible [13]. In the future, additional validation is needed, both by continuing our own project and by external educational game researchers and educators. The transformation from the semi-formal model to the Statechart model is also planned to explore model verification via simulation/animation using commercial tool support.

References

1. Gee, J.P.: What video games have to teach us about learning and literacy. Macmillan, U.S.A. (2003)
2. Adams, E.: Fundamentals of Game Design, 2nd edn. New Riders Publishing (2010)
3. Object Management Group, OMG Model Driven Architecture (MDA) Guide Version 1.0.1 (2003), http://www.omg.org
4. Dormans, J.: The Effectiveness and Efficiency of Model Driven Game Design. In: Herrlich, M., Malaka, R., Masuch, M. (eds.) ICEC 2012. LNCS, vol. 7522, pp. 542–548. Springer, Heidelberg (2012)
5. Tang, S., Hanneghan, M.: Fusing Games Technology and Pedagogy for Games-Based Learning Through a Model Driven Approach. In: Proceedings of the 2011 IEEE Colloquium on Humanities, Science, and Engineering Research, pp. 380–385 (2011)
6. Sauer, S., Engels, G.: UML-based Behavior Specification of Interactive Multimedia Applications. In: Proceedings of the IEEE 2001 Symposia on Human Centric Computing Languages and Environments, pp. 248–255 (2001)
7. Truong, K., Hayes, G., Abowd, G.: Storyboarding: an empirical determination of best practices and effective guidelines. In: Proceedings of the 6th Conference on Designing Interactive Systems, pp. 12–21 (2006)
8. Pollack, S.L., Hicks, H.T., Harrison, W.J.: Decision tables: theory and practice. Wiley-Interscience (1971)
9. Object Management Group, OMG Unified Modelling Language, version 2.2 (2009), http://www.omg.org
10. World Wide World Consortium, Extensible Markup Language (XML) 1.0, 4th edn. (August 2006), http://www.w3.org/TR/xml/
11. Longstreet, C., Cooper, K.: A meta-model for developing simulation games in higher education and professional development training. In: Proceedings of the IEEE 17th International Conference on Computer Games, pp. 39–44 (2012)
12. Cooper, K., Longstreet, C.: Towards Model-driven Game Engineering for Serious Educational Games: Tailored Use Cases for Game Requirements. In: Proceedings of the IEEE 17th International Conference on Computer Games, pp. 208–212 (2012)
13. Riebisch, M., Hübner, M.: Refinement and Formalization of Semi-Formal Use Case Descriptions. In: Proceedings on the 2nd Workshop on Model-Based Development of Computer Based Systems: Appropriateness, Consistency and Integration of Models (2004)

Measuring and Improving the Completeness of Natural Language Requirements

Alessio Ferrari[1], Felice dell'Orletta[2], Giorgio Oronzo Spagnolo[1],
and Stefania Gnesi[1]

[1] ISTI-CNR, Pisa, Italy
{alessio.ferrari,giorgio.oronzo.spagnolo,stefania.gnesi}@isti.cnr.it
[2] ILC-CNR, Pisa, Italy
felice.dellorletta@ilc.cnr.it

Abstract. [**Context and motivation**] System requirements specifications are normally written in natural language. These documents are required to be *complete* with respect to the input documents of the requirements definition phase, such as preliminary specifications, transcripts of meetings with the customers, *etc.* In other terms, they shall include all the *relevant concepts* and all the *relevant interactions* among concepts expressed in the input documents. [**Question/Problem**] Means are required to *measure* and *improve* the completeness of the requirements with respect to the input documents. [**Principal idea/results**] To *measure* this completeness, we propose two metrics that take into account the relevant terms of the input documents, and the relevant relationships among terms. Furthermore, to *improve* the completeness, we present a natural language processing tool named COMPLETENESS ASSISTANT FOR REQUIREMENTS (CAR), which supports the definition of the requirements: the tool helps the requirements engineer in discovering relevant concepts and interactions. [**Contribution**] We have performed a pilot test with CAR, which shows that the tool can help improving the completeness of the requirements with respect to the input documents. The study has also shown that CAR is actually useful in the identification of specific/alternative system behaviours that might be overseen without the tool.

Keywords: Requirements analysis, requirements completeness, requirements quality, natural language processing, terminology extraction, relation extraction.

1 Introduction

The starting point of a requirements definition process is very rarely a blank paper. More often, several input documents are placed on the desk of the requirements engineer, from legacy system documentation to reference standards, from transcripts of meetings with the customers to preliminary specifications. The content of these documents has to be taken into account when writing the requirements [1, 2], since it settles the background on which the future system

C. Salinesi and I. van de Weerd (Eds.): REFSQ 2014, LNCS 8396, pp. 23–38, 2014.

can start to take its form. Such input documents are normally written in natural language (NL), and suitable natural language processing (NLP) tools can help identifying all the information that is relevant for the requirements. NLP approaches have been proposed in the past to identify significant abstractions that can aid the requirements process (e.g., [3, 4]). However, none of the existing approaches considers the *completeness* of the requirements with respect to the existing documentation. A requirements document that does not include the relevant information of the input documents - i.e., it is *incomplete* - could bring to several problems: if the missing information resides in the transcripts of meetings with the customers, the product might not address the customer's expectations; if some information is overseen from the reference standards, the resulting product might not comply to the norms; when concepts from legacy documentation and preliminary specifications are not taken into account, re-work on the product or on the process artifacts is hard to avoid.

In this paper, we propose a NLP-based approach to *measure* and *improve* the completeness of a requirements specification with respect to the input documents of the requirements definition process. A requirements document is *complete* with respect to the input documents if all the *relevant concepts* and *interactions* among concepts expressed in the input documents are also treated in the requirements. We refer to this type of completeness as *backward functional completeness*. In order to measure such completeness, we provide two metrics that take into account the relevant terms and relevant relations among terms of the input documents. Furthermore, we provide a NLP approach to automatically extract such terms and relations. A prototype tool named COMPLETENESS ASSISTANT FOR REQUIREMENTS (CAR) has been developed, which suggests relevant information during the requirements definition phase, and automatically computes the degree of completeness of the requirements specification produced.

We evaluate the effectiveness of the approach with a pilot test, which is also used as a reference example in the remainder of the paper. The pilot test concerns the definition of the requirements for an Automatic Train Supervision (ATS) component of a Communications-based Train Control system (CBTC). CBTC systems are signalling and control platforms tailored for metro, standardized by the IEEE Std 1474.1-2004 [5]. These systems provide automatic train protection, train monitoring, and automated train driving. The ATS component of a CBTC is a centralized system that monitors and regulates the movement of the trains. The system automatically routes trains, and sends them speed profiles that shall be followed while moving through the railway network. It is normally equipped with a user interface where the ATS operator can view the position of all the trains, their schedule, and other information.

From the pilot test, we find that the CAR tool actually helps in improving the completeness of the requirements specification with respect to the input documents – in our case, the ATS reference standard. The tool suggests relations about concepts that do not appear evident while reading the input document, and facilitates the identification of specific/alternative behaviours of the ATS system.

The paper is structured as follows. In Sect. 2, we give some background on requirements specifications completeness. In Sect. 3, the research questions addressed by the current paper are presented. In Sect. 4, we introduce two metrics to evaluate the backward functional completeness of a requirements specification. In Sect. 5, the CAR tool is described. Sect. 6 presents the evaluation of the approach through a pilot test. Sect. 7 provides conclusions and future works.

2   Defining and Measuring Completeness

In general, a requirements specification is complete if all the necessary requirements are included [6]. Several works have been presented in the literature to *define* and to *measure* the completeness of a requirements specification. In this paragraph, we review some definitions, which give a framework to understand the concept of *backward functional completeness* provided by the current paper.

Completeness. A largely agreed definition of completeness of a requirements specification can be found in Boehm [7]. The definition states that a complete specification shall exhibit five properties: 1) No To-be-determined (TBD) items 2) No nonexistent references 3) No missing specification items (e.g., missing interface specifications) 4) No missing functions 5) No missing products (i.e., part of the actual software that are not mentioned in the specification).

Internal/External Completeness. The definition is further conceptualized by Zowghi and Gervasi [8]. The first two properties defined by Bohem [7] are associated to *internal completeness*, and the second three properties to *external completeness*. Internal completeness can be measured by considering solely the information included in the specification. Instead, measuring external completeness requires additional information provided by domain experts, for example in the form of a domain model.

Feasible Semantic Completeness. A more formal definition of external completeness - referred as *semantic completeness* - is given in Lindland et al. [9]. They look at the requirements specification as a *conceptual model M*, and they state that M has achieved semantic completeness if it contains all the statements about the domain D that are correct and relevant (i.e., $D \setminus M = \emptyset$). They observe that total semantic completeness cannot be achieved in practice, and they define the concept of *feasible semantic completeness* as $D \setminus M = S \neq \emptyset$. The set S is composed of correct and relevant statements, but there is no statement in S such as the benefit of including it in the specification exceeds the drawback of including it.

Functional Completeness. A further refinement of the concept, which goes toward the definition of a completeness measure, is provided by España et al. [10]. In line with the observations of Zwoghi and Gervasi [8], the authors argue that, in order to compute the feasible semantic completeness, a reference model M_r shall be defined to conceptualize the domain D. By focusing on functional requirements, they consider the subset $FM_r \subset M_r$, which is a model of the functional requirements. Such a model is composed of functional encapsulations F_r, roughly "functions", and linked communications LC_r, roughly "messages". More formally, $F_r = F_r \cup LC_r$.

A functional requirements specification FM shall be compared against this reference model FM_r to evaluate its completeness. Therefore, the specification FM shall be regarded as a composition of functional encapsulations F and linked communications LC (i.e., $FM = F \cup LC$). The introduced concepts are used to define two aspects of *functional completeness*:

- *functional encapsulation completeness:* all functional requirements specified in the reference model have been specified in the model (i.e., $F_r \setminus F = \emptyset$).
- *linked communication completeness:* all linked communications specified in the reference model have been specified in the model (i.e., $LC_r \setminus LC = \emptyset$).

In order to provide metrics associated to these aspects, the authors define the degree of functional encapsulation completeness as $degFEC = |F|/|F_r|$, and the degree of linked communication completeness as $degLCC = |LC|/|LC_r|$. In practice, computing these metrics requires the definition of a reference model for the functional requirements in terms of functions and linked communications.

3 Motivation

Besides the one applied by España et al. [10], several other measures for functional requirements completeness have been proposed in the literature (e.g., [11–15]). Nevertheless, the majority of such metrics deal with functional completeness defined with respect to the future implementation of the system[1]. Indeed, domain models [10], ontologies [15], identification of components [14], identification of system states [12], or expert analysis [11] are required to compute this kind of completeness. In other terms, domain experts are called to foresee a possible implementation of the system, possibly through a reference functional model FM_r. According to this vision, we refer to this kind of completeness as *forward functional completeness*. Instead, in our work we wish to focus on the completeness of the requirements with respect to the available input documents of the requirements definition process. The input documents might be transcripts of meeting with customers, preliminary specifications, reference implementation standards, or any other information specifically regarding the system under development. We refer to the completeness of a functional requirements specification with respect to the input documents as *backward functional completeness*.

Backward functional completeness is achieved by a functional requirements specification when (1) all the *relevant concepts* expressed in the input documents are treated in the requirements specification; (2) all the *relevant interactions* among concepts expressed in the input documents are treated in the requirements specification.

---

[1] One exception is [13], where completeness is evaluated against higher-level requirements.

Consider for example the input document of our pilot test [5]. The document contains the sentence *"An ATS system shall have the capability to automatically track, maintain records of, and display on the ATS user interface the locations, [...], the train schedule and [...]"*. Besides the other content, such a sentence tells that the ATS user interface is supposed to display the schedule of the trains. Therefore, the requirement specification is expected to include the concepts of "ATS user interface" and "train schedule". Furthermore, requirements shall be provided that define the *interaction* among the two concepts (i.e., the fact that the ATS user interface shall display the train schedule).

Achieving backward functional completeness ensures that no relevant information contained in the input documents is left out from the specification. Measuring this type of completeness can give higher confidence on the quality of the specification. Therefore, a metric is required to measure this kind of completeness. Furthermore, we are also interested in establishing whether a positive correlation holds between such completeness and the completeness of the specification with respect to the system to be (i.e., the *forward functional completeness*).

Bearing these observations in mind, we define three research questions, which are addressed by the current paper: **RQ1.** How to *measure* the backward functional completeness of a requirements specification document? **RQ2.** How to *improve* the backward functional completeness of a requirements specification document? **RQ3.** Does the backward functional completeness help in improving the *forward functional completeness* of the specification?

The first question is answered by computing two completeness metrics that consider the number of relevant terms that are used in the input documents, and the number of relevant relations among terms (Sect. 4). Roughly, a document is more complete than another if more relevant terms and more relevant relations are included in the document. The second question is answered through a prototype tool that suggests relevant terms to be included in the requirements, and that considers the relations among terms (Sect. 5). The third question is answered through a pilot test, where we have evaluated the forward functional completeness of the requirements produced with the proposed tool, and without the proposed tool (Sect. 6).

4   Metrics for Backward Functional Completeness

Measuring the backward functional completeness of a requirements specification requires the definition of specific metrics (**Research Question 1**). Here, we define two metrics. The first one, named *degree of concept completeness*, measures how many relevant concepts that are expressed in the input documents are treated also in the specification. The second one, named *degree of interaction completeness*, measures how many relevant interactions that are expressed in the input documents are treated also in the specification.

More formally, we define the two metrics as follows. Let T be the set of relevant concepts expressed in the input documents, and let $Q \subseteq T$ be the set of such concepts expressed in the requirements specification. We define the *degree of concept completeness* of a requirements document $\mathcal{D}$ with respect to a set of input documents $\mathcal{I}$ as $degCC(\mathcal{D}, \mathcal{I}) = |Q|/|T|$.

Now, let U be the set of relevant interactions among concepts expressed in the input documents, and let $R \subseteq U$ be the set of relevant interactions among concepts expressed in the requirements specification. We define the *degree of interaction completeness* of a requirements document $\mathcal{D}$ with respect to a set of input documents $\mathcal{I}$ as $degIC(\mathcal{D}, \mathcal{I}) = |R|/|U|$.

Given a requirements document and the corresponding input documents, we would like to compute the two metrics in an automated manner.

We argue that the relevant concepts expressed in the input documents can be approximated with the relevant *terms* included in such documents. Furthermore, relevant interactions among concepts can be approximated with the relevant *relations* among terms. Therefore, we define a NLP approach to automatically identify relevant terms and relations among terms in the input documents.

4.1   Identification of Relevant Terms

The proposed method for the identification of relevant terms is based on a novel natural language processing approach, named *contrastive analysis* [16], for the extraction of *domain-specific terms* from natural language documents. In this context, a *term* is a conceptually independent linguistic unit, which can be composed by a single word or by multiple words. For example, consider the document that we have used in our pilot test [5]. In such document, "Automatic Train Supervision" is a term, while "Supervision" is not a term, since in the textual documents considered in our study it often appears coupled with the same words (i.e., "train", "route"), and therefore it cannot be considered as conceptually independent.

The *contrastive analysis* technology aims at detecting those terms in a document that are *specific* for the domain of the document under consideration [16, 17]. Roughly, contrastive analysis considers the terms extracted from domain-generic documents (e.g., newspapers), and the terms extracted from the domain-specific document to be analysed. If a term in the domain-specific document highly occurs also in the domain-generic documents, such a term is considered as domain-generic. On the other hand, if the term is not frequent in the domain-generic documents, the term is considered as domain-specific.

In our work, the documents from which we want to extract domain-specific terms are the input documents of the requirements definition phase. The proposed method requires two steps. First, conceptually independent expressions (i.e., *terms*) are identified (*Identification of Terms*). Then, *Contrastive Analysis* is applied to select the terms that are domain-specific.

Identification of Terms. Given a set $\mathcal{I} = \{I_1, \ldots, I_n\}$ of input documents, we aggregate the documents in a single input document I. From this document, which collects the content of all the input documents, we identify a ranked list of *terms*. To this end, we perform the following steps.

1. POS Tagging: first, Part of Speech (POS) Tagging is performed with an english version of the tool described in [17]. With POS Tagging, each word is associated with its grammatical category (*noun, verb, adjective*, etc.).

2. Linguistic Filters: after POS tagging, we select all those words or groups of words (referred in the following as *multi-words*) that follow a set of specific POS patterns (i.e., sequences of POS), that we consider relevant in our context. For example, we will not be interested in those multi-words that end with a preposition, while we are interested in multi-words with a format like <*adjective, noun, noun*> (such as "Automatic Train Supervision").

3. C-NC Value: terms are finally identified and ranked by computing a "termhood" metric, called C-NC value [16]. This metric establishes how much a word or a multi-word is likely to be conceptually independent from the context in which it appears. The computation of the metric is rather complex, and the explanation of such computation is beyond the scope of this paper. The interested reader can refer to [16] for further details. Here we give an idea of the spirit of the metric. Roughly, a word/multi-word is *conceptually dependent* if it often occurs with the same words (i.e., it is *nested*). Instead a word/multi-word is *conceptually independent* if it occurs in different context (i.e., it is normally accompanied with different words). Hence, a higher C-NC rank is assigned to those words/multi-word that are conceptually independent, while lower values are assigned to words/multi-words that require additional words to be meaningful in the context in which they are uttered.

After this analysis, we have a ranked list of k words/multi-words that can be considered *terms*, together with their ranking according to the C-NC metric, and their frequency (i.e., number of occurrences) in I. The more a word/multi-word is likely to be a *term*, the higher the ranking.

Contrastive Analysis. The previous step leads to a ranked list of k terms where all the terms might be *domain-generic* or *domain-specific*. With the contrastive analysis step, terms are re-ranked according to their domain-specificity. To this end, the proposed approach takes as input: 1) the ranked list of terms extracted from the document I; 2) a second list of terms extracted from a set of documents that we will name the *contrastive corpora*. The contrastive corpora is a set of documents containing domain-generic terminology. In particular, we have considered the Penn Treebank corpus, which collects articles from the Wall Street Journal. The reasonable assumption here is that a term that frequently occurs in the Wall Street Journal is not likely to be a domain-specific term of the domain of a technical requirements specification. The new rank $TRank(t)$ for a term t extracted from the document I is computed according to the function [16]:

$$TRank(t) = \log(f(t)) \cdot \left(\frac{f(t)}{\frac{F_c(t)}{N_c}}\right)$$

where $f(t)$ is the frequency of the term t extracted from I, $F_c(t)$ is the sum of the frequencies of t in the contrastive corpora, and N_c is the sum of the frequencies of all the terms extracted from I in the contrastive corpora. Roughly, if a term is less frequent in the contrastive corpora, it is considered as a *domain-specific term*, and it is ranked higher. Consider again our pilot test. After the contrastive analysis, a term such as "train" – which is highly frequent in the document (57 occurrences), but is also frequent in the contrastive corpora – is ranked lower than "ATS user interface". Indeed, this term has 8 occurrences in the document, but is uncommon in the contrastive corpora.

After this analysis, we have a list of terms, together with their ranking according the function $TRank$, and their frequency in I. The more a term is likely to be domain-specific, the higher the ranking. From the list, we select the terms that received the higher ranking. The choice shall be made according to a *domain relevance threshold* τ. If $TRank(t) \geq \tau$ the term will be selected as *relevant*. The value of τ is defined over normalized values, where the rank of each term is divided by the maximum value of $TRank$. The selection of τ shall be performed by a domain expert after reviewing the lists of terms extracted. Normally, a value of $\tau = 0.99$ allows selecting most of the relevant terms.

Assuming that the set of selected terms $\bar{T}$ provides an approximation of the relevant concepts of the input documents T, we can approximate the degree of concept completeness as $degCC(\mathcal{D}, \mathcal{I}) \approx |\bar{Q}|/|\bar{T}|$, where $\bar{T} = \{t \subset I : TRank(t) \geq \tau\}$, and $\bar{Q} = \mathcal{D} \cap \bar{T}$. For example, in our case study, we have $|\bar{T}| = 67$ relevant terms extracted from the input documents (see Table 1 for examples). In the first experiment, the requirements produced by subject A included $|\bar{Q}| = 46$ of such terms. Therefore $degCC(\mathcal{D}, \mathcal{I}) \approx 68.7\%$.

4.2   Identification of Relevant Relations

In order to identify relevant relations among terms, we first select all the terms t extracted in the previous step, regardless of their ranking. Then, we search for possible relations among such terms. We state that there is a relation $u = (t_j, t_h)$ between two terms t_j, t_h if such terms appear in the same sentence or in neighboring sentences. In our case, we select the previous and the following sentence. In order to give a rank to such relation, we use the Log-likelihood metric for binomial distributions as defined in [18]. The explanation of such metric is beyond the scope of this paper. Here, we give an idea of the spirit of the metric. Roughly, a relation holds between two terms if such terms frequently appear together. Moreover, the relation is stronger if the two terms do not often occur with other terms. In other words, there is a sort of *exclusive relation* among the two terms. For each couple of terms t_j, t_h occurring in neighboring sentences of the input document I, we associate a rank according to the Log-likelihood metric, which represents the degree of their relation $u = (t_j, t_h)$:

$$RRank(u) = \text{Log-likelihood}(t_j, t_h)$$

In our pilot test, the term "re-routing of trains" has a relation with "movement of trains" and with "ATS user interface". However, the relation is stronger (i.e., more exclusive) with the former ($RRank = 14.88$ *vs* $RRank = 8.85$), since the latter often occurs with other terms. Indeed, the ATS user interface is required to show several information, besides those concerning re-routing of the trains.

After this analysis, we have a list of relations, together with their ranking according the function $RRank$. From the list, we select the terms that received the higher ranking. The choice shall be made according to a *relation degree threshold* ρ. If $RRank(u) \geq \rho$, the relation will be selected as *relevant*. The selection of ρ shall be performed by a domain expert after reviewing the lists of relations extracted with the proposed method. Normally, a Log-likelihood above 10.83 is recommended to select only relevant relations. However, lower thresholds can be chosen, if more relations are required.

Assuming that the set of selected relations $\bar{U}$ provides an approximation of the relevant interactions U in the input documents, we can approximate the degree of interaction completeness as $degIC(\mathcal{D}, I) \approx |\bar{R}|/|\bar{U}|$, where $\bar{U} = \{u \in \bar{T} \times \bar{T} : RRank(u) \geq \rho\}$, and $\bar{Q} = (\mathcal{D} \times \mathcal{D}) \cap \bar{U}$. For example, in our case study, we have $|\bar{U}| = 316$ relations extracted from the input documents (see Table 2 for examples). In the first experiment, the requirements produced by subject A included $|\bar{R}| = 54$ of such relations. Therefore $degIC(\mathcal{D}, I) \approx 17.1\%$.

5 A Word-Game to Support Requirements Definition

We would like to provide means to improve the backward functional completeness of a requirements specification (**Research Question 2**). We argue that the backward functional completeness of a requirements specification is normally hampered by two problems: (1) *missing concepts:* the person who writes the requirements might forget to consider relevant concepts of the problem, either because she postpones their analysis, or because they are unclear and hard to specify, or because the input documents include too many concepts to consider them all; (2) *missing concept interaction:* when one writes a requirement, she might be concentrated on the specific function that she is defining, and oversee possible interactions among elements.

We have implemented a prototype tool named COMPLETENESS ASSISTANT FOR REQUIREMENTS (CAR), which addresses these problems by automatically suggesting possible relevant terms and possible relevant relations among terms to be used in the requirements. The relevant terms and relations are extracted from the input documents (e.g., transcripts of meeting with the customers, reference standards, preliminary requirements) according to the approach explained in Sect. 4. Therefore, the tool starts with a set $\bar{T}$ of relevant terms, and a set $\bar{U}$ of relevant relations. Furthermore, the degree of concept completeness and the degree of interaction completeness is computed at run-time while the requirements manager writes down the requirements.

Fig. 1 shows the interface of CAR. The figure is used as a reference example to explain the working principles of the tool. The example, adapted from our pilot test, concerns the definition of the requirements for an Automatic Train Supervision (ATS) system. An ATS system is a component of a metro control system that takes care of monitoring and routing trains. Furthermore, an ATS provides capabilities to remotely issue commands to the trains. The input document, in the example, is a reference international standard [5], which is used

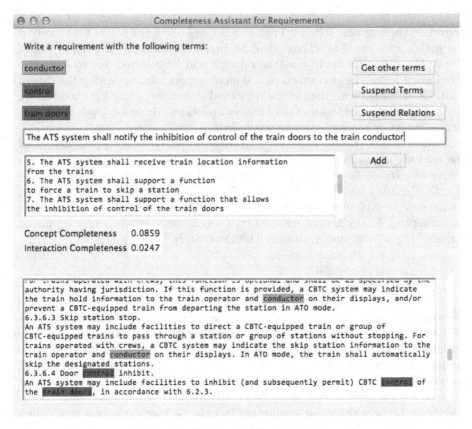

Fig. 1. User interface of the tool

as a starting point to write the requirements for the ATS system. In general, the tool can work with any kind of natural language input document, such as interviews, transcripts of meetings with the customers, etc.

The tool is a sort of word-game. The main steps of the game are summarized below:

1. The tool suggests to write a requirements with three terms. The first term (conductor , in Fig. 1) is extracted from the set of relevant terms, while the other two terms (control , train doors) are extracted from the set of relevant relations. The three terms are also highlighted in the original document, which is loaded to the bottom frame of the interface. In the current version of the tool, the extraction is random. Nevertheless, smarter approaches can be devised that choose the terms by taking into account their relevance, their position, or the previously written requirements.
2. The user writes a requirement, possibly using the three terms suggested. An example requirement that employs the three terms is *"The ATS system shall notify the inhibition of* control *of the* train doors *to the train* conductor".*

Then, the user adds the requirement to the central panel by pressing the button **Add**. It is worth noting that a requirement like the one presented above could not be deduced by simply reading the text of the input document. It is actually an additional behaviour inspired by the suggested terms. Indeed, a relation between the "conductor" and the "train doors" was not specified in the original input document, as one can see from the fragment displayed in Fig. 1.

3. The system checks if the user used any relevant term or relevant relations, and consequently increases the degree of **Concept Completeness** and the degree of **Interaction Completeness**. These values are computed as $|\bar{Q}|/|\bar{T}|$ and $|\bar{R}|/|\bar{U}|$, respectively, as explained in Sect. 4.1 and 4.2. When relevant concepts are found within the requirement, these are added to the set $\bar{Q}$. When relevant relations are found, these are added to the set $\bar{R}$. The current values of the metrics are shown below the panel that lists the requirements.

4. The system automatically suggest other terms to be used in the following requirement.

If a relevant term or relation is suggested twice, and the user does not employ it in the requirement, such term/relation is marked as *not relevant*. Therefore, the completeness scores are adjusted consequently (i.e., $|\bar{T}|$ or $|\bar{U}|$ are decreased).

In some cases, the user might not be interested in writing a requirement that includes all the suggested terms. In other cases, the user might want to focus on the suggested terms/relations to write more than one requirement. With the normal behaviour of the tool, new terms/relations would be automatically suggested in these cases after pressing the button **Add**. As explained, if such terms/relations are not used, they are marked as *not relevant*, and will not be presented anymore among the suggestions. Therefore, we added the **Suspend Terms** and **Suspend Relations** buttons, to suspend the automated suggestion of terms and relations, and prevent the tool from marking them as not relevant.

If new relations among terms are reported in a requirement, these new relations shall be added to the relevant relations $\bar{U}$. In our case, the relations between "conductor" and the other two terms are added to $\bar{U}$. Similarly, if some terms are used that were not identified as relevant in the initial analysis, such terms shall be stored among the relevant terms $\bar{T}$. These situations do not influence the computation of the backward completeness (also $|\bar{Q}|$ and $|\bar{R}|$ increase like $|\bar{T}|$ and $|\bar{U}|$). Nevertheless, we argue that storing and reviewing the new concepts and relations can help understanding if the requirements specification provides additional information with respect to the input documents.

6   Pilot Test

We have performed a pilot test to assess the effectiveness of the proposed approach, and to evaluate the correlation between the backward functional completeness and the forward functional completeness (**Research Question 3**) of a requirements specification.

In the pilot test, the first and third author, referred as subject A and subject B, were required to write requirements for an ATS system, according to the generic requirements provided by the standard IEEE Std 1474.1-2004 [5].

The requirements have been written with the support of the tool, and without the support of the tool. The goal was to compare the degree of backward functional completeness and the degree of forward functional completeness achieved in the two cases.

More specifically, the pilot test required four steps, which are described below.

1. Input document reading: the chapter concerning the ATS of the IEEE Std 1474.1-2004 [5] - about 5 pages long - was used as input document for the requirements definition task. Subject A and B were asked to read the input document to have a first understanding of the general needs of the system.

2. Tool set-up: from the input document, 67 relevant terms and 316 relevant relations have been automatically extracted. To this end, a threshold of 99% and a threshold of 10 were chosen as domain relevance threshold τ, and relation degree threshold ρ, respectively. In Table 1 and 2, we provide representative examples of relevant terms and relevant relations extracted from the document. These terms and relations have been fed into the tool to support the definition of the requirements.

3. Requirements definition Phase 1: subject A and B were asked to write the requirements. Subject A operated with the support of the tool, and subject B operated without the tool. The requirements definition lasted one hour.

4. Requirements definition Phase 2: subject A and B were asked again to write the requirements. Subject B operated with the tool, and subject A operated without the tool until they produced the same amount of requirements produced in the previous step (i.e., if a subject produced n requirements in Phase 1, he should have produced n requirements also in the Phase 2). Given a subject, this choice allows comparing the completeness scores achieved in the two phases on the same amount of requirements.

The subjects chosen for the test - first and third author - were involved in the definition of the principles of CAR, while the approach for term/relation extraction was defined and implemented by the second author only. Therefore, we argue that the expectations of the two test subjects on the success of the solution had a limited influence on the result of the test. Indeed, they did not know which types of terms/relations would be considered relevant by the tool, and could not influence the test by avoiding the usage of relevant terms/relations when the tool was not used. This is especially true for Subject B, who performed his first experiment without the tool. But it is also true for Subject A, since during the first experiment he viewed only a limited part of the terms/relations extracted by the tool (i.e., the suggested terms/relations).

6.1   Quantitative Evaluation

We evaluated the results of the test by computing the backward functional completeness of the produced requirements for the two subjects. Then, we computed the forward functional completeness according to the metrics provided by España

Table 1. Examples of relevant terms

Term	TRank (%)	Freqency
CBTC	100.0	44
ATS	$99.99999 + 0.99769 \times 10^{-6}$	43
ATS system	$99.99999 + 0.8456 \times 10^{-6}$	19
ATS user interface	$99.99999 + 0.29614 \times 10^{-6}$	8
train location	$99.99999 + 0.1231 \times 10^{-6}$	7
train	$99.99999 + 0.1185 \times 10^{-6}$	57
conductor	$99.99997 + 0.73215 \times 10^{-6}$	8
station	$99.99979 + 0.57378 \times 10^{-6}$	12

Table 2. Examples of relevant relations

Relation	RRank	Freqency
(conductor, ATS system)	35.1402383629	6
(ATS user interface, position of trains)	17.9938334306	2
(station, train at station)	16.1777267317	2
(speed regulation function, service brake rates)	14.8834871304	1
(train fault reporting, train health data)	14.8834871304	1
(re-routing of trains, movement of trains)	14.8834871304	1
(equipment, supplier)	13.1023727742	2
(ATS user interface, movement authorities)	12.4872415276	2
(station departure time, train service)	12.1108984081	1

et al. [10]. The degree of functional encapsulation completeness $degFEC$, and the degree of linked communication completeness $degLCC$ require the definition of a reference model for the system. In our case, we have employed a preliminary system specification where functions and linked communications were listed. The reference model defines 21 functions and 10 linked communications for the ATS system. The document was edited in the context of the Trace-IT project, a project for technology-transfer, which involves ISTI-CNR and a medium-sized railway signalling company. It is worth noting that the reference model was provided *before* the definition of the method presented in this paper. Table 3 summarizes the results of the test.

Backward functional completeness. We see that, for both subjects, the backward functional completeness, estimated with $degCC$ and $degIC$, is higher when the tool is employed ($\Delta degCC = 12.7\%$ and $\Delta degIC = 8.6\%$ in average). Therefore, in our pilot test, the usage of the tool actually helped in improving the backward functional completeness of the requirements specification. Furthermore, we argue that if a larger amount of input documents would be employed, the benefit given by the usage of the tool would be even more evident. The CAR tool helps in the navigation of the input documents. Without tool support, coherent navigation would be hardly practicable in the case of many documents. Moreover, with a larger amount of information, the statistics that bring to the set of relevant terms/relations would be more accurate, and the consequent suggestions given by the tool would be more meaningful.

Table 3. Results of the pilot tests

Subject	Num. Reqs	Tool	$degCC$	$degIC$	$degFEC$	$degLCC$
A	36	Yes	68.7%	17.1%	47.6%	40%
		No	52.3%	12.8%	61.9%	50%
B	21	Yes	67.2%	24.5%	47.6%	50%
		No	58.2%	11.6%	33.3 %	50%

Forward Functional Completeness. Conflicting results have been found concerning the effectiveness of the approach with respect to forward functional completeness, estimated through $degFEC$ and $degLCC$. Indeed, we see that subject A achieved a lower value for both metrics when using the tool with respect to the values obtained when the tool was not employed ($\Delta degFEC = -14.3\%$, $\Delta degLCC = -10\%$). Instead, subject B achieved a higher value for $degFEC$ when using the tool ($\Delta degFEC = 14.3\%$), while equivalent values for $degLCC$ were obtained in Phase 1 and 2. Therefore, from our test, we cannot identify a positive correlation between the degree of backward functional completeness and the degree of forward functional completeness. Instead, we argue that the results obtained might be related to the *order* that was followed by the two subjects in performing the tasks. Subject A performed the experiment with CAR *before* writing the requirements without the tool, while for subject B was the other way around. Both subjects achieved a higher degree of completeness during Phase 2. Basically, a higher degree of completeness was obtained when the subjects acquired a higher confidence with the topic of the requirements, since they already defined requirements for the system in Phase 1.

6.2 Qualitative Evaluation

We have performed a qualitative analysis of the produced requirements to understand which were the main differences between the requirements produced with CAR and those produced without the tool. Interesting results have been found. We have identified two main differences: 1) requirements produced with CAR tend to be more specific, while requirements produced without the tool are more high-level; 2) requirements produced with CAR tend to identify alternative behaviors of the system. Representative examples of requirements produced *without* the support of the tool by subject A are:

- R_1. *The ATS system shall send the desired speed profile to the trains*
- R_2. *The ATS system shall have the capability to define temporary speed restrictions for the trains*
- R_3. *The ATS system shall implement the functionality of train routing*

These requirements are quite generic, and do not add too much content compared to the input document. Instead, more specific requirements are produced with the tool. For example, the following requirement was produced when the tool suggested the term "emergency brake application" and the relations < "response", "wet rail" >: *The ATS system shall adjust the speed profile of the trains in* response *to* wet rail *conditions in order to avoid* emergency brake application". Such requirement can be regarded as a specialization of R_1 and R_2, since it explains the specific condition (i.e., the wet rail) that requires temporary speed restrictions. The following requirement is an example of an alternative behavior identified with the support of the tool. In this case, the relations suggested was < "re-routing", "service disruptions" >: *The ATS system shall be capable of supporting* re-routing *of trains in response to* service disruptions *".* This requirement shows an alternative behavior (i.e., re-routing) of the routing functionality identified by requirement R_3. According to this preliminary analysis, we argue that the proposed tool can play a complementary role during requirements definition. Indeed, it can be used as a support tool to identify specific cases, and alternative behaviors that tend to be overseen in requirements definition approaches based solely on the analysis of the input documents.

7   Conclusions

In this paper, the novel concept of *backward functional completeness* of a requirements specification has been defined as the completeness of a specification with respect to the input documents of the requirements definition process. Metrics to measure such completeness have been provided, as well as a NLP-based tool named CAR to improve it. Further development of the principles of CAR are currently under analysis. We would like to give a *type* to the relations that are extracted from the input documents. For example, "ATS user interface" and "train schedule" are related in our input document, and their relation is of type "display". Furthermore, we would like to explore different approaches for choosing the terms to be suggested to the user of CAR. Such approaches should also take into account the structure of the input documents, the structure of the requirements specification itself, and the requirements previously written by the user. Other similarity metrics, such as the *cosine similarity*, are currently under analysis to evaluate the relations among the terms.

After improving the principles of CAR, we plan to assess the tool with both academic and industrial case studies. In particular, we plan to consider systems of different domains, as well as different types of input documents, in order to identify possible refinements and domain-specific optimizations of the approach.

Acknowledgements. This work was partially supported by the PAR FAS 2007-2013 (TRACE-IT) project.

References

1. Rayson, P., Garside, R., Sawyer, P.: Recovering legacy requirements. In: Proc. of REFSQ 1999, pp. 49–54 (1999)
2. Pohl, K., Böckle, G., Van Der Linden, F.: Software product line engineering: foundations, principles, and techniques. Springer (2005)
3. Goldin, L., Berry, D.M.: Abstfinder, a prototype natural language text abstraction finder for use in requirements elicitation. Autom. Softw. Eng. 4(4), 375–412 (1997)
4. Ambriola, V., Gervasi, V.: On the systematic analysis of natural language requirements with CIRCE. Autom. Softw. Eng. 13(1), 107–167 (2006)
5. IEEE: IEEE Standard for Communications Based Train Control (CBTC) Performance and Functional Requirements. IEEE Std 1474.1-2004 (Revision of IEEE Std 1474.1-1999) (2004)
6. Lauesen, S.: Software Requirements: Styles and Techniques. Addison-Wesley (2002)
7. Boehm, B.: Verifying and validating software requirements and design specifications. IEEE Software 1(1), 75–88 (1984)
8. Zowghi, D., Gervasi, V.: The three cs of requirements: Consistency, completeness, and correctness. In: Proc. of REFSQ 2002, pp. 155–164 (2002)
9. Lindland, O., Sindre, G., Solvberg, A.: Understanding quality in conceptual modeling. IEEE Software 11(2), 42–49 (1994)
10. España, S., Condori-Fernandez, N., Gonzalez, A., Pastor, O.: Evaluating the completeness and granularity of functional requirements specifications: A controlled experiment. In: Proc. of RE 2009, pp. 161–170 (2009)
11. Yadav, S.B., Bravoco, R.R., Chatfield, A.T., Rajkumar, T.M.: Comparison of analysis techniques for information requirement determination. Commun. ACM 31(9), 1090–1097 (1988)
12. Davis, A., Overmyer, S., Jordan, K., Caruso, J., Dandashi, F., Dinh, A., Kincaid, G., Ledeboer, G., Reynolds, P., Sitaram, P., Ta, A., Theofanos, M.: Identifying and measuring quality in a software requirements specification. In: Proc. of SMS 1993, pp. 141–152 (1993)
13. Costello, R.J., Liu, D.B.: Metrics for requirements engineering. J. Syst. Softw. 29(1), 39–63 (1995)
14. Menzel, I., Mueller, M., Gross, A., Dörr, J.: An experimental comparison regarding the completeness of functional requirements specifications. In: Proc. of RE 2010, pp. 15–24 (2010)
15. Kaiya, H., Saeki, M.: Ontology based requirements analysis: lightweight semantic processing approach. In: Fifth International Conference on Quality Software (QSIC 2005), pp. 223–230 (2005)
16. Bonin, F., Dell'Orletta, F., Montemagni, S., Venturi, G.: A contrastive approach to multi-word extraction from domain-specific corpora. In: Proc. of LREC 2010, pp. 19–21 (2010)
17. Dell'Orletta, F.: Ensemble system for part-of-speech tagging. In: Proc. of Evalita 2009, Evaluation of NLP and Speech Tools for Italian (2009)
18. Dunning, T.: Accurate methods for the statistics of surprise and coincidence. Comput. Linguist. 19(1), 61–74 (1993)

(Semi-) automatic Categorization
of Natural Language Requirements

Eric Knauss[1] and Daniel Ott[2]

[1] Department of Computer Science and Engineering
Chalmers | University of Gothenburg, Sweden
`eric.knauss@cse.gu.se`
[2] Research and Development, Daimler AG
P.O. Box 2360, 89013 Ulm, Germany
`daniel.ott@daimler.com`

Abstract. Context and motivation: Requirements of todays industry specifications need to be categorized for multiple reasons, including analysis of certain requirement types (like non-functional requirements) and identification of dependencies among requirements. This is a pre-requisite for effective communication and prioritization of requirements in industry-size specifications. **Question/problem:** Because of the size and complexity of these specifications, categorization tasks must be specifically supported in order to minimize manual efforts and to ensure a high classification accuracy. Approaches that make use of (supervised) automatic classification algorithms have to deal with the problem to provide enough training data with excellent quality. **Principal ideas/results:** In this paper, we discuss the requirements engineering team and their requirements management tool as a socio-technical system that allows consistent classification of requirements with a focus on organizational learning. We compare a manual, a semi-automatic, and a fully-automatic approach for the classification of requirements in this environment. We evaluate performance of these approaches by measuring effort and accuracy of automatic classification recommendations and combined performance of user and tool, and capturing the opinion of the expert-participants in a questionnaire. Our results show that a semi-automatic approach is most promising, as it offers the best ratio of quality and effort and the best learning performance. **Contribution:** Our contribution is the definition of a socio-technical system for requirements classification and its evaluation in an industrial setting at Mercedes-Benz with a team of ten practitioners.

Keywords: requirements, classification, categorization, natural language.

1 Introduction

In current industry specifications it is essential to categorize requirements, partly because of their growing size and complexity [1], but also to allow for a number

C. Salinesi and I. van de Weerd (Eds.): REFSQ 2014, LNCS 8396, pp. 39–54, 2014.

of requirements related activities [2]: Identification of requirements of different kinds (e.g. technical or non fun-functional requirements) is a necessity (1) for having specific guidelines for developing and analyzing these requirement types, (2) for architectural decisions, (3) for identifying equipment needed, its quantity and permitted suppliers, and (4) for identifying dependencies among these requirements, especially to detect risks and for scheduling needs during the project. Related to this, Knauss et al. [3] propose an automatic classifier for identifying security-related requirements early in the project, which is crucial in order to prevent substantial security problems later [4–6]. More recent, Ott [7] also reports the need to categorize requirements for inspection tasks to support reviewers with the detection of consistency or completeness defects over large document sets. Note that in this work, we use the term *classification* to refer to the specific algorithmic task of mapping requirements to topics and *categorization* to refer to general goal of establishing a good mapping between requirements and topics for a specification.

Efficient classification can enable focussed communication and prioritization of requirements. As the examples show, categorization of requirements allows filtering relevant requirements for a given important aspect. Considering large specifications, for example in the automotive domain (a single specification at Mercedes-Benz can consist of up to 50.000 requirements and headings [8]), it is necessary to minimize the manual efforts in categorization tasks. Automatic classification is promising [3, 7], but depends on a sufficient amount of high quality training data which is not available in many realistic scenarios.

Contribution: In this work, we model a socio-technical system for requirements classification, consisting of the requirements engineering team and their requirements management tool. This socio-technical system allows different modes of operation, ranging from full-automatic over semi-automatic to manual classification of requirements. Our model has a special focus on learning, i.e. gaining shared understanding of a classification scheme in a team and generating high quality training data. For example, our semi-automatic approach learns and adjusts its suggestions with each new requirement according to the user's choices.

We explore the performance of the different operation modes of the socio-technical system in an experiment in cooperation with Mercedes-Benz, driven by the following research questions:

- RQ1: If applied to a new specification domain, how are the *relative quality* levels that can be achieved with the three operation modes *fully-automatic*, *semi-automatic*, and *manual classification*?
- RQ2: If applied to a new specification domain, how high are the *relative efforts* of these operation modes?

Our results suggest that the semi-automatic approach is most promising: it offers significantly better quality than the fully automatic approach, causes less effort than the manual approach, and in addition generates valuable training data as a by-product. In Section 2 we describe related work. Thereafter, we present our model of a socio-technical system (the planned user interactions and classification mechanisms) in Section 3. Section 4 gives a short overview of our technical solutions and we present the exploratory experiment with Mercedes-Benz in Section 5. We discuss the results in Section 6 and conclude the paper with an outlook on future research in this field.

2 Related Works

In this section, we discuss a spectrum of approaches for classification of requirements. On the one side of this spectrum are approaches that are based on purely manual classification, as supported by most state-of-the-art requirements management tools. Analysts specify the classification of requirements in a user-defined attribute. As one such example, Song and Hwong [2] report about their experiences with manual categorizations of requirements in a contract-based system integration project. The contract for this project contains over 4,000 clauses, which are mostly contract requirements.

On the other side of the spectrum are approaches that classify requirements only based on automatic classification. Examples include QuARS tool by Gnesi et al. [9], which automatically detects linguistic defects like ambiguities, using an initial parsing of the requirements. Thereby, QuARS creates a categorization of requirements to topics as a byproduct.

Especially when based on machine learning, such approaches face the problem to obtain large enough training sets in sufficient quality. Knauss et al. [3] evaluate to what extent security-relevant requirements can be automatically identified in specifications based on Naive Bayesian Classifiers. Accordingly, satisfactory results can be achieved, if both training and testing data were derived from the same specification. This is probably due to the fact that writing style and domain specific concepts have a strong impact on the classifier's performance. Ott [7] reports similar results for automatic classification of requirements in multiple categories for supporting review activities. For this reason, Ko et al. [10] propose to automatically create the training data for topic classification. Based on a clustering algorithm they categorize requirements and use these to train Naive Bayesian classifiers. Their evaluation results are promising, but only based on small English and Korean specifications (less than 200 sentences).

Hussain et al. [11] developed the tool LASR that offers an interactive modus for supporting groups in annotation tasks. By not relying on a fully automatic classification approach they mitigate the problem of insufficient training data. In contrast to our work, they try to support a group in collaboratively creating and agreeing on a categorization, whereas we focus on supporting single annotators with a special focus on cost and quality, as well as continuous improvement.

3 Socio-technical Requirements Classification

We define a topic as any crosscutting concern that demands for the ability to filter related requirements. Examples include qualitative requirements, such as performance or security-relevance, and crosscutting design issues or constraints such as regulatory concerns. A requirement can be assigned to a set of topics. Technically, this can be done by adding an attribute *topic* to the requirement and specify relevant topics as a comma separated list.

When requirements are categorized into topics, certain tasks (e.g. creating a security concept, reviewing, prioritizing) become much simpler. As shown by related work, automatic topic classification of natural language requirements is technically feasible but prone to writing style and domain specificity. The main reason for these problems is the lack of sufficient training data in high quality. Thus, the integration of such algorithms in the requirements specification process needs to be considered carefully.

To get a good categorization, the socio-technical system needs to support four main use cases: It should support the author of a requirements document in choosing topics during the documentation of requirements, it should propose relevant topics when the user chooses a topic for a given requirement, it should allow the user to add new topics to the socio-technical system, and it should support assigning topics to a set of requirements that are already documented.

A system for requirements categorization needs to be able to learn, because otherwise it could not adjust to domain specific concepts or writing style. This learning can be observed on several levels. First, users learn a suitable system of topics during working with the requirements. Second, the classification system itself should learn from previous classifications and gain more and more accuracy in proposing relevant topics.

The value of requirements categorization depends on its quality. For example, consider designing a security concept. In this case it is very important that all security relevant requirements are identified. Moreover, the value of the topic classification needs to be higher than the cost to create it.

Figure 1 shows our model of a socio-technical system for requirements classification which can offer different modi of operation. First of all, it allows *manual classification* (automatic classification support = no), the modus with the highest level of freedom. Users can specify a number of requirements, then classify them, before they continue with the specification. We assume that this modus can generate a high quality categorization at high cost.

Secondly, it allows to rely on *fully automatic classification* (in Figure 1: automatic classification support = yes, user confirms classification = no). By eliminating the need for human intervention, the cost to create the classification is minimal (consequently, the dashed transitions in Figure 1 are unusual in this modus. Instead, the user would write the specification and then finalize it by triggering the automatic classification). As has been shown before [7], this approach is highly effective, if enough high quality training data is available, i.e. classified requirements in a closely related domain. Even though this is not unlikely in product centered or software evolution scenarios, there will often be situations where such training data is not available. Consequently, quality of fully automatic topic classification might just be too low for many tasks.

Thus, we are especially interested in a third modus, the *semi automatic classification*. In this case the system recommends relevant topics and allows the user

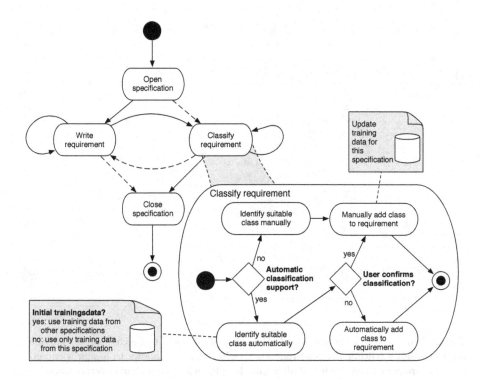

Fig. 1. A socio-technical system for requirements classification

to interact by confirming or rejecting recommendations (automatic classification support = yes, user confirms classification = yes). This interaction can be used to train supervised learning algorithms as discussed in the following section, thus generating high quality training data for future versions of this specification.

The screenshot in Figure 2 shows a prototype of a supporting tool for the socio-technical requirements classification system. The prototyp allows working on data from typical requirements management tools, e.g. an authentic, publicly available specification for a door control unit [7] stored in IBM Doors, as shown in the figure. Users can add, remove, and edit requirements. If the user selects or changes a requirement r_1, the prototype updates the recommendation list (3 in Figure 2). If the user selects another requirement r_2, the prototyp analyses the user's topic classification of requirement r_1 and updates its training data accordingly. Depending on the modus, parts of the UI are deactivated and hidden, e.g. the recommendation list in manual modus or both lists in fully automatic modus.

4   Text Classification Algorithms

In requirements engineering and management, text classification algorithms can be used to categorize huge document landscapes to certain topics: In past

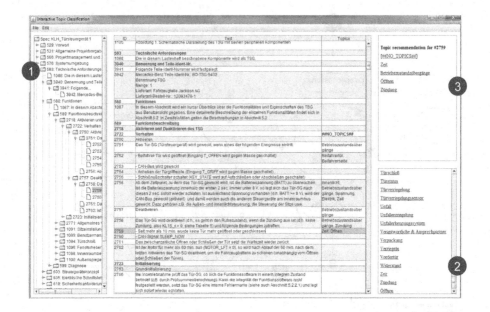

Fig. 2. Prototype of a specification tool as part of the socio-technical system. The main area (1) allows editing the requirements specification, (2) allows to assign a category to a requirement from the list of all available categories, (3) a shorter recommendation list allows to asign recommended categories.

research [7], we showed at typical large-scale, German automotive specifications of Mercedes-Benz that an automatic classification using text classification is possible with sufficient quality. Therefore, we identified a well-working combination of pre-, post-processing, and classification steps, out of many alternatives. We will use this combination in the current work, too.

Figure 3 shows details to the individual processing steps. The chosen pre-processing, post-processing, and classification steps have many alternatives, but after a comparison, we got the best results with the illustrated setting in previous work for German natural-language specifications from Mercedes-Benz [7]. A more detailed description to the individual process steps can also be found in this previous work.

Fig. 3. Processing Steps

The **support vector machine** (SVM) approach works as follows (based on Witten et al. [12]) : A nonlinear mapping is used to transform the training data into a higher dimension. Within this new dimension, the classifier searches for the optimal separating hyperplane, which separates the class of topic relevant and topic irrelevant requirements. If a sufficiently high dimension is used, data from two classes can always be separated by a hyperplane. The SVM finds the maximum-margin hyperplane using support vectors and margins. The maximum-margin hyperplane is the one with the greatest separation between the two classes.

The maximum-margin hyperplane can be written as [12]:

$$x = b + \sum_{i \text{ is support vector}} \alpha_i * y_i * a(i) \cdot a$$

Here, y_i is the class value of training instance $a(i)$, while b and α_i are numeric parameters that have to be determined by the SVM. $a(i)$ and a are vectors. The vector a represents a test instance, which shall be classified by the SVM.

Based on external training data (manually classified requirements), the SVM then calculates for each topic such a maximum-margin hyperplane with the greatest separation between the training requirements belonging to the topic and the ones that do not. With this hyperplane the SVM can assign a new requirement to the topic or not.

In the pre-processing step **k-gram indexing** [13], each word of each requirement is separated in each ongoing combination of k letters and the classifier is then trained with these k-grams instead of the whole words. For example, a k-gram indexing with k = 4 separates the word "require" to "requ", "equi", "quir", "uire".

The post-processing step called **topic generalization** takes the structure of Mercedes-Benz specifications into account. All specifications at Mercedes-Benz are written using a template, which provides a generic structure and general requirements, and are filled later with system specific contents. Because of this structure, we assume that if a heading was assigned to a topic, then we can also assign each of the requirements and subheadings below it to this topic. This allows to relate requirements represented by tables or figures (i.e. elements that are not accessible to text classification at all) to the topics of their headings. Tables are implemented as OLE objects in our requirement management tool, so the content of a table is not accessible to our algorithms.

5 Evaluation

5.1 Research Method

The purpose of this experiment is to test in which way automatic classification helps to reduce effort and to increase quality of topic classifications in industrial requirements specifications. We are also interested in learning effects. For this reason, we explore the impact of *initial training* and *user/tool interaction* on *learning*, i.e. changes of effort and quality over time.

Based on our model of the socio-technical classification system (Figure 1), we defined the following independent variables: *Automatic classification support* can be activated or deactivated. *Initial training* of the automatic classifier might provide better suggestions in the beginning, but take longer to adjust to a special problem domain. *User confirms classification* determines if the user confirms the classification and potentially overrides automatic classifications.

We monitored the following dependent variables: *effort* to provide a requirements specification with topic classification and *quality* of the topic classification. Finally, we controlled for the quality of the requirements specification itself.

In previous work, we showed the fully automatic classification of requirements to multiple topics with satisfactory results, when high quality training data is available [7]. In contrast, we are now applying the socio-technical classification system to new specifications, in different domains, and with new authors. We are especially interested in how difficult it is to adjust the approach to such new environments and if we can derive new training data during that process.

Based on our research questions on effort and quality of the different operation modes of the socio-technical classification system, the independent and dependent variables lead us to the following *hypotheses*:

H1: Automatic classification leads to lower quality than manual classification.
H2: Automatic classification leads to less effort than manual classification.
H3: Starting with an initially trained classifier leads to better classifications than starting with an untrained automatic classifier.
H4: An untrained classifier adjusts faster to the problem domain than an initially trained classifier.
H5: The combination of automatic classification and user confirmation leads to higher quality of classifications than automatic classification.
H6: The combination of automatic classification and user confirmation leads to less effort than manual classification.

We evaluated our hypotheses in an experiment and semi-structured follow-up interviews with the participants (especially for determining a good ratio of $\frac{effort}{size}$ for practical use). For this experiment, we define four different (sets of) treatments (Table 1).

Our model of the socio-technical system offers four relevant modi of interaction for categorizing requirements while writing a requirements specification,

Table 1. Four relevant sets of treatments of independent variables

Treatment	Automatic classification support	Initial training	User confirms classification
T1	no	no	yes
T2	yes	yes	no
T3	yes	no	yes
T4	yes	yes	yes

which are defined by specific values of the independent variables (treatments). Treatment 1 describes the manual modus of interaction, where requirements are written and classified in parallel without any tool support. Treatment 2 describes the fully automatic operation of the socio-technical system, where users are not involved with classification. This treatment provides us with a baseline on how good the automatic classifier performs on the requirements that are specified during the experiment.

Together, Treatment 1 and 2 allowed us to control for particularities resulting from specific writing styles of the participants. These treatments did not require us to observe the interaction of humans and the system, but provided us with a baseline for the two established operation modi manual and fully automatic: We established a *ground truth* based on (manual) expert classification of all requirements written in the experiment and measured classification quality by comparing against it. To ensure sufficient quality of the ground truth, we let two experts classify the requirements iteratively and measure their agreement in their classification. If the agreement level is below a threshold (based on inter-rater agreement, e.g. Cohen's Kappa [14]), the raters need to discuss situations where they disagree and improve for the next iteration.

Treatment 3 defines the semi-automatic classification modus, where requirements authors write requirements and classify them interactively. In this case, the classification tool was not initialized with any training data and needed to learn the classification from the user. Treatment 4 is equal to 3, except that in this case the classification tool was initialized with training data from other requirements specifications. Both, in Treatment 3 and 4, the socio-technical system learned through interaction between user and classification tool. For Treatment 3 and 4, we randomly assigned the participants in the experiment (controlling only for similar levels of experience in both groups) and provided them with an exemplary implementation of our classification tool prototype that was configured according to the treatment.

5.2   Participants and Data Collection

The participants of the experiment were ten developers from Mercedes-Benz with a typical mix of experience (relatively new to expert). Each participant wrote approximately 100 - 300 functional and interface requirements for different parts of two car systems, an outside light system and a speed control system. During the writing tasks, they categorized the requirements with the semi-automatic approaches described in section 5.1. For the categorization tasks we provided the participants with a list of topics relevant for the specification domain in advance. This list consists of 62 topics like, for example, "speed", "ignition", or "communication" which are suitable for supporting specific review tasks [7].

To compare the results of this semi automatic classification with manual classifications, two independent persons manually classified these requirements later. The manual classification of requirements to topics was done by separating the data into parts of 150 objects. Each of these parts was then manually and independently classified by two persons and then synchronized in a review session using Cohen's Kappa [14] as an aid. Cohen's Kappa is a statistical measure to calculate the inter-rater agreement between two raters, who each classify n items to x categories. If the agreement level is below a threshold (< 0.9), the raters need to discuss situations, where they disagree and improve for the next iteration.

For the fully automatic classification (Treatment T2) and the semi automatic classification (Treatment T4) with trained classifier we used the same training data. We derived this training data from additional documents describing the outside light system and the speed control system and from two public specifications of previous work [15]. All in all we used approximately 2,000 requirements for training. The additional documents with descriptions of these two systems were also provided during the experiment to help participants describing the functionality of their parts of the systems.

5.3   Descriptive Statistics

Our experiment provided us with three sources of data. Firstly, we compared the endresults with our ground truth (see Section 5.1). Secondly, the prototype of our supporting classification tool was logging all interactions between user and tool. This allowed us to compare how often a user accepts a recommendation. Finally, the questionnaire provided us with insights into the opinion of our expert classifiers.

Endresults vs. Ground Truth. Table 2 shows the recall and precision results of of the 10 participants (last three columns). Column 2-4 present the results of Treatment 2 (the fully automatic classifications), applied to the requirements specidied by our participants. The first 5 rows show results for requirements specifications that were created with Treatment 3 (semi-automatic classification without initial training). The last 5 rows show the results for Treatment 4.

Table 2. Analyses Results

participant	automatic			semi-automatic		
	recall	precision	f-measure	recall	precision	f-measure
T3: P1	0.42	0.36	0.39	0.30	0.77	0.43
T3: P2	0.55	0.58	0.57	0.15	0.66	0.25
T3: P3	0.62	0.45	0.52	0.83	0.76	0.79
T3: P4	0.48	0.46	0.47	0.80	0.89	0.84
T3: P5	0.50	0.42	0.46	0.82	0.91	0.87
T4: P6	0.43	0.33	0.37	0.56	0.76	0.65
T4: P7	0.47	0.56	0.51	0.49	0.73	0.59
T4: P8	0.47	0.33	0.39	0.40	0.72	0.51
T4: P9	0.56	0.46	0.51	0.90	0.69	0.78
T4: P10	0.46	0.33	0.38	0.34	0.57	0.43

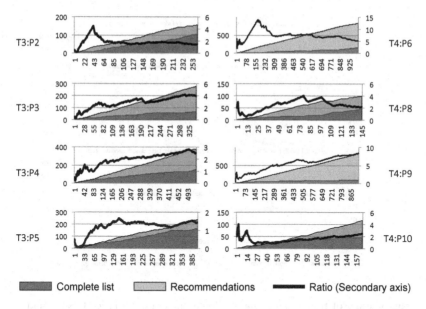

Fig. 4. Results of telemetry: Cumulative amount of user picks from *complete list*, *recommendations*, and *ratio* between both

Telemetry. During the experiment, each participant could categorize a requirement by either choosing the category from a complete list of all categories, or by accepting a recommendation. Our prototype logs such events and we accumulate how many categories were assigned with each method in Figure 4 (note that telemetry data of two participants was corrupted and is missing).

The figure shows that our participants only preferred the full list over the recommendations for the first 20-30 categorizations, if at all. Later, they tend to assign categories from the recommendation list significantly more often.

Figure 4 also shows the ratio between both ways of assigning categories to requirements. It appears that in both groups this ratio typically ends up around the Factor 2, i.e. twice as many categories are assigned based on recommendations. In Group 3 (left hand side), the ratio is a little bit lower, which might have been caused by the insufficient amount of training. The trajectories in Group 4 seem to have in common that during the first 30 categorizations, a depression occurs (the ratio drops drastically).

Questionnaires. Figure 5 shows an excerpt from our questionnaire results, where our participants report on their trust in the automatic classification. Participants in Treatment 4 were more optimistic towards automatic classification. The confidence of participants in Treatment 3 even decreased.

In similar question blocks we asked whether the participants were happy with amount, quality, and improvement rate of the recommendations (Treatment 4:

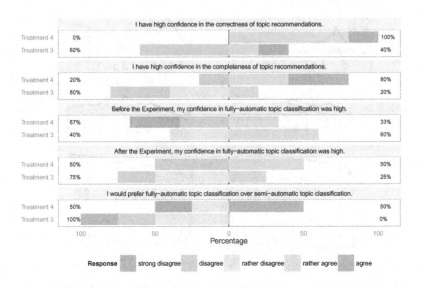

Fig. 5. Excerpt from questionnaire: Confidence in automatic classification

answer was generally positive, Treatment 3: less positive and recommendations were not found helpful), whether they think that the semi automatic approach would scale for real world specifications and if they would like to work with such a tool (answer was yes for both treatments), and whether their ability to do the topic classification improved (inconclusive for the scope of this experiment). We also controlled for usability issues of our prototype (see Section 6.4)

6   Discussion

6.1   Performance of Fully Automatic Classification (H1 and H2)

With respect to (H1) – automatic classification leads to lower quality than manual classification – the results in Table 2 confirm hypothesis and observations we made in previous work [7]. Typical goals for sufficient classification quality (e.g. recall > 70% and precision > 60% as proposed for example in [3, 7]) are never met. This is due to the fact that training data from a specification in one domain was used to classify requirements in another specification and domain, leading to a drastic loss of quality of the automatic classification.

Concerning the comparison of effort for manual and automatic classification (H2), the naive answer is of course yes: The effort of automatic classification (ca. 5 min for initialization with training data and < 1 min for classification) is lower than the effort of manual classification (> 1 hr). However, this does not include the effort to create training data in sufficient quality. For the task of creating training data, we employed similar to the manual classification of the experiment data two experts that iteratively classified and compared their classification results with Cohen's Kappa to increase the classification quality. From our experience with the public and confidential DCU [7], we know that such a high quality manual classification of a typical specification with 2000-3000 requirements takes at least 150hrs. In the context of this experiment, we used similar amounts of training data and again the total effort for creating this data was at least 150hrs. Since training is not necessarily portable from one application of the tool to another, this effort will not pay off over time.

6.2   Cold Start and Ability to Adjust to Domain (H3 and H4)

Concerning the question if initial training of the classifier leads to better classifications (H3), we get mixed results. The boxplot in Figure 6 (left) compares results of semi-automatic classifications by participants with Treatment T3 and T4 with our ground truth. Surprisingly, the deviation of classification results is smaller, but the median of the f-measures is lower, if initial training data (T4) was used.

We were also interested in how quick the recommender system adjusts to a new domain (H4). Our data does not allow to give a clear answer to this. However, it is noteworthy, that participants working with Treatment T4 did encounter some phase of depression during the first 30 classifications, where the ratio of accepted recommendations per classification drastically dropped (Figure 4). This is probably due to the fact that participants were initially having high confidence in the recommendations and realized only later that better classifications were available. The confidence (and ratio) dropped, before it was slowly re-established. This phenomen is not as clearly visible for participants with Treatment T3, where recommendations in the beginning were obviously suboptimal. In addition, participants of T3 mention the phenomen that every topic they choose is automatically recommended in the next requirement, regardless of the content (due to the lack of negative training data). Thus, participants seemingly circumvent the phase of over-confidence.

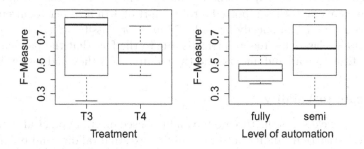

Fig. 6. Comparison of classification quality between treatments (left) and level of automation (right)

The overview of the responses in Figure 5 shows a mixed picture for this hypothesis. Participants that were confronted with Treatment 3 (with no initial training data) lost confidence in the automatic classification and strongly oppose fully automatic approaches. Participants that worked with Treatment 4 are indecisive about favouring the semi or fully automatic approach, but slightly gained confidence in the automatic classification.

In summary, all participants generally liked the semi automatic approach and participants with Treatment 4 gave even better ratings than those with Treatment 3. This is no wonder, since the initial suggestions in Treatment 3 were random and therefore not useful. Participants seemed to be more sceptic about recommendations in this situation, leading to a better overall classification performance. In contrast, the higher trust in the recommendations by participants in Treatment 4 lead to more consistent quality and results.

6.3   Performance of Semi-automatic Approach (H5 and H6)

We were interested if the semi automatic approach leads to better quality than the fully automatic (H5) and to less effort than the manual approach (H6).

For (H5), the box plot in Figure 6 on the right indicates that indeed the semi-automatic classification is better (in comparison to our ground truth). In fact, the f-measures in Table 2 are always better for the semi automatic approaches compared to the full-automatic classification in the same row.

The telemetry shown in Figure 4 shows that our participants accepted recommendations roughly twice as often as not (ratio ≥ 2), leaving about $\frac{1}{3}$ of cases where the automatic classification could be improved in the semi-automatic work modus and indicates a quality improvement of the semi automatic approach.

In the questionnaire, we asked our participants to give us the (1) total number of hours, as well as hours (2) for specifying and (3) classifying the requirements.

With respect to (H6) we need to compare these times with typical times for classifying requirements manually. At Mercedes-Benz these times are frequently normalized by number of requirements. Due to their experience, the raters in our experiment were able to classify 150 requirements in 4 h, which equals 1.6 min per requirement. Our participants had less experience with classification of requirements. In average, they reported a total effort of 3.76 min per requirement, consisting of 2.99 min for specifying and 0.77 min for classifying it. This significant speedup in classifying requirements is due to the fact that the participants needed less time to read and understand the requirements they had just written.

6.4   Threats to Validity

In this section, we discuss the threats to validity based on Runeson et al.'s classification in construction validity, internal validity, external validity and reliability [16]. One obvious threat of the **construction validity** is the manual classification. There is no unique classification and it is reviewer dependent. By using Cohens' Kappa we slightly mitigated this threat, but is still there. Another question is, whether there are no better algorithms for our text classification tasks, better/additional pre- and post-processing steps or better/additional ways to automatically extract training data, but the results show that we have at least chosen promising candidates. Usability issues of the prototype might be a confounding factor and threat to the **internal validity**. We controlled for this factor by doing System Usability Scale test [17] which showed that no major problems affected the outcome. Concerning the **external validity**, there are limitations in the transferability of our results on natural language specifications drawn from the Mercedes-Benz passenger car development to specifications from other companies in the automotive industry or even to specifications from other industries because of different specification structures, the content and complexity of the specifications, and other company specific factors. In addition, because of the German language, we may have advantages with certain pre-processing steps compared to other languages, while other well known pre-processing steps, for example stemming, do not work on our data sets [7].

In our study we aimed at investigating a socio-technical system for classifying requirements in an industrial setting. We prioritized working in an industrial setting with professional requirements analysts and real world requirements over statistical significance. In our setup, we did not plan to work with enough participants to achieve statistical significance in one of our hypotheses. Thus, the **reliability** of our results has to be considered low, as a different choice of participants with similar background might lead to different results.

7   Conclusion and Outlook

In this paper, we introduced a model of a socio-technical system for requirements classification, which consists of a requirements engineering team and their requirements management tool with automatic classification support. The model offers three different operation modes and we argue that the semi-automatic classification can mitigate some major problems in automatic requirements classification: According to our exploratory study it offers a reasonable ratio of effort and quality when compared with the alternatives. It supports organizational learning in that it automatically adjusts to new domains. Thus, it mitigates the problem of insufficient training data that impedes the use of fully automatic classification approaches in many industrial settings. During the evaluation, we learned first hand how difficult it is to agree on a specific classification scheme in a team. The semi automatic approach seems to offer an advantage over the manual approach in that the recommendations transport some shared knowledge across the team. Future work should investigate these effects. We hope that others will profit from our model of a socio-technical requirements classification system as well as from its empirical exploration.

References

1. Regnell, B., Svensson, R.B., Wnuk, K.: Can we beat the complexity of very large-scale requirements engineering? In: Rolland, C. (ed.) REFSQ 2008. LNCS, vol. 5025, pp. 123–128. Springer, Heidelberg (2008)

2. Song, X., Hwong, B.: Categorizing requirements for a contract-based system integration project. In: Requirements Engineering Conference (RE), pp. 279–284. IEEE (2012)
3. Knauss, E., Houmb, S., Schneider, K., Islam, S., Jürjens, J.: Supporting requirements engineers in recognising security issues. In: Berry, D. (ed.) REFSQ 2011. LNCS, vol. 6606, pp. 4–18. Springer, Heidelberg (2011)
4. Neumann, P.G.: Requirements-related risks in critical systems. In: Proceedings of the 4th International Conference on Requirements Engineering (ICRE 2000), Schaumburg, IL, USA, p. 3 (2000)
5. Chung, L.: Dealing with Security Requirements During the Development of Information Systems. In: Rolland, C., Cauvet, C., Bodart, F. (eds.) CAiSE 1993. LNCS, vol. 685, pp. 234–251. Springer, Heidelberg (1993)
6. Dubois, E., Wu, S.: A framework for dealing with and specifying security requirements in information systems. In: Katsikas, S., Gritzalis, D. (eds.) SEC. IFIP Conference Proceedings, vol. 54, pp. 88–99. Chapman & Hall, Boca Raton (1996)
7. Ott, D.: Automatic requirement categorization of large natural language specifications at mercedes-benz for review improvements. In: Doerr, J., Opdahl, A.L. (eds.) REFSQ 2013. LNCS, vol. 7830, pp. 50–64. Springer, Heidelberg (2013)
8. Houdek, F.: Challenges in Automotive Requirements Engineering. In: Industrial Presentations at REFSQ 2010, Essen (2010)
9. Gnesi, S., Lami, G., Trentanni, G., Fabbrini, F., Fusani, M.: An automatic tool for the analysis of natural language requirements. International Journal of Computer Systems Science & Engineering 20(1), 53–62 (2005)
10. Ko, Y., Park, S., Seo, J., Choi, S.: Using classification techniques for informal requirements in the requirements analysis-supporting system. Information and Software Technology 49, 1128–1140 (2007)
11. Hussain, I., Ormandjieva, O., Kosseim, L.: Lasr: A tool for large scale annotation of software requirements. In: Second IEEE International Workshop on Empirical Requirements Engineering (EmpiRE), pp. 57–60. IEEE (2012)
12. Witten, I., Frank, E., Hall, M.: Data Mining: Practical Machine Learning Tools and Techniques: Practical Machine Learning Tools and Techniques. Morgan Kaufmann (2011)
13. Hollink, V., Kamps, J., Monz, C., De Rijke, M.: Monolingual document retrieval for european languages. Information Retrieval 7(1), 33–52 (2004)
14. Carletta, J.: Squibs and discussions assessing agreement on classification tasks: The kappa statistic. Computational Linguistics 22(2), 249–254 (1996)
15. Ott, D., Raschke, A.: Review improvement by requirements classification at mercedes-benz: Limits of empirical studies in educational environments. In: IEEE Second International Workshop on Empirical Requirements Engineering (EmpiRE), pp. 1–8. IEEE (2012)
16. Runeson, P., Höst, M.: Guidelines for conducting and reporting case study research in software engineering. Empirical Software Eng. 14(2), 131–164 (2009)
17. Brooke, J.: SUS: A quick and dirty usability scale. In: Jordan, P.W., Thomas, B., Weerdmeester, B.A., McClelland, A.L. (eds.) Usability Evaluation in Industry. Taylor and Francis, London (1996)

A Systematic Literature Review of Requirements Modeling and Analysis for Self-adaptive Systems

Zhuoqun Yang[1], Zhi Li[2,3], Zhi Jin[3], and Yunchuan Chen[1]

[1] Institute of Mathematics, Academy of Maths and Syst. Sci., Chinese Academy of Sciences,
Haidian Dstr, Beijing 100190, P.R. China
zhuoqun.y@gmail.com, yunchuan001@163.com
[2] Software Engineering Dept., College of Computer Science and Information Technology
Guangxi Normal University, Guilin, Guangxi 541004, P.R. China
zhili@gxnu.edu.cn
[3] Key Laboratory of High Confidence Software Technologies (MoE), Peking University
Ministry of Education, Beijing 100871, P.R. China
zhijin@sei.pku.edu.cn

Abstract. [**Context and motivation**] Over the last decade, researchers and engineers have developed a vast body of methodologies and technologies in requirements engineering for self-adaptive systems. Although existing studies have explored various aspects of this topic, few of them have categorized and evaluated these areas of research in requirements modeling and analysis. [**Question/Problem**] This review aims to investigate what modeling methods, RE activities, requirements quality attributes, application domains and research topics have been studied and how well these studies have been conveyed. [**Principal ideas/results**] We conduct a systematic literature review to answer the research questions by searching relevant studies, appraising the quality of these studies and extracting available data. The results are derived by synthesizing the extracted data with statistical methods. [**Contributions**] This paper provides an updated review of the research literature, enabling researchers and practitioners to better understand the research trends in these areas and identify research gaps which need to be further studied.

Keywords: systematic literature review, self-adaptive systems, modeling method, RE activity, requirements quality attribute

1 Introduction

Self-adaptive systems (SASs) are able to adjust their behaviors in response to the dynamic changes in the environment and themselves. Due to the inherent volatility of the deployed environment and frequent interactions between software systems and the environment, SASs are faced with the challenges of meeting demands on some quality attributes, such as fault-tolerance, replaceability, etc. To maintain these attributes, we need to build adaptation mechanisms in SASs for endowing them with the capability of self-reconfiguring, self-healing, self-protecting and self-optimizing, which are

C. Salinesi and I. van de Weerd (Eds.): REFSQ 2014, LNCS 8396, pp. 55–71, 2014.

known as self-* properties [1]. Therefore, when developing SASs, engineers should take both domain logic and adaptation logic into account.

Requirements engineering (RE) is known as the first stage in the lifecycle of software development, aiming at defining domain logic, identifying stakeholders' needs and documenting information for subsequent analysis and implementation [2]. Different from traditional RE, RE for SASs focuses more on defining adaptation logic, since SASs need adaptation mechanisms. Thus, during RE for SASs, engineers must address what changes in the environment and the system themselves to be monitored, what to adapt, when to adapt and how to adapt. Requirements modeling is a fundamental activity in RE. Various kinds of artifacts produced during the modeling process are involved in the latter analysis, such as specifying requirements, diagnosing requirements, verifying requirements, etc.

Over the last decade, researchers and engineers have developed a vast body of work on requirements modeling and analysis for SASs. Existing studies [3-7] have summarized some of the achievements, provided insight in this field and outlined challenges in each direction. However, to the best of our knowledge, no systematic study has been performed on categorizing and evaluating these emerged modeling methods and corresponding RE activities. Thus, there is no clear view on where the researches are conducted and where the results are published, to what extend each kind of modeling method or RE activity is studied, how the method is evaluated, how the quality of studies varies against each method and what the most active topics are.

The objective of this paper is to systematically investigate the research literature of requirements modeling and analysis for self-adaptive systems, summarize the state-of-the-art research trends, categorize the used modeling methods and relevant RE activities, classify the quality attributes and application domains, assess the quality of current studies and generate the most active research topics. To conduct the investigation and report analysis results, we adopt the research methodology of systematic literature review [8] [9] in the evidence-based software engineering paradigm [10].

The rest of the paper is structured as follows. Section 2 briefly describes the systematic review and the protocol underpinning this study, followed by the presentation of the analysis results in Section 3. Section 4 discusses the results and threats to validity, followed by the conclusions and discussions on future work in Section 5.

2   Research Method

Evidence-based software engineering (EBSE) aims to improve decision making related to software development and maintenance by integrating current best evidence from research with practical experience and human values [11]. The core tool of the evidence-based paradigm is the Systematic Literature Review (SLR), which is a systematic methodology of defining answerable research questions, searching the literature for the best available evidence, appraising the quality of the evidence, collecting and aggregating available data for answering the identified questions. The whole process of SLR is presented in Figure 1. To complete SLR, three phases are needed: planning, conducting and reporting. During the planning phase, a protocol is produced for defining basic review procedures, on which the conducting phase should depend.

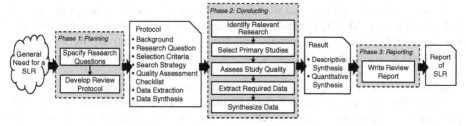

Fig. 1. Process of Systematic Literature Review

Due to the limitation of space, a detailed account of our SLR protocol is beyond the scope of this paper, but can be found in [12], which is available online.

2.1   Research Questions

The high-level goal of this literature research is to review the existing research work in the literature of requirements modeling and analysis for self-adaptive systems. To achieve this goal, we refine it into seven answerable questions in Table 1. These questions can be categorized into four types: a) publication type is related to the questions that are related to publication information, such as published time, venues and authors; b) content type contains the questions that should be answered by extracting the corresponding data from the texts of papers; c) quality type consists of the questions which are answered by assessing the quality of papers; d) topic type includes the questions which are related to the topics of relevant studies.

Table 1. Research Questions and Corresponding Types

Research question	Type
RQ1: What is the time/venue/research group/region distribution of the publications?	Publication
RQ2: What modeling methods and RE activities are studied? RQ3: What requirements quality attributes and application domains are involved?	Content
RQ4: Which methods are better applied and have more rigorous evaluation? RQ5: Which RE activities are presented and discussed more detailedly?	Quality
RQ6: What topics can we generalize based on the content of selected studies? RQ7: What is the relationship between topics and modeling methods?	Topic

2.2   Search Process

Figure 2 presents the mechanism underpinning the search process. The objective of the search process is to identify relevant studies based on search strategies. Defining search strategies includes defining search sources and defining search strings.

Search sources consist of some search engines, e.g. IEEE Xplore, and publication venues. Search engines are chosen for conducting automated search, which means researchers use these online databases to thoroughly retrieve relevant studies with some search strings adapted to the given search syntax and rules. Publication venues are chosen for conducting manual search, in which researchers manually scan conference proceedings or journals for relevant studies.

To improve the reliability and the repeatability of our study, we adopt the quasi-gold standard (QGS) [13] method, which is a set of known studies established by manual search within certain venues and time span, to objectively define search strings and evaluate the performance of search strings. The retrieved results from automated search complement manual search by expanding the coverage of the relevant studies. Moreover, we conduct the "snowball" search, which means investigators scan the references in each paper derived by manual search and automated search and pick out the most relevant ones. Therefore, the final set of relevant studies consists of search results from manual search, automated search and "snowball" search.

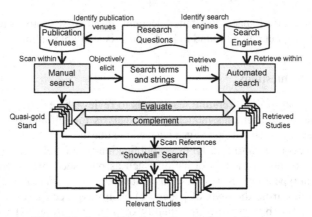

Fig. 2. Mechanism Underpinning the Search Process

Defining Selection Criteria. Inclusion criteria and exclusion criteria are defined for selecting relevant studies. Retrieved papers are firstly checked with exclusion criteria. If one paper meets any one of the exclusion criteria, i.e. C5 **OR** C6 **OR** C7 **OR** C8, it will be excluded. The remaining papers are checked with inclusion criteria. If one paper meets all the inclusion criteria, i.e. C1 **AND** C2 **AND** C3 **AND** C4, then it will be included.

Table 2. Inclusion and Exclusion Criteria

Inclusion criteria	Exclusion criteria
C1: Published time between 2003.1-2013.9	C5: In the form of books
C2: Focus on requirement modeling and analysis for self-adaptive systems.	C6: In the form of editorial, abstract, keynote, poster or a short paper (less than 6 pages)
C3: Related to concrete RE activity	C7: Opinion pieces or Position papers
C4: Involve concrete modeling methods and evaluation to the methods	C8: Focus on summarizes the existing research work, e.g. roadmap or survey

Defining Selection Procedure. We use the above criteria for establishing QGS from the manual search and deriving relevant studies from the automated search and the "snowball" search. The selection procedure consists of three rounds:

- Round 1: We first scan each paper by title, aiming to eliminate any irrelevant papers. Any paper that any researcher thinks should be included or is unsure about should be kept in the set of candidate papers for Round 2.
- Round 2: Scan the abstracts of candidate papers from Round 1 and appraise each paper with selection criteria. Any paper that any researcher considers should be included or is unsure about should be kept in the set of candidate papers for Round 3.
- Round 3: Look through the full texts of the candidate papers from Round 2 and assess each paper with the selection criteria. Any paper on which researchers cannot reach agreement should be resolved by a joint meeting.

During the selection procedure, we also consider duplicate papers and repeat studies. A duplicated paper refers to the same paper that can be retrieved from more than one search engine. In this situation, we retain only one of the duplicates in the final set of relevant studies and remove all the duplication. A repeated study means the same study published in more than one venue with the same authors' order or different authors' order. In this situation, we remove the repeated studies and retain the most comprehensive or the most recent version, except for answering RQ1.

Defining Search Sources. Search engines function as the databases for the automated search and the digital library where publication venues are provided. To ensure thorough retrieval, we choose six search engines that cover the RE literature: ACM Digital Library, IEEE Xplore, Science Direct, Springer, EI Compendex and Web of Knowledge.

Publication venues consist of a collection of proceedings and journals where the community tend to publish their research results. To ensure the quality of this study, we choose the qualified conferences and journals (Table 3) according to the Australian ERA (Excellence in Research for Australia) Outlet Ranking [14].

Establishing QGS. The manual search is conducted by two researchers individually and should be terminated when the Kappa value depicts a good or very good agreement. We scan all papers in the chosen venues by title, abstract and full texts with the selection criteria. The Kappa value is above 0.8, which indicates good agreement [15] and disagreement is eliminated by discussion with other investigators. Finally, the QGS is established by aggregating the selected results of two researchers. Table 3 provides the frequency and percentage of the 61 papers that compose QGS.

Defining Search Strings. Search terms are derived by using text mining. A frequency analysis of information of papers in QGS is undertaken followed by a statistical analysis of most frequently occurring words or phrases by using QDA Miner and WordStat [16]. We import the title-abstract-keyword segment of each paper in to QDA Miner and derive search strings (Table 4). The use of the search strings can be combined with Boolean operator as: S1 **AND** (S2 **OR** S3 **OR** S4 **OR** S5 **OR** S6 **OR** S7 **OR** S8 **OR** S9 **OR** S10).

Table 3. Publication Venues and Paper Frequency

Conference	Frequency	%	ERA	Journal	Frequency	%	ERA
SEAMS	12	27%	N/A	REJ	4	25%	B
RE	6	14%	A	JSS	3	19%	A
RE@runtime	5	10%	N/A	SESAS	2	19%	N/A
REFSQ	5	10%	B	ASEJ	1	6%	A
ICSE	4	8%	A	IST	1	6%	B
MODELS	4	8%	B	SoSyM	1	6%	B
ASE	3	6%	A	TAAS	1	6%	B
ICAC	2	6%	B	ToSEM	1	6%	A
CAiSE	2	4%	B	TSE	0	0%	A
FSE	2	4%	A	ESE	0	0%	A
SASO	1	2%	N/A	—	—	—	—
Total	46	100%		Total	15	100%	

Table 4. Derived Search Strings

Item	Search string
S1	("self-adaptive systems" **OR** "dynamically adaptive systems" **OR** "adaptive system" **OR** "Adaptive software" **OR** "self-adaptive software" **OR** "adaptive service" **OR** "web systems" **OR** "socio-technical system" **OR** "self-adjusting systems" **OR** "autonomic computing" **OR** "self-adapting software")
S2	"model requirements" **OR** "modeling requirements" **OR** "Requirements modeling"
S3	"specify requirements" **OR** "specifying requirements" **OR** "requirements specifying" **OR** "requirements specification"
S4	"monitor requirements" **OR** "monitoring requirements" **OR** "requirements monitoring"
S5	"aware requirements" **OR** "requirements-aware" **OR** "requirements awareness" **OR** "requirements-awareness"
S6	"diagnose requirements" **OR** "diagnosing requirements" **OR** "requirements diagnosing" **OR** "requirements diagnosis"
S7	"detect requirements" **OR** "detecting requirements" **OR** "requirements detection"
S8	"verify requirements" **OR** "verifying requirements" **OR** "requirements verifying" **OR** "requirements verification"
S9	"requirements" **AND** ("self-adaptation" **OR** "self-reconfiguration" **OR** "self-repair" **OR** "self-healing" **OR** "self-tuning" **OR** adaptation **OR** configuration **OR** reconfiguration **OR** "decision making" **OR** "decision-making" **OR** "adaptation behavior" **OR** "behavior")
S10	"evolution requirements" **OR** "requirements evolution"

Automated Search and Evaluating Search Strings. We conduct automated search within each search engine by splitting and inputting the strings according to the search syntax demanded. After eliminating disagreement, we finally record 79 papers and 47 of them can be found in QGS (Figure 3).

Quasi-sensitivity is an important criterion for evaluating the quality and efficiency of search strategies [13]. It refers to the proportion of relevant studies covered by the QGS. Thus, the value of our quasi-sensitivity is 77.04% (47/61), which is between 72%~80%. It means that the search strategies are acceptable according to [13].

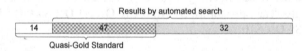

Fig. 3. Relationship between QGS and Automated Search Results

2.3   Quality Assessment Checklist

To answer RQ4 and RQ5, a quality assessment checklist (Table 5) is defined based on the assessment items introduced in [9] and [17]. We use the checklist to evaluate whether a method or an activity is maturely or rigorously conveyed in the literature.

Table 4. Quality Assessment Checklist

Assessment question	Optional answer and score
A1: How clearly is the problem of study described?	Explicitly=1/Vaguely=0.5/No description=0
A2: How clearly is the research context stated?	With references =1/Generally=0.67/ Vaguely=0.33/No statement=0
A3: How detailedly is the modeling method conveyed?	Step by step=1/Relatively detail=0.67/ Generally=0.33/Vaguely conveyed=0
A4: How detailedly is the RE activity elaborated?	Explicitly=1/General steps=0.67/ Vaguely=0.33/Disorderly=0
A5: How rigorously is the method evaluated?	Simulation=1/Detailed case study=0.67/ General case study=0.33/No evaluation=0
A6: How explicitly are the contributions presented?	Explicitly=1/Generally=0.5/No presentation=0
A7: How explicitly are the limitations discussed?	Explicitly=1/Generally=0.5/No discussion=0
A8: How explicitly are the insights and issues for future work stated?	With recommendations=1/Generally=0.5/ No statement=0

2.4   Data Extraction

To answer RQ1, corresponding information can be extracted directly from the papers. To answer RQ2, we extend the modeling method category presented in [2], investigate RE activities at requirements time, design time and runtime. To answer RQ3, we classify requirements quality attributes based on ISO 9126 Software Quality Characteristics [18]. Application domains can be elicited from the motivating example of each paper. To answer RQ4 and RQ5, we read full texts and appraise each paper according to the quality assessment checklist. To answer RQ6 and RQ7, we extract text segments, coding texts, and translate codes into topics or themes [19, 20].

More details on how the data is extracted and synthesized can be found in [21] and the theory underpinning the extraction process is elaborated in our protocol [12].

3   Results and Discussion

RQ1: What is the time/venue/research group/region distribution of the publications?

After the search process, we select a total of 101 relevant papers, in which 11 of them are identified as repeated studies. The time distribution of the studies is provided in Figure 4. Publication venue distribution can be found in Table 3.

To derive the research group and region distribution, we investigate the authors' affiliations. The results depict that the selected papers are from 29 research groups in 13 regions and the researchers are from 43 groups in 17 regions. Most of these papers are from European countries (58/101), followed by American countries (25/101) and Asian countries (18/101). Figure 5 and Figure 6 present the top 10 research groups and regions with the frequency of published papers and corresponding researchers.

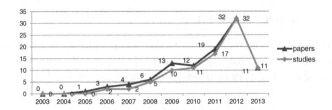

Fig. 4. Time Distribution of Selected Papers and Studies

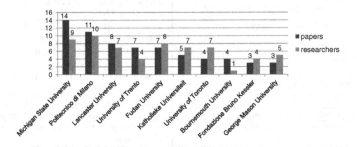

Fig. 5. Top 10 Research Groups and Researchers

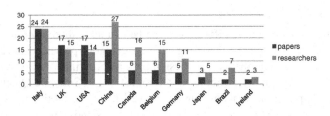

Fig. 6. Top 10 Region and Researchers

RQ2: What modeling methods and RE activities are studied?

Figure 7 presents the modeling methods and the corresponding frequency of studies. These modeling methods are categorized and synthesized according to the objective of modeling activities, including requirements, context and system. Goal-oriented methodologies, including KAOS [25], i* [26] and Tropos [27], are the most popular requirements modeling methods in the literature. They can clearly describe stakeholders' intension and systems' requirements. Temporal logic, including LTL [28], CTL [29] and FBTL [30] are always used as specification languages. They are utilized to specify the properties that should be held by the system. When modeling context, context models [31] are always built to capture the environmental properties. Z notation [32] is used to specify systems' behavior. Transition systems including Markov Chain [33], Petri Net [34] and DDN [35] are adopted to describe systems' states and state transitions. In addition, UML models [36] are also used to model systems' behavior. Problem frame, feature model and feedback control mechanism are more close to design level. Business process model and domain-specific model focus more on business logic and domain logic, respectively.

Figure 8 presents the categories of RE activities and the corresponding frequency of studies. RE activities are classified into activities at requirements time, activities at design time and activities at runtime. Activities at requirements time focus on modeling and specifying requirements [30], modeling adaptation mechanism [37] and verification [38]. Activities at design time mainly aim to map requirements model to architecture model [39] or derive design decisions based on requirements [40]. Activities at runtime include achieving adaptation through MAPE loop [41], runtime verification [33], runtime reconfiguration [42] and runtime evolution [43].

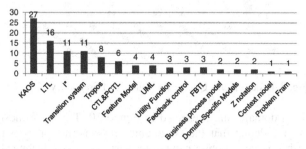

Fig. 7. Modeling Methods and Corresponding Frequency of Studies

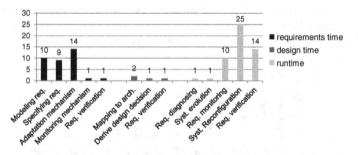

Fig. 8. RE activities and Corresponding Frequency of Studies

Challenges in Modeling Methods and RE Activities. Figure 7 depict that context modeling in RE for SASs still lacks study. The modeling method proposed in [31] may inspire us to work out other innovative context models. Promising research topics related to context may include: model and specify context uncertainty, reasoning with context uncertainty and requirements-driven adaptation with context uncertainty. Figure 8 depicts that there are research gaps in mapping requirements to architectures. Promising research topics may include: requirements-driven architecture adaptation and requirements-driven evolution.

RQ3: What requirements quality attributes and application domains are involved?

We investigate the requirements quality attributes (Figure 9) related to SASs according to ISO 9126. We do not intend to elaborate the definitions of these quality attributes, but reveal the relations implied behind. According to [18], adaptability and replaceability belong to portability. These two quality attributes are involved in the studies of building adaptation mechanism or runtime adaptation. Analyzability is considered in the studies of monitoring or diagnosing requirements. Time behavior and resource behavior are always concerned in the evaluation of the adaptation process. Reliability is studied in the work on the topic of verification. Fault tolerance is always derived by relaxing the requirements. Security is discussed in security requirements engineering. Understandability is involved in the study of producing more understandable requirements model.

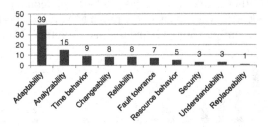

Fig. 9. Requirements Quality Attributes and Frequency of Studies

The application domains are presented in Figure 10. The top 5 most widely cited application domains depict that the community concentrate on investigating online applications, web services, mobile computing systems, social-technical systems and smart living systems. We find the common characteristic of this application domain is that they all need to interact with other software, systems or the human. These results will benefit researchers and practitioners to choose the most appropriate demonstrations and design the most reasonable experiments for their research work.

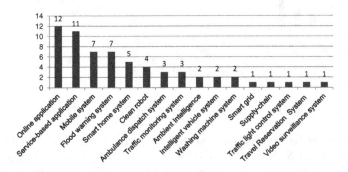

Fig. 10. Application Domains and Frequency of Studies

Challenges in Requirements Quality Attributes and Application Domains. Figure 9 shows the gaps in research on security requirements engineering, adaptation mechanisms that can provide explanations to the human and compositional adaptation. Researchers can also consider other quality attributes, e.g. recoverability. Besides, the application domain should be chosen to underpin the quality attributes.

RQ4: Which methods are better applied and more rigorously evaluated?
    Relevant studies are appraised according to the quality assessment checklist (Table 5). Figure 11 depicts that KAOS and i* both have relatively low score, because some of modeling methods and adaptation mechanisms proposed based on KAOS or i* lack rigorous evaluation. The highest scored logic is CTL&PCTL, for they are widely used

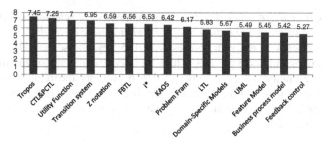

Fig. 11. Quality Score of Modeling Methods

to model system properties for model checking, which is inherently a rigorous approach. Domain-specific models, UML models, feature model, business process model and feedback control need more exploration and more rigorous evaluation.

RQ5: Which RE activities are presented and discussed more detailedly?

Figure 8 depicts the first three activities at requirements time and the last three activities at runtime are almost explored in more than 10 studies. Therefore, the scores of these activities are more convincing than others'. In these six activities, requirements verification at runtime has the highest score, for the verification process is always based on rigorous reasoning or mathematical methods. System reconfiguration at runtime comes after runtime verification, because this process is related to decision making and the evaluation process is always elaborately designed. The next is runtime monitoring, which also includes rigorous analysis processes. The three activities at requirements time are lower scored because they are always involved in qualitative studies and most of the evaluations are based on qualitative demonstrations.

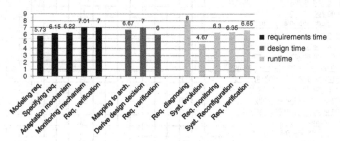

Fig. 12. Quality Score of RE activity

Challenges in Quality of Research. To achieve more precise and more effective adaptation decisions, we expect to derive quantitative models and quantitative representations during requirements modeling and analysis. Therefore, we should incorporate research results in other disciplines into RE for SASs. Fuzzy set theory, probabilistic theory and probability theory can be applied to describing uncertainties of both requirements and context. Control theory can be utilized to design adaptation mechanisms in SASs. Optimization theory, decision theory and game theory can be used to derive adaptation decisions. In this way, the quality of modeling methods and RE activities may get improved.

RQ6: What topics can we generalize based on the content of selected studies?
RQ7: What is the relationship between topics and modeling methods?

We code segments of relevant studies with 135 key phrases and 44 of them are kept after removing duplicate phrases. Then, these codes are categorized into 7 topics according to the content of each paper. Table 6 presents the relationship between topics and the related modeling methods. The bar in the table indicates the relative frequency of each method. One study may have more than one code and adopt more than one modeling method.

Table 6. Relationship between Topics and Modeling Methods

Topic	Item	KAOS	i*	Tropos	Feature Model	Context model	Problem Frame	UML	Business process model	Domain-Specific Model	Transition system	LTL	CTL&PCTL	FBTL	Z notation	Utility Function	Feedback control
Modeling requirements, contexts and systems	context modeling and analysis	1		1		1											
	defining SAS development framework			2													
	describing adaptation in feedback loop									1							1
	modeling adaptation mechanism	5	2	1				1	1	1							
	model adaptation with security requirements	2															
	modeling and resoning on NFR							1									
	modeling domain requirements for SAS								1								
	modeling requirements evolution	1															
	modeling RE activities of SAS		1														
	modeling security requirements	1															
	modeling systems behavior										1						
	modeling variant of self-adaptive systems								1								
	cope with requirements changes			2													
	customize software with preferences	1															
Specifying adaptive elements	specifying and managing self-* properties														1		
	specifying adaptation mechanism									1							
	specifying adaptation semantics	3									2						
	specifying adaptive programs										2						
	specifying adaptive requirements	1															
	specifying self-adaptive systems							1			1				1		
Dealing with uncertainty	addressing environmental uncertainty	1						1									
	decision making with uncertainty		1								2					1	
	mitigating uncertainty through adaptation	1	1										1				
	modeling sources of uncertainty		1														
	modeling uncertainty in requirements														1		
Verification and validation	QoS verification										1		1				
	requirements modeling and validation										1						
	validating the qualities of system										1	1					
	validating requirements at design time												1				
	verifying NFR at runtime										1		1				
	verifying adaptive programs										3						
	verifying requirements at runtime										3	1	3				
Monitoring and detecting	monitoring requirements	2		1							1					1	1
	detecting inconsistency within contextual req.			1													
	detecting requirements violation	1									1					1	
Adaptation and decision making	self-tunning with unanticipated changes					1											
	dealing with runtime variability reconfiguration					1											
	requirements-driven runtime reconfiguration	5	2	1		2											1
	runtime evolution by dynamic reconfiguration	1											1				
	runtime reconfiguration with model evolution							1									
	decision making to protect security req.	1															
	optimizing design decision			1													
	trade-off between FR and NFR						1										
mapping	mapping requirements model to arch. model		1								2						

Challenges in Research Topics

Researchers can refer to this table for investigating how different modeling methods are applied to a certain research topic. They can also explore how a certain modeling method can be adopted into different research topics. The blank areas in the table present research gaps in requirements modeling and analysis for self-adaptive systems. Promising topics may include: quantitative reasoning with NFR, modeling adaptation behavior with transition systems, runtime verification with context uncertainty. Indeed, to generate new topics or new motivation, a flexible way is incorporating uncertainty into the existing topics, since uncertainty has been a first-class concept in requirements engineering for self-adaptive systems.

4   Threats to Validity

Potential Bias. During conducting the review, researcher's bias may affect the analysis results. We adopt Kappa coefficient to assess the selection results and categorizing results of different researchers. When there is disagreement, we eliminate it by conducting a joint meeting and discussing with external researchers.

Internal Threats. Internal threats to validity deal with systematic errors in design and conduct of the review. To reduce this threat, we establish a rigorous protocol in advance and the protocol is reviewed by external reviewers. When conducting the review, the participants are divided into two groups. The final results are derived by integrating their individual results together.

External Threats. There may be some threats to external validity with respect to the generalization of the conclusions of this study. We note that with the increasing number of works in the literature we cannot guarantee complete capture of all the material in this area. There are still numerous unpublished papers, which cause the decrease of paper frequency in 2013 (Figure 4). We diminish this threat by taking into account all the primary venues in this area and integrating manual search, automated search and "snowball" search together to get the final set of relevant studies.

5   Related Roadmaps and Surveys

During the last decade, roadmaps and surveys of the literature have summarized the achievements and provide insight is this field. Cheng, et al. [5] and Salehie, et al. [7] are both highly qualified roadmaps in the literature. The former one presented challenges of software engineering for self-adaptive systems in four aspects: modeling dimensions, requirements, engineering and assurances. The latter one provided more details and insights in requirements engineering, design, implementation and test. More recently, Weyns, et al. [22] summarized several interesting research areas based on the research results of SEAMS from 2006 to 2011 and Dagstuhl seminar in 2008. Besides, they [23] also investigated the formal methods used in self-adaptive systems with research work between 2000 to 2011. Moreover, Patikirikorala, et al. [24] summarized various kinds of control engineering approaches used in designing self-adaptive systems with the publications between 2000 to 2010.

Different from these works, our review not only investigates the modeling methods and RE activities, but also explores how well these methods and activities are conveyed. In addition, we consider a wider time span and more publication venues for ensuring the coverage of existing research work. We present the state-of-the-art research trends and research gaps based on rigorously statistical results, which we hope to make this review more reliable than others. We believe that the SLR methodology we have adopted can make our review more trustworthy.

6   Conclusion and Future Work

The objective of this systematic literature review is to summarize the state-of-the-art trends of research on requirements modeling and analysis for self-adaptive systems. We found that most of these research works are from European countries and American countries, where the research groups produce more results than groups in other regions. A total of 16 modeling methods are used in 11 RE activities, and about 10 requirements quality attributes are studied, while adaptability is the most frequently concerned attribute. Online applications and service-based systems are the mostly cited application domains. It is found that some of the modeling methods need more exploration and most of the qualitative studies need more rigorous evaluation. The results of thematic synthesis (Table 6) show the gaps in using these modeling methods. In addition to these statistical results, we also analyzed the reasons implied behind the results and put forward some promising challenges implied by the results.

Our future work focuses on further investigating the relationship between requirements modeling methods and RE activities, the relationship between requirements quality attributes and modeling methods, and the relationship between requirements quality attributes and RE activities. Furthermore, we will also explore how the modeling methods and RE activities are evaluated in case studies and how the application domains are chosen for illustration. We also plan to publish all the research details and the relevant studies in the form of journal paper for helping researchers and practitioners better understand our research results and the research literature.

Acknowledgements. We thank Prof. Barbara A. Kitchenham and her team at Keele University for reviewing our protocol and all the received advice. This research is supported by the National Natural Science Foundation of China under Grant Nos 61232015 and 91318301. This research is also supported in part by the Natural Science Foundation of Guangxi Province under Grant No. 2012GXNSFCA053010.

References

1. Ganek, A.G., Corbi, T.A.: The dawning of the autonomic computing era. IBM Syst. J. 42, 5–18 (2003)
2. Nuseibeh, B., Easterbrook, S.: Requirements engineering: a roadmap. In: ICSE 2000 Proceedings of the Conference on The Future of Software Engineering, pp. 35–46 (2000)
3. Kephart, J.O., Chess, D.M.: The Vision of Autonomic Computing. Computer 36, 41–50 (2003)

4. Dobson, S., Denazis, S., Fernandez, A., Gaiti, D., Gelenbe, E., Massacci, F., Nixon, P., Saffre, F., Schmidt, N., Zambonelli, F.: A survey of autonomic communications. ACM Trans. Auton. Adapt. Syst. 1, 223–259 (2006)
5. Cheng, B.H.C., et al.: Software Engineering for Self-Adaptive Systems: A Research Roadmap. In: Cheng, B.H.C., de Lemos, R., Giese, H., Inverardi, P., Magee, J. (eds.) Software Engineering for Self-Adaptive Systems. LNCS, vol. 5525, pp. 1–26. Springer, Heidelberg (2009)
6. de Lemos, R., Giese, H., Müller, H.A., Shaw, M., Andersson, J., Litoiu, M., Schmerl, B., Tamura, G., Villegas, N.M., Vogel, T., Weyns, D., Baresi, L., Becker, B., Bencomo, N., Brun, Y., Cukic, B., Desmarais, R., Dustdar, S., Engels, G., Geihs, K., Göschka, K.M., Gorla, A., Grassi, V., Inverardi, P., Karsai, G., Kramer, J., Lopes, A., Magee, J., Malek, S., Mankovskii, S., Mirandola, R., Mylopoulos, J., Nierstrasz, O., Pezzè, M., Prehofer, C., Schäfer, W., Schlichting, R., Smith, D.B., Sousa, J.P., Tahvildari, L., Wong, K., Wuttke, J.: Software Engineering for Self-Adaptive Systems: A Second Research Roadmap. In: de Lemos, R., Giese, H., Müller, H.A., Shaw, M. (eds.) Software Engineering for Self-Adaptive Systems. LNCS, vol. 7475, pp. 1–32. Springer, Heidelberg (2013)
7. Salehie, M., Tahvildari, L.: Self-adaptive software: Landscape and research challenges. ACM Trans. Auton. Adapt. Syst. 4, 1–42 (2009)
8. Brereton, P., Kitchenham, B.A., Budgen, D., Turner, M., Khalil, M.: Lessons from applying the systematic literature review process within the software engineering domain. Journal of Systems and Software 80, 571–583 (2007)
9. Kitchenham, B., Charters, S.: Guidelines for performing Systematic Literature Reviews in Software Engineering. EBSE Technical Report (2007)
10. Kitchenham, B.A., Dyba, T., Jorgensen, M.: Evidence-based software engineering. In: 26th International Conference on Software Engineering, pp. 273–281 (2004)
11. Dyba, T., Kitchenham, B.A., Jorgensen, M.: Evidence-based software engineering for practitioners. IEEE Software 22, 58–65 (2005)
12. Protocol for A Systematic Literature Review of Requirements Modeling and Analysis for Self-adaptive Systems,
https://www.dropbox.com/s/t6i4ock5g11zo2x/SASProtocol.pdf
13. Zhang, H., Babar, M.A., Tell, P.: Identifying relevant studies in software engineering. Information and Software Technology 53, 625–637 (2011)
14. ERA Outlet Rankings Access,
http://lamp.infosys.deakin.edu.au/era/?page=hmain
15. Landis, J.R., Koch, G.G.: The measurement of observer agreement for categorical data. Biometrics 33, 159–174 (1977)
16. QDA Miner V4 and WordStat V6, http://provalisresearch.com/products/
17. Dybå, T., Dingsøyr, T.: Empirical studies of agile software development: A systematic review. Information and Software Technology 50, 833–859 (2008)
18. ISO 9126 software quality model definition,
http://www.sqa.net/iso9126.html
19. Cruzes, D.S., Dyba, T.: Recommended Steps for Thematic Synthesis in Software Engineering. In: International Symposium on Empirical Software Engineering and Measurement, pp. 275–284 (2011)
20. Cruzes, D., Mendonca, M., Basili, V., Shull, F., Jino, M.: Extracting Information from Experimental Software Engineering Papers. In: 26th International Conference of the Chilean Society of Computer Science, pp. 105–114 (2007)

21. Extracted Data of Systematic Literature Review of Requirements Modeling and Analysis for Self-adaptive Systems, https://www.dropbox.com/s/1ksksvcyjsxhg0n/SASData.xlsx

22. Weyns, D., Iftikhar, M.U., Malek, S., Andersson, J.: Claims and supporting evidence for self-adaptive systems: A literature study. In: ICSE Workshop on Software Engineering for Adaptive and Self-Managing Systems, pp. 89–98 (2012)

23. Weyns, D., Iftikhar, M.U., de la Iglesia, D.G., Ahmad, T.: A survey of formal methods in self-adaptive systems. In: 5th International Conference on Computer Science and Software Engineering, pp. 67-79 (2012)

24. Patikirikorala, T., Colman, A., Han, J., Liuping, W.: A systematic survey on the design of self-adaptive software systems using control engineering approaches. In: ICSE Workshop on Software Engineering for Adaptive and Self-Managing Systems, pp. 33–42 (2012)

25. Dardenne, A., van Lamsweerde, A., Fickas, S.: Goal-directed requirements acquisition. Sci. Comput. Program. 20, 3–50 (1993)

26. Yu, E.S.K.: Towards modelling and reasoning support for early-phase requirements engineering. In: 3rd International Symposium on Requirements Engineering, pp. 226–235 (1997)

27. Castro, J., Kolp, M., Mylopoulos, J.: Towards requirements-driven information systems engineering: the Tropos project. Information Systems 27, 365–389 (2002)

28. Zhang, J., Cheng, B.H.C.: Using temporal logic to specify adaptive program semantics. Journal of Systems and Software 79, 1361–1369 (2006)

29. Filieri, A., Ghezzi, C., Leva, A., Maggio, M.: Self-adaptive software meets control theory: A preliminary approach supporting reliability requirements. In: 26th International Conference on Automated Software Engineering (ASE), pp. 283–292 (2011)

30. Whittle, J., Sawyer, P., Bencomo, N., Cheng, B.H.C., Bruel, J.-M.: RELAX: a language to address uncertainty in self-adaptive systems requirement. Requir. Eng. 15, 177–196 (2010)

31. Ali, R., Dalpiaz, F., Giorgini, P.: A goal-based framework for contextual requirements modeling and analysis. Requir. Eng. 15, 439–458 (2010)

32. Weyns, D., Malek, S., Andersson, J.: FORMS: Unifying reference model for formal specification of distributed self-adaptive systems. ACM Trans. Auto. Adapt. Syst. 7, 1–61 (2012)

33. Filieri, A., Ghezzi, C., Tamburrelli, G.: A formal approach to adaptive software: continuous assurance of non-functional requirements. Form. Asp. Comp. 24, 163–186 (2012)

34. Zhang, J., Cheng, B.H.C.: Model-based development of dynamically adaptive software. In: The 28th International Conference on Software Engineering, pp. 371–380 (2006)

35. Bencomo, N., Belaggoun, A.: Supporting Decision-Making for Self-Adaptive Systems: From Goal Models to Dynamic Decision Networks. In: Doerr, J., Opdahl, A.L. (eds.) REFSQ 2013. LNCS, vol. 7830, pp. 221–236. Springer, Heidelberg (2013)

36. Goldsby, H.J., Cheng, B.H.: Automatically Generating Behavioral Models of Adaptive Systems to Address Uncertainty. In: Czarnecki, K., Ober, I., Bruel, J.-M., Uhl, A., Völter, M. (eds.) MODELS 2008. LNCS, vol. 5301, pp. 568–583. Springer, Heidelberg (2008)

37. Cheng, B.H., Sawyer, P., Bencomo, N., Whittle, J.: A Goal-Based Modeling Approach to Develop Requirements of an Adaptive System with Environmental Uncertainty. In: Schürr, A., Selic, B. (eds.) MODELS 2009. LNCS, vol. 5795, pp. 468–483. Springer, Heidelberg (2009)

38. Weyns, D.: Towards an integrated approach for validating qualities of self-adaptive systems. In: The 2012 Workshop on Dynamic Analysis, pp. 24–29 (2012)

39. Pimentel, J., Lucena, M., Castro, J., Silva, C., Santos, E., Alencar, F.: Deriving software architectural models from requirements models for adaptive systems: the STREAM-A approach. Requir. Eng. 17, 259–281 (2012)
40. Morandini, M., Penserini, L., Perini, A.: Towards goal-oriented development of self-adaptive systems. In: Proceedings of the 2008 International Workshop on Software Engineering for Adaptive and Self-Managing Systems, pp. 9–16 (2008)
41. Wang, Y., Mcilraith, S.A., Yu, Y., Mylopoulos, J.: Monitoring and diagnosing software requirements. Automated Software Engg. 16, 3–35 (2009)
42. Yiqiao, W., Mylopoulos, J.: Self-Repair through Reconfiguration: A Requirements Engineering Approach. In: 24th International Conference on Automated Software Engineering, pp. 257–268 (2009)
43. Inverardi, P., Mori, M.: Requirements models at run-time to support consistent system evolutions. In: 2nd International Workshop on Requirements@Run.Time, pp. 1–8 (2011)

Requirements-Driven Social Adaptation: Expert Survey

Malik Almaliki[1], Funmilade Faniyi[2], Rami Bahsoon[2], Keith Phalp[1], and Raian Ali[1]

[1] Bournemouth University, UK
[2] University of Birmingham, UK

Abstract. **[Context and motivation]** Self-adaptation empowers systems with the capability to meet stakeholders' requirements in a dynamic environment. Such systems autonomously monitor changes and events which drive adaptation decisions at runtime. Social Adaptation is a recent kind of requirements-driven adaptation which enables users to give a runtime feedback on the success and quality of a system's configurations in reaching their requirements. The system analyses users' feedback, infers their collective judgement and then uses it to shape its adaptation decisions. **[Question/problem]** However, there is still a lack of engineering mechanisms to guarantee a correct conduction of Social Adaptation. **[Principal ideas/results]** In this paper, we conduct a two-phase Expert Survey to identify core benefits, domain areas and challenges for Social Adaptation. **[Contribution]** Our findings provide practitioners and researchers in adaptive systems engineering with insights on this emerging role of users, or the crowd, and stimulate future research to solve the open problems in this area.

Keywords: Requirements Engineering, Adaptive Systems, Social Adaptation.

1 Introduction

In self-adaptive software community there has been a great deal of emphasis on architectures to support design and development of adaptation, models for anticipating and reacting to changes in the managed system and methods for verifying properties of these systems [1,2]. Ultimately, self-adaptivity is a meta-computing capability which enables a system to reason about itself and its dynamic environment so that it can formulate the right decisions to reach stakeholders' requirements [3].

While success on these foundational fronts has contributed significantly to the field, the role of users in the adaptation process has only recently become a main focus. This can be partly attributed to lessons learnt from successfully deployed self-adaptive systems such as Rainbow [4], where it was found that the adaptation process was not transparent to users. An example of such transparency limitations can be illustrated by the insufficient explanation offered by self-adaptive system about why a course of actions was chosen instead of alternative actions to meet the users' requirements.

Early research in self-adaptive systems limited users' ability to steer adaptation with the good intention of maximizing system autonomy and minimizing human efforts. However, this would lead to adaptation decisions that were valid but only temporarily since users were not given a voice in the iterative validation of these decisions after software was deployed [5]. Consequently, one of the identified research challenges in the engineering of self-adaptive software systems road map is:

C. Salinesi and I. van de Weerd (Eds.): REFSQ 2014, LNCS 8396, pp. 72–87, 2014.
© Springer International Publishing Switzerland 2014

[To devise a way of] *"analysing feedback types from human-computer interaction and devising novel mechanisms for exposing the control loops to the users, keeping the users of self-adapting systems in the loop to ensure their trust"* [1].

Although the role of users in the adaptation process has recently been recognized [5,6,7,8], there is still a lack of consensus and holistic approaches on how to engage the users and the crowd in that process. In this paper, we address this problem and conduct an expert survey to gather and analyse the knowledge of experts in adaptive systems research. We give the acquisition of users' feedback a special focus due to its vital role in enabling this kind of adaptation. Our survey provides practitioners and researchers in self-adaptive systems with insights and challenges to consider when involving users, individually or as a crowd, in the adaptation process.

The paper is structured as follows. In Section 2 we briefly discuss Social Adaptation. In Section 3 we describe the study's objectives and design. In Section 4 and Section 5 we present the results of the first and second phase of the survey, respectively. We discuss threats to validity in Section 6 and conclude the paper in Section 7.

2 Social Adaptation

Social Adaptation is defined as a system's autonomous ability to analyse users' feedback and choose an alternative behaviour which is collectively shown to be the best for meeting requirements in a context [5]. Social Adaptation claims to have the benefit of improving the transparency of the self-adaptive system and raising users' trust in it, since users are treated as first-class entities in both the engineering and also the operation of such systems. In fact, over time of using the software, users may be able to shape the decision-making process in a way that can only be done by today's experts.

Some researchers have pursued similar visions under themes such as requirement-aware self-adaptive systems [9], requirement monitoring at run-time [3], and social adaptation in pervasive software systems [6]. All these efforts adhere to a notion of representing users' requirements or trust relationship among users (in [6]) as run-time objects that can be used by the system to reason about the adaptation process. Other researchers use the term of socially-adaptive software differently to refer to software agents which are socially adaptive in the sense of their ability to comply to social norms, e.g. [10]. Social Adaptation, as described in [5], is unique in the sense that instead of catering to the requirement of a user or subset of users at run-time, it harnesses the "wisdom of the crowd" to adapt the system in a way that is deemed best by end-users' collective judgement rather than the decisions of an elite group of users or those of developers. To put it another way, Social Adaptation pursues the goal of a democratic-like, consensus-based social approach to adapting software systems to meet users' requirements.

In Social Adaptation, users act as monitors and provide software with information via their feedback. This introduces a range of challenges for the engineering of this human-based monitor. Reviewing the literature, we could not identify systematic approaches for feedback acquisition at runtime. The impact of users' feedback and how users behave when providing feedback is still ambiguous as discussed in [11].

The lack of engineering processes for feedback acquisition would lead to poorly designed feedback collection mechanisms and this could harm the quality of collected feedback, users' experience and the quality of adaptation and evolution decisions [7]. Owing to its importance, our Expert Survey will give a particular focus on the engineering challenges of feedback acquisition in Social Adaptation.

3 Expert Survey Design

The study's objectives were to poll the opinion of experts on (i) the principles and primitives for enabling Social Adaptation (ii) the role of users' feedback in steering software adaptation, and (iii) the engineering of software-based feedback acquisition.

3.1 Experts Selection

Experts selection can have a high effect on the survey outcomes and the acceptability of the result in the wider community [12]. Since we are tackling a multidisciplinary research area and in order to have a diversity of viewpoints, we targeted experts from Requirement Engineering and Adaptive Systems research community with additional focus on at least one different related domain: HCI, Human Factors in Computing, Psychology, Privacy and Security Engineering, Socio-Technical Systems Engineering and Social Computing. Our inclusion criteria allowed for experienced participants who are knowledgeable in their respective fields, evidenced by proven publication track record. Although the majority of our experts work in academia, they either worked in industry previously or were engaged in collaborative projects involving industrial partners. To make sure these participants had sufficient experience and knowledge about the discussed issue, some assessment questions regarding their knowledge and experience were asked at the beginning of the questionnaire.

According to expert elicitation practitioners, the number of experts to be included should be at least six, otherwise we would not be confident about the quality of the conclusions and their generalizability [13]. In the first phase of our survey 35 experts were invited; 29 forms were returned. Considering the average actual time taken to complete the survey (35 minutes), the size of the form and the amount of effort required to complete it, we consider this as a good response rate. In the second phase we invited the 29 experts who participated in the first phase and only 21 forms were returned. We invited additional 5 experts so that we got a total of 26 forms completed.

3.2 Design, Test and Distribution of the Survey

We used online questionnaires as a data collection method for our study because our experts were widely distributed geographically (five countries). The questionnaire contained both types of questions: open-ended questions and close-ended questions. The open-ended questions were used to ensure that we minimize the risk of missing significant information and to give participants a space to include information they felt was relevant. Closed questions were employed to ensure that we get a high response rate and to put less effort on participants when answering the questionnaire [14].

Survey questions were deduced and extracted from two talks, given by two of the authors, followed by a brainstorming session on Requirements-driven Social Adaptation. The sessions took place on March 2013 as a part of a project meeting, which included academics in the computing departments of three universities. The participants set included 12 researchers who have a variety of relevant expertise including Requirements Engineering, Self-adaptive Systems, Dynamic Software Product Lines, Cloud Computing, Machine Learning and Human Factors in Computing.

The questions focused on the value and benefits of Social Adaptation for both developers and clients, its application areas, whether it has to be autonomous or semiautonomous and its technical development challenges. A good part of the discussion focused on the acquisition of users' feedback, how to engineer it, and whether it should be adaptive as well. The survey script contained 25 questions discussing and investigating these points.

Questionnaires need to be tested on typical respondents before the actual data collection stage begins to ensure their readiness and clarity [15]. Our questionnaire was tested first on three respondents who met our inclusion criteria. After the test and revision, experts were sent an email containing a brief description of our purpose of the survey and asking them to participate in the Expert Survey. We gave a period of two weeks for them to come back to us with their input. Surprisingly, the response rate was high (29 out of 35) which is an indicator that the field is relevant and timely especially to Requirements Engineering which is a primary research area of our surveyed experts.

4   First Phase Results

The returned survey forms were analysed and responses were cleaned up and irrelevant/inconsistent answers were excluded. A descriptive analysis on the quantitative part of the survey was conducted to describe the data and to get the feel of it. A qualitative analysis was applied to the open-ended questions of the survey which included coding the response and creating categories to identify patterns and trends in the responses.

4.1   Social Adaptation Benefits and Value

Social Adaptation claims to offer valuable benefits for both developers and users. This claim raises important questions that need to be addressed by experts. The following 4 questions attempt to dig a little deeper, that is to understand, not only to what extent Social Adaptation is beneficial but also to understand better the nature and context of those benefits among different groups. The questions also vary in their focus. In brief, Q1 to 3 consider benefits for developers and clients or users with Q4 attempting to consider areas that are either particularly fruitful or, in contrast do not offer particular benefits.

> *Q1: How would you rate the benefits of Social Adaptation: (a) For software developers? (b) For software clients.*

Beneficiary / Rating	High	Medium	Low
Developer	13	14	2
Client	20	8	1

A rating of *Low* implies Social Adaptation is not beneficial; *Medium* implies that there are benefits but not necessarily significant; significant benefits are rated as *High*. There is a consensus among experts that Social Adaptation, if realised, is a useful concept to developers (93% chose medium/high) and clients (96% chose medium/high). The higher perceived benefit to clients is perhaps not surprising, as users will have more active role in steering the adaptation process.

Q2: What are the benefits of Social Adaptation for software developers?

Social Adaptation, as indicated by experts' responses, offers valuable benefits for both developers and users of adaptive software. **[Finding 2.1]** Acquired knowledge through users' feedback can be used to build and refine models used by the system or to improve the accuracy of reactive or predictive adaptive algorithms for various aspects of the self-adaptive system. New knowledge may also reveal latent requirements that were not known before. Developers of self-adaptive systems can therefore use Social Adaptation to: (1) improve problem resolution tactics by identifying bugs and scenarios that cause software crashes and poor performance, (2) better prioritise requirements and maximise the productivity of limited development resources, (3) identify the distribution of software use across age groups, geo-location, time of day etc., and (4) build knowledge-bases of contextual profiles, which are hard to elicit at design time where the users have not used the system in real settings yet.

In contrast to Q1, where the numbers are revealing; this open question gave us a great deal of insightful comments from the expert survey. In terms of benefits, respondents noted that Social Adaptation: *"Provides insights from the user perspective to software developers on aspects of the system that need to change."* (EX24). *"Learning about and adapting to new (or un-elicited) requirements and making software more aware of new contexts seamlessly."* (EX25). *"Up-to-date knowledge - accessible unobservable knowledge - able to react to new events (in a faster way) - more knowledge shared knowledge"* (EX1). *"Considering adaptation early avoids making hard and expensive changes afterwards when the system is running."* (EX12).

[Finding 2.2] Future socially-driven adaptive systems may disrupt the current development paradigm of self-adaptive systems, in terms of time to market or deploy, by reducing the upfront effort in design phase to the barest minimum. By taking the socialized view of adaptation, the system will only provide a platform for users to express their preferences, whilst design decisions are collectively made by users at run-time. This indeed makes Social Adaptation different from other approaches (e.g. Agile software development) in which the variability points of the software and execution environment will be learnt at run-time based on feedback provided by users which makes. This is a realistic assessment since users of today's software system vary widely in their preferences (perhaps, influenced by culture, norms, age group, location etc). Designers of adaptive systems will focus on engineering open, configurable, and extensible platforms, instead of debating functionality choices.

Q3: What are the benefits of Social Adaptation for users?

The ultimate goal of Social Adaptation is to satisfy users' requirements efficiently by enabling users to steer and tailor the adaptation process. Our experts agreed that Social Adaptation was of most benefit to users. This correlates with responses to the first question. [**Finding 3.1**] The benefits cited included improved trust (users feel their voice is considered), [**Finding 3.2**] user satisfaction (software behaves according to users' judgement), [**Finding 3.3**] transparency (adaptation decisions is visible to users), and [**Finding 3.4**] confidence in self-adaptive system *"1- Acknowledgement of clients' opinion 2 Visible involvement of clients in the adaptation"* (EX22), *" Having a software with an adaptive behaviour based on similar users / past experience and participation / involvement in a community is very gratifying to many users"* (EX5).

The data also revealed that the involvement of users and their ability to collectively configure the software on the fly at run-time could result in users perceiving the software as a partner rather than a tool *"Clients will have more user-friendly software as a result of the analysis performed on information received from them. Their confidence and trust in the adaptive systems may grow. They will be able to provide focused and real-time feedback to the developers which can in return empower them."* (EX3). Indeed this is consistent with the overarching objective of self-adaptation, where the software is expected to adapt to users' needs and not the other way around. Since Social Adaptation is a group-based adaptation, the software will be able to quickly adapt to group norms and beliefs, without the conventional maintenance-evolution phases.

Experts also indicated that users' involvement should be accommodated under some constraints and users should not be always involved in shaping and validating software adaptation. Restricting users' involvement is due to a negative effect on users' experience (e.g. annoyance), which might arise when involving them too much *"if every system would ask often to confirm something, the end-users would be overwhelmed and they would not react at all"* (EX1).

Aside from the apparent benefits of Social Adaptation to users (as listed above), one unusual finding is the perceived impact on the software life-cycle of self-adaptive software systems. The idea of fully automated user-driven evolution or reduced human involvement in the evolution process already raises many challenges. An example of these challenges could be the way users' feedback is being collected and analysed by the system. The findings and challenges in this area will be discussed in another question.

Q4: Can you nominate certain areas and application domains where Social Adaptation: (a) has distinguished benefits (b) should not be used?

A common theme raised by our respondents was the need for a user-centred or human-oriented software and user bases in which preferences of the entire user population collectively steer the adaptation. We classify the identified application areas as follows:

- [Finding 4.1] **Mobility intensive systems** where software is used in different contexts, e.g., driving navigation systems *"Telecom industry will be highly interested in such applications, Content intensive applications"* (EX10).
- [[Finding 4.2] **Large-scale systems** such as SaaS clouds, where the software is in global demand and developers are unable to elicit preferences of groups of users distributed around the world *"Any software system that has a very large community of users, e.g., smartphone applications."* (EX7).
- [Finding 4.3] **Real time management systems** where crowd-sourcing will empower the system monitor and enhance the decision making. For example,

evacuation scenarios or congestion management at train stations or airports "- *unobservable areas - areas with lots of traffic and different end-users and needs (airport, central train stations, shopping malls) - mobile devices (apps with unknown end users)"* (EX1).

- **[Finding 4.4] Highly interactive systems:** These are software that is frequently used for variety of purposes where it is hard to know a priori how users will judge quality in the diverse contexts of use and human-computer interaction. Mobile, pervasive, and social networking applications fall into this category of highly interactive systems. *"Systems with repetitive tasks. The driving navigation system is a good example. Perhaps an operating system, adapts to common usage. Also embedded electronics like refrigerators, heating, etc. could adapt to behaviour without criticality."* (EX14).
- **[Finding 4.5] Prototyping tools** in moderately dynamic systems, where feedback from Social Adaptation can be used to infer user needs before a final implementation is carried out. Here, there is an assumption that the rate of adaptation is relatively controllable by human development effort after the final system is deployed *"in prototyping for requirements engineering activities possibly, to find out which model to focus on in the actual implementation"* (EX16)

Our experts considered Social Adaptation inapplicable in the following domains:

- **[Finding 4.6] Critical systems** where wrong Social Adaptation could result in disaster or huge financial loses.
- **[Finding 4.7] Security sensitive applications**.
- **[Finding 4.8] Non- or less-interactive systems** under the control of centralised authorities such as payroll system or an embedded system. A comment from an expert in regard to areas outside the scoop of Social Adaptation *"Safety Critical Systems where real-time data input may results in disasters e.g. a nuclear power plant. High Secure Systems - that is sealed/closed systems e.g. military missile systems."* (EX3).

It is interesting to uncover the subtle difference between "personalised" adaptation and "social" adaptation as evident in candidate application areas listed above. The former refers to a type of user-driven adaptation where the objective is to meet the requirement of user(s) with mutual non-conflicting preferences. Crucially, some users may choose not to conform to popular opinion, therefore, they should be given the freedom to deviate from the choice deemed best by the group (e.g. for some privacy reasons). On the other hand, social adaptation is a different concept as the preferences of the entire user base (including conflicting ones) is collectively used by the system to adapt in a way deemed best for the group. Figure 1 illustrates the difference between these concepts. Applying Social Adaptation in the previous domains is a promising opportunity to empower adaptation quality. The reason is that the potential to get a wide range and large volume of users' feedback is high and that the users' feedback is meaningful as the interaction between users and the software is intensive.

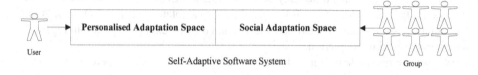

Fig. 1. Personalised Adaptation Versus Social Adaptation in Self-Adaptive Software

4.2 Challenges to Supporting Benefits to Developers and Users

Utilising on-line Learning: The role of on-line learning is a key in realising open platforms for socially-driven adaptation since there is a question of: how do we build a system when little is known about the users of the system. Existing work in the self-adaptation literature mainly uses learning-based approaches to model decision-making about computational configurations at run-time (e.g. [16,17]). Unlike these efforts, the role of learning here is that of learning user trends, behaviours, and adaptively resolving conflicts among user preferences at run-time. Since user behaviour and preferences are not static, i.e. users themselves evolve, a fully open social-adaptation platform should empower users to decide the protocols and resolution tactics for their collaboration. Consequently, **[Challenge 1]** there is the problem of identifying what learning models to use for enabling user interaction and conflict resolution at run-time and **[Challenge 2]** how the process of mining users' feedbacks should be conducted to inform recommendations which are consistent with the system's requirements.

Gauging User Involvement: The challenges include **[Challenge 3]** how to measure users' involvement with the system as a main descriptor of their feedback, **[Challenge 4]** identifying the degree to which users are allowed to configure the software on the fly at run-time and **[Challenge 5]** and specifying restrictions for their involvement (e.g. users can provide feedback after a certain period of use).

Monitoring Adaptation Spaces: From Figure 1, it can be observed that while a user is able to independently tune parameters in his/her personalised adaptation space, the system's social adaptation space, which also affects the user, is a product of a collective configuration. **[Challenge 6]** The research challenge here is to develop models and languages to allow users to specify their preference on the way their requirements are reached (e.g. when to rely on the crowd and when to take their personal choices). Another challenge **[Challenge 7]** is to develop mechanisms to allow software to deduce such users' preference without getting them explicitly involved.

4.3 Implementation Choices (Autonomy and Feedback Acquisition)

The following questions dig much deeper and attempt to look at issues to consider in implementing Social Adaptation, with Q5 examining autonomy and Qs 6-8 focussing on aspects and developments challenges of users' feedback acquisition process since it plays a significant role in enabling Social Adaptation.

> *Q5: Knowing that relying on Social Adaptation is a user's choice, are there cases where software should still ask users to confirm its adaptation decision?*

The degree of autonomy in socially-adaptive systems has been always debated. Should the system take an autonomous full control on the adaptation process? Or should the user interfere sometimes? We extract, analyse and discuss experts' opinion in regard to autonomy in Social Adaptation.

96% of the respondents agree that user confirmation is essential before an adaptation action autonomously suggested by software is allowed to impact the system. The remaining 4% claim that adaptation actions should not require user confirmation since this is why self-adaptive systems are autonomous *"User should be not too much bothered. Moreover I think that user identification should be automatic in the mechanism adopted to get user feedback."* (EX20).

Even though the consensus tilts towards user involvement in confirming adaptation actions, many experts believe that the answer to this question is not a binary (yes or no). In many cases, the choice of whether user should be involved depends on the type of services provided by the adaptive system (e.g. its criticality), the implication of the action on user's privacy, security, and financial spending. Also, "nice to have" autonomous social adaptation actions should not outweigh core functionalities of the system, hence users need to choose what is important to them in each context.

Q6: Can the quality of collected feedback be affected by the way it is collected?

All respondents agreed that the way feedback is collected has an effect on the quality of the feedback. The exact implication of the collection mechanism can be manifested in terms of:

- **[Finding 6.1] Time:** Asking users for feedback when they are busy may result to poor responses or it may be discarded. Finding the right time to ask for feedback is important *"Asking in a busy moment of the end-user will result in only yes/no answers. Asking if the end-user is bored will result maybe in creative feedback, but not necessarily high quality."* (EX1).
- **[Finding 6.2] User interface:** Short, concise, clear questions should be preferred to long, complicated ones. The user interface should allow users to express their biases using wider band of options, such as Likert scale [18], rather than conventional yes or no options.
- **Finding 6.3] Language:** The phrasing of the question, for example based on the language proficiency of the user, will determine how users interpret and respond to questions. Even for experienced users, misinterpretation is sometimes inevitable due to the ambiguity inherent in natural languages *"simple interfaces are essential, avoid long texts or complicated questions. Things such as "like" and "dislike" may be especially effective"* (EX5).
- **[Finding 6.4] Quality of users:** This involves asking the right user population for feedback and ensuring the size of users is representative of the group characteristics *"Is it the right user group? How representative is the feedback? User profiles? Can you capture user's perception or viewpoint of the question asked? How is the feedback question phrased? Any domain specific language?"* (EX3).
- **[Finding 6.5] User's mood:** Some interesting responses suggest strongly that the mood of users should be factored into the feedback acquisition process. While the mood of users may impact the quality of feedback, it is still hard to monitor the

emotional state of users (e.g. happy, bored, excited, angry etc.) during feedback acquisition. Perhaps advances in recognizing emotions through facial expression [19] could be helpful in this area.

Q7: Is the development feedback acquisition mechansims technically challenging?

Experts stress that developing software-based feedback acquisition poses a variety of technical challenges due to changing context of use and users' evolvement. Almost two-thirds (65%) of the responses indicated that the users selection and interaction style is a key challenge which includes incentivising users to give feedback, when to ask for feedback, who to ask for feedback, how to interact with users without annoying them and the usability degree when giving feedback *"Uncertainty, building a user-friendly interface, convincing the user of the importance of it."* (EX7). *"The design should incentivize impatient and ignorant users to give feedback. Implementation would not be the problem, designing is the main challenge."* (EX18).

Responses also indicated that, engineering of users' feedback acquisition is a multidisciplinary process and it has a potential usefulness and strong relationships with various domains such as, Requirement Engineering, Ubiquitous systems, HCI, Context-aware systems Social Science, Psychology, Recommendation Systems and Machine learning.

From the various experts' answers to the engineering challenges of a software-based feedback acquisition we can deduce that the engineering of an adaptive software-based feedback acquisition stands out as a technically challenging process. The first step of gathering feedback already raises many questions: What type of feedback should be asked of users? How should feedback be cleansed, represented, processed, filtered, and selectively adopted for use by the systems? If users are relied upon to steer the adaptation process, then the system must be equipped with capabilities to cope with the ambiguity flaws of natural languages.

Additionally and in relation to the findings of the previous question (Q6), the extracted engineering challenges of the feedback acquisition can also be considered as factors that can affect negatively/positively the quality of collected feedback. Addressing these challenges can possibly improve the quality of collected feedback. For example, developing an incentive scheme for users might improve the quality of their given feedback.

Q8: If feedback acquisition is adaptive, what could be the adaptation drivers?

Context is important for the choice of feedback acquisition methods, and experts agreed that an adaptive feedback acquisition mechanism is a necessary enabler to decide ways of acquiring feedback. Some possible drivers for such adaptive mechanism suggested were:

- **[Finding 8.1] User experience:** E.g. usage frequency. This could inform how often users should be asked for feedback. For example, a less frequent user may find providing feedback meaningless, since they hardly use the software in the first place *"Usage information of user's laptop (or other smart devices). E.g. if a user is browsing web sites or watching a video, probably he/she is free."* (EX17).

- **[Finding 8.2] Application constraints:** Such as the application model, domain model, and level of interactivity of the software are likely to influence ways of acquiring feedback *"this should include several components, including a user model, application model, domain model, and a general feedback or adaptation model."* (EX8).
- **[Finding 8.3] Direct enquiry:** Involves asking the users if they wish to provide feedback, if yes, how often they wish to do so and what methods they would like to use for providing such feedbacks *"Ask the user what they prefer. When is the best time to give feedback, what form would they like?"* (EX14).

  The identified trend here is that drivers of adaptive feedback acquisition should not be studied in isolation. Such drivers may trade-off against each other. A user that provides feedback frequently, for example, will only find answering the direct enquiry questions useful, as a way of improving his/her feedback provision.

4.4 Research Challenges to Implementing Social Adaptation

Degree of Autonomy: It is interesting to observe that although experts advocate that Social Adaptation is useful for meeting users' requirements, autonomously, based on the crowd feedback, they still believe individual users should be in the loop during the decision-making process of their software. **[Challenge 8]** It raises the question of how much control users are willing to surrender to software systems. For example, in modern autopilot assistant systems, pilots take a supervisory role while software controls the flight of airplanes. The challenge here seems to be psychological in nature, since users are happy to trust the system when they are involved in the decision-making. Does this mean users trust their own socially-generated decisions less than expert knowledge encoded in systems such as Auto-pilot? Suppose, users were able to collaboratively fly an aircraft, would it land safely? Perhaps, this trustworthiness issue is why experts believe that Social Adaptation should not be used in critical systems but in less critical systems (See Q4).

Impact of Collection Approach and Importance of Mood: Investigation into the impact of user mood on the quality of feedback in specific application domains may require evidences from psychology *"This is mainly a psychological issue, finding the right time and modality and give incentives to the user for providing a good feedback"* (EX5). Advances in neuroinformatics could be helpful in this area. Some experts suggest that feedback should only be requested for features that are frequently used by the user. **[Challenge 9]** This will require mechanisms for monitoring user's feature usage statistics/trends and using these results to inform which feedbacks are requested from the user.

[Challenge 10] Some domain-specific feedback acquisition languages and mechanisms might be needed. Some feedback mechanisms may work better in some application areas than others. This challenge is akin to problem in requirement elicitation based on application areas and user experience. Perhaps some lessons can be learnt from the requirements community to address this challenge.

[Challenge 11] Additionally, we could turn to mature fields like HCI to learn how interfaces are built to gather feedback from users in a variety of contexts or even to use innovative features such as voice-based feedback acquisition rather than purely text which might make the process easier and more enjoyable for users *"[users] will provide more feedbacks to a system that can support voice recognition than others without this feature."* (EX17).

Impact of User Selection and Interaction Styles: In a software-based feedback acquisition, a further important challenge is catering for the users selection and inter-action style. More specifically, there are challenges in the following aspects [**Challenges 12-18**]: 1) modelling users styles (including incentives, 2) deciding when to ask for feedback, 3) deciding what type of feedback to ask for, 4) deciding with whom to interact, 5) deciding how to interact and avoid annoying or confusing users, 6) deciding how to design for maximized usability in feedback acquisition and 7) deciding how to ensure trust and reliability of acquired feedback.

Feedback Acquisition Drivers: [**Challenge 19**] The challenge here is indeed the need to identify the relevant drivers of the adaptive acquisition of users feedback and [**Challenge 20**] engineer these drivers in a way that is non-intrusive to users. In addition, Social Adaptation is applicable and useful in various domains and the availability of a systematic approach for engineering an adaptive users' feedback acquisition is highly valuable. It could bring promising benefits for users and developers in the different domain where adaptation is recommended and, perhaps, different disciplines like marketing and e-commerce. [**Challenge 21**] Therefore, the development of an application-independent framework for an adaptive users' feedback acquisition is also a key challenge of users' feedback acquisition.

5   Second Phase Results

From our Expert Survey responses, we were able to deduce and extract a set of core findings and challenges in the area of Social Adaptation and engineering of users' feedback acquisition. In order to confirm the set of extracted findings and the degree of relevance and difficulty of our extracted challenges to the Requirements Engineering research community, we conducted a second phase survey. We invited the 29 experts who responded in the first phase and 21 forms were returned. Then we invited 5 new experts who attended at least one of the seminars given by one of the authors on Social Adaptation. They all responded which made a total of 26 completed form in this phase.

The survey was designed and delivered following our approach in designing the previous Expert Survey (see Section 3). Before experts answer the survey, they were given a brief reminder about the purpose of our first-phase Expert Survey and then a brief description about the second-phase survey and the purpose of it. In addition, a brief description before each set of challenges was given to highlight why it was extracted/identified as a challenge to give a clearer vision to experts before answering the questions.

The questions were developed to discuss and gather experts' opinion in regard to the following three points:

– Confirming our findings of the first phase. We focused on the debatable findings which did not receive a high percentage of consensuses in the first phase. We marked the findings using the tag [**Finding x.y**] in Section 4. We gave three options for each finding: *Agree*, *Partially Agree*, and *Disagree*.

– Measuring the degree of challenge in each of the extracted challenges (we marked the challenges using the tag [**Challenge x.y**] in Section 4). We gave the following three options: *[Ch: A]*: It is challenging and it requires significantly new approaches, *[Ch: B]*: It is challenging but it can still be solved by extending and customizing existing approaches. *[Ch: C]*: It is not really challenging and solutions already exist in the literature.
– Measuring the relevance degree of each challenge to the area of Requirement Engineering (RE). We gave the experts three options here: *[RE: A]*: It is very relevant to RE research. *[RE: B]*: It is not strictly relevant to RE research, but having a solution for it is still beneficial to RE. *[RE: C]*: The challenge and solution are not relevant to RE research and practice.

The following tables present a summary of our second survey findings.

Table 1. The confirmation of experts on the findings of the first phase

Finding	Agree	Partially	Disagree	Finding	Agree	Partially	Disagree
[2.1]	50%	46%	4%	[4.6]	81%	15%	4%
[2.1]	69%	27%	4%	[4.7]	34%	54%	12%
[3.1]	65%	34%	4%	[4.8]	50%	38%	12%
[3.2]	73%	27%	0%	[6.1]	92%	8%	0%
[3.3]	38%	58%	4%	[6.2]	85%	15%	0%
[3.4]	58%	31%	11%	[6.3]	88%	12%	0%
[4.1]	69%	23%	8%	[6.4]	77%	19%	4%
[4.2]	50%	38%	12%	[6.5]	69%	31%	0%
[4.3]	46%	46%	8%	[8.1]	81%	19%	0%
[4.4]	85%	15%	0%	[8.2]	65%	30%	4%
[4.5]	65%	27%	8%	[8.3]	50%	46%	4%

In Table 2, a high degree of challenge is given to engineering challenges related to enabling users to steer the adaptation process and the degree in which they are willing to steer it (e.g. challenge 6 and 8). This high degree of challenge is perhaps due to the lack of models and languages for enabling users to express their adaptation preferences and the lack of studies on the degree of autonomy in socially-adaptive systems. Another noticeable high degree of challenge was given to challenges related to engineering feedback acquisition for different application areas and empowering adaptivity in it (e.g. challenge 10, 19 and 20). The reason behind this high degree of challenge could be the obvious lack of systematic approaches for engineering feedback acquisition.

In addition, challenges related to users' involvement, feedback collection and interaction styles and feedback mining to inform adaptations show a high degree of relevance to RE (e.g. challenge, 2, 5, 6, 10, 13, 14 and 16). This high degree is perhaps because experts believe that users' involvement in the adaptation process, ability to provide feedback in their preferable way and the system's ability to react to their feedback accordingly is a user' requirement that should be systematically engineered and efficiently met.

Table 2. The challenge degree and the relevance to RE of each of the challenges of the first phase

Challenges	[Ch:A]	[Ch:B]	[Ch:C]	[RE:A]	[RE:B]	[RE:C]
[1]	46%	46%	7%	50%	42%	8%
[2]	15%	77%	7%	65%	27%	8%
[3]	38%	54%	7%	42%	46%	12%
[4]	27%	57%	15%	50%	42%	8%
[5]	15%	65%	19%	61%	35%	4%
[6]	61%	34%	7%	84%	11%	4%
[7]	50%	50%	0%	50%	42%	8%
[8]	58%	34%	7%	65%	27%	7%
[9]	15%	77%	7%	57%	27%	15%
[10]	61%	35%	4%	69%	31%	0%
[11]	15%	54%	30%	27%	57%	15%
[12]	42%	50%	8%	46%	34%	19%
[13]	35%	50%	15%	65%	27%	7%
[14]	19%	58%	23%	62%	34%	4%
[15]	24%	50%	8%	50%	42%	8%
[16]	31%	61%	8%	65%	23%	12%
[17]	35%	46%	19%	54%	38%	8%
[18]	35%	57%	7%	58%	35%	7%
[19]	58%	42%	0%	46%	50%	4%
[20]	54%	46%	0%	54%	42%	4%
[21]	46%	46%	8%	50%	46%	4%

6 Threats to Validity

Our expert survey has three main threats to validity:

- The first threat is one of the common issues when designing a questionnaire and relates to ensure whether the questions were understood by all experts as intended. This threat is somehow addressed as we conducted a pilot test on typical respondents then some questions were revised and modified to ensure clarity. This was done for both phases of our survey.
- The second relates to the low percentage of our experts who have industrial experience in adaptive systems. The reason is that adaptive systems are not yet widely applied in industry and much of the work is still in academia. This could mean that our results are flavoured with more judgements coming from academia than industry.
- The third relates to the fact that Social Adaptation is a forward-looking way of developing adaptive systems. This would mean that the answers of our experts are fairly speculative. However, given that most of the elements of this domain as well as the survey questions are directly related to the main areas of expertise of our experts (e.g. requirements engineering, adaptive systems, HCI, and social computing) we would consider that the answers are good enough to draw credible insights.

7   Conclusion

This paper has synthesized findings from a two-phase Expert Survey of 29 experts in the first phase and 26 experts in the second phase on the topic of Social Adaptation and the challenges posed by the mechanisms for collecting user feedback, to steer the adaptation process. The consensus among experts is that Social Adaptation is a highly beneficial concept to both developers and clients of self-adaptive systems. However, enabling Social Adaptation is a technically challenging process due to the lack of models and mechanisms for enabling such a concept. Engineering approaches are highly needed for Social Adaptation to empower users' involvement in shaping adaptation decisions and to systematically develop the feedback collection process and interaction styles as well as feedback mining. The paper has highlighted research challenges in the areas of providing an enabling platform for Social Adaptation and the design of adaptive feedback acquisition mechanisms that fits user context.

Acknowledgement. The research was supported by an FP7 Marie Curie CIG grant (the SOCIAD Project) and by Bournemouth University through the Fusion Investment Fund (the BBB and the VolaComp projects) and the Graduate School PGR Development Fund. We would also like to thank Sarah Williams for insights on conducting qualitative research.

References

1. Cheng, B.H.C., et al.: Software engineering for self-adaptive systems: A research roadmap. In: Cheng, B.H.C., de Lemos, R., Giese, H., Inverardi, P., Magee, J. (eds.) Software Engineering for Self-Adaptive Systems. LNCS, vol. 5525, pp. 1–26. Springer, Heidelberg (2009)
2. Oreizy, P., Gorlick, M.M., Taylor, R.N., Heimhigner, D., Johnson, G., Medvidovic, N., Quilici, A., Rosenblum, D.S., Wolf, A.L.: An architecture-based approach to self-adaptive software. IEEE Intelligent Systems and Their Applications 14(3), 54–62 (1999)
3. Fickas, S., Feather, M.S.: Requirements monitoring in dynamic environments. In: Proceedings of the Second IEEE International Symposium on Requirements Engineering, pp. 140–147. IEEE (1995)
4. Cheng, S.W., Huang, A.C., Garlan, D., Schmerl, B., Steenkiste, P.: Rainbow: Architecture-based self-adaptation with reusable infrastructure. In: International Conference on Autonomic Computing, pp. 276–277. IEEE (2004)
5. Ali, R., Solis, C., Omoronyia, I., Salehie, M., Nuseibeh, B.: Social adaptation at runtime. In: Maciaszek, L.A., Filipe, J. (eds.) ENASE 2012. CCIS, vol. 410, pp. 110–127. Springer, Heidelberg (2013)
6. Esfahani, N., Malek, S.: Social computing networks: a new paradigm for engineering self-adaptive pervasive software systems. In: Proceedings of the 32nd ACM/IEEE International Conference on Software Engineering, vol. 2, pp. 159–162. ACM (2010)
7. Pagano, D., Brügge, B.: User involvement in software evolution practice: A case study. In: Proceedings of the 2013 International Conference on Software Engineering, ICSE 2013, pp. 953–962. IEEE Press, Piscataway (2013)
8. Ali, R., Solis, C., Salehie, M., Omoronyia, I., Nuseibeh, B., Maalej, W.: Social sensing: When users become monitors. In: Proceedings of the 19th ACM SIGSOFT Symposium and the 13th European Conference on Foundations of Software Engineering, ESEC/FSE 2011, pp. 476–479. ACM, New York (2011)

9. Sawyer, P., Bencomo, N., Whittle, J., Letier, E., Finkelstein, A.: Requirements-aware systems: A research agenda for re for self-adaptive systems. In: The 18th IEEE International Requirements Engineering Conference (RE), pp. 95–103. IEEE (2010)

10. Van Riemsdijk, B.: Socially adaptive software. Awareness Magazine (2013)

11. Pagano, D., Maalej, W.: User feedback in the appstore: An empirical study. In: The 21st IEEE International Requirements Engineering Conference (RE), pp. 125–134 (2013)

12. Linstone, H.A., Turoff, M.: The delphi method. Addison-Wesley Reading, MA (1975)

13. Cooke, R.M., Probst, K.N.: Highlights of the Expert Judgment Policy Symposium and Technical Workshop. Resources for the Future, Washington, DC (2006)

14. Leung, W.C.: How to design a questionnaire. Student BMJ 9(11), 187–189 (2001)

15. Franklin, S., Walker, C.: Survey methods and practices. Statistics Canada, Social Survey Methods Division (2003)

16. Elkhodary, A., Esfahani, N., Malek, S.: Fusion: a framework for engineering self-tuning self-adaptive software systems. In: Proceedings of the Eighteenth ACM SIGSOFT International Symposium on Foundations of Software Engineering, pp. 7–16. ACM (2010)

17. Tesauro, G., Jong, N.K., Das, R., Bennani, M.N.: A hybrid reinforcement learning approach to autonomic resource allocation. In: The IEEE International Conference on Autonomic Computing, ICAC 2006, pp. 65–73. IEEE (2006)

18. Likert, R.: A technique for the measurement of attitudes. Archives of Psychology (1932)

19. Adolphs, R.: Recognizing emotion from facial expressions: Psychological and neurological mechanisms. Behavioral and Cognitive Neuroscience Reviews 1(1), 21–62 (2002)

A Requirements Monitoring Infrastructure for Very-Large-Scale Software Systems

Michael Vierhauser, Rick Rabiser, and Paul Grünbacher

Christian Doppler Laboratory MEVSS
Johannes Kepler University Linz, Austria
michael.vierhauser@jku.at

Abstract. **[Context and motivation]** Approaches for requirements monitoring check the compliance of systems with their requirements during operation. **[Question/problem]** Despite many advances, requirements monitoring remains challenging particularly for very-large-scale software systems (VLSS) with system-of-systems architectures. **[Principal ideas/results]** In this research preview we describe key characteristics of industrial VLSS and discuss implications for requirements monitoring. Furthermore, we report on our ongoing work of developing a requirements monitoring infrastructure addressing these characteristics. **[Contribution]** Our infrastructure supports runtime monitoring of requirements across systems; variability management of requirements-based monitors; and the integration of monitoring data from different sources in a VLSS.

Keywords: Requirements monitoring, very-large-scale software systems.

1   Introduction

Many very-large-scale software systems are systems of systems (SoS) with decentralized control; support for multiple platforms; inherently volatile and conflicting requirements; continuous evolution and deployment; as well as heterogeneous, inconsistent, and changing components [1,9,12,13]. Due to their scale the behavior of VLSS cannot be fully tested or predicted and only emerges during operation. This means that detecting violations of requirements and desired properties at runtime plays an important role. Different research communities have developed approaches for monitoring system properties at runtime. Examples cover requirements monitoring [11, 15], complex event processing [17], or runtime verification [3,8] to name but a few. However, it has been reported that simply applying existing approaches and techniques to large-scale systems will likely lead to problems [1, 9]. The size, scale, and heterogeneity of VLSS imply significant challenges for requirements monitoring: for instance, different technologies and architectural paradigms need to be considered. VLSS also operate in a complex environment and interact with third-party and legacy systems. Furthermore, requirements in VLSS exist at different levels and across different

C. Salinesi and I. van de Weerd (Eds.): REFSQ 2014, LNCS 8396, pp. 88–94, 2014.

systems and are defined in different artifacts, which are owned by diverse stakeholders. The requirements are often overlapping, conflicting, or cross-cutting and
cannot easily be allocated to the involved systems. Still, when different systems
are composed, their requirements need to be aligned to satisfy the overall VLSS
requirements.

In our ongoing research we are developing an infrastructure for monitoring
requirements in VLSS. The infrastructure will provide capabilities for monitoring
requirements across systems in the VLSS during development and operation.
It will also address variability management of requirements-based monitors to
support different system variants and versions. Event models are used as a unified
representation of monitoring data collected from the involved systems. Our work
is carried out in cooperation with Siemens VAI Metals Technologies (SVAI) in the
context of VLSS for metallurgical plants in the domain of industrial automation.
In this research preview paper we present a brief problem description based on
an industrial example and summarize our ongoing work.

2 Industrial Motivation and Challenges

VLSS automating metallurgical plants in the iron and steel making industries
provide capabilities for production planning, material tracking and optimization,
as well as basic hardware automation. Metallurgical plants comprise different
mechanical systems each relying on complex interdependent software systems
sizing up to several million lines of code. For instance, our industry partner
Siemens VAI provides a wide range of software-intensive systems for operating blast furnaces, electric arc furnaces, continuous casting machines, or rolling
mills in steel plants. These self-contained software systems are engineered independently. However, there are manifold dependencies that need to be considered
when planning their joint operation. Rolling mills in a plant, for example, depend
on the production capacity of the casting machines while the casting machines
rely on the material input they receive from steel making. The VLSS is further connected to legacy or third-party systems. The requirements of all these
systems are often cross-cutting and interrelated. Requirements about the production capacity of the caster for example are related with requirements about
the production speed of the rolling mills. Similarly, the requirements about ladle handling in the caster system are related with the requirements on finishing
ladles in the steel making system.

Although such dependencies are carefully managed during development, it is
crucial to monitor them also during runtime to detect inaccurate and erroneous
behavior. While the production process is monitored by operators in control
rooms, the consequences of operator settings can have unforeseen effects on the
automation software. For instance, the cut length defined by an operator of the
caster system might conflict with some required plan characteristics, or the ladle
finished event might be lacking from steel making. There are also dependencies
between requirements at different levels, such as the machine level and the automation level. For instance, the minimal length allowed for cutting a steel slab

in the caster system might depend on the maximum load capacity of the cranes available in the plant.

Numerous research areas have proposed approaches addressing these issues. *Requirements monitoring* approaches allow determining compliance of a system with its requirements during runtime. Monitors are used to detect possible violations and serve as a starting point for revealing the root cause of problems. For instance, Robinson [15] describes a framework for checking a software system using requirements defined as constraints in the Object Constraint Language. Cleland-Huang et al. [4] describe a framework for event-based traceability to uncover errors between distributed artifacts. *Complex event processing (CEP)* [10] is an approach for monitoring arbitrary business processes. It aims at combining event streams gathered from multiple sources to infer events or patterns of events. Event patterns are typically described by implementing rules in some higher programming language or in an Event Description Language. *Runtime verification* approaches in various peculiarities have been proposed as viable solution for monitoring and verifying system properties. For instance, Calinescu et al. [3] emphasize the need for quantitative runtime verification in the context of self-adaptive systems. They propose a three-staged process of monitoring, analysis, and planning. A system model is verified to detect violations of requirements. Ghezzi et al. [8] present the SPY@RUNTIME approach that relies on behavior models which are represented by finite state automata. An initial model is inferred in a setup phase and then used at runtime to detect changes.

While these approaches provide important building blocks for requirements monitoring in VLSS their focus is typically on single systems. However, VLSS are frequently systems of systems which have recently received more attention in the literature. For instance, Dahmann and Baldwin [6] distinguish between *directed* SoS which are centrally managed (cf. our industrial example), *collaborative* SoS in which the systems voluntarily collaborate to fulfill the agreed purposes, *virtual* SoS with little or no central management authority and highly emergent behavior, as well as *acknowledged* SoS which share a common management and resources but remain in independent ownership.

The characteristics of VLSS [1], however, impose a number of additional challenges for requirements monitoring: *Operational independence* of their constituent systems, meaning that the systems in the VLSS are only weakly integrated and often have not been designed with their interaction in mind. Current requirements monitoring approaches do not adequately support monitoring across different systems in VLSS. *Managerial independence and stakeholder diversity*, meaning that the systems are developed, maintained, and put into operation by independent teams and often even by multiple different companies. However, current requirements monitoring approaches are not designed to offer their capabilities to different independent teams and stakeholders. *Evolutionary independence*, meaning that the different systems in a VLSS evolve independently and at different speeds, which requires their continuous validation to avoid unexpected behavior. This strengthens the need for requirements monitoring after changes. Furthermore, it is important to manage the variability of the monitoring solutions to cover different system variants. *Emergent behavior*, leading to challenges in predicting the effects of cumulative actions and interactions of the constituents of a VLSS and making it difficult to define the requirements to be monitored. It has been reported that simply applying existing approaches and techniques to large-scale systems will likely lead to problems [1, 9]. Boehm and Lane [2], for instance, reported that traditional 20th century development processes do not work well on developing large-scale software-intensive systems with system-of-systems architectures.

3   Infrastructure Capabilities for Requirements Monitoring in VLSS

We are developing an infrastructure for requirements monitoring that provides different services for stakeholders developing or using tools for diagnosing problems in VLSS. The infrastructure aims at replacing the perspective of "building a house" with the perspective of "building a city" [14].

The infrastructure provides capabilities to support engineers who instrument systems in a VLSS. Engineers can register probes in the infrastructure to collect information about events and related data at runtime. Monitored events and data are stored in a unified event model. Different systems in a VLSS can be instrumented using arbitrary techniques and the probes provide information about events and data to the unified model. Based on the requirements, engineers can define monitors using constraints about the event model to detect violations. Furthermore, our infrastructure provides capabilities for variability management to allow the customization of constraints, probes, and monitors. Engineers can use the services provided by our infrastructure to develop custom solutions for specific use cases. For instance, we are currently using the infrastructure to develop a tool that allows service engineers to display monitored events and constraint violations. More specifically, our infrastructure will support the following activities:

Define requirements of different systems to be monitored. Requirements are documented in arbitrary artifacts such as specification documents, developer documentation, or models and need to be selected and refined by requirements engineers to allow their monitoring. The infrastructure (cf. Fig. 1–A) supports the definition of requirements using a domain-specific language (DSL) to monitor constraints across system boundaries. In our example of the VLSS in metallurgical plants, such a constraint could define that "prepare casting" requires that "ladle finished" has occurred. The first is handled in the steelmaking system while the latter is managed in the continuous casting system. In our industrial context, people defining and maintaining constraints are engineers and project managers who are familiar with third-generation programming languages. Our current prototype implementation thus uses an embedded DSL with Java as a host language. Additionally, we are currently evaluating other constraint languages such as the OCL regarding their usefulness in our context. Our implementation also allows to add constraints at runtime, making it possible to monitor emerging requirements.

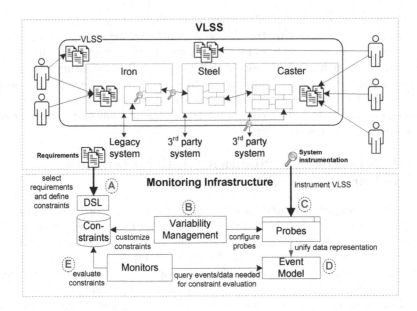

Fig. 1. Key elements of our Requirements Monitoring Infrastructure for VLSS

Define variability of probes, constraints, and monitors. To overcome the often
tedious and error-prone task of adapting constraints and monitors to specific systems the monitoring infrastructure provides integrated variability management
(cf. Fig. 1–B). For instance, certain constraints might be relevant in specific
system configurations only and some monitors might need to be deactivated to
reduce unnecessary overhead. Our example constraint could be customized, for
instance, by defining a specific time span in which the "prepare casting" event
must follow the "ladle finished" event in a particular plant. We will use our existing approach for variability management [7] to provide these capabilities. More
specifically, we plan to represent the variability of probes, events, and constraints
using decision-oriented variability models [5]. This allows us to define different
variants and versions of probes, events, and constraints to ease the adaptation
of the infrastructure. We plan integrate the DOPLER tool suite [7] with the
monitoring infrastructure for that purpose.

Register probes collecting and aggregating data from the instrumented system.
The infrastructure provides capabilities for implementing probes to allow instrumentation of the VLSS at various levels (cf. Fig. 1–C). For example, it is
necessary to retrieve information about the interaction between different components, different systems forming the VLSS, or between the systems and legacy
systems or third-party systems. Our model-based approach for data collection
allows managing this diversity.

Define event models for different systems. Our event model (cf. Fig. 1–D) allows
a unified representation of arbitrary data collected from various systems in the

VLSS to abstract from concrete systems and instrumentation techniques. The model allows, for example, to capture data about system events, related event data, and event dependencies across systems. For instance, the steelmaking system could be monitored to recognize a "ladle finished" event, while the "prepare casting" event would be detected in the caster system.

Formalize requirements and define monitors. Monitors can be defined to evaluate the defined constraints (cf. Fig. 1–E). Runtime monitoring presumes continuous (re-)evaluation of constraints as the system and its environment are subject of continuous change. Thus, an incremental evaluation strategy is advisable to ensure fast evaluation feedback to users in case of deviations from the desired behavior. Our prototype infrastructure utilizes an incremental consistency checker we used in our previous work in the area of product line models [16].

4   Summary and Outlook

In this research preview we discussed our ongoing work on requirements monitoring in VLSS. We identified problems and challenges that hamper the application of approaches for single systems in a VLSS environment. We propose an infrastructure for flexible constraint and monitor definition and management that considers variability. Our infrastructure provides three novel features: runtime monitoring of requirements across systems to detect violations of requirements that cannot be found by considering only single systems; variability management of requirements-based monitors to support the customization of constraints and their related monitors to specific systems; and the integration of monitoring data from different sources in a VLSS to ease the analysis of erroneous behavior (e.g., by engineers that were not involved in original development).

We are currently implementing the described infrastructure and are frequently evaluating prototypes with industrial users. We already have developed the event model as well as prototypes of several probes to instrument VLSS on different layers. Furthermore, we started implementing different event viewers to filter, search, and visualize collected events and data. Our next steps are the definition and evaluation of constraints as well as the persistence of monitored system events and data. In parallel, we are working on the variability management support for constraints and monitors.

Acknowledgements. This work has been conducted in cooperation with Siemens VAI Metals Technologies and has been supported by the Christian Doppler Forschungsgesellschaft, Austria.

References

1. Boehm, B.: A view of 20th and 21st century software engineering. In: 28th International Conference on Software Engineering, Shanghai, China, pp. 12–29. ACM (2006)

2. Boehm, B., Lane, J.: 21st century processes for acquiring 21st century software intensive systems of systems. Cross Talk 19(5), 4–9 (2006)
3. Calinescu, R., Ghezzi, C., Marta: Kwiatkowska, Z.: Raffaela Mirandola. Self-adaptive software needs quantitative verification at runtime. Communications of the ACM 55(9), 69–77 (2012)
4. Cleland-Huang, J., Chang, C.K., Christensen, M.: Event-based traceability for managing evolutionary change. IEEE Transactions on Software Engineering 29(9), 796–810 (2003)
5. Czarnecki, K., Grünbacher, P., Rabiser, R., Schmid, K., Wąsowski, A.: Cool features and tough decisions: A comparison of variability modeling approaches. In: 6th International Workshop on Variability Modelling of Software-Intensive Systems, Leipzig, Germany, pp. 173–182. ACM (2012)
6. Dahmann, J.S., Baldwin, K.J.: Understanding the current state of us defense systems of systems and the implications for systems engineering. In: 2nd Annual IEEE Systems Conference, Montreal, Canada, pp. 1–7. IEEE (2008)
7. Dhungana, D., Grünbacher, P., Rabiser, R.: The DOPLER meta-tool for decision-oriented variability modeling: A multiple case study. Automated Software Engineering 18(1), 77–114 (2011)
8. Ghezzi, C., Mocci, A., Sangiorgio, M.: Runtime monitoring of component changes with Spy@Runtime. In: 34th International Conference on Software Engineering, Zurich, Switzerland, pp. 1403–1406. IEEE (2012)
9. Keating, C.B., Padilla, J.J., Adams, K.: System of systems engineering requirements: challenges and guidelines. Engineering Management Journal 20(4), 24–31 (2008)
10. Luckham, D.C.: Event processing for business: Organizing the real-time enterprise. John Wiley & Sons (2011)
11. Maiden, N.: Monitoring our requirements. IEEE Software 30(1), 16–17 (2013)
12. Maier, M.W.: Architecting principles for systems-of-systems. Systems Engineering 1(4), 267–284 (1998)
13. Ncube, C.: On the engineering of systems of systems: Key challenges for the RE community. In: Workshop on Requirements Engineering for Systems, Services and Systems-of-Systems, Trento, Italy, pp. 70–73. IEEE (2011)
14. Northrop, L.: Ultra-large-scale systems: Challenges and promising research areas. Journal of Software Technology 11(4) (2008)
15. Robinson, W.N.: A requirements monitoring framework for enterprise systems. Requirements Engineering 11(1), 17–41 (2006)
16. Vierhauser, M., Grünbacher, P., Egyed, A., Rabiser, R., Heider, W.: Flexible and scalable consistency checking on product line variability models. In: 25th IEEE/ACM International Conference on Automated Software Engineering, Antwerp, Belgium, pp. 63–72. ACM (2010)
17. Völz, M., Koldehofe, B., Rothermel, K.: Supporting strong reliability for distributed complex event processing systems. In: 13th International Conference on High Performance Computing & Communication, Banff, Canada, pp. 477–486. IEEE (2011)

State of Practice of User-Developer Communication in Large-Scale IT Projects

Results of an Expert Interview Series

Ulrike Abelein and Barbara Paech

Institute of Computer Science, University of Heidelberg, Im Neuenheimer Feld 326,
69120 Heidelberg, Germany
{abelein,paech}@informatik.uni-heidelberg.de

Abstract. [**Context and motivation**] User participation in software development is considered to be essential for successful software systems. Especially missing direct communication between users and developers can cause various issues in large-scale IT projects.[**Question/Problem**] We want to understand current practices of user–developer communication in large-scale IT projects, the factors for, and consequences of communication gaps, and what experts suggest to prevent them. [**Principal ideas/results**]: We conducted a series of semi-structured interviews with twelve experts. The experts work on the coordination of Business and IT and describe their experiences gained in 69 large-scale IT projects. The analysis of our interviews showed that direct user–developer communication is limited and that no commonly used method for the user–developer communication in the design and implementation activity exists. [**Contribution**]: The interviews helped us to understand current practices and issues resulting from missing communication. Furthermore, we can confirm the need for a method enhancing user–developer-communication in large-scale IT projects.

Keywords: user–developer communication, collaboration, coordination issues, software development, large-scale IT projects, expert interviews.

1 Introduction

User participation and involvement (UPI) are widely studied in different fields, such as information systems (IS), human-computer-interaction (HCI), and requirements engineering (RE). Many empirical studies revealed that an increase in UPI and in particular in user-developer communication (UDC) in software (SW) development increases system success [10]. The terms "user participation" and "user involvement" are often used interchangeably, but there are also publications that distinguish between them. In our study, we use the two separate definitions of [2]. Thus, we define user involvement as a 'psychological state of the individual, defined as the importance and personal relevance of a system to a user' and user participation as 'behaviors and activities users perform in the system development process'. User participation takes place when the end user takes an active part in the development or design process

C. Salinesi and I. van de Weerd (Eds.): REFSQ 2014, LNCS 8396, pp. 95–111, 2014.
© Springer International Publishing Switzerland 2014

together with the designer [12]. User-Developer Communication is a specific form of user participation and we define it as communication, evaluation, and approval activities that take place between users and IS staff [2], also the frequency, content and direction of that communication [7].

For example, Amoako-Gympah and White found a positive correlation derived from the level of communication between the users and the IS team towards user satisfaction as a measurement for system success [1]. In addition, Barki and Hartwick [2–4] studied the dependencies between the user-IS relationship on UPI and confirmed that informal and formal communication of users with the IS team and senior management significantly influences the management of a software project and the system design, but not necessarily the satisfaction with the system [3, 4]. McKeen et al. [9] investigated contingency factors for user satisfaction and found that UDC is an independent predictor for user satisfaction. There are several methods to support UPI in software development projects and an analysis of practices of proposed solutions in our previously conducted systematic mapping study on UPI showed the importance of the setup of structures to enable communication within these methods [10]. For example, several authors suggest to clarify roles of users and mediators to reduce communication barriers [11–15]. However we did find method that supports UDC in the design and implementation phase of software development.

Begier [16] mentions that it is important to keep people (e.g. users) informed and to give them timely feedback. Particularly in the design and implementation phase, Kautz [17] suggests to have weekly feedback meetings with onsite customers during the presentations of working software. Several research studies on agile methods have targeted communication problems in software development (e.g. [12, 18]).

However, we have seen from our experience as a management consultant for IT projects that a lot of large-scale IT projects still use traditional methods, i.e. the waterfall approach. Therefore, we wanted to understand current practices of large-scale IT projects, mainly with a focus on projects using traditional development methods.

We define *large-scale IT projects* as projects which at least fulfill two or more of the following characteristics: large amount of users (over 1000 users), rollout of the system in multiple countries or business units, large budget (over 1 million EUR), project duration of one year minimum (12 calendar months).

For the term *user-developer communication,* we build upon a definition of [2], and include: 'all interaction (e.g. communication, evaluation, or approval activities) that take place between the users and developers of an IT project; we also include communication interactions that are mediated through project management.'

The role of a user includes all users from the (business) organization using the new system and their managers for approval interactions [19]. The role developer includes all IT personnel, e.g. designers, architects, coders, IT managers that are involved in the software development project.

There are other studies on communication issues and structures (e.g., regular meetings or workshops) in software development [20–22]. However, none of these studies focusses on UDC in large-scale IT projects.

We conducted an interview series with experts in large-scale IT projects to find out how and how well large-scale IT projects support UDC. In particular, we are interested to answer the following research questions:

RQ 1: Do users and developers communicate in large scale IT projects?
RQ 2: What are possible organizational obstacles that prevent large-scale
T projects from implementing UDC?
RQ 3: What factors might cause communication gaps between users and de-
velopers and what are the consequences of these communication gaps?
RQ 4: What do experienced practitioners suggest to overcome the obstacles
for the implementation of UDC and to eliminate the factors that cause com-
munication gaps?

So far, the research on UDC in large-scale IT projects provides only limited empirical insights from practitioners. We do believe that it is important to consider their perspectives and knowledge on the existing communication between users and developers and why they think it is hard to implement processes that ensure effective cooperation between the two parties. This is especially essential for the design of methods to improve UDC in large-scale IT projects.

The paper is structured as follows. In Section 2, we present related work and in Section 3, we explain the research method of the interviews and the data of the interview partners. We present the results and the discussion on the state of practice of UDC in large-scale IT projects in Section 4. Further, in Section 5, we describe the threats to validity. We conclude our work and describe future areas for research in section 6.

2   Related Work

In the introduction we referenced research on the importance of UDC: Here we present other empirical studies, which explored communication in various software development projects or settings. None of the presented studies focuses on the communication from the developer to the users in large-scale IT projects, but we will compare their results to ours and discuss similarities in Section 4. An interesting study has been done by Bjarnason et al. in 2011 [20]. They empirically studied communication gaps in terms of their root causes, causes, and effects with practitioners in one large company that develops market-driven software. However, the study focuses on the communication of requirements and as the context was market-driven software development, the results do not include communication with customers, i.e. users of the software. Stapel and Schneider [23] propose an approach of how to manage knowledge on communication and information flows in global software projects. They identified poor communication as a main obstacle to successful collaboration. However, they focus on distributed development settings and not on large-scale IT projects. Marczak et al. [24] explored information flow patterns in requirement-dependent social networks. In particular, they studied communication and coordination in cross-functional teams that work on the same or on interrelated requirements. They only looked into the communication between IT personnel and did not study the communication with the users. Lastly, Gallivan and Keil [25] studied the UDC process in a software project that failed despite a high level of user involvement. They found out that communication gaps occurred because the developers were not informed about the underlying reasons of why the users did not accept the software system. However, their results are based on only one project, and thus include insights from a limited perspective.

3   Research Method

In order to answer our research questions, we conducted a series of interviews with twelve experts in large-scale IT projects from October until December 2012. The first interview was used as a prototype interview, in order to refine the questionnaire and estimate the time frame. We conducted qualitative interviews, which is the most important data gathering tool in qualitative research and is extensively used in IS research [26]. The interviews were semi-structured, which means they were based on a questionnaire (see Appendix), but we improvised and changed the order of questions whenever the discussion moved in another direction, as recommended by [26]. In the following, we describe the identification of the experts, the interview process, and the data analysis.

Identification of Experts. In order to ensure the right target group for our interviews, we developed a role description for people working on the coordination of Business and IT (Table 1). We believe that people fulfilling this description have a project management perspective and thus are knowledgeable about existing communication structures between developers and users. In addition, we wanted to ensure that our interview partners were experts in large-scale IT projects with experience in one or more large-scale IT projects. As we wanted to support projects using traditional methods, we searched for experts who ideally have been involved in projects not using/applying agile methods, but did not limit our search to those. As consultants are typically not involved in the whole IT project timeline, we set a minimum time of three months of participation. We used these role descriptions together with some information about our research area and the goals of the interviews to contact possible interview partners. We mainly used already existing relationships of all the authors to contact possible experts.

Table 1. Role description

Coordinator between Business and IT
<ul><li>Involved in more than 1 large-scale IT project</li><li>Ideally experiences in projects with no usage of agile development methods</li><li>Involved for at least 3 months in the projects (for consultants)</li><li>Person (internal or consultant) who had a leading role in the development/ implementation/customizing in a large-scale IT project and was involved in discussions with users during the project or in change request management after go-live OR who had a leading role in the requirements analysis, concept development, or project management in a large-scale IT project and was involved in defining requirements and in discussions with developers during the project and/or involved in the change request process after go-live</li></ul>

Overall, we could attain twelve experts for our interview series. The educational background of the interview partners is very widespread (Table 2). Furthermore, the study background covered seven different areas, with half of them in IT- related subjects (4 in Computer Science and 2 in Information Technology).

Table 2. Overview of base data of experts

No.	Role in Company	Perspective (Industry)	Educational Background	# of Projects
1	Project manager	Internal IT (Pharma)	Mathematics	15
2	Business project manager	Management consulting	Business Administration and Engineering	6
3	Developer, architect, requirements engineer	IT consulting	Computer Science	3
4	Business project manager	Management consulting	Mechanical Engineering	3
5	Developer, head of research department	IT consulting	Computer Science	5
6	IT project manager	IT consulting	Information Technology	6
7	Business project manager	Internal IT (Insurance)	Mathematics	2
8	Head of IT Strategy	Internal IT (Public Sector)	Computer Science	3
9	IT project manager	IT consulting	Computer Science	4
10	CEO	Management Consultant and Software Company	Physics	14
11	IT project manager	IT consulting	Apprenticeship as Bank Clerk	5
12	Head of IT Strategy	Internal IT (Insurance)	Information Technology	3
			Sum / Average	**69** / 6
			Min - Max	2 - 15

Seven experts are employed by IT or management consultancies, four experts work in internal IT departments of large organizations, and one expert works for software providers. If we consider the current roles of the experts within their companies, we can see that all experts have a leading role, which enables them to have a broad overview of IT projects. We also asked the interview partners in how many large-scale IT projects they were involved. On average, the interview partners were involved in six large-scale IT projects (minimum two projects and maximum 15 projects) throughout their carriers in various roles (e.g. developer, project manager, architect, requirement engineer, consultant, quality manager), which ensures a wide expertise of all of them.

In order to get an overview of the previous experience of the experts and to understand what large-scale IT projects are performed in practice, we asked the interview partners about the main characteristics of their projects respectively *System Type, Development Type, Industry, Project Length, Project Volume, Number of Users, Rollout in Countries/Business Units, Development Method, Role/Task*. Even though the experts could not name all characteristics of each project (also for confidentiality reasons), we were able to record data of 42 projects (see Appendix Figure 1).

Interview Process. Four interviews were done in person; the other eight interviews were conducted via telephone. The average time for one interview was 90 min, with a minimum of 44 minutes and a maximum of 125 minutes. In total, we collected about 18 hours of interview time. In the interviews, we explained the purpose of our research on UDC. We asked the interview partners about their experience in large-scale IT projects (see questionnaire in Appendix). With regard to our research questions, we did a mapping of the interview questions to the research questions. RQ 1 corresponds to question 6. RQ 2 and 3 correspond to question 7 and RQ 4 to question 8. Within the interviews we used different terms and formulations than in the RQs, in order to ensure understandability for our practice experts.

Data Analysis. All interviews were recorded with the permission of the interviewees and transcribed for analysis purposes. Three experts reviewed their transcripts and all experts validated the derived results, i.e. reviewed them and approved for publication. We coded the interviews which helped us in the analysis of the results [27]. We built a code tree based on our research questions with descriptive codes and extended and reorganized the code tree in two cycles of coding [27]. We used the software MaxQ-DA and therefore were able to also do cross-interview or cross-code analysis (e.g. between the factors for communication gaps and ideas to overcome the factors). For the representation we use tables, which show the descriptive codes and the corresponding number of occurrences in the interviews (see Section 4). One occurrence means an expert did describe something in an interview that we mapped to a descriptive code. Thus it is possible to have two occurrences for one research question in one interview. For example, if in one interview an expert described the factors for communication gaps 'Lack of motivation of developers or users' and 'Lack of common language between Business and IT', we counted one occurrence for each of the descriptive codes. However, we ensured that each descriptive code got a maximum of one occurrence per interview. Thus, it is not possible to have more than twelve occurrences per descriptive code.

4   Results and Discussion

In this section, we describe the interview results on current communication structures (e.g., meetings, reports, workshops) in large-scale IT projects. We use tables, which show the descriptive codes and the corresponding number of occurrences in the interviews (for detailed explanation see Section 3). Within each subsection, we first present the results and the table and then discuss and compare them to the existing literature. To answer our research questions, we analyzed whether the interview partners experienced UDC in large-scale IT projects (section 4.1.). We report on organizational obstacles (section 4.2.), factors for communication gaps, and consequences of these communication gaps within the IT projects (section 4.3.). And, we describe the experts' ideas to overcome these obstacles and factors for communication gaps (section 4.4.).

4.1   Existence of UDC in Large-Scale IT Projects (RQ 1)

To understand the current practice of UDC in large-scale IT projects, we asked all interview partners, what communication took place within their projects. We wanted to understand UDC on a detailed level, thus asked exactly who communicated with whom in the project. Overall, only three experts reported of projects where communication between users and software coders (i.e. developers) took place. However, two of these three experts also participated in projects where no direct communication between those parties existed. Hence, eleven experts told us about large-scale IT projects, in which they did not experience direct communication between software coders and users (Table 3). In total, less than one fifths of all 69 projects our experts were involved in had any communication between users and developers.

Nevertheless, some projects had other forms of UDC, such as: communication between the IT consultant and the users, communication between the architect and the users, or communication between the requirements engineer and the expert users (not users, but rather business personnel with broad context knowledge or a management role). Even though our analysis of existing methods for UPI in the systematic mapping study [10] indicated that methods affect all activities of software development, we learnt from our interview partner that in practice most of the communication is done either in the early or the late activities of software development (i.e. in specification or acceptance).

Table 3. Existence of direct communication between developers and users

Existence of UDC (Descriptive Code)	# of Int. [1]
Communication between software coders (i.e. developers) and users	3
No communication between software coders (i.e. developers) and users	11
Other forms of communication with users	
Communication between IT consultant and users	3
Communication between architect and users	2
Communication between requirements engineer and expert user	2

Based on the experiences of our experts, we can conclude that direct communication between developers and users does not exist in most large-scale IT projects. This is in contrast to Chang et al.'s results [5], who found that the presence of mutual influence among IT staff and users, which enables open and direct communication and coordination, is significantly associated with project performance. However, their context was not within large-scale IT projects. The reported setup of communication between requirements engineers and expert users is in line with Kanungo and Bagchi [6], as they suggest moving user participation upstream in the implementation process and using representatives of user groups. The finding that most of the communication is done either in the early or the late activities of software development shows a lack of communication in the middle of the development, i.e. in the design and implementation activity. Even though, there are suggested methods in literature, e.g. Kautz [17] and Korkola [15] suggest to have weekly feedback meetings with onsite customers during working software presentations or at least mid-iteration communication with users, our findings show that the implementation of such methods is limited in practice.

---

[1] Number of interviewees that mentioned an experience mapped to descriptive code.

4.2   Organizational Obstacles for UDC (RQ 2)

We identified four obstacles whereof three concern the users or access to them (Table 4). In total, we did discuss the topic of organizational obstacles with half of the experts; the other experts did not mention any organizational obstacles. Firstly, two experts mentioned that users are not a homogeneous group, but different user groups or business units with often different opinions and organizational power within a company. In such cases, developers (and other IT personnel) face an additional challenge, as they need to mediate between these groups. Secondly, it seems to be hard to find user representatives with the right qualification and knowledge for an IT project. We think, this can be explained by the fact that knowledgeable key users are very important for the business operations and thus will not be released to fulfill tasks within IT projects. Thirdly, one expert mentioned that in several projects the real users are not defined during the project, thus the developers (and other IT personnel) cannot access them. Fourthly, one expert reported that no mediators were available to establish and uphold the relationship between the users and the developers.

Table 4. Organizational obstacles for implementing communication with users

ID	Organizational Obstacles (Descriptive Code)	# of Int.
O1	Different opinions between user groups	2
O2	Get the right user representatives for large-scale projects	2
O3	No access to users/users unknown	1
O4	Lack of local mediators	1

The obstacles O1 and O2 correspond with the findings of Bjarnason et al. [20], who also identified scale effects through complex products and large organization. In addition, they describe gaps between roles over time through distributed environment as root causes for communication gaps. Even though they studied a different setup without direct contact to users, these obstacles also seem to be present for UDC. Obstacle O4 is supported by the findings of Marczak et al., who studied communication and coordination in cross-functional teams that work on the same or interrelated requirements [24]. They found out that the power of information flows lies with a few key members who control information flows between dependent networks. Our findings indicate that this is also true for UDC.

4.3   Factors for and Consequences Caused by Communication Gaps (RQ 3)

We identified three factors for communication gaps and four consequences caused by communication gaps (Table 5). Common factors for communication gaps are 'lack of motivation of either the users or the developers', as well as the 'lack of a common language between the business and IT side'. Another factor, which is somehow related to both of the other factors, is lack of appreciation between these two sides. The consequences most frequently named among interviewees is the misunderstanding of requirements, i.e. developers either interpret requirements in a wrong way or users do not specify requirements on a detailed level and are later surprised by the results.

Table 5. Factors for and consequences caused by communication gaps

ID	Factors for communication gaps (Descriptive Code)	# of Int.
F1	Lack of motivation of developers or users	4
F2	Lack of common language between Business and IT	4
F3	Lack of appreciation between Business and IT	1
	Consequences caused by Communication Gaps (Descriptive Code)	**# of Int.**
C1	Misunderstanding of requirements	8
C2	Ad-hoc changes required due to unclear requirements	3
C3	Increased implementation cost	3
C4	Increased test effort due to rework	1

This also often leads to the need of ad-hoc changes or, as one expert named it, a 'scope creep' during implementation. In addition, increased implementation cost or test effort were named as consequences of communication gaps.

The results of RQ 3 show that the consequences are severe as misunderstandings and ad-hoc changes have an impact on cost and schedule of the project. The factor F1 is similar to Bjarnason et al.'s [20] identified effect of "low motivation to contribute to requirements work" and F2 is a commonly known issue in IT projects. However, the factor F3 of missing appreciation has not been described so far and is also interesting, as the required actions to improve appreciation between IT and Business are different from overcoming barriers of a common domain language. The identified consequences C1 and C2" are in line with Bjarnason et al's effect [20] described as "problems with the system requirements specification". C3 and C4 are similar to their effect "wasted effort". However, it is quite interesting that our results show that the experts stated a clear connection between communication gaps and increased implementation costs and a higher test effort. In addition, the consequences C1 to C4 correspond to the named benefits of UPI [10], such as improved quality due to more precise requirements and the prevention of expensive features.

4.4 Ideas to Overcome Obstacles for the Implementation of UDC and Factors for Communication Gaps (RQ 4)

In total, the experts suggested twelve different approaches to overcome factors for communication gaps or obstacles. We classified these approaches into three categories, user-centered approaches, developer-centered approaches, and organizational approaches. We mapped them in our analysis phase to the addressed factors for communication gaps and organizational obstacles wherever possible and identified similar approaches from the literature (Table 6). The user-centered approaches are ideas that include the involvement of the user. The second category clusters ideas that have to be realized by the developer. The third category of organizational approaches is for ideas that need to be considered in the setup of the project organization and management.

Table 6. Ideas to overcome obstacles or factors for communication gaps

Cate-gory	Ideas (Descriptive Code)	# of Int	Litera-ture	ID	Addressed Fac-tor/Obstacle
User-cen-tered ap-proach es	Presentation of (UI) prototypes or proof of concepts to users	3	[14, 28, 29]	O2	Get the right user repre-sentatives for large-scale projects
	House tours in different business units with running SW	1	[17, 30]	F2	Lack of common lan-guage between business and IT
	Description of added value to users to increase acceptance	1	n/a		
	Incentive system for the participation of business users	1	[31]	F1	Lack of motivation of developers or users
				O2	Get the right user repre-sentatives for large-scale projects
	Involvement of users in the organiza-tion of rollout and change manage-ment	1	n/a	O2	Get the right user repre-sentatives for large-scale projects
Devel-oper-cen-tered ap-proach es	Developers must mediate between different user groups	2	[13]	O1	Different opinions be-tween user groups
				O4	Lack of local mediators
				F2	Lack of common lan-guage between Business and IT
				F3	Lack of appreciation between Business and IT
	End-to-end feature responsibility of developers	1	n/a	F2	Lack of common lan-guage between Business and IT
	Developer writes informal description of how to implement requirements.	1	n/a		
	Obligation to justify all technical decisions with functional need	1	n/a		
Orga-niza-tional ap-proach es	Usage of test data early in project	2	[32]		n/a
	Agile methods e.g. frequent review meetings	2	e.g. [17, 33]		
	Definition of usability guidelines to avoid detailed UI discussions	1	n/a		

In the first category of user-centered approaches, five ideas were named.

One idea is to show the users prototypes (often called 'proof of concept' by the ex-perts). One expert described a successful project: the software was very complex, therefore the project members wrote down all requirements in large workshops with about 50 users and then invited two vendors to build up prototypes as a 'proof of con-cept' before the actual design and implementation activity began. The users were highly involved in this activity, as the vendors presented the status of the prototype in regular meetings to them. At the end of the proof of concept activity, a prototype, implementing about 80% of the functionality, had been built and was aligned with the users. The vendor selected for implementation could proceed with implementing the rest of the requirements, integrating the prototypes into the system's landscape, and building up the data structures. Even though this is a promising approach, the expert mentioned that it will be hard to implement in large-scale IT projects such as an ERP implementation, because those systems' functionality is too wide for a prototype ap-proach. Nevertheless, two other experts suggested showing users mockups or even integrate users as beta customers within the software development by showing them running prototypes. In general, this idea of using prototypes is not new and has been described in the literature, e.g.[14, 28, 29]. However, the detailed description of how such an approach was used within a real-life IT project can be helpful for the research community.

Another suggested approach that is similar to the prototype approach described above is to do house tours with running software. The difference to the proof of concept approach is that after about half of the actual implementation time, the project team presents the running software in different business units to different users. This approach allows small changes of the system based on user feedback and it ensures an early change and expectation management with the users. A similar approach has been described by [17, 30]. They call it "road shows" and suggest having onsite users conducting them with other users.

One approach in response to the factor 'lack of common language between business and IT' was to explain the added value of the system to the users. The expert suggests doing that with posters, result descriptions, and several meetings with the users.

To include users in the rollout and change management planning was also named by an expert. According to the expert, this leads to a higher integration of users in the project. For these two suggestions, we could not identify an approach from the literature, thus these are particularly interesting findings for the design of a new method.

The last suggestion in that category has been for years in the head of one of our interview partners, namely to create an incentive system for the participation of business users. The expert wants to overcome the factor 'lack of motivation of users' and the obstacle 'get the right user representatives for large-scale projects'. One issue, in the opinion of the expert, is that users are not rewarded either through promotions or higher wages for their work in IT projects in addition to their usual daily work. This lack of appreciation leads to a low interest and thus low involvement of the user. A similar idea has been presented by Finck et al. [31] They suggested an incentive system for the software evolution activity, i.e. after the first rollout of a system.

In the category of developer–centered approaches, four ideas were named.

Especially in response to the obstacle 'different opinions between user groups," two experts recommended that developers need to mediate between different user groups. As different user groups (e.g. the finance and the marketing department) often have different opinions, the developers need to solve their communication gap and dissolve their disagreement.

In addition, one interview partner referred to the factor 'lack of appreciation between Business and IT' and 'lack of common language between Business and IT' by explaining: "Most (non IT) users do not think in structures…thus the IT personnel need to learn to talk in examples to explain their structure, even though it is not relevant to them." Therefore, this expert suggests always having someone in the project, who has experience with the to-be-implemented business domain. This person can then fulfill the mediator role. In general, the idea to clarify roles and mediators is described in the literature, e.g. [13], but to assign/fill this role to/with a developer is a new suggestion. With reference to the factor 'lack of common language between Business and IT', one expert suggested to ensure end-to-end feature responsibility for each developer. That means, you do not need a developer who is responsible for one technical cross over area, e.g. database or UI, you rather need a developer who is responsible for the implementation of one use case, including the UI, the business logic, the database, and the interfaces.

A similar approach is to oblige the developer to write an informal description of how to implement a given requirement so the users should be able to read and understand information related to implementation. Before the implementation starts, this informal description must be aligned with the users. We think this also helps to mitigate all the above mentioned four consequences of communication gaps. In order to mitigate the lack of a common language, one interesting approach is the obligation for developers to justify all technical decisions with a functional need. For example, the need for another database can only be justified with a higher service level for the business unit, but not out of narcissistic technical preferences of a developer. The last three developer-centered approaches have so far not been described in the UPI literature. Thus, it is important to include these suggestion is future work of methods to improve UDC.

In the category of organizational approaches three ideas were named.

The usage of test data very early in the software development process is supposed to give the users a possibility to challenge the logic and the quality of the system. One expert suggested using extreme test data to provoke situations where complications can occur. Another expert suggested having usability tests with real data as early as possible within a large-scale IT project, which has also been suggested in [32].

Another suggested approach was, to use agile methods, e.g. have weekly or monthly meetings (often called sprint meetings) together with user representatives. Even though this expert suggested this approach, he also reported that those meetings had not been a success, which he attributes to the too finely-grained level, i.e. on a bug tracker level. This was too detailed for the users and they lost attention after two minutes. Furthermore, these meetings had been held as a telephone conference which, according to the expert, is not the ideal setting. Agile methods including a high level of feedback towards the users have been described extensively in the literature, e.g., [17, 33].

In addition, one expert mentioned that it is not only important to involve users by offering workshops or by showing prototypes to them, but also to ensure clear guidelines for the user interface. This is particularly important in terms of the user interface, as several unnecessary discussions about screen details occur in meetings with users. The expert also mentioned that if these guidelines are missing this can have high cost implications for the project.

Overall, we can conclude that the experts' ideas try to overcome all factors for communication gaps (F1 – F3) and the organizational obstacles (O1, O2, O4), except obstacle O3, namely the "lack of access to users". Nevertheless, the experts did not report of a successful, sustainable solution to overcome the communication gaps in large-scale IT projects and in particular in the design and implementation phase.

5   Threats to Validity

We analyzed threats to validity based on the scheme suggested from Runeson [34].

Construct validity – as described in the research method section, the interviews were semi-structured thus interviewees and interviewer could influence the direction of the discussion, which sometimes led to the fact that we did not pose all questions of our interview guideline explicitly. Furthermore, eight interviews were conducted via telephone, which prevents visual cues and sometimes limited the understanding. We mitigated that threat through the recording of all interviews. This also enabled us to rewind for the transcripts in the case of poor acoustic reception.

Internal validity – we relied on our personal relationships for the identification of experts, this can be a threat to internal validity, as three of the experts knew the interviewer before the interviews and therefore they might be biased. However, the majority of the experts did not know the interviewer.

External validity – a possible threat to external validity is that we only interviewed twelve experts. Nevertheless, the experts' backgrounds were very widespread and they all had been involved in a minimum of two large-scale IT projects. Therefore, we are confident that our results show a broad overview of communication structures in large-scale IT projects and can be transferred to other projects outside of the experiences of our interviewees.

Reliability – The interviews as well as the coding of the interviews were conducted by one person. On the one hand, this ensured the consistency of the interviews and their analysis. On the other hand, it can also be a threat to the reliability, as another researcher could interpret the results in another direction.

6   Conclusion

In this paper, we reported on the results of an interview series with experienced practitioners in large-scale IT projects. We conducted twelve semi-structured interviews, transcribed all interviews and coded them with descriptive codes based on our research questions. Our experts described experiences from 69 large-scale IT projects, which ensure widespread experience. In the context of our larger research on UDC in large-scale IT projects, we wanted to determine how and how well large-scale IT projects support UDC.

With regard to current communication structures in large-scale IT projects, the results of the study indicate that *direct communication between developers and users does not exist in most large-scale IT projects*. The experts describe some setups for communication with the users, e.g. communication between IT consultant and users, but none of them seems to focus on our research target the design and implementation activity.

The identified obstacles for implementation and factors for communication gaps seem to be in line with the literature [20, 35], e.g. lack of motivation of user or developer or a lack of a common language of Business and IT. However, an interesting result is that the experts stated a clear connection between communication gaps and increased implementation costs and a higher test effort.

We classified the ideas from experts to overcome the obstacles in *user-centered approaches*, e.g. show user prototypes, *developer-centered approaches*, e.g. developers must mediate between different user groups and *organizational approaches*, e.g. use test data early in the project. Some of the suggestions have also been described in the literature, however the detailed descriptions of which setup was successful in large-scale IT projects and the developer-centered approaches are important findings for our future work. The experts did not report on a successful, sustainable solution to overcome the communication gaps in large-scale IT projects and in particular to improve UDC in the design and implementation activity.

In our future work, we plan to detail our method to support UDC in large-scale IT projects. We already published a first proposal and a descriptive classification of user-relevant decisions in two other papers [36, 37] Furthermore, we plan to evaluate the implementation feasibility as well as measure the benefits of the method in a case study in a large-scale IT project.

Acknowledgement. We would like to thank all experts for their time and support of this research.

References

1. Amoako-Gyampah, K., White, K.: User involvement and user satisfaction: An exploratory contingency model. Inf. Manag. 25, 25–33 (1993)
2. Barki, H., Hartwick, J.: Measuring User Participation, User Involvement, and User Attitude. MIS Q. 18, 59 (1994)
3. Hartwick, J., Barki, H.: Communication as a dimension of user participation. IEEE Trans. on. Prof. Comm. 44(1), 21–36 (2001)
4. Hartwick, J., Barki, H.: Delineating the dimensions of user participation: A replication and extension. Rev. Lit. Arts Am. (1997)
5. Chang, K., Shin, T., Klein, G., Jiang, J.J., Sheu, T.S.: User commitment and collaboration: Motivational antecedents and project performance. Inf. Softw. Technol. 52, 672–679 (2010)
6. Kanungo, S., Bagchi, S.: Understanding User Participation and Involvement in ERP Use. J. Manag. Res. 1, 47–64 (2000)
7. Kristensson, P., Gustafsson, A., Witell, L.: Collaboration with Customers – Understanding the Effect of Customer–Company Interaction in New Product Development. In: 2011 44th Hawaii International Conference on System Sciences, pp. 1–9. IEEE (2011)
8. Kujala, S., Kauppinen, M., Lehtola, L., Kojo, T.: The Role of User Involvement in Requirements Quality and Project Success. In: 13th IEEE Int. Conf. Requir. Eng., pp. 75–84 (2005)
9. McKeen, J., Guimaraes, T., Wetherbe, J.: The Relationship between User Participation and User Satisfaction: An Investigation of Four Contingency Factors. MIS Q. 18, 427–451 (1994)
10. Abelein, U., Paech, B.: Understanding the Influence of User Participation and Involvement on System Success – a Systematic Mapping Study. Empir. Softw. Eng. (2014), doi:10.1107/S10664-013-9278-4
11. Amoako–Gyampah, K., White, K.: When is user involvement not user involvement? Inf. Strateg. Exec. J. 13, 40–45 (1997)
12. Hope, K., Amdahl, E.: Configuring designers? Using one agile project management methodology to achieve user participation. New Technol. Work Employ 26, 54–67 (2011)
13. Eckhardt, A.: Lost in Translation?! – The Need for a Boundary Spanner between Business and IT. In: SIGMIS–CPR 2010, Vancouver, BC, Canada, May 20-22, pp. 75–82 (2010)
14. Humayoun, S.R., Dubinsky, Y., Catarci, T.: A Three–Fold Integration Framework to Incorporate User – Centered Design into Agile Software Development. In: Kurosu, M. (ed.) HCD 2011. LNCS, vol. 6776, pp. 55–64. Springer, Heidelberg (2011)

15. Korkala, M., Abrahamsson, P., Kyllönen, P.: A Case Study on the Impact of Customer Communication on Defects in Agile Software Development. In: Abrahamsson, P., Kyllonen, P. (eds.) AGILE 2006, pp. 76–88. IEEE (2006)

16. Begier, B.: Evolutionally Improved Quality of Intelligent Systems Following Their Users' Point of View. In: Nguyen, N.T., Katarzyniak, R., Chen, S.-M. (eds.) Advances in Intelligent Information and Database Systems. SCI, vol. 283, pp. 191–203. Springer, Heidelberg (2010)

17. Kautz, K.: Investigating the design process: participatory design in agile software development. Inf. Technol. People. 24, 217–235 (2011)

18. Takats, A., Brewer, N.: Improving Communication between Customers and Developers. In: Agil. Dev. Conf. Database Conf., pp. 243–252 (2005)

19. Carmel, E., Whitaker, R.D., George, J.F.: PD and joint application design: a transatlantic comparison. Commun. ACM. 36, 40–48 (1993)

20. Bjarnason, E., Wnuk, K., Regnell, B.: Requirements are slipping through the gaps — A case study on causes & effects of communication gaps in large–scale software development. In: 2011 IEEE 19th International Requirements Engineering Conference, pp. 37–46. IEEE (2011)

21. Stapel, K., Knauss, E., Schneider, K., Zazworka, N.: FLOW Mapping: Planning and Managing Communication in Distributed Teams. In: 2011 IEEE Sixth Int. Conf. Glob. Softw. Eng., pp. 190–199 (2011)

22. Marczak, S., Kwan, I., Damian, D.: Social Networks in the Study of Collaboration in Global Software Teams, pp. 7–8 (2007)

23. Stapel, K., Schneider, K.: Managing knowledge on communication and information flow in global software projects. Expert Syst., doi: 10.1111/j.1468-0394.2012.00649.x (2012)

24. Marczak, S., Damian, D., Stege, U., Schröter, A.: Information Brokers in Requirement–Dependency Social Networks. In: 2008 16th IEEE Int. Requir. Eng. Conf., pp. 53–62 (2008)

25. Gallivan, M.J., Keil, M.: The user–developer communication process: a critical case study. Inf. Syst. J. 13, 37–68 (2003)

26. Myers, M.D., Newman, M.: The qualitative interview in IS research: Examining the craft. Inf. Organ. 17, 2–26 (2007)

27. Saldana, J.: The Coding Manual for Qualitative Researchers (Google eBook) (2009)

28. Cohen, S., Dori, D., De Haan, U.: A Software System Development Life Cycle Model for Improved Stakeholders' Communication and Collaboration. Int. J. Comput. Commun. Control 5, 20–41 (2010)

29. Dean, D., Lee, J., Pendergast, M., Hickey, A., Nunamaker, J.: Enabling the Effective Involvement of Multiple Users: Methods and Tools for Collaborative Software Engineering. J. Manag. Inf. Syst. 14, 179–222 (1998)

30. Martin, A., Biddle, R., Noble, J.: An Ideal Customer: A Grounded Theory of Requirements Elicitation, Communication and Acceptance on Agile Projects. In: Agile Software Development: Current Research and Future Directions, pp. 111–141. Springer, Berlin (2010)

31. Finck, M., Gumm, D., Pape, B.: Using Groupware for Mediated Feedback. In: Proceedings of the Eighth Conference Biennial Participatory Design Conference 2004: Artful Integration: Interwearing Media, Toronto, Canada, July 27-July 7, vol. 2 (2004)

32. Teixeira, L., Saavedra, V., Ferreira, C., Santos, B.: Using Participatory Design in a Health Information System. In: Conf. Proc. Annu. Int. Conf. IEEE Eng. Med. Biol. Soc., pp. 5339–5342 (2011)

33. Korkala, M., Pikkarainen, M., Conboy, K.: Combining Agile and Traditional: Customer Communication in Distributed Environment. In: Šmite, D., Moe, N.B., Ågerfalk, P.J. (eds.) Agility Across Time and Space, pp. 201–216. Springer, Heidelberg (2010)
34. Runeson, P., Host, M., Rainer, A., Regnell, B.: Case Study Research in Software Engineering. Wiley–Blackwell (2012)
35. Harris, M., Weistroffer, H.: A New Look at the Relationship between User Involvement in Systems Development and System Success Development and System Success. Commun. Assoc. Inf. Syst. 24, 739–756 (2009)
36. Abelein, U., Paech, B.: A proposal for enhancing user–developer communication in large IT projects. In: Proceedings of the 5th International Workshop on Cooperative and Human Aspects of Software Engineering (CHASE 2012) at the ICSE 2012, Zurich (June 2, 2012)
37. Abelein, U., Paech, B.: A Descriptive Classification for End User –Relevant Decisions of Large–Scale IT Projects. In: 2013 6th International Workshop on Cooperative and Human Aspects of Software Engineering (CHASE) (2013)

7   Appendix

Interview questionnaire
1. What is your role in your company? What is your educational background?
2. How many large IT projects (either large amount of users, multiple countries or business units involved, large budget, project duration minimum of 1 year, e.g. ERP implementation) have you been involved in?
3. What were the main characteristics of these projects (type of system, project length, amount of users)?
4. What was your role and what were your tasks within these projects?
5. Would you classify yourself on the IT or on the Business side?
6. Was there communication between users and developers of the project? If yes in what setup did the communication take place? In what SW activities of the project did the communication take place?
7. Did you experience any issues/consequences in these projects that might be caused by communication gaps? If yes, please specify the issues. In what SW activities did the issues occur?
8. What would you do to prevent these issues in your next project?

Base Data of Large-scale IT Projects

Characteristics	min	max	average
Project length [years]	1	18	5,7
Project volume [million EUR]	1	500	145
Amount of users	40	1.600000	430.325
Rollout units	1	1000	112

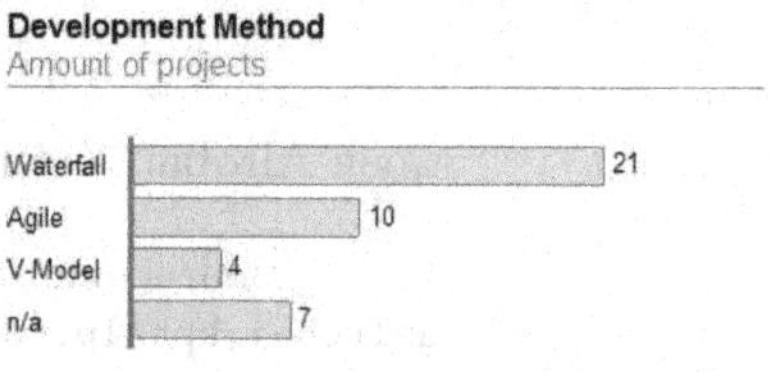

Development Method
Amount of projects

Waterfall	21
Agile	10
V-Model	4
n/a	7

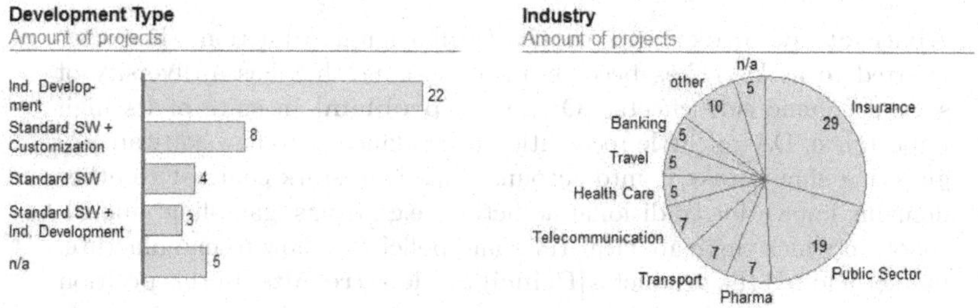

Development Type
Amount of projects

Ind. Development	22
Standard SW + Customization	8
Standard SW	4
Standard SW + Ind. Development	3
n/a	5

Industry
Amount of projects

Insurance 29
Public Sector 19
other 10
Banking 5
Travel 5
Health Care 5
Telecommunication 7
Transport 7
Pharma 7
n/a 5

Fig. 1. Base Data of Large-Scale IT Projects

Digital Addiction:
A Requirements Engineering Perspective

Amen Alrobai, Keith Phalp, and Raian Ali

Bournemouth University, UK
{aalrobai,kphalp,rali}@bournemouth.ac.uk

Abstract. [**Context and motivation**] Digital Addiction, (hereafter referred to as DA), has become a serious issue that has a diversity of socio-economic side effects. [**Question/problem**] In spite of its high importance, DA got little recognition or guidance as to how software engineering should take it into account. This is in stark contrast to other domains known for traditional addiction (e.g., drugs, gambling, and alcohol) in which there are clear rules and policies on how to manufacture, market and sell the products. [**Principal ideas/results**] In this position paper, we suggest that software engineering in general and requirements engineering in particular need to consider DA as a first class concept in developing software systems. [**Contribution**] As an early step in this area, we conduct an empirical investigation of DA by reviewing the literature and analysing web discussion forums on the topic and use that to design a mind-map of its main causes. We also provide a basic model to articulate the DA problem from requirements perspective and elaborate research challenges for a future work.

Keywords: Digital Addiction, Requirements Engineering.

1 Introduction

Digital Addiction (DA) can be described as a significant degree of dependent behaviour that is triggered and facilitated by software products. It can lead to both pleasure and relief of discomfort, but unfortunately, in a way that can harm a person socially, physically and psychologically. However, despite its impact on society, DA is still considered outside the boundary of the software engineering community. That is, unlike the situation with drugs or alcohol, software engineering has, so far, not been charged with the responsibility for dealing with or mitigating the effects of DA.

DA is still seen as a problem on the user's side, rather than the responsibility of the software or the software developers. Hence, the problem of DA is typically articulated in a way that makes the solution entirely within the domain of other disciplines, such as psychology, sociology and health care. For example, Beard [1] highlighted different factors related to the content, style of use and activity. Widyanto and Griffiths [2] emphasized the addiction 'on' rather than 'to' the Internet. As such, the Internet is treated as a single entity, without considering

C. Salinesi and I. van de Weerd (Eds.): REFSQ 2014, LNCS 8396, pp. 112–118, 2014.

the features of the applications used, the way they are designed or the goals and values they help to achieve. Similarly, software is still seen, implicitly, as just a medium in which its requirements, features, values and design are not studied as primary causes of DA. In contrast, this paper suggests that the study of these factors inherently belongs to the early stages of developing software; namely requirements engineering. DA strongly relates to the requirements of users in the first place. People use software as a means to reach certain requirements, however, while doing so, they may get addicted.

There are a variety of different perspectives and debates on DA. While some works view it as a mental disorder, others believe that it is no more than a personal choice [2]. Similar debate could be found for tradition addiction [3]. However, individuals' exposure to technology advancements has led to patterns of use that seem to match the criterion of Diagnostic and Statistical Manual of Mental Disorders (DSM). Therefore, the American Psychiatric Association has added this type of addiction as an Appendix in DSM-5, which is the latest version of DSM. Such a debate in the application domain is not new to the world of software engineering, e.g., we still lack consensus in a variety of domains, such as Green Computing, Digital Citizenship and Agent Computing. For this reason, we would encourage approaches that do not interfere with the decision-making about DA, but rather provide tools and platforms to facilitate taking those decisions effectively.

DA has roots in the software design, the requirements or goals for which this software is being used and the context of use. Other latent causes relate to the personal, physiological and mental characteristics of the user, over which we, as software engineers, have little control. However, we may still aim to accommodate these factors in the design of software, similar to disciplines like design for accessibility and universal design [4]. We contend that software engineering is required to attempt to provide ways to develop software that do not lead to addiction and to accommodate users who are genuinely vulnerable to addictive behaviour.

DA raises new challenges to software engineering in general and requirements engineering in particular. This paper argues for novel approaches, which are able to cater for the diversity, subjectivity and also the private nature of information related to DA. We review the literature and analyse a discussion thread in a set of online forum discussions about DA and present a mind-map articulating the causes of DA. Some of these causes are within a software engineering remit. Finally, we use our findings to suggest a foundation, or baseline ontology for DA, and propose areas of research on DA for the software and requirements engineering community.

2   Empirical Investigation of DA

There are already existing studies on sub-areas of DA (internet addiction [2] and game addiction [5,6]) which focus on the perception of users and those user characteristics which lead to DA. However, crucially, these studies do not focus on the peculiarities of the object on which DA is centred, i.e., the software. This lack of consideration of the software motivated us to carry out our own investigation by reviewing the literature to identify those factors that appeared to lead to DA and then to analyse discussion forums on DA which we found in widely accessed and well-reputed websites to validate and enhance our initial findings. In doing so, we identified a range of factors and then classified them under five main categories, namely; software-mediated activity, attractiveness, personal, cultural and situational. The last three categories are directly related to qualities of the software while the personal and cultural dimensions are factors that would fit studies in psychology and sociology. Our findings are summarized in Figure1.

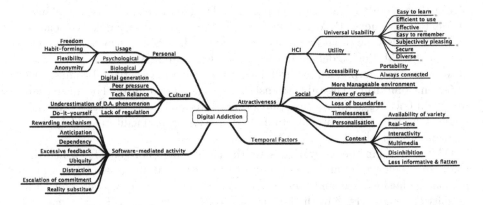

Fig. 1. A mind-map for Digital Addiction

This mind-map merely provides answers for the "what" question, that is, what has an impact on DA? Ultimately we might hope that studying user experience (UX) could, ideally, provide insights on the "why" question. Several studies, e.g., [7,8,9,10], showed that user experience is not negatively affected even when social software such as YouTube, Facebook, Wikipedia have poor compliance to usability principles [11]. Therefore, to understand the true nature of DA, the broader scope of UX may need to incorporate not only the "felt experience" such as "pleasure, curiosity, and self- expression", but also what users gain, rightly or wrongly, from particular behaviours. To some extent, we could see these users as using the 'addictive' behaviour to satisfy some 'internal' requirement (an aspect which we explore more fully below). Hence, it may not be enough simply to describe the associations among aspects of the software and specific, possibly addictive, behaviours, but rather to understand the nature of the satisfaction and how it relates to user's internal and private requirements, and their individual values.

However, whilst ultimately wanting to reach such rich understanding, a more pragmatic, or medium term, view would be that, even should we not be able to understand fully, say the psychological reasons for why certain features appear to trigger or exacerbate particular addictive behaviours, we could still learn which features have those impacts. That is, from a behavioural perspective, we should be able to learn to produce software products that are less likely to stimulate addictive behaviours. Hence, in having such an engineering goal, we turn again to consideration of DA from a requirements perspective.

3 Digital Addiction: A Requirements Perspective

There is a wide debate on the meaning of DA [2]. In brief there is a general agreement on the existence of the phenomenon but different viewpoints on its nature. In order to make practical progress, for a discipline like requirements engineering, we suggest a working definition. Hence, we take the initiative here and define DA from a requirements perspective as:

Digital Addiction is the excessive use of certain software-mediated operations to reach certain requirements. This includes the case when the use itself is compulsive or impulsive and also the case when the user cannot switch to other available alternatives to reach the same requirements without a good reason.

Requirements Engineering is the natural place in which users' goals and values are captured and analysed. Users' goals and values are different in that the values are 'cognitive representations' of the goals and are able to sustain users' positive emotion towards a software design [12]. On the other hand, goals are the explicit requirements that users can express. In terms of DA, values are very hard to identify due to their private nature. For example, increasing the number of followers in a social network, e.g., Twitter, is the explicit *goal* for some users, while raising the reputation in the virtual community is the latent *value*. If we can validate such values, we might help users to switch to another goal and/or alternative software design, perhaps less addictive, as long as it still can satisfy that value. Understanding what and how to do to achieve that is a requirements challenge in the first place.

A further challenge is whether we can help stakeholders to articulate these hidden requirements. Conventional elicitation methods, such as workshops, interviews and focus groups, suffer from a threat to validity when used for DA. This is due to the private nature and the tacit nature of users' values. To handle this, we suggest exploiting techniques that enable stakeholders, say addicts, to communicate through a lifelong collaborative and social activity, e.g. designated forums, and facilitate capturing this knowledge at runtime. Techniques like Crowdsourcing [13] used in the context of obtaining knowledge about software, as in [14], could be promising here.

One might argue that design time surveys can provide similar results. However, these requirements are dynamic as users' interactions with the system evolve with time, e.g., due to changes in different factors including users' familiarity with the software, the competitive technology or peer pressure. Hence, addiction not only arises from software features, but also depends on the interaction with the software in a particular context (technical, environmental and social). The fact that DA is both dynamic and context dependent makes it necessary to have more novel elicitation technique to sustain the validity of elicited DA knowledge. Software could utilize that knowledge from addicts at runtime and use it to switch to a behaviour shown by the users to be less-addictive or addiction-free. Such adaptation is called Social Adaptation [15] and it aims to harness the "wisdom of crowd" [16] in the context of software adaptation.

Social networking websites provide a wide range of features that have distinct functional traits such as tagging, likes, notifications, walls, and new features will continue to emerge. Kietzmann et al. [17] presented the Honeycomb framework as an attempt to define social media based on the peculiarity of their activities. The framework consists of seven functional blocks, identity, conversations, sharing, presence, relationships, reputation and groups. This contribution aimed to help firms to understand the engagement needs of their audiences. Such approach could provide a starting point and help to analyse software features, mainly social features, based on the addiction aspects (see Figure 1) the users' engagement requirements and values.

In our preliminary suggested approach, we first create links between users' values and requirements and analyse the software features against the mind-map factors. This analysis can be done individually, by user, or collectively through designated social platform or community of interests. The challenge is on how to adapt and provide users with alternative feature configuration that are less addictive whilst at the same time maintain users' values and requirements. We can view this as a particular kind of Dynamic Software Product Lines [18] where the addictive aspects of features, as shown by users feedback or patterns of use, could be the driver for adaptation. Figure 2 shows the meta-model which contains the main concepts of our suggested direction.

We emphasise that there is a fine line between a commitment to a task or a high level of satisfaction with software and DA. As requirements engineering we cannot, and perhaps should not, impose our definition of an addictive behaviour. Hence, we advocate that users, individually or in groups, provide and update that knowledge. Developing that user-led knowledge elicitation is an obviously challenging problem.

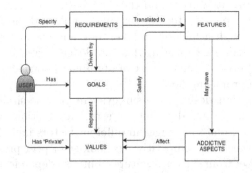

Fig. 2. DA from Requirements Perspective

4   Challenges and Future Work

Having articulated a vision for Requirements Engineering accommodating DA, we note that there are still a number of significant challenges, notably, those outlined below.

- Diversity of both Software and Users: both product features and user diversity in terms of their needs and patterns of use justify the need for enabling users to act as modellers to express personal perception toward software. A key challenge is to develop the social platform to act as a communication channel so we understand better addiction sources and stimuli within the different users groups and software features.
- Elicitation: DA relates heavily to users perceptions, expectations and personal requirements which are not easy to express in words for most users, i.e. tacit [19], fuzzy in nature and also very sensitive and private. This maximizes the challenge of capturing DA knowledge even via Crowdsourcing.
- We have identified some addictive aspects of different social software products. Questions remain as to how, or even whether, users would like to be aware of DA when they have it, what decisions would be taken by software and what other decisions are to be taken by users when the software is running? This introduces also ethical and legal issue on the accountability and responsibility of software, developers, and users.
- From a developer's (business) perspective, user's satisfaction should not be compromised. Thus, how can we, as software engineers, regulate addiction or even prevent it without affecting negatively users' experience?
- Our work focuses on the software as a core entity within DA. However, complementary work should be conducted to look at a particular set of personality traits that make individuals predisposed to DA.

5   Conclusions

Digital Addiction (DA) is as a growing and important societal issue. In this paper we suggest the need to recognise DA, and our responsibilities for it within Requirements Engineering (RE). We also suggest some potential approaches to incorporating consideration of DA within RE and articulate key challenges for DA. We expect a multidisciplinary research to address the many diverse aspects of DA aiming to develop addiction-aware software. Our future work will investigate approaches which allow not only experts but also users to contribute knowledge on the addictive aspects of a software. We anticipate that this will lead to a more holistic view of the reasons and potential treatment of DA.

Acknowledgement. The research was supported by an FP7 Marie Curie CIG grant (the SOCIAD Project) and by Bournemouth University through the Fusion Investment Fund (the BBB and the VolaComp projects) and the Graduate School PGR Development Fund.

References

1. Beard, K.W., Yarnall, C.: Internet addiction in children and adolescents. Computer Science Research Trends, 59–70 (2008)
2. Widyanto, L., Griffiths, M.: Internet addiction: a critical review. International Journal of Mental Health and Addiction 4(1), 31–51 (2006)
3. Davies, J.B.: Myth of Addiction. Routledge (2013)
4. Story, M.F.: Maximizing usability: the principles of universal design. Assistive Technology 10(1), 4–12 (1998)
5. Schüll, N.D.: Addiction by Design: Machine Gambling in Las Vegas. Princeton University Press (2012)
6. Park, S., Hwang, H.S.: Understanding online game addiction: Connection between presence and flow. In: Jacko, J.A. (ed.) HCI International 2009, Part IV. LNCS, vol. 5613, pp. 378–386. Springer, Heidelberg (2009)
7. Hart, J., Ridley, C., Taher, F., Sas, C., Dix, A.: Exploring the facebook experience: a new approach to usability. In: Proceedings of the 5th Nordic Conference on Human-Computer Interaction: Building Bridges, pp. 471–474. ACM (2008)
8. McCarthy, J., Wright, P.: Technology as experience. Interactions 11(5), 42–43 (2004)
9. Silva, P.A., Dix, A.: Usability: not as we know it? In: Proceedings of the 21st British HCI Group Annual Conference on People and Computers: HCI... but not as we know it, vol. 2, pp. 103–106. British Computer Society (2007)
10. Thompson, A.J., Kemp, E.A.: Web 2.0: extending the framework for heuristic evaluation. In: Proceedings of the 10th International Conference NZ Chapter of the ACM's Special Interest Group on Human-Computer Interaction, pp. 29–36. ACM (2009)
11. Rosson, M.B., Carroll, J.M.: Usability engineering: scenario-based development of human-computer interaction. Morgan Kaufmann (2002)
12. Kujala, S., Väänänen-Vainio-Mattila, K.: Value of information systems and products: Understanding the users' perspective and values. Journal of Information Technology Theory and Application 9(4), 23–39 (2009)
13. Howe, J.: The rise of crowdsourcing. Wired Magazine 14(6), 1–4 (2006)
14. Ali, R., Solis, C., Salehie, M., Omoronyia, I., Nuseibeh, B., Maalej, W.: Social sensing: When users become monitors. In: Proceedings of the 19th ACM SIGSOFT Symposium and the 13th European Conference on Foundations of Software Engineering, ESEC/FSE 2011, pp. 476–479. ACM, New York (2011)
15. Ali, R., Solis, C., Omoronyia, I., Salehie, M., Nuseibeh, B.: Social Adaptation at Runtime. In: Maciaszek, L.A., Filipe, J. (eds.) ENASE 2012. CCIS, vol. 410, pp. 110–127. Springer, Heidelberg (2013)
16. Surowiecki, J.: The wisdom of crowds. Random House Digital, Inc. (2005)
17. Kietzmann, J.H., Hermkens, K., McCarthy, I.P., Silvestre, B.S.: Social media? get serious! understanding the functional building blocks of social media. Business Horizons 54(3), 241–251 (2011)
18. Hallsteinsen, S., Hinchey, M., Park, S., Schmid, K.: Dynamic software product lines. Computer 41(4), 93–95 (2008)
19. Gacitua, R., Ma, L., Nuseibeh, B., Piwek, P., Roeck, A.D., Rouncefield, M., Sawyer, P., Willis, A., Yang, H.: Making tacit requirements explicit. In: Second International Workshop on Managing Requirements Knowledge (MaRK 2009) (September 2009)

Feedback-Aware Requirements Documents for Smart Devices

Erik Kamsties[1], Fabian Kneer[1], Markus Voelter[2], Burkhard Igel[3], and Bernd Kolb[3]

[1] Dortmund University of Applied Sciences and Arts,
Emil-Figge-Str. 42, 44227 Dortmund, Germany
{erik.kamsties,fabian.kneer}@fh-Dortmund.de
http://www.fh-dortmund.de
[2] independent/itemis, Germany
voelter@acm.org
[3] itemis AG, Germany
{igel,kolb}@itemis.de

Abstract. [**Context/ Motivation**] A smart device is a software-intensive system that operates autonomously and interacts to some degree with other systems over wireless connections. Such systems are often faced with uncertainty in the environment. Runtime representations of requirements have recently gained more interested to deal with this challenge and the term *requirements at runtime* has been established. Runtime representations of requirements support reasoning about the requirements at runtime and adapting the configuration of a system according to changes in the environment. [**Questions/Problems**] The research question is how the results of runtime monitoring of requirements and the system's decisions about changes in the configuration are communicated back to the requirements engineer to better understand the environment. There is a gap between the written requirements document and the dynamic requirements model inside the system. This problem is exacerbated by the fact that a requirements document are mostly informal while the dynamic requirements model is formal. [**Principal ideas/results**] This paper introduces an approach to bridge the gap between development time and runtime representations of requirements in order to keep them consistent and to facilitate better understanding. We propose to weave the feedback from the runtime system into requirements documents using a domain-specific language that largely retain the informal nature of requirements. An annotated requirements document helps get a better understanding of the system's actual behavior in a given environment. The approach is implemented using mbeddr, a novel set of domain-specific languages for developing embedded systems, and illustrated using a running example.

Keywords: Smart Device, Embedded System, Domain-specific Language, mbeddr, Requirements at Runtime, Self-Adaptivity.

1 Introduction

Runtime representations of requirements have received increased interest over the last years. Runtime representations are the basis for reflection on requirements, that is to

C. Salinesi and I. van de Weerd (Eds.): REFSQ 2014, LNCS 8396, pp. 119–134, 2014.
© Springer International Publishing Switzerland 2014

understand, explain, and modify requirements at runtime, in order to deal with continuously changing environmental needs [1] – a significant challenge for today's software-intensive systems.

We propose in this paper an approach for relating *runtime* representations of requirements with *development time* representations. The goal is to gain insights into how requirements evolve over time and how the system is actually used from the perspective of a requirements engineer. The focus is on resource-constrained embedded systems.

For the development time representation, we use mbeddr[1], a set of modular domain-specific extensions to the C programming language. mbeddr is also capable of representing requirements, it stores them along with code and maintains traceability. That is, mbeddr provides an integrated view on requirements and implementation in C, which are maintained in the same formalism and same tool (see Fig. 1). Requirements documents can be generated from mbeddr in the usual formats (e.g., HTML, PDF).

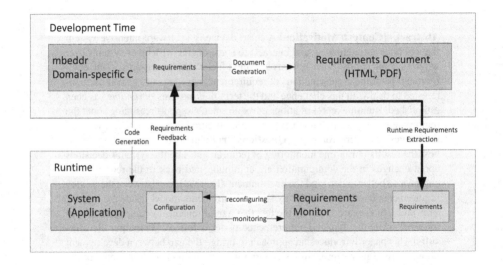

Fig. 1. Bridging the gap between development time and runtime artifacts

For the runtime representation of requirements, we make use of a goal-oriented approach. The runtime requirements (i.e., the goal model) are extracted from the development time requirements expressed in mbeddr. A requirements monitor utilizes the runtime requirements. That is, the monitor is able to spot violations of assumptions the system imposes on its environment and is able to recalculate a configuration for the system based on the runtime requirements.

If environmental changes results in an update of the configuration, then this feedback is woven into the mbeddr development time requirements. These changes are highlighted after re-generation also in the PDF/HTML requirements document.

A code generation step is part of our approach, as shown in Fig. 1. During development time, a developer creates an *implementation* of the application using the mbeddr

---

[1] http://mbeddr.wordpress.com/

domain-specific C language. The system itself is then generated from the domain-specific C code. The code generator adds some hooks for requirements monitoring.

Contribution. The contribution of this paper is a formal, tool supported link between the development time and runtime representations (bold arrows in Fig. 1). The benefit is two-fold. First, a requirements engineer better understands the adaptations of systems as they run in the field. Second, a user can be better informed about the actual system behavior.

Structure. The remainder of this paper is organized as follows. Section 2 outlines the background of our research. Section 3 introduces mbeddr and explains how it is used as an development time representation for requirements and for domain-specific code generation. Section 4 discusses the runtime representation of requirements and the missing link between the two representations. Our approach is illustrated using a running example of a vacuum cleaner. Section 5 reviews the related work. Section 6 concludes with a summary and an overview on our future work.

2 Background

Embedded Systems. The focus of our work is in particular on smart systems, which are a subclass of embedded systems. Embedded systems impose heavy constraints on software. First, as these systems are mass-produced, the capabilities of the hardware are optimized to the purpose of the respective system. That is, the power of the CPU and the memory size are limited. We often see 8-bit microcontrollers running at 16 MHz and providing 256 KB flash memory (e.g., in wireless sensor networks). Embedded Linux systems come with a 32-bit typically clocked at 400 MHz or higher and 512 MB of memory. Constraints on energy consumption prohibit more powerful hardware, since many embedded systems run on batteries. The C programming language is prevalent.

Smart systems are embedded systems that collaborate with each other, typically over wireless connections. For example, a warning about an iced bridge may be passed through a sequence of vehicles. The systems are only loosely coupled and a smart system must adapt its behavior to the current situation (e.g., when there are not enough networked cars available).

Self-adaptive Systems. Many embedded systems act autonomously, that is they make decisions without the confirmation of a human operator. The software cannot be easily maintained or tuned to changing conditions manually. Therefore, there is a need for adaptivity. However, adaptivity conflicts with other design goals such real-time behavior, safety considerations, and the resource constraints mentioned above.

A self-adaptive system has the ability to dynamically and autonomously reconfigure its behavior in order to respond to changing environmental conditions [1]. We consider a self-adaptive system as consisting of two parts: the system and a requirements monitor (see Fig. 1). The system implements the development time requirements. The requirements monitor contains a requirements model, which is a machine-processable representation of the system's requirements. The requirement model is the basis for computing new configurations at runtime in case of environmental changes. Often, a goal-oriented model is used for this purpose (see Related Work in Sec. 5).

3   Development Time Representation Using mbeddr

mbeddr is an open source project supporting embedded software development based on incremental, modular domain-specific extension of C. It also supports languages that address other aspects of software engineering such as requirements or documentation. Fig. 2 shows an overview, details are in [2] and [3].

We selected mbeddr for the development time representation of requirements, because it provides an integrated, model-driven approach for dealing with development artifacts such as requirements, component-based design, and code. Moreover, it is geared to the embedded domain, it allows for code generation for the abstractions in the domain (e.g., state machines).

3.1   mbeddr Overview

mbeddr builds on the JetBrains MPS language workbench[2], a tool that supports the definition, composition and use of general purpose or domain-specific languages. MPS uses a projectional editor, which means that, although a syntax may look textual, it is *not* represented as a sequence of characters which are transformed into an abstract syntax tree (AST) by a parser. Instead, a user's editing actions lead *directly* to changes in the AST. Projection rules render a concrete syntax from the AST. Consequently, MPS supports non-textual notations such as tables, and it also supports unconstrained language composition and extension – no parser ambiguities can ever result from combining languages (see [4] for details).

The next layer in mbeddr is an extensible implementation of the C programming language (C99, ISO/IEC 9899:1999) in MPS. On top of that, mbeddr ships with a library of reusable extensions relevant to embedded software. As a user writes a program, he can

User Extensions	to be defined by users										
Default Extensions	Test Support	Decision Tables							Glossaries	Use Cases & Scenarios	
	Compo-nents	Physical Units	State Machines	State Machine Verification	Decision Tables	Contracts					
Core	C core			Model Checking	SMT Solving	Dataflow Analysis	Visual-ization	PLE Variability	Documen-tation	Requirements & Tracing	
Platform	JetBrains MPS										
Backend Tool	C Compiler, Debugger and Importer		NuSMV	Yices	CBMC	PlantUML					
	Implementation Concern			Analysis Concern			Process Concern				

Fig. 2. mbeddr rests on the MPS language workbench. Above it, the first language layer contains an extensible version of the C programming language plus special support for logging/error reporting and build system integration. On top of that, mbeddr comes with a set of C extensions (components, state machines, units) plus cross-cutting support for requirements, traceability, documentation, visualization and variability.

---

[2] http://jetbrains.com/mps/

import language extensions from the library into his program. Major extensions include test cases, interfaces and components, state machines, decision tables and data types with physical units. For many of these extensions, mbeddr provides an integration with static verification tools (model checking state machines, verifying interface contracts or checking decision tables for consistency and completeness; see also [5]).

3.2 Requirements in mbeddr

mbeddr exploits language engineering to provide a powerful tool for embedded software engineering: the vast majority of problems is solved by providing domain-specific languages that express different aspects of the overall system. This is also true for requirements. Requirements are captured using an extensible language specific to the *requirements domain*. Like any other requirements management tool, the mbeddr requirements language primarily describes requirements with a short title, a unique ID and a prose description (see Fig. 3). However, it also supports a number of unique features, which we utilize in our approach:

- Extensibility: The mbeddr requirements language can be extended in any direction. That is, we are able to add e.g., goal-oriented modeling (see Sec. 3.3).
- The *right* degree of formality: Most industrial embedded systems are specified using a mixture of formal and informal/semi-formal representations of requirements. This observation imposes a challenge to our goal of requirements feedback: how to feed formal[3] results from executing a system into the requirements if requirements are described informally? mbeddr supports *partial formalization* by formal concepts that are introduced directly into informal requirements.
- Traceability and consistency: As requirements and code are maintained by mbeddr, traceability is supported between requirements and to other artifacts. If informal requirements are partially formalized (e.g., using parameters), mbeddr maintains consistency between requirements and code such that a change of a parameter in the code changes the value in the requirement and vice versa. We extend traceability in our approach towards runtime representation of requirements.

3.3 Extension of mbeddr to Deal with Runtime Requirements

We extend mbeddr to cover *parameters*, *optional requirements*, and *i* goal models* [6] to establish the missing link between development time and runtime requirements. These extensions are discussed below. As a running example throughout the paper, we use a vacuum cleaner case study that was originally introduced in [7] and [1].

Parameters. The use of parameters in functional requirements is a common technique for embedded systems e.g., to enforce adaptability regarding a technical environment, or particular customers. Parameters are added to the original mbeddr requirements language in a way so they can be embedded in the requirements prose description ([8] explains how to do this). Like variables in programs, parameters have a name, a type

---

[3] We use the term *formal* here in the sense of *machine-readable* as it is usually done in model-driven engineering.

and an initial value. Fig. 3 shows an example: the Requirement RE3 is completely informal, except for a formal concept *parameter* called maxSuction and annotated as @param.

Optional Requirements. Some requirements for an embedded system are considered optional. That is, the respective function can be enabled or disabled at runtime. We assume in the following that these requirements are initially *enabled* and become *disabled* at runtime if a conflict arises between requirements due to change in the environment. RE1 and RE2 in Fig. 3 are optional.

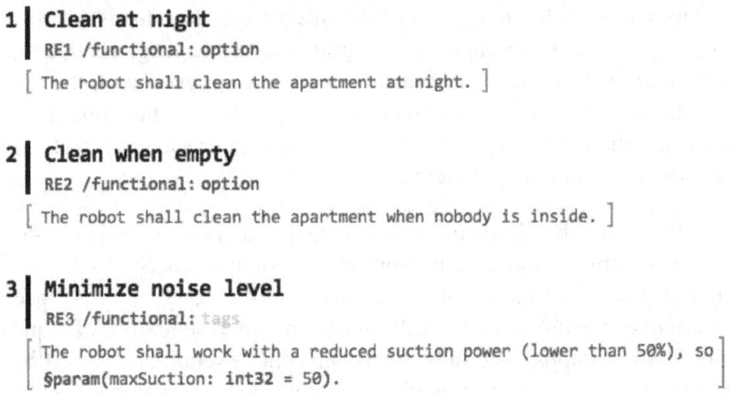

1 | **Clean at night**
RE1 /functional: option
[The robot shall clean the apartment at night.]

2 | **Clean when empty**
RE2 /functional: option
[The robot shall clean the apartment when nobody is inside.]

3 | **Minimize noise level**
RE3 /functional: tags
[The robot shall work with a reduced suction power (lower than 50%), so
§param(maxSuction: int32 = 50).]

Fig. 3. Example requirements with parameters and an *option* attribute

i* Goal Models. We use an i* goal model to resolve possible conflicts at runtime. For this purpose, we developed a new mbeddr language module to describe a goal model and to link it to the requirements. The goal model is basically a textual description of the classic i* goal model shown in Fig. 5 therefore we do not provide an example.

Finally, the exchange of information between mbeddr at development time and an embedded system at runtime needs consideration. From a practical viewpoint, this means that we need to exchange information between a machine used for development (host) and an embedded system (target). The exchange is currently realized using XML files. Listing 1 shows part of the information sent from mbeddr to the embedded system derived from the requirements in Fig. 3 (again, the goal model is omitted).

Listing 1. XML representation with optional requirements and a parameter

```
1  <parameters>
2    <requirement option="true" name="RE1" />
3    <requirement option="true" name="RE2" />
4    <requirement name="RE3">
5      <param name="maxSuction" type="int32">50</param>
6    </requirement>
7  </parameters>
```

4   Runtime Representation of Requirements

This section describes our runtime representation of requirements. The runtime requirements are maintained by a requirements monitor as mentioned in Sec. 2. The requirements monitor shown Fig. 1 consists of three components: (1) monitor, (2) requirements model, and (3) impact analyzer. Fig. 4 illustrates the relationships between these components. In the following, we explain briefly the interaction of the components.

The *monitor* is implemented by a rule engine, which monitors assertions. *Assertions* are Boolean conditions describing assumptions about the environment, which usually should be fulfilled. If an assertion fails, a requirement may be violated and the *impact analyzer* is invoked. The impact analyzer assesses which parts of the *requirements model* are affected and whether a change in the model is really necessary. Sometimes a change is postponed in order to keep a different, but more important goal satisfied. If a change is necessary, a new *configuration* is computed and the *system* switches to that new configuration eventually. The monitor registers itself at the system and gets invoked when a relevant environmental property observed by the system changes.

The technical details of the concept shown in Fig. 4 are described in the remainder of this section.

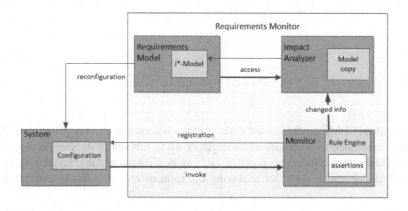

Fig. 4. Concept for runtime representation and monitoring of requirements

4.1   Requirements Model

To represent requirements at runtime we use the i* goal-oriented modeling language [6]. A simple implementation of i* is provided by the openOME[4] tool. We use its meta model which is defined based on the Eclipse Modeling Framework[5](EMF).

We extend the openOME meta model with a new attribute *Priority* of a goal. The attribute is defined as an enumeration with the values *VeryLow, Low, High, VeryHigh,*

---

[4] https://se.cs.toronto.edu/trac/ome/
[5] http://www.eclipse.org/modeling/emf/

Unknown. The attribute is needed for the impact analyzer, which must find the goal with the highest priority to decide how to change the requirements model to maintain the satisfaction of this goal. Fig. 5 shows an i* model for the vacuum cleaner. The elements *task*, *goal*, *soft goal* and *resource* have an attribute *EvaluationLabel* which represents the satisfaction of that element. Note that in Fig. 5 goals have the additional attribute *Priority*.

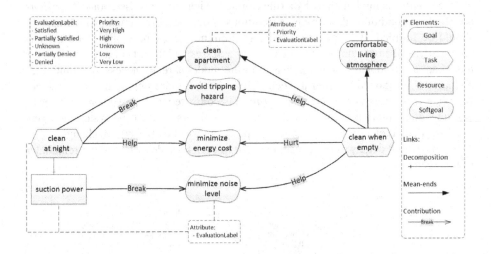

Fig. 5. i* model of the vacuum cleaner

The extended i* EMF model is used as the runtime representation of requirements. This model is developed by a requirements engineer using mbeddr at development time, it is imported by the requirements monitor, and can be changed and displayed at runtime. The underlying source code for accessing the runtime requirements is generated by EMF.

4.2 Monitor

The monitor observes assertions. An assertion is a Boolean condition on parameters which is evaluated by the rule engine. For example, in Listing 2 the parameter is *time*. The assertion fails if the current time is not between *timeMin* and *timeMax*.

An assertion is evaluated on the current values of parameters. For this purpose, these parameters are observed by the monitor according to the Observer pattern: the monitor registers itself as an observer to the system and gets a notification whenever one of the parameters change.

An assertion is assigned to the requirements model. We define two kinds of assertions. The first is assigned to a soft goal. If the assertion breaks, the satisfaction of the assigned soft goal is set to *Denied*. Otherwise, the satisfaction is set to *Satisfied*. The second kind of assertion is assigned to a contribution link. If the assertion breaks, the assigned contribution link is set to a new type. This new type is determined by a developer and is stored along with the assertion. In the case of a fulfilled assertion, the type is set to *unknown*.

The following assertions are defined for the vacuum cleaner i* model:

1. No tripping hazard
2. Lowest energy cost between 22 and 8 o'clock
3. Noise level too high when suction power over 50%

Assertion 1 is assigned to the contribution link between the elements *clean at night* and *avoid tripping hazard*. If the assertion breaks, the new type of the contribution link shall be *break*. Assertion 2 is important to satisfy the soft goal *minimize energy cost*. It means this soft goal can only be satisfied between 22 and 8 o'clock. Assertion 3 is described in the next subsection.

To implement the rule engine we use Roolie[6], a framework that supports defining, changing and checking rules at runtime. Listing 2 is the Roolie representation of Assertion 2.

Listing 2. Implementation of a rule with Roolie

```
boolean passes = time > timeMin && time < timeMax;
```

4.3 Impact Analyzer

The impact analyzer is notified by the monitor when an assertion breaks: the notification contains the affected soft goal (or contribution link) and its new satisfaction (or new type). This change is first applied to a copy of the requirements model to avoid premature changes.

The impact analyzer performs an evaluation of the requirements model based on the model evaluation process for i* proposed by Grau et al. [7]. This process starts at the affected soft goal (or the soft goal connected to the affected contribution link), traverses all elements of the requirements model, and ends when all satisfactions have been recomputed.

Fig. 6 shows an example calculation for the vacuum cleaner. Assume Assertion 1 is broken, which is assigned to the contribution link between *clean at night* and *avoid tripping hazard* (bold contribution link). The type of the contribution link changes to *break*. From the target *avoid tripping hazard* of this contribution link we start to compute the satisfactions of the other model elements.

Rules for Computing the Satisfaction of an Element.   The satisfaction for a *goal* is calculated over the mean-ends link. The mean-ends link is an *or*-relationship between a goal and one or more tasks. The goal satisfaction is taken from the highest satisfaction of one of the linked tasks. In Fig. 6 the goal *clean apartment* gets the satisfaction from the task *clean when empty*.

---

[6] http://roolie.sourceforge.net/
[7] http://istar.rwth-aachen.de/tiki-view_articles.php

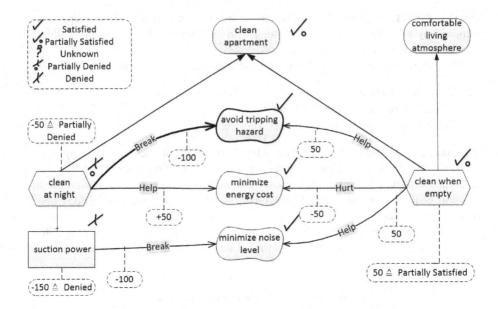

Fig. 6. i* model with computed satisfaction of elements

A *task* can have decomposition links to a task, goal, soft goal, or resource. This is an *and*-relationship. Every linked element must be satisfied to satisfy the task. So, all elements get the satisfaction of the task. In Fig. 6, the resource *suction power* gets the satisfaction from the task *clean at night*.

The value of the *contribution link* must be determined from the desired satisfaction of the target and the type of the contribution. The result is the value the source must have in this relationship to get the desired satisfaction of the target. Fig. 7 shows how to combine a soft goal satisfaction and a contribution link type. The values were derived in a pragmatic fashion. In the example in Fig. 6, the satisfaction *partiallyDenied* is computed for the task *clean at night*. It is the result of the sum of the assigned contribution links. The results are 50 (combination of *help* and *satisfied*) and -100 (combination of *break* and *satisfied*, see Fig. 7)

	Denied	Partially Denied	Unknown	Partially Satisfied	Satisfied
Break	100	50	0	-50	-100
Hurt	50	50	0	-50	-50
Some-	50	50	0	-50	-50
Unknown	0	0	0	0	0
Some+	-50	-50	0	50	50
Help	-50	-50	0	50	50
Make	-100	-50	0	50	100

Fig. 7. Combination of soft goal satisfaction and contribution link type

Delay Reconfigurations. The evaluation process above results in new satisfaction values of goals (and other elements), which in turn would lead to a new configuration. To avoid premature reconfigurations, the threshold of an assertion can be relaxed at runtime under specific conditions described by the procedure in Listing 3. Thus, a reconfiguration can be delayed.

Listing 3. Pseudocode for the delay of changes

```
1   if (assertion_has_threshold() == false) {
2       change_original_requirements_model(); // reconfigure
3       return;
4   }
5   old_number = number_of_satisfied_goals(); // before change
6   old_priority = sum_of_priorities_of_satisfied_goals();
7   change_copy_of_requirements model();
8   new_number = number_of_satisfied_goals(); // after change
9   new_priority = sum_of_priorities_of_satisfied_goals();
10
11  if (old_number < new_number)
12      change_original_requirements_model(); // reconfigure
13  else
14      if (old_priority > new_priority)
15          relax_threshold(); // delay
16      else
17          change_original_requirements_model(); // reconfigure
```

An assertion cannot be relaxed if there are no thresholds as in Assertion 1 (see Lines 1-4 in pseudocode of Listing 3). Otherwise, the impact of a change is tested on the a copy of the requirements model (Lines 5-9). Under specific conditions described in Lines 11-17, the system is reconfigured or the threshold of an assertion is relaxed. An assertion has the ability to incrementally relax the threshold. The step size and the maximum threshold are predefined by a developer.

For example, Assertion 3 is assigned to the soft goal *minimize noise level* and can be relaxed by changing the threshold from 50% to 60%. Consequently, the change to the requirements model is delayed to assure the satisfaction of a goal with a high priority.

Generate Configurations. Finally, the impact analyzer generates a new configuration for the system. A configuration is a new assignment of values to parameters and options of the runtime requirements shown in Listing 1. For a requirement assigned to a task with a positive satisfaction, the option is set to *true*. For a requirement assigned to a task with a negative satisfaction, the option is set to *false*. In the example, the *option* attribute of Requirement *RE1* is set to *false*, i.e., the function *clean at night* is disabled in the new configuration. *RE2* remains *true*.

4.4 System

The system, i.e., the embedded software, reads sensor data and writes to actuators. Two additional interfaces are required. First, the system provides an interface to allow for monitoring parameters. The monitor can register itself with this interface and gets a notification if a parameter changes its value.

Second, the system provides an interface to read a new configuration after a modification of the requirements model. When the system is started up, it reads a configuration generated by the requirements monitor.

This configuration contains parameter values and which functions are active under the current environmental situation. The state of a function is related to the enabled or disabled state of a requirement (see Listing 1).

4.5 Requirements Feedback

The information about changes is collected by the requirements monitor and is sent to mbeddr at some point in time (note that we are doing a post-mortem analysis of a system using mbeddr). This is the last step in our feedback cycle shown in Fig. 1. The information is again represented using XML and contains the concrete parameter values, enabled requirements, and the changes to the goal model.

It is important to note that there is a 1-to-many relationship between development time and runtime requirements, i.e., the development time requirements receive feedback from many runtime instances. Thus, a system identifier is added to the feedback, see Listing 4.

Listing 4. XML file with system identification

```
1   <parameters systemID="42">
```

Finally, the feedback file is imported by mbeddr. The parameter values are stored as child nodes of the parameter definition in the requirements description, separately for each system ID. In mbeddr, the requirements engineer can use a filter to focus on a specific system and show the values of the parameters directly in the requirements. It is also possible to inspect all parameter values of all systems that provided feedback.

Fig. 8 shows the change of the requirements from Fig. 3. Now the requirements RE1 and RE2 have a value for the option tag. For the system with the ID 42, requirement RE1 is disabled and requirement RE2 is enabled. Also, for system 42, the value of the *maxSuction* parameter is 50.

mbeddr supports generating requirements documents (e.g., HTML or PDF) from mbeddr requirements. This generator is modified in order to highlight the changes that happened at runtime so that a requirements engineer is able to better understand how systems evolve.

4.6 Scenario

The following scenario illustrates how the system, monitor, impact analyzer, and requirements model interact in a given situation.

The vacuum cleaner cleans different surfaces in an apartment. Depending on the environment and prioritization of the goals, one of the realization strategies is selected. Assume the robot cleans at night. A person walks into the apartment. Now, because of a power failure the lights switch off. The following steps are carried out:

Requirements vacuum_cleaner3

doc config: test		filters:
class: runtime-requirements for 42		imports:
Abstract: [ ]		

1 | **Clean at night**
RE1 /functional: option=false
[The robot shall clean the apartment at night.]

2 | **Clean when empty**
RE2 /functional: option=true
[The robot shall clean the apartment when nobody is inside.]

3 | **Minimize noise level**
RE3 /functional: tags
[The robot shall work with a reduced suction power (lower than 50%), so $param(maxSuction = 50).]

Fig. 8. Requirements with Feedback

1. The monitor notices a change in the apartment and triggers the rule engine.
2. The rule engine checks all assertions and notices that Assertion 1 *no tripping hazard* is broken.
3. The rule engine informs the impact analyzer that the contribution link must be set to *break*.
4. The changes are applied to a copy of the model and the satisfaction of each element is calculated.
5. Both goals are satisfied by the task *clean when empty* (see Fig. 6). This means the copy became the original model.
   (a) The information about the change is stored in a file.
   (b) mbeddr imports this file and weaves the information into the requirements (see Listing 8).
   (c) This definition is used to generate a requirements document in PDF or HTML with highlighted deltas.
6. From the new requirements model the analyzer generates a new configuration for the system where *clean at night* is disabled and *clean when empty* is enabled.
7. The system reads the configuration and switches to the new strategy.

5   Related Work

Many approaches have been developed to deal with adaptivity, including neural networks, rule engines, and dynamic decision networks. In the domain of embedded systems, adaptive fuzzy controllers are a typical solution. These approaches can be subdivided into approaches targeting *continuous* and *discrete* systems. The focus of our work is on discrete systems. Thus, neural networks and fuzzy controllers are not further discussed.

The following discussion of related work in adaptivity in RE follows the reference model shown in Fig. 4. For the *requirements model* most authors [1, 9–13] use a goal-orientated model such as KAOS [14], i* [6] or an extension such as Tropos [15] or adaptiveRML [9]. The system is usually attached to the requirements model using *domain assumptions* [1, 9–11, 16], *claims* [12], or *assertions* [13]. Assertions are monitored by a monitor system such as Flea [13], ReqMon [10, 17], or SalMon [10, 18].

The work by Fickas et al. [13, 16], Robinson et al. [17, 19], and Wang et al. [6] showed that it is important to use a representation of requirements at runtime. But this work does not support *adaption* at runtime. The solutions proposed by Baresi et al. [20], Oriol et al. [10, 18] and Qureshi et al. [9] support adaption, they can switch between different services at runtime.

Qureshi et al. [9] introduced a visual language called AdaptiveRML to model and analyze requirements in adaptive systems. They tried to handle premature changes of the model with monitor configurations for the assertions that can be modified at runtime. Their solution also supports goal reasoning, which mean that the impact on the goals are evaluated before an adaption is performed.

Oriol et al. [10] are working on notifications to involve users in decision processes, for example which type of connectivity should be used (Wi-Fi, Bluetooth, etc.). Also new monitor configurations can be generated from the runtime requirements.

Further research aims at improving the decision process by using dynamic decision networks (DDNs). Bencomo et al. [7] transfer an i* goal model into a DDNs to get a more dynamic representation of the requirements. The DDNs choose tasks with dynamically evolving nodes instead of the static contribution links. The weights of the notes are initialized with the domain knowledge inside the i* model. These weights are refined through a learning process at runtime. The work of Bencomo et al. focuses on a better learning process and to improve the adaption support. Premature changes shout be avoided and the system must learn to handle the unknown environment at runtime.

Our approach is based on previously mentioned work, but focuses on the *traceability* between development time and run time requirements. In this respect, the use of a DDN is an interesting approach, but the outcome of the learning process inside the network cannot be retranslated in terms of runtime requirements changes. Thus, changes cannot be traced back to the development time requirements.

Because we work in the area of embedded systems we have to handle resource constraints as mentioned in Chapter 2. The approaches from Oriol, Qureshi, Robinson, and Wang are all based on service-oriented architectures, which are not well established in the area of embedded systems.

6   Discussion

This paper identifies a problem in a RE, which arises for self-adaptive systems: how are possible changes to the runtime requirements communicated to requirements engineers and users?

The goal of our work is from the perspective of a requirements engineer to gain insights into how requirements evolve over time and how the system is actually used. One challenge lies in the representation of requirements at development time in a way they can be easily extracted and used at runtime. The feedback from the system to the development time requirements imposes another challenge, as requirements are represented as a mixture of informal and formal representations. However, the feedback from system is formal.

We proposed an approach to establish the missing link between development time and runtime representations of requirements in the context of embedded systems. Especially smart/embedded systems are interesting, as a human operator is often not available to give a confirmation to a system's decision. Thus the system must decide autonomously.

We suggested in this paper a concept for making adaptivity explicit. Nevertheless, discrete adaptivity can also be "programmed" directly into an application. The benefits of an *explicit* documentation of adaptivity are similar to the benefits of an explicit documentation of variability in case of software product lines: understanding and communication are improved. Changes in the runtime requirements (due to changes in the environment) are communicated to a requirements engineer. This leads eventually to a better understanding of the environment.

Our future work addresses the communication of the changes to the users and the formalization and monitoring of further aspects of requirements (beside parameters) such as conditions and relations between requirements. Regarding embedded real-time systems in particular, execution times, violations of deadlines, etc. are of interest. This information can also be collected at runtime and feed back into the requirements. MPS provides tables for a visualization of this more complex information. Further work is also underway on how to automatically resolve conflicts in goal models. Finally, a case study is planned in the context of an industrial research project on automotive software development tool chains.

References

1. Bencomo, N., Whittle, J., Sawyer, P., Finkelstein, A., Letier, E.: Requirements reflection: requirements as runtime entities. In: 2010 ACM/IEEE 32nd International Conference on Software Engineering, vol. 2, pp. 199–202 (2010)
2. Voelter, M., Ratiu, D., Kolb, B., Schaetz, B.: Journal of Automated Software Engineering (2013)
3. Voelter, M., Ratiu, D., Schaetz, B., Kolb, B.: mbeddr: an extensible c-based programming language and ide for embedded systems. In: Proc. of the 3rd Conf. on Systems, Programming, and Applications: Software for Humanity, SPLASH 2012, pp. 121–140. ACM, New York (2012)
4. Voelter, M.: Language and IDE Development, Modularization and Composition with MPS. In: Lämmel, R., Saraiva, J., Visser, J. (eds.) GTTSE 2011. LNCS, vol. 7680, pp. 383–430. Springer, Heidelberg (2013)
5. Ratiu, D., Voelter, M., Schaetz, B., Kolb, B.: Language Engineering as Enabler for Incrementally Defined Formal Analyses. In: FORMSERA 2012 (2012)
6. Wang, Y., McIlraith, S., Yu, Y., Mylopoulos, J.: Automated Software Engineering 16, 3 (2009)
7. Bencomo, N., Belaggoun, A.: Supporting decision-making for self-adaptive systems: From goal models to dynamic decision networks. In: Doerr, J., Opdahl, A.L. (eds.) REFSQ 2013. LNCS, vol. 7830, pp. 221–236. Springer, Heidelberg (2013)

8. Voelter, M.: Integrating prose as a first-class citizen with models and code. In: 7th Workshop on Multi-Paradigm Modelling (2013)
9. Qureshi, N.A., Jureta, I.J., Perini, A.: Towards a requirements modeling language for self-adaptive systems. In: Regnell, B., Damian, D. (eds.) REFSQ 2011. LNCS, vol. 7195, pp. 263–279. Springer, Heidelberg (2012)
10. Oriol, M., Qureshi, N.A., Franch, X., Perini, A., Marco, J.: Requirements monitoring for adaptive service-based applications. In: Regnell, B., Damian, D. (eds.) REFSQ 2011. LNCS, vol. 7195, pp. 280–287. Springer, Heidelberg (2012)
11. Sawyer, P., Bencomo, N., Whittle, J., Letier, E., Finkelstein, A.: Requirements-aware systems: A research agenda for re for self-adaptive systems, in. In: 2010 18th IEEE International Requirements Engineering Conference (RE), pp. 95–103 (2010)
12. Welsh, K., Sawyer, P., Bencomo, N.: Towards requirements aware systems: Run-time resolution of design-time assumptions, in. In: 2011 26th IEEE/ACM International Conference on Automated Software Engineering (ASE), pp. 560–563 (2011)
13. Feather, M., Fickas, S., Van Lamsweerde, A., Ponsard, C.: Reconciling system requirements and runtime behavior. In: Proceedings of the Ninth International Workshop on Software Specification and Design, pp. 50–59 (1998)
14. van Lamsweerde, A.: Requirements Engineering - From System Goals to UML Models to Software Specifications. Wiley (2009)
15. Brinkkemper, J., Mylopoulos, J., Solvberg, A., Yu, E.: Tropos: A framework for requirements-driven software development (2000)
16. Fickas, S., Feather, M.: Requirements monitoring in dynamic environments. In: Proceedings of the Second IEEE International Symposium on Requirements Engineering, pp. 140–147 (1995)
17. Robinson, W.: Implementing rule-based monitors within a framework for continuous requirements monitoring. In: Proceedings of the 38th Annual Hawaii International Conference on System Sciences, HICSS 2005, p. 188a (2005)
18. Oriol, M., Marco, J., Franch, X., Ameller, D.: Monitoring adaptable soa-systems using salmon. In: Workshop on Service Monitoring, Adaptation and Beyond (Mona+), pp. 19–28 (2008)
19. Robinson, W.: Requirements Engineering 11, 17 (2006)
20. Baresi, L., Pasquale, L.: Live goals for adaptive service compositions. In: Proceedings of the 2010 ICSE Workshop on Software Engineering for Adaptive and Self-Managing Systems, SEAMS 2010, pp. 114–123. ACM, New York (2010)

INCREMENT: A Mixed MDE-IR Approach for Regulatory Requirements Modeling and Analysis*

Nicolas Sannier and Benoit Baudry

Inria Rennes Bretagne Atlantique
Campus de Beaulieu
35042 Rennes Cedex, France
{nicolas.sannier,benoit.baudry}@inria.fr

Abstract. **[Context and motivation]** Regulatory requirements for Nuclear instrumentation and control (I&C) systems are first class requirements. They are written by national safety entities and are completed through a large documentation set of national recommendation guides and national/international standards. **[Question/Problem]** I&C systems important to safety must comply to all of these requirements. The global knowledge of this domain is scattered through these different documents and not formalized. Its organization and traceability relationships within this domain is mainly implicit. As a consequence, such long lasting nuclear I&C projects set important challenges in terms of tacit expertise capitalization and domain analysis. **[Principal ideas/results]** To tackle this domain formalization issue, we propose a dual Model-driven Engineering (MDE) and Information Retrieval (IR) approach to address the nuclear regulatory requirements domain definition, and assisted traceability based on the acquired requirements model. **[Contributions]** In this paper, we present the Connexion metamodel that provides a canvas for the definition and capitalization of the nuclear regulatory requirements domain. We also present an hybrid MDE/IR-based approach, named INCREMENT, for acquiring, modeling and analyzing these regulatory requirements. This approach is supported by a tool that is developed in the context of the CONNEXION project, which gathers French major nuclear I&C industrial actors.

Keywords: Nuclear Instrumentation and Control Systems, Regulatory Requirements, Standards, Metamodeling, Traceability, Information Retrieval.

1 Introduction

In addition to their systems requirements, systems with high level of security, privacy, or safety must also conform to regulatory requirements. For example, in the avionics domain, most regulators impose the application and compliance to

---

* This work is partially supported by the French BGLE Project CONNEXION.

C. Salinesi and I. van de Weerd (Eds.): REFSQ 2014, LNCS 8396, pp. 135–151, 2014.

the RTCA DO-178B/C. All healthcare related products in the USA must comply with the Health Insurance Portability and Accountability Act (HIPAA). Costs of noncompliance and incentives toward conformance are significant [1,2] and many initiatives, such as OPENCOSS [3], have emerged to tackle the regulatory requirements compliance issue from the safety certification perspective.

In the nuclear domain, regulatory requirements are completed using a large set of national recommendation guides and national/international standards. Putting these requirements in an international context showed important gaps between requirements and practices in different countries [4]. Since January 2011, the French nuclear industry and academic partners have joined forces in the CONNEXION project[1] to develop the major innovations in the design and implementation of the future nuclear power plants' Instrumentation and Control (I&C) systems. One aspect of the project consists in the formalization and the understanding, from a high level global perspective, of regulatory requirements the nuclear industry partners has to face in their licensing projects.

In this paper, we aim to address the following research questions. (1) How to formalize and organize the domain knowledge in a way that is relevant from an industrial experts perspective? (2) Once formalized, How to browse and manipulate this knowledge? (3) As the domain is large, not formalized, and hard to handle, can we analyze this domain and retrieve traceability links between regulatory requirements?

To tackle these questions, we propose a mix of Model-driven Engineering (MDE) and Information Retrieval (IR) to respectively address domain formalization and requirements traceability. The paper contributions are organized around the INCREMENT approach (Instrumentation aNd Control Regulatory Requirement Modeling Environment) that respectively addresses the challenges previously introduced. In particular, they consist in: **(1) the domain formalization** by proposing a metamodel that allows a high level capitalization of a requirements corpus and its organization. This metamodel was built through intensive interactions with our industrial partners. **(2) A tool-support basis** to gather partial knowledge from the textual documents, and manipulate such models. This tool basis is evaluated with both empirical and industrial feedback. **(3) The proposal of an original hybrid approach, mixing both metamodeling and information retrieval** to support better domain analysis and that has been empirically evaluated.

The remainder of the paper is organized as follows. Section 2 presents the I&C Regulatory requirements global picture as well as an illustrative example. In section 3, we present the metamodel that supports the INCREMENT approach. Section 4 presents the environment we built on top of the metamodel while section 5 discusses the hybridization MDE-IR in our approach and the empirical evaluation of its benefits. In section 6, we expose threats to validity of our work. Section 7 reviews related work while section 8 concludes the paper.

---

[1] http://www.cluster-connexion.fr

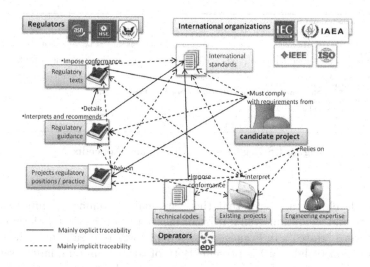

Fig. 1. Global picture of the Nuclear Regulatory Requirements Domain

---

Requirements for Software in Category 1E Programmed Systems
Reliability
Reliability is addressed within qualitative perspectives
Ea 2.1 Software design and documentation shall allow performing verification and validation methods in order to demonstrate ... An acceptable practice, related to methods and techniques of verification, is described in chapters 6 (verification) and 7 (software/component integration) of the IEC 60880 publication (1986) ...
Similarly, simulation is an acceptable technique for the validation of the executable program, especially for time performances. This technique can be combined with prescriptions of chapter 8 of IEC 60880 publication (1986).

Fig. 2. V&V in French regulatory text RFS II.4.1.a

2   Analyzing Nuclear Regulatory Requirements in the Large: An Example

Figure 1 proposes a global picture of the nuclear regulatory landscape in terms of concepts and traceability concerns. To illustrate the heterogeneity of the domain (different stackholders, different perspectives, different levels of details), we propose ask a simple question and browse the corpus to find out elements related to it. More details are proposed in our previous work [5], and we recall it for the sake of clarity regarding the paper contribution.

Considering specific analysis such as finding V&V regulatory requirements in safety systems for different countries, one should initially think that these requirements are close enough to be compared. We propose an example of what nuclear operators have to face from the regulatory text perspective, and refine it to the normative level in two different contexts: France and USA.

At the Regulatory Level. In France, in the RFS (basic safety rule) II.4.1.a (2000), the requirements or principles are written in French. About the concern Verification and Validation, Figure 2 proposes a translation. In the USA, we shall consider the 10CFR50 and in particular following excerpt in Figure 3.

Par55a(a)(1): Codes and Standards
(a) Quality standards, ASME Codes and IEEE standards, and alternatives.
(1) Structures, systems, and components must be designed, fabricated, erected, constructed, tested, and inspected to quality standards commensurate with the importance of the safety function to be performed. ...
(h) Protection and safety systems.
(2) Protection systems. For nuclear power plants ... must meet the requirements stated in either IEEE Std. 279 ... or in IEEE Std. 603-1991 ...
(3) Safety systems. Applications ... must meet the requirements for safety systems in IEEE Std. 603-1991 and the correction sheet dated January 30, 1995.
Appendix A to Part 50–General Design Criteria for Nuclear Power Plants
I. Overall Requirements
Criterion 1- Quality standards and records.
Structures, systems, and components important to safety shall be designed, fabricated, erected, and tested to quality standards commensurate with the importance of the safety functions to be performed. ...

Fig. 3. US Regulation: 10CFR50 and Appendix A

At this level, we can agree that there are mainly common points regarding verification and validation even if it is not mentioned in the US regulation (apart from the word "tested". In France, independent V&V is already explicit. Fitness to specification (validation) is present. Both of them mention quality assurance programs. The notion of compliance with standards is expressed everywhere with more or less importance. Software safety life cycle is approached using different terms or enumeration of activities in the US, fitness to specification, V&V methods in France). We also observe the emergence of different level of application of standards as acceptable approaches (FR, USA), best in process and applicability (USA) and mandatory items (USA).

At the Regulatory Guidance Level. There is no document at this level in France. Nevertheless, the RFS explicitly mention that use of Chapter 6, 7 and 8 of the IEC60880 (1986) are acceptable practices for software V&V of category 1E systems. The French safety authority has endorsed the RCC (Rules for Design and Construction) series issued by EDF (considered as a technical operator code in Figure 1). In particular, RCC-E (for electrical devices) requires conformance with several international standards such as IEC60880, IEC62138, etc. depending on the safety function category performed by the software. In the US, it is described partially into the regulatory guide 1.168 that will later lead us to the analysis of the IEEE standard 1012.

At the Normative Level. The next step finally leaves us with two documents from the IEC and IEEE community. If both IEC60880 and IEEE1012 deal with software validation and verification, the chosen perspective of description is rather different.

IEC 60880 (chapter 8) deals with: 1. independence of the verification; 2. verification plan; 3. design verification; 4. implementation verification (with both general purpose and application-oriented languages and respective test reports); 5. configuration of pre-developed software. IEEE 1012 deals with: 1. software V&V processes: management, acquisition, supply, development, operation, maintenance; 2. software V&V reporting, administration and documentation; 3. detailing a software V&V plan outline.

If we want to sum the two standards, IEC 60880 expresses objectives to reach whereas IEEE 1012 details activities to perform to reach these objectives.

More generally, there is a gap between the IEC corpus, which is specifically written by the IEC subcommittee SC45-A and that issues nuclear specific to nuclear industry and IEEE standards which are not always nuclear specific.

This example describes two different regulatory practices with their own particularities and the issue is to formalize this domain if we want to be able to compare them [6]. We address in next section our first research question, concerning the domain formalization issue.

3 Formalizing the Nuclear Requlatory Requirements Domain

3.1 Toward a Domain Specific Modeling Approach in the Industry

One major issue when working with industrial partners is their level of adoption of MDE or, at least, modeling concerns [7]. In the CONNEXION project, we face research and development engineers with very heterogeneous background, from senior project leaders with mainly low expertise on modeling to junior and senior engineers with or without knowledge in MDE neither in requirements engineering (or from the Systems Engineering point of view).

The key question here is to propose a modeling approach that meet our partners' intuition of how the domain should be represented and that is close to their current practice. As a consequence, we decided to go through a classic MDE-based approach and the creation of a domain specific metamodel.

3.2 The Connexion Metamodel

In figure 4, we propose an excerpt of the Connexion metamodel we built with our industrial partners in the CONNEXION project. This metamodel[2] structures the different kind of elements one may find while looking at the nuclear regulations.

1. **Modeling Regulations Atomic Elements.** Though our industrial partners mainly focus on requirements, they also want to put these requirements in context and keep the document structural information. The metamodel does not only focus on requirements and its different specializations but also on side elements such as definitions, recommendations, descriptive texts, etc. This whole set of typed elements (*TypedElement*), contained into a *TypedElementCorpus* are acquired through the documentation or may be tacit knowledge (*NonWrittenElement*) acquired from past or existing projects.
2. **Modeling the Regulatory Hierarchy.** We defined the different types of documents and their structure that we handle in the project. It goes from the different regulatory documents to standards as well as documents from the licensee (engineering documents, technical codes, etc.). These documents are modeled as a *Corpus* of refinable *Documents* and possess a composite structure of refinable *DocumentFragments*.

---

[2] A more detailed version as well as specific perspectives are available at http://wp.me/P1tUd5-6I

3. **Modeling Clustering of Elements.** Built as-is, the proposed requirements referential includes an important amount of information that must be organized. To analyze this set of elements, Different kinds of wrappers are required. These *TypedElementWrappers* define: (1) structural similarities that clusters *TypedElements* regarding their nature (regulatory, normative, engineering), but also (2) thematic similarities within a *Topic* collection, (3) large general elements that are specific to a *Project* or a more general *GenericProject*.

4. **Modeling the Bridge between Requirements, Architecture and Qualification.** As high level ambiguous requirements [8,9], it is very difficult to cope with the traditional set <Requirement, Architecture, Qualification>. The architecture part is addressed separately in the CONNEXION project with a specific metamodel. However, we link the architecture elements through the satisfaction of design rules, that are industry-based clauses. It is the same process for qualification and certification concerns while defining a justification. As a consequence, we have defined high level *DesignRules* that allow an indirect validation of the related requirements as well as *Justifications* to address the safety evidence process. These concerns are close to the actual OMG proposal around the SAEM/SACM standard metamodels [10].

5. **Modeling Elements Interactions.** Carlhamre et al. [11] defined a set of interdepencies in order to address requirements prioritization and planning. However, regulatory requirements are more abstract, more complex and cannot be seen in terms of marketable or temporal priority.

   To tackle the traceability concern we highlighted in figure 1, we propose a set of traceability links where comparison links are made to define equivalence between or conflicting elements. On the other hand, the interaction links are made to describe relationships within the requirements domain. We have defined two families of *Interactions*: *ElementsComparisons* that describe equivalence and conflict links, as well as *ElementInteractions* that describes inter-requirements relationships such as basic *References* or more evaluated *Generalization, Contribution* relationships. These relationships are complementary to those defined by Zhang et al[12] or Maxwell et al.[13].

For the nuclear industry, which owns a very precise vocabulary, determining the correct metamodel often depends on the terminology of terms and concepts. The metamodel fitness is built among a long iterative process. To the best of our knowledge, the process of building a domain specific modeling language in the industry has not much been assessed in terms of activity length or number of iterations. We mainly spent two years of interviews and meetings to built and provide examples for this metamodel with various minor (new attributes, renaming attributes) and major changes (brand new concepts, major concept shifts). For the major changes, we had three different versions of the metamodel.

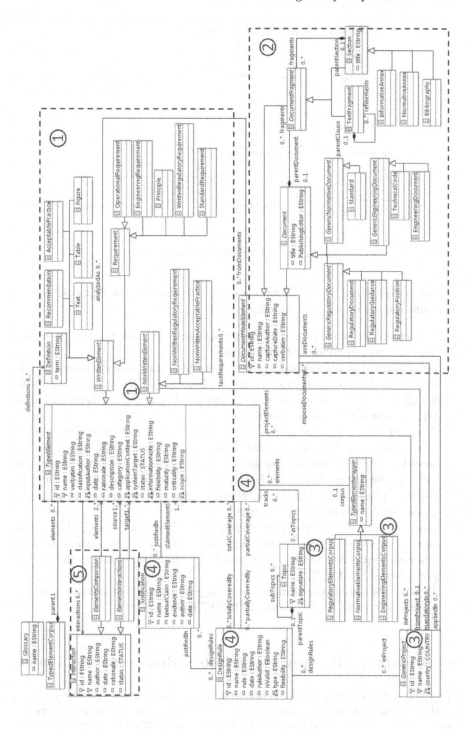

Fig. 4. The Connexion Metamodel

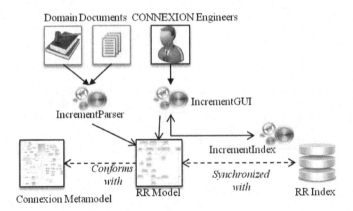

Fig. 5. The INCREMENT Contribution

If we analyze the different factors for our major changes, the following aspects had some impact on the metamodel life cycle:

- Concepts arise or change from the natural, mutual, and iterative process of domain understanding and elicitation.
- Being proactive and proposing concepts or providing examples may help to make domain experts describe tacit knowledge [14]. Clustering requirements within topics is a natural practice as the number of requirements grows up but was not determined explicitly.
- Academic and industrial definitions or visions upon particular concepts can co-exist but may lead to the final choice or definition modification. We observed a significant granularity gap between our visions of topic/theme definitions. We defined topics or themes as a set <topic name, topic signature, tracks>, which is close to the Gotel proposition [15] instead of an industrial hierarchical and composite structure.
- Basic state of the art concepts and structures may not ensure their adoption as experts are very demanding concerning their own domain lexicon. They may question academic approaches though concepts are similar but not expressed in the "correct" way.
- Experts are also involved in different projects where they acquire new perspectives or ideas related to the CONNEXION project.

4 Breathing Life into a Regulatory Requirements Model

Providing a domain metamodel is one first thing. Making this metamodel manageable for nuclear engineers and ensure its adoption, with a concrete representation, is one another, and much more difficult, point. For the nuclear industry, most of our partners do read and interpret UML diagrams. However, it's hard for them understand (meta)modeling. In particular, our partners wrongly associate metamodels, models that conform to them and tooling that manipulate and exploit models.

This metamodel allows to formalize the I&C regulatory requirements domain. However, CONNEXION engineers require additional features in order to provide ways to populate and analyze models that are the concrete domain representations and knowledge capitalization. To this end, we have proposed different software solutions that leverage the metamodel and, in addition to the Connexion metamodel, form the global INCREMENT approach (Fig. 5. In particular, we propose:

- *IncrementParser* as a configurable parser, that allow us to extract information from the regulation and model them as Connexion model elements.
- *IncrementGUI* is a graphical environment for the model browsing and analysis and is presented in Fig. 6.
- *IncrementIndex* is a model-based indexing and searching engine. It leverage the metamodel information to propose an indexing step based on the model elements. We address this concern in the next section.

A Parser for Systematic Requirements Model Acquisition. Despite the variety of documents, regulation can be organized with respect to reading rules, which allow the readers to have a systematic and efficient reading of the document. Some rules may be explicit, written in the documents, or implicit and provided by domain experts such as keywords. It is worth noticing that these reading rules are specific to each document and may evolve from one another.

It is possible to automate the extraction of textual information and generate an instance of the metamodel, leveraging the reading rules. To perform the extraction task, we have developed a configurable parser (IncrementParser) that uses, for each document, a set of regular expressions that defines the parsing rules to determine the different fragments types while reading the input file. All clauses of standards are then typed and generated as model elements.

This tool was evaluated on the acquisition of 8 international nuclear standards, and validated by sampling. We provide some details in Table 1. 1. software sys-

Table 1. Details from the 8 Acquired International Standards

Standard	1st year of publication	# of pages	Structure	Reqts.	Recoms.	Defs.	Ind. documents
IEC60880-2006	1986	110	15 sections and 10 normative or informative annexes	308	92	43	939
IEC60987-2007	1989	30	13 sections and 3 informative annexes	53	17	18	219
IEC61226-2009	2009	32	7 sections and 1 informative annex	67	12	22	261
IEC61500-2009	1996	14	10 sections	43	10	8	136
IEC61513-2011	2001	98	8 sections and 5 informative annexes	238	48	62	1098
IEC62138-2004	2004	47	6 sections	180	48	36	555
IEC62340-2007	2007	22	9 sections + 1 informative annex	46	4	26	226
IEC62566-2011	2011	52	17 sections + 2 informative annexes	243	33	14	646
totals	405	107 1st level structures	1178 structural elements	264	94	229	4080

tems performing category A functions (IEC 60880), B and C functions (IEC 62138); 2. hardware design requirements (IEC 60987); 3. classification of safety functions (IEC61226); 4. data communication (IEC 61500); 5. general criteria for I&C systems (IEC 61513); 6. common cause failure (IEC 62340); and 7. development of HDL-programmed Integrated Circuits (IEC62566).

These 8 standards cover a large scope from very general concerns (IEC 61513, IEC 60880, IEC 62138) to very precise ones (IEC 62340, IEC 62566). Publication dates vary from 2001 to 2011 but first publication record start in 1986. These 8 standards illustrate the diversity of the documentation in terms of temporal evolution, scope heterogeneity, amount of statements, etc.

An Environment for the Corpus Browsing and Analysis. *IncrementGUI*, illustrated in Fig. 6, proposes a domain description over three dimensions. The left part proposes to navigate the model through the different wrappers: TypedElements, semantic wrappers, topics, projects, interactions, design rules, and justifications. The center part details the content of these wrappers and focus on the elements types and verbatims. The right part proposes a detailed and navigable view of the selected element through its attributes and its references.

We originally proposed a first prototype to represent such requirements models with a diagram perspective, which exhibits interactions, similarly to the the visualization proposed by Carlhamre et al. [11]. However, this perspective was not adopted as very far from their common vision of requirements and what they

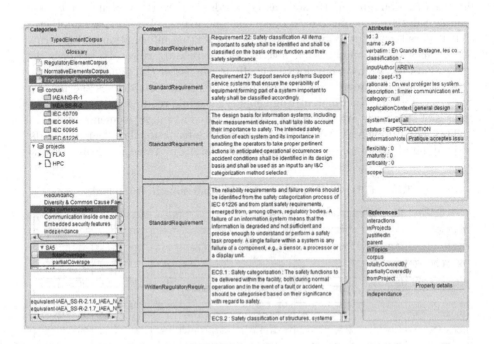

Fig. 6. The Increment environment

would like to manipulate. In particular, they wanted to manipulate the textual documents they are used to read and analyze. The second proposition is based on the IncrementGUI interface (Fig. 6), and is based on a requirements library metaphor with a strong focus put on elements verbatim.

IncrementGUI layout had a "sufficient correctness", said differently, the prototype was close enough of the industrial intuition of what the domain concepts and the supporting tool should be. The prototype is currently under evaluation regarding navigation and the basic CRUD (create, read, update, delete) features.

Though we had a domain formalization through the metamodel, acquired from the documentation and domain experts, we also wanted to perform analyses on this domain. In particular, we wanted to be able to search within our documentation and ease the definition of topics or retrieve requirements. Due to the textual nature of our model elements, these features were not possible at the modeling level. However, information retrieval techniques for requirements traceability offer such analysis capability. In next section, we propose to describe our hybridization of MDE and IR for requirements analysis and traceability concerns.

5   Hybridizing MDE and IR in the Tool

In a previous work [16], we presented the challenges to keep both a model and a index synchronized in order to have a consistent use of information retrieval on such requirements models. Basically, the main concept of indexing engines is based around the Document, and its fields. Fields are textual entries that may describe any property of the document, its verbatim among others, but without any further semantics such as typing, structure, references, etc.

Fig. 7 describes the mapping we operated to perform the hybridization. The Clusters of the Metamodel can be used as different indexes. Model element types are stored as a field as well as TypedElement and DocumentModelElement attributes. By the way, instead of slicing flat standard documents, we use the Connexion model as root for a richer indexation, provided the elements attributes.

One major drawback of Information retrieval approaches, in particular, TF-IDF similarity scoring, is the huge amount of false positives candidate links that are generated [17]. In the literature, this is handled through the use of an arbitrary cut-off value upon the document's score below which, the document is not considered as a valuable candidate link [18].

Fields inherited from the model, in particular type and classification, can be used efficiently to filter the candidate link generation and remove inconsistent document while searching this large amount of documents. In particular, our metamodel defines not only requirements but a substantial set of different concepts that are also indexed as they may provide contextual information upon their neighbor requirements. With large requirement index such as we have, removing inconsistent information from the expert further operation is crucial as it prevents the expert from rejecting inconsistent (by construction) elements.

Table 2 presents the results of our experiments regarding the search space reduction while leveraging the model information against a standard approach

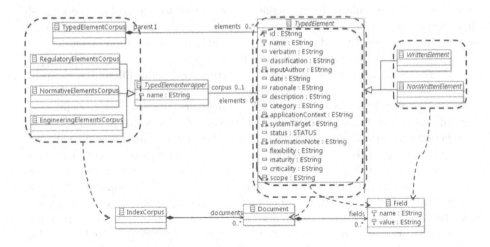

Fig. 7. Hybridizing MDE and IR

with an empirically defined cut-off value (0.2). It proposes a comparison between a « standard » information retrieval TF-IDF similiarity scoring based on a simple index (set of flat documents, without any information but the documents text) (left half) and the same scoring based on our model-based index with richer information provided by the model (right half). In particular, the table provides, respectively, the total number of retrieved documents, the number of candidate links (documents whose score are above the cut-off value), the number of retrieved requirements and recommendations, and the proportion on "noise" (documents that are not requirements or recommendations). The right half proposes the number of retrieved documents and the number of requirements and recommendations using our model-based index. Finally we propose an evaluation of our approach concerning the search space reduction against the standard approach.

The cut-off value has a rather low impact on the "noise" removal. Worse, it also cuts possible consistent elements, from a typing point of view. On the other side, the model-based index does not remove these elements and also remove the related noise (which are type inconsistent) and further reduced the research space, compared to the standard approach, at an average 65% more. This tends to show that our model-based pruning heuristic performs much better than an arbitrary cutoff-value in our particular context.

6   Threat to Validity

External Threats. Our study is based on an empirical analysis and informal industrial feedbacks on our work. However, we have not evaluated the consistency and the adoption of the tool at a larger scale. We plan to extend this evaluation

Table 2. Leveraging the Model's Information to Reduce the Number of Candidate Links

query	links	candidates	Rqts/Rcms	% noise	links	Rqts/Rcms	reduction
	\multicolumn{4}{Standard Index (with a cutoff value)}			Model-based Index		
config. mngt.	438	221	72	67,42	106	106	52,04%
cmon. cause failure	602	154	17	88,96	115	115	25,32%
specification	668	576	216	62,5	216	216	62,5%
independence	102	64	14	78,13	14	14	78,13%
validation	404	347	96	72,33	96	96	72,33%
verification	555	445	169	62,02	171	171	61,57%
quality assurance	421	259	84	67,57	106	106	59,07%
defence in depth	141	81	8	90,12	14	14	82,72%
integration	280	237	65	72,57	65	65	72,57%
self supervision	125	92	25	72,83	25	25	72,83%
modification	271	214	70	67,29	70	70	67,29%
diversity	114	103	16	84,47	16	16	84,47%

with more formal and quantitative measures in a more advanced dissemination phase.

Internal Threats. We progressively defined the metamodel according to our interviews with experts and analysis of the domain. As our partners have no experience in metamodeling, we have to manage this task and further empirically validate it with them.

Construction Threats. The metamodel is still evolving. Factors of change we identified can be biased with our partners' MDE practice, though many factors are known from the RE community. The metamodel evolution is more related to adding new concepts or refining and organizing concepts. We have not observed inconsistent concepts or associations. Our partners are highly experiences I&C experts and they do know what concepts have to be defined and then refined.

7 Related Work

On Using Models and Indexes. To the best of our knowledge, there is no existing work that proposes requirements traceability using information retrieval that is based on a domain metamodel and its instances. Recently, Dumitru et al. [19] or Tung et al. [20] mined Softpedia products information to propose enhanced recommending systems. These approaches mined static contents that do not require further synchronization accordingly to a more changing and dynamic model. Moreover, these approach did not address traceability but recommendations and were not concerned with the search space reduction issue but with small and precise information.

On MDE Approaches for Requirements Modeling and Analysis. Apart of the popular goal-oriented approaches such as KAOS [21], i* [22] that are specification oriented, or URN [23] that has been recently standardized, more domain specific modeling languages have been proposed. Some are based on UML/SysML profiling. Panesar et al., in CRESCO, proposed a UML profil for the certification task and was specific to the IEC 61508 standard [24]. In a similar approach, Zoughbi et al. proposed a UML profile that was specific to the requirements to code traceability within the DO-178B perspective [25]. In a different context, de la Vara and Panesar proposed the metamodel SafetyMet [3] and aimed to fit a more general purpose but was activity-driven. Helming et al. [26,27] had different concern and dealt with requirements models version management with EMFStore in Unicase. All these work did not take into account the diversity of concepts and traceability issues that are contained in regulations. They did not also embrace the global domain in the large, but focus, at most, one specific standard, or very specific requirements analyses.

On Regulatory Requirements Analysis. About regulatory requirements and compliance concerns, extensive studies had been done in healthcare domain and, particularly around HIPAA. In [28], production rules are developed to translate regulatory texts and formalize forms of legal knowledge and ambiguity. In [29], the authors derive rights and obligations from HIPAA and compare different stakeholders' interpretations. In [30], specific legal statements from multiple jurisdictions are refined using a requirement specification language. Statements are then neighbored and similar ones are organized to identify gaps, conflicts and try to reconcile them. In [13], the authors focus on explicit external cross-reference links and propose a legal cross-reference taxonomy. In [31], the authors use User Requirements Notation (URN), a combination of NFR and i* frameworks and use-case maps, to model both the regulation and a hospital business process. All these works, however, did not consider regulatory requirements in the large but focused, in the small, very specific aspects of a regulations such as privacy or data breaches analyses.

On Requirements Traceability and Information Retrieval. Natural language processing (NLP) and information retrieval approaches have been previously used for Requirements Analysis. At the system's scale, it has been pioneered by Sawyer et al. [32] within the REVERE project and distinguish between requirements types. Kiyavitskaya et al. [33] use GaiusT to extract rights, obligations, on both HIPAA and equivalent Italian regulations. It relies on text decomposition in a parse tree. Cleland et al. [34,35,36] use NLP and probabilistic techniques to trace regulatory requirements from HIPAA in several software applications. Leuser and Ott [37] also wanted to tackle requirements traceability in large specifications in the automotive domain at Daimler, but leverage specifications in controlled natural language and already formalized domain knowledge. Tackling the candidate link generation is a major issue in the IR community. Niu and Mahmoud proposed to rely on clustering algorithm to sort between good and bad quality clusters [17]. Our approach is based on a pre-processing enrichment of the documents, synchronized with the model information and can be seen as a complementary work.

8   Conclusion

In this paper, we addressed the question of formalizing the regulatory requirements for the nuclear domain. In this domain, nuclear I&C engineer face a large amount of regulatory and normative requirements as well as tacit practices. All these requirements express multiple different concerns, scatter and hinder the domain knowledge capitalization.

In the context of the CONNEXION project, we iteratively defined a metamodel that defines the different domain concepts as well as its organization. We proposed an Hybrid MDE/IR approach and a tool to assist engineers in the quest for the domain navigation, manipulation, and analysis. We evaluated the hybridization of MDE and IR in terms of non arbitrary candidate link search space management. For the particular nuclear I&C domain, we have shown an average 65% reduction of this search space, without having to rely on a cut-off value.

As the CONNEXION goes on, our current work is on an improvement of the definition in the metamodel of tacit (non written) requirements and practices. We also plan to address the requirements variability inside such requirements Metamodel. In particular, we want to address the meaning of regulatory requirements variability, find the good variability formalism and evaluate the impact of requirements variability in terms of design rules validity and architecture design.

References

1. Otto, P.N., Antón, A.I., Baumer, D.L.: The choicepoint dilemma: How data brokers should handle the privacy of personal information. IEEE Security & Privacy 5(5), 15–23 (2007)
2. Maxwell, J.C., Antón, A.I., Swire, P.: Managing changing compliance requirements by predicting regulatory evolution. In: RE 2012, pp. 101–110 (2012)
3. de la Vara, J.L., Panesar-Walawege, R.K.: Safetymet: A metamodel for safety standards. In: Moreira, A., Schätz, B., Gray, J., Vallecillo, A., Clarke, P. (eds.) MODELS 2013. LNCS, vol. 8107, pp. 69–86. Springer, Heidelberg (2013)
4. RHWG, W.R.H.W.G.: Harmonisation of reactor safety in wenra countries. Technical report, WENRA (2006)
5. Sannier, N., Baudry, B.: Defining and retrieving themes in nuclear regulations. In: RELAW 2012, pp. 33–41. IEEE (2012)
6. Johnson, G.: Comparison of iec and ieee standards for computer-based control systems important to safety. In: IEEE Nuclear Science Symposium Conference Record, vol. 4, pp. 2474–2481. IEEE (2001)
7. Hutchinson, J., Rouncefield, M., Whittle, J.: Model-driven engineering practices in industry. In: ICSE 2011, pp. 633–642 (2011)
8. Kamsties, E.: Understanding ambiguity in requirements engineering. In: Engineering and Managing Software Requirements, pp. 245–266. Springer (2005)
9. Breaux, T.D., Antón, A.I.: Analyzing regulatory rules for privacy and security requirements. IEEE Trans. Software Eng. 34(1), 5–20 (2008)
10. OMG: Documents associated with software assurance evidence metamodel (saem) version 1.0 - beta 1, http://www.omg.org/spec/SAEM/1.0/Beta1/ (2010)

11. Carlshamre, P., Sandahl, K., Lindvall, M., Regnell, B.: och Dag, J.N.: An industrial survey of requirements interdependencies in software product release plannin. In: RE 2001, pp. 84–93 (2001)
12. Zhang, W., Mei, H., Zhao, H.: A feature-oriented approach to modeling requirements dependencies. In: RE 2005, pp. 273–284 (2005)
13. Maxwell, J.C., Antón, A.I., Swire, P.: A legal cross-references taxonomy for identifying conflicting software requirements. In: RE 2011, pp. 197–206. IEEE (2011)
14. Sawyer, P., Gervasi, V., Nuseibeh, B.: Unknown knowns: Tacit knowledge in requirements engineering. In: RE 2011, p. 329 (2011)
15. Gotel, O., Morris, S.J.: Out of the labyrinth: Leveraging other disciplines for requirements traceability. In: RE 2011, pp. 121–130 (2011)
16. Sannier, N., Baudry, B.: Toward multilevel textual requirements traceability using model-driven engineering and information retrieval. In: MoDRE 2012, pp. 29–38 (2012)
17. Niu, N., Mahmoud, A.: Enhancing candidate link generation for requirements tracing: the cluster hypothesis revisited. In: RE 2012, pp. 81–90. IEEE (2012)
18. Chen, X., Grundy, J.: Improving automated documentation to code traceability by combining retrieval techniques. In: ASE 2011, pp. 223–232. IEEE Computer Society (2011)
19. Dumitru, H., Gibiec, M., Hariri, N., Cleland-Huang, J., Mobasher, B., Castro-Herrera, C., Mirakhorli, M.: On-demand feature recommendations derived from mining public product descriptions. In: Proceedings of the 33rd International Conference on Software Engineering, ICSE 2011, pp. 181–190. ACM, New York (2011)
20. Thung, F., Wang, S., Lo, D., Lawall, J.: Automatic recommendation of api methods from feature requests. In: ASE 2013, pp. 290–300 (2013)
21. van Lamsweerde, A.: Requirements Engineering - From System Goals to UML Models to Software Specifications. Wiley (2009)
22. Yu, E.S.: Towards modelling and reasoning support for early-phase requirements engineering. In: Requirements Engineering, RE 1997, pp. 226–235. IEEE (1997)
23. Amyot, D., Mussbacher, G.: User requirements notation: The first ten years, the next ten years (invited paper). Journal of Software (JSW) 6(5), 747–768 (2011)
24. Panesar-Walawege, R.K., Sabetzadeh, M., Briand, L.C.: A model-driven engineering approach to support the verification of compliance to safety standards. In: ISSRE 2011, pp. 30–39 (2011)
25. Zoughbi, G., Briand, L.C., Labiche, Y.: Modeling safety and airworthiness (rtca do-178b) information: conceptual model and uml profile. SOSYM 10(3), 337–367 (2011)
26. Li, Y., Narayan, N., Helming, J., Koegel, M.: A domain specific requirements model for scientific computing. In: ICSE 2011, pp. 848–851 (2011)
27. Helming, J., Koegel, M.: Managing iterations with unicase. In: ICSE 2010, pp. 313–314 (2010)
28. Maxwell, J.C., Antón, A.I.: Developing production rule models to aid in acquiring requirements from legal texts. In: RE 2009, pp. 101–110 (2009)
29. Breaux, T.D., Antón, A.I., Doyle, J.: Semantic parameterization: A process for modeling domain descriptions. TOSEM 18(2) (2008)
30. Gordon, D.G., Breaux, T.D.: Reconciling multi-jurisdictional legal requirements: A case study in requirements water marking. In: RE 2012, pp. 91–100 (2012)
31. Ghanavati, S., Amyot, D., Peyton, L.: Towards a framework for tracking legal compliance in healthcare. In: Krogstie, J., Opdahl, A.L., Sindre, G. (eds.) CAiSE 2007. LNCS, vol. 4495, pp. 218–232. Springer, Heidelberg (2007)

32. Sawyer, P., Rayson, P., Garside, R.: Revere: Support for requirements synthesis from documents. Information Systems Frontiers 4(3), 343–353 (2002)
33. Kiyavitskaya, N., Zeni, N., Breaux, T.D., Antón, A.I., Cordy, J.R., Mich, L., Mylopoulos, J.: Automating the extraction of rights and obligations for regulatory compliance. In: Li, Q., Spaccapietra, S., Yu, E., Olivé, A. (eds.) ER 2008. LNCS, vol. 5231, pp. 154–168. Springer, Heidelberg (2008)
34. Cleland-Huang, J., Czauderna, A., Gibiec, M., Emenecker, J.: A machine learning approach for tracing regulatory codes to product specific requirements. In: ICSE 2010, pp. 155–164 (2010)
35. Mirakhorli, M., Shin, Y., Cleland-Huang, J., Çinar, M.: A tactic-centric approach for automating traceability of quality concerns. In: ICSE 2012, pp. 639–649 (2012)
36. Cleland-Huang, J., Heimdahl, M., Huffman Hayes, J., Lutz, R., Maeder, P.: Trace queries for safety requirements in high assurance systems. In: Regnell, B., Damian, D. (eds.) REFSQ 2011. LNCS, vol. 7195, pp. 179–193. Springer, Heidelberg (2012)
37. Leuser, J., Ott, D.: Tackling semi-automatic trace recovery for large specifications. In: Wieringa, R., Persson, A. (eds.) REFSQ 2010. LNCS, vol. 6182, pp. 203–217. Springer, Heidelberg (2010)

Systematic Elaboration of Compliance Requirements Using Compliance Debt and Portfolio Theory

Bendra Ojameruaye and Rami Bahsoon

University of Birmingham, UK
{Beo136,r.bahsoon}@cs.bham.ac.uk

Abstract. [**Context and motivation**] Eliciting compliance requirements often results in requirements, which might not be satisfied due to uncertainty and unavailability of resources. The lack of anticipation of these factors may increase the cost of achieving compliance. [**Question/problem**] Managing compliance is an investment activity that requires making decisions about selecting the right compliance goals under uncertainty, handling the obstacles to those goals and minimising risks. [**Principal ideas/results**] (1) We define the concept of technical debt for managing compliance and we explore its link with obstacles to compliance goals. (2) We propose goal-oriented method and obstacles handling with a portfolio-based thinking for systematically managing obstacles and refining compliance goals. [**Contribution**]We use an exemplar to illustrate and evaluate the approach. The results show that our approach can provides analysts and compliance managers with an objective tool to assess and rethink their investment decisions when elaborating compliance requirements.

Keywords: Compliance requirements, compliance debt, Economics-driven software Engineering.

1   Introduction

Compliance refers to an organization's responsibility to operate in agreement with established laws, regulations, standards, and specifications [1]. Security requirements need to be aligned with the relevant laws and other prevailing regulations to control compliance and non-compliance issues; conversely, compliance is one of the driving factors for eliciting security requirements. Though the correlation between compliance and the likelihood of security breaches is unclear, data from Verizon's PCI compliance report shows that organisations that suffered data loss, as a common example of a security breach, were much less likely to be compliant.

While compliance goals capture desired properties, obstacles to those goals capture undesirable ones, which are likely to cause situations of incompliance. The violation may place the system and the organisation at risk. Managing compliance is ultimately an investment activity that requires value-driven decision making – about selecting the right compliance goals and handling the obstacles to those goals for mitigating risks. Analysts and managers often disagree about decisions on how to invest limited resources into compliance goals that are crucial to the business sustainability as they

C. Salinesi and I. van de Weerd (Eds.): REFSQ 2014, LNCS 8396, pp. 152–167, 2014.

do not generate revenue and their value tends to be invisible. The value is usually questioned and the situation is aggravated in organisations that must balance very limited resources with requirements that have visible value chain. It has been acknowledged that the selection of requirements have an impact on the system's success [1] [2]. Consequently, the choice of requirements selected and how obstacles to those requirements are resolved will significantly determine the extent to which the compliance goals are achieved along with their cost and likely risks.

The need to prioritise and resolve obstacles for the compliance goals is necessary to manage cost, create value, sustain the solution and reduce risk. Though it could be possible to use existing requirements prioritisation techniques to prioritise obstacles, such as the Analytical Hierarchy Process (AHP) [3] [4], these techniques do not clearly include uncertainty and incomplete knowledge of the real world [5]. Factors such as minimising cost and risk generally have a higher impact on creating value [5]. The management of compliance goals and their obstacles handling shall anticipate for uncertainty, cost, incomplete knowledge, likely risks and the associated trade-offs.

The novel contribution of this paper is as follows. We introduce the concept of *Compliance Debt*. Compliance Debt is a form of a technical debt, which is result of neglected compliance when engineering requirements of software. We propose an economics-driven solution, which elaborates on the notion of obstacles handling in goal-oriented requirements engineering by using portfolio-based thinking and compliance debt analysis to systematically manage compliance goals and their obstacles. This stems from the necessity to anticipate potential hindrances that may block the fulfilment of the compliance goals and to resolve those obstacles at the best cost with minimum risk, while accounting for uncertainty. In this context, we posit that obstacles and their resolution decisions may introduce compliance debt that needs to be managed for creating value and mitigating risks. One way to reason about compliance debt in relation to goals and obstacles is to characterise it as the gap between what level of compliance can be achieved with the available resources and the hypothesised "ideal" environments, where the goals are successfully achieved. In addition, obstacles which can be temporarily tolerated can be deemed as compliance debt, which needs to be managed for risk. In finance, a portfolio denotes a collection of assets (investments) by an investor, usually used as a strategy for minimising risk and maximising returns [6]. The goal of modern portfolio theory is to select the combination of assets using a formal mathematical procedure that can minimise risk for an expected level of return on investment while accounting for uncertainty of the real world. This can be applied to the process of managing compliance goals and obstacles management, where analysts make decisions on what compliance obstacles are most critical and likely to expose the business into risk. Likely risk will also inform investment decisions in handling the obstacles for compliance. Portfolio has been cited as one of the promising techniques for predicting and managing compliance debt in software engineering. Our portfolio-based approach determines the optimum selection of obstacles that needs to be managed for risks along with the compliance debt that can be tolerated. Combining goals and obstacles analysis with portfolio-based analysis provide systematic means for elaborating compliance requirements, handling their obstacles and likely compliance debt. The approach is value driven, risk-aware, and systematic; it leverage on influential work in goal-oriented requirements and obstacles handling. It uses portfolio thinking to make the link between obstacles, risks and compliance debt explicit and transparent to compliance mangers and security requirements engineers. The approach allocates resources to resolving obstacles as well as looks at their resolution tactics and the associated compliance debts, risk and value trade-offs. The objective is to inform the decision of investment in compliance, derive more realistic compliance requirements based on their economics, risks and compliance debt.

The remainder of this paper is organised as follows: Section 2 provides the motivation and background material on goal oriented requirement engineering, obstacles, compliance debt and portfolio management. Section 3 explores the link between compliance debt and obstacles and presents a modified obstacle analysis technique that integrates portfolio reasoning and compliance debt management. Section 4 evaluates the effectiveness of our approach using an example. Section 5 concludes the paper and explores directions for future work.

2   Motivation and Related Work

We refer to closely related work to motivate the need for our approach. We explore concepts, which are necessary for understanding our contribution.

2.1   Managing Compliance Using Goal-Driven Requirement Engineering

Organizations' heavy reliance on information systems (IS) requires them to manage the risks associated with those systems. Today, risks related to information security are a major challenge for many organizations, since these risks may have dire consequences, including corporate liability, loss of credibility, and monetary damage [7]. Ensuring information security compliance has become one of the top managerial priorities in many organizations [8]. The need for compliance arises when stakeholders establish that there is a need to operate in agreement with established laws, regulations, standards, and specifications [9] so as to protect themselves from any risk, cost or loss of value involving the consequences of non-compliance. Compliance goals express this need, describing the risk to be prevented. It is vital to elicit from these regulations and standards, prioritised information security compliance requirements that can be satisfied with the available resources. These requirements shall respond stakeholders' needs.

Compliance requirements can be considered as non-functional or quality requirements. These requirements do not have simple true or false satisfaction criteria; rather their level of satisfaction can vary [10]. Although compliance requirements are crucial to the business sustainability, they do not have clear link to revenue generation. Henceforth, the benefits and returns of compliance investments are difficult to comprehend and visualize. The value is usually questioned and the situation is intensified in projects that must balance very limited resources. Satisfying a compliance requirement can depend on the risk value attached to not complying with that requirement.

Furthermore, compliance is difficult to measure as it can crosscut many concerns within a system. This makes the measurement for compliance hard to simplify and bound the problem space. Furthermore, compliance involves a dynamic mix of changing regulations, interaction between different stakeholders in the organisation. Another challenge, which faces compliance managers is ensuring that the specified compliance requirements are neither too idealist nor too weak with respect to business goals [11] as well as finding trade-offs between achieving compliance requirements and the available resources.

Goal-orientation is a widely used approach for managing requirements [11]. *Van Lamsweerde* [12] presented a detailed study of Goal-oriented requirements engineering. A goal is an objective or a *"statement of intent that a system should satisfy"* [12] and requirements are represented in the form of goals. Goals range from high-level business objectives, to well-defined compliance properties. Agents are components, which are capable of performing operations to satisfy goal [11]. In requirement engineering, goal driven approaches focuses on why the system needed, expressing the justification for a specific requirement.

While goals capture the objectives to be satisfied, obstacles capture undesired properties that may prevent the goal from being satisfied [13] [11]. An obstacle obstructs a goal if the obstacle negates the goal in the domain [13].

There is need to apply proven requirement engineering methods and demonstrate how best to apply these methods within the context of analysing legal regulatory requirements. Requirements for compliance are derived from a variety of sources and the need to include security policies among those information sources has been recognized as important [14]. Researchers have investigated different methods for analysing security requirements using goals [15] [16], with more recent work focusing on the extraction of requirements from security policies [14] [17]. The work of Anton and Breaux [14] takes this further by systematically extracting rights and obligations from legal texts. These techniques recognise the need to manage compliance requirements; however, none of these attempts to have linked compliance to value creation under uncertainty.

An important contribution is the work of Burgemeestree et al [18], they discussed how value-based augmentation theory can be applied to formalising compliance decision. This approach models a control system and the justification for compliance decisions/choosing control in a state transition diagram. It operationalizes legislations into control objectives and identifies the control measures. This approach also takes into account the organisational context of the legislation. Although this approach helps to formalise compliance decisions, it does not present a value-based approach for managing uncertainty

2.2   Portfolio Management and Requirements

Modern Portfolio theory [19] was introduced in 1952 by Harry Markowitz. The goal of modern portfolio theory is to select the combination of assets using a formal mathematical procedure that can minimise risk for an expected level of return on investment while accounting for uncertainty of the real world. In finance, a portfolio denotes a collection of weighed compositions of assets (investments) by an investor, usually used as a strategy for minimising risk and maximising returns.

Portfolio theory attempts to show the benefits of holding a diversified portfolio of risky assets rather than assets selected individually. The theory can also assist in determining the optimal strategy for diversification of assets to minimise risk and maximise return. This is can be linked to the process of analysing compliance obstacles, where analysts make decisions on which obstacles should be resolved given a certain amount of resources for minimum risks.

In modern portfolio theory, the risk of a portfolio R_P is determined by the individual risks associated with each asset R_1, the weight of each asset in the portfolio W_1 and the correlations between the assets P_{IJ}. These correlation coefficients range from -1 (a perfectly negative correlation between the two items) to +1 (a perfectly positive correlation and 0 indicates no relationship between the items.

$$Rp = \sqrt{\sum_{i=1} w1^2 R1^2 + \sum_{i=1}^{m} \sum_{j=2}^{m} WiWjRiRjPij} \tag{1}$$

The link between selection of requirements and market value using portfolio has been first explored by [5]. They proposed market driven, systematic, and more objective approach to supplement the selection of requirements, which accounts for uncertainty and incomplete knowledge in the real world using portfolio reasoning [5]. Our use of portfolio is different: We identify an optimal portfolio of obstacles to be resolved along with their resolution tactics. We employ the analysis on the gaol and elaboration levels. We explicitly look at linking compliance goals and their resolutions to risk and compliance debt.

2.3   Technical Debt, Compliance Debt, Obstacles and Portfolio

Cunningham used the Technical debt metaphor in his 1992 report [4] to describe a situation in which long-term code quality is traded for short-term gain. The link between technical debt and financial analysis using portfolio analysis has been explored [20], Seaman et al. discussed four decision approaches to deal with Technical debt: Cost-Benefit Analysis, Analytic Hierarchical Process (AHP), Portfolio Management Model and Options. In addition, [21] proposed an approach using portfolio theory to diversify the allocation of web services in the cloud. However, none of the available work has looked at compliance debt as a type of technical debt in compliance management and goal-obstacles analysis for compliance. The concept of linking compliance debt as types of technical debt to compliance goals and their obstacles using portfolio thinking is novel. We identify an *optimal* portfolio of obstacles to be resolved. We then quantify the likely compliance debt that may be incurred by selecting different obstacle resolution tactics when elaborating compliance goals and understanding the link to value.

3   Analysing Compliance Obstacles Using Portfolio Reasoning and Compliance Debt.

Brown el al. opined that "like financial debt, compliance debt incurs interest payments in the form of increased future costs owing to earlier quick and dirty design and implementation choices" [22]. The term compliance debt has been developed broadly and has covered wider aspects associated with the overall systems development life cycle.

Unlike previous work, we introduce a new dimension of using compliance debt as a decision factor for elaborating and managing compliance goals through obstacles handling. We incorporate compliance debt analysis at the goal refinements and obstacles resolution levels. While compliance goals capture desired objectives, obstacles to those goals capture undesirable properties that may obstruct those goals, which are likely to cause situations of incompliance. The violation may place the system and the organisation at risk. Compliance debt can inform the obstacle analysis process and the decision for investing in resolving obstacles at early stages of the requirements and the goal definition and elaboration lifecycle. Our objective is to avoid inappropriate selection of obstacles resolution decisions that are not value- and risk-driven and debt-aware. The key principle here is to tackle and manage the increased and unjustified compliance debt, which can be associated with the selection and consequently the inappropriate resolution tactics of the compliance obstacles, expressed in risk, cost and value. We assume that compliance debt can vary with the different obstacle resolution tactics that can be used for realising compliance. Each tactic can deliver its own trade-offs for risk, value, cost and compliance debt reduction.

3.1   Reasoning of Compliance Debt in Handling Obstacles for Compliance

We now define relationship between obstacles and compliance debt more precisely; the integration of compliance debt and portfolio reasoning as an obstacle analysis and resolution method is then discussed. We suggest a predictive approach for anticipating and managing compliance debt at the goal refinements and obstacle analysis stages. A predictive approach can be applied during the early stages of the engineering process to predict the debt, its impact on compliance, when it will be incurred, when it will pay off, and the interest if any. Classical approaches to managing compliance debt in software development lifecycle tend to be retrospective. Unlike retrospective approaches, predictive approaches allow planning.

Compliance debt in compliance management can be traced back to requirements – the way requirements are engineered, elicited, selected, prioritised and analysed. Compliance is difficult to measure as compliance policies are often open to different interpretations and are subjective. This makes it difficult to simplify and bound the problem space. Compliance involves a dynamic mix of changing regulations and lack of insight into historical performance of security operations as well as the interaction between different stakeholders in the organisation. As a result, the solutions chosen to aid compliance may not completely meet the requirements. Fixes may be required reengineer the solution to better meet requirements or compliance will be required introducing compliance debt that needs to be managed. This particularly makes the process of goals elaboration for compliance through obstacles resolution prone to compliance debt. Compliance debt can be linked to the resolution tactics used and their appropriateness, resources used, expertise, etc. Moreover, the absence of historical performance data, metrics and benchmarks for compliance makes managing and assessing compliance, resolving obstacles for compliance a mere difficult exercise. The trial and error handling of the process can introduce unnecessary compliance debt in situations when the costs of managing compliance (capital and operational costs) tends exceed that of the generated value and the risk tends to prevail. Furthermore, compliance debt can occur accidentally when poor and quick decisions for managing and resolving obstacles for compliance may add a value in the short-term but can introduce long-term debt. Compliance debt may be intentionally incurred when corrective measures for compliance becomes unavoidable.

One way to understand compliance debt in relation to goals and obstacles is to characterise it as the gap between what can be achieved with the available resources and the hypothesised "ideal" environments, where the goals are successfully achieved. Uncertainty about whether or not a decision is appropriate or will have an associated penalty may incur a compliance debt. In this sense, compliance debt can be considered as a particular type of risk; the problem of managing compliance debt boils down to managing risk and making informed decisions [20]. Obstacles resolution decisions are examples of these decisions. Obstacles can be resolved by generating alternative resolutions and selecting one resolution among the different alternatives. Compliance debt may also occur when the obstacle is tolerated and nothing is done to completely resolve the obstacles and consequently the likely risks. If the risk materializes, the system may accumulate interest signalling debt. We can attribute compliance debt in obstacle analysis to different obstacle resolution tactics, this can also be seen as the cost of reducing or tolerating the obstacle to the cost of eliminating that obstacle. We can manage compliance debt at the obstacle level by switching from one obstacle resolution alternative to another, while considering cost, risk and value.

3.2   Portfolio-Based Approach for Managing Compliance Debt

We now examine the integration of portfolio reasoning and compliance debt in obstacle analysis and resolution. Once obstacles have been identified, they need to be assessed and prioritised. We assert that the risk value of an obstacle is the product of the likelihood of the obstacle occurring and its criticality. We describe an approach for allocating resources for resolving obstacles as well as selecting the obstacle resolution tactic by considering the amount of compliance debt that each obstacle may incur and the interest that might accumulate as the deciding factors.

Consider a compliance goal that has been specified and its obstacles have already been identified, the basic steps of our value and risk-aware approach for elaborating the compliance requirements can be stated as follows:

• **Prioritise Obstacles that Needs to be Resolved:** The fundamental component of this approach is to put the obstacles in a "list". Each item includes the obstacle, the goal it obstructs, and estimates of the *expected interest amount* and *interest probability* as well as an estimate of the *principal*. The principal refers to the cost required to completely resolve the obstacle, the interest probability refers to the likelihood that the obstacle will occur and the interest amount is the extra cost that will be required if this obstacle is not resolved as well as the cost of the consequence. Since it is uncertain that extra cost will be required, we use expected interest amount and interest probability to capture the uncertainty. Every obstacle has a risk value. We can prioritise the obstacles by quantifying the risk value of the obstacles. The value of an obstacle is the product of the likelihood of the obstacle occurring and the criticality.

$$R_O = I_P * I_A \tag{2}$$

$$V_O = P * I_P * I_A \tag{3}$$

Where R_o is the risk value of the obstacle, V_O is the value of the obstacle, P is the principal; I_P is the likelihood that the obstacle will occur and I_A the extra cost that will be needed if this obstacle is not resolved as well as the cost of the consequence. For simplicity, these (P, I_P, I_A) are assigned values of high (3), medium (2), or low (1). Initially, when a debt item is created, the principal, expected interest amount, interest standard deviation and correlations with other debt items can be estimated subjectively according to the maintainer's experience. These rough estimates can be adjusted later using historical data. Historical effort data can be used to achieve a more accurate estimation as the more accurate and detailed the data is, the more reliable the approach.

• **Determine the Weight of Each Asset in the Portfolio:** Some obstacle may be resolved to a certain degree but may not fully. In order to optimize the global risk of the portfolio and find the optimum solution, we need to find how much weight should be invested in resolving each obstacle to construct a low risk portfolio. This can be calculated using a non-linear optimisation technique or the AHP [3].

• **Determine the Correlation Coefficient:** Since we will apply the Modern Portfolio Theory model to decision making in selecting and prioritising the obstacles, we need to include "correlations with other debt items" as a property to be estimated. We use the idea of correlation coefficients to represent the correlation between two obstacles, these correlation coefficients range from -1 (a perfectly negative correlation between the two items) to +1 (a perfectly positive correlation). For simplicity, we speculate that the correlation coefficient would be either1, 0, or -1 for most pairs of the obstacles. For more accurate analysis, the correlations could be determined through dependency analysis.

•**Evaluate the Portfolio of Obstacles to be Resolved:** Since compliance requirements do not have simple true or false satisfaction criteria; but are satisfied up to a level [10], we can determine how well the obstacles to a goal needs to be resolved with the available resources. With the measurements of the value of the obstacles as described above, all input information for the portfolio approach is ready. We can start making decisions using the portfolio approach. Each obstacle O_1 has a risk value R_1, a cost P_1 and W_1 as the weight of the obstacle. Based on these values, we can then decide on how many instances of the obstacles to the goal need to be resolved so that global risk of the goal being obstructed is reduced.

$$\sum_{i=1} Ep = 1 \tag{4}$$

$$Rp = \sqrt{\sum_{i=1} w1^2 R1^2 + \sum_{i=1}^{m} \sum_{j=2}^{m} WiWjRiRjPij} \tag{5}$$

• **Evaluate and Select the Best Resolution Tactic:** Evaluating and selecting the best resolution tactic is a core activity for resolving the obstacles in the compliance requirement elaboration process. We evaluate the resolution alternatives by considering the amount of compliance debt that each resolution tactic may incur as the deciding factor. We calculate and assign the compliance debt of each alternative, so that the sum of the alternatives is 1.

• As with selecting the obstacles, we put the resolution tactics in a "list". This contains items, each of which represents an obstacle resolution tactic for resolving a specific obstacle. Each item includes the goal, the obstacle which it is meant to resolve, the resolution tactic, an estimate of the principal, estimates of the expected interest amount and interest probability. The principal refers to the cost required by the resolution tactic; the interest is the extra cost that will be needed if this resolution tactic does not fully mitigate the risk of the obstacle as well as the cost of the consequences. For simplicity, these (principal, interest probability, and interest amount) are assigned values of high (3), medium (2), or low (1).

• We formulated the value of the resolution tactic using the following equation:

$$R_T = P * I_P * I_A \tag{6}$$

Where R_T is the cost of the resolution tactic, P is the principal, I_P is the interest probability and I_A is the interest amount.

• From our earlier explanation of the compliance debt metaphor in relation to goals and obstacles as the gap between what can be achieved with the available resources and the hypothesised "ideal" environments where the goals are successfully achieved. We formulate the value of the compliance debt using (6):

$$T_D = IR_T - R_T \tag{7}$$

Where T_D is the compliance debt, IR_T is the cost of an "ideal" resolution tactic and R_T is the cost of the selected resolution tactic. The ideal value is context dependent. The ideal value is application and business dependent. Assuming security engineers and architects voted for Tactic *IR* as the ideal resolution tactic. T_D for any other tactic is calculated as the gap between value of tactic k (IR_T) and the value of the tactic in question.

This technique provides decision makers with a metric for reasoning about compliance debt in conjunction with obstacle resolution tactics. The process of goal refinement and elaboration through obstacle analysis and handling is iterative and continuous. Our technique can inform the decision for further refinements for compliance and the need for further resolutions of the obstacles for managing debt.

The metric can also inform the desirable stopping criteria for the refinements and resolution processes. Using compliance debt and portfolio thinking, we put risk, added value and cost in the heart of refinements and elaboration process.

4   Illustrative Example

We use a hypothetical case referred to as *SmartBank* to exemplify and evaluate the approach. We describe the steps for managing compliance debt in engineering security compliance through obstacle analysis and goal refinements for *SmartBank*. We extend on the goal elaboration for *SmartBank* [23]. We describe how portfolio theory and compliance debt can assist the process of resolving obstacles and elaborating security requirements. The initial goal model is shown in Figure 1. The goal tree shows the goal tree and obstacles that may prevent the security goal from being achieved. Blue parallelograms show the goals and green parallelograms are the obstacles obstructing those goals. Hexagons represent agents. We assume OR-refinement as any of obstacles can obstruct the compliance goal. Looking at one scenario for the simplicity of exposition, SmartBank is bound by the data protection act which prohibits personal data from being stored outside its country of operation. With cloud computing, the user has very little knowledge about where the data is stored; hence this becomes a potential obstacle.

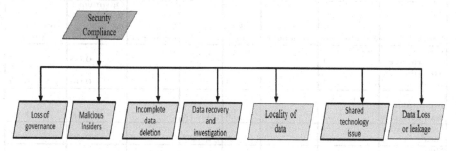

Fig. 1. Portion of the goal elaboration for Smart Bank

Identifying Compliance Obstacles: - Table 1 shows an obstacle to the "*locality of data*" goal from the goal model in figure 1

Table 1. Obstacles to Achieving Goal 1

Goal	Obstacle	Agent
Achieve [Store Personal Data in United Kingdom]	Data centre not located in the United Kingdom Subcontracting to another cloud provider as a backup plan	Cloud Provider

In this table, the cloud provider (agent) is shown to be responsible for the goal of storing data within the United Kingdom. We have thereby obtained the obstacles to this goal of storing data in the United Kingdom. In defining this obstacle, we took into consideration that cloud providers generally do not specify where the data will be stored.

Assessing and Selecting the Obstacles Using Portfolio Theory: Once obstacles have been identified, they need to be assessed, prioritised and be allocated with re- sources for resolving them. We can prioritise the obstacles by quantifying the risk value of the obstacles. The value of an obstacle is the product of the likelihood of the obstacle occurring and the criticality. In order to optimize the global risk of the port- folio and find the optimum solution, we calculated how much weight should be in- vested in resolving each obstacle to construct a low risk portfolio. This is calculated using their relative risk value in an optimisation algorithm. These weights imply that we will be able to construct the minimum risk portfolio for resolving the obstacles by allocation x-unit of resources. For this example, we assume no correlations between the obstacles.

$$Rp = \sqrt{\sum_{i=1} W1R1} \qquad (8)$$

Table 2. Obstacle Analysis

Obstacle	Likelihood	Criticality	Risk Value	R1 (%)	Cost / Principal	Optimum Weights % (W1) (AHP)	Amount to be invested
Loss of governance	1	3	3	9.09	1	0.06	0.54
Malicious Insiders	1	3	3	9.09	2	0.06	0.54
Incomplete data deletion	3	2	6	18.18	1	0.16	1.45
Locality of data	3	3	9	27.27	2	0.40	3.59
Shared technology issue	3	2	6	18.18	3	0.16	1.45
Data Loss or leakage	2	3	6	18.18	3	0.16	1.45
Portfolio Risk Value				**12.01%**			

Assuming we have 9 units of resources available for resolving the obstacle, we can either decide to resolve the obstacles based on their priority using AHP (3) or their cost. If the obstacles to be resolved are selected based on their AHP priority, we will allocate the 9 units of resources to the resources with the highest priorities. Using this approach, we will be left with a combined risk of *18.2%* for the obstacles not resolved (i.e. we resolved the obstacle by doing nothing).

On the other hand, if the obstacles to be resolved are selected based on their cost, we will allocate the 9 units of resources to the cheapest obstacles to resolve. Using this approach, we will be left with a risk of *18.2%* for the obstacle not resolved.

From the results allocation process in table 2, It can be concluded that portfolio based approach has the minimum risk profile *(12.01%)* because it utilizes the concept portfolio to diversify the allocation of resources to resolving the obstacles instead of resolving just some of the obstacles based on priority alone.

Instead of focusing the investment on resolving some of the obstacles, the approach spreads the investment into a portfolio of multiple obstacles. The diversifying process is a risk mitigating strategy. This is believed to be a powerful risk mitigating strategy in situations where analysts and compliance managers lack the experience and make ad hoc decisions, which fail to justify the choice of obstacles to be resolved under uncertainty. In such context, the conclusion would have been different if portfolio was not in use: the analyst may have focused the investment on prioritised obstacles that may be driven by cost, time, risk profile and resources. The result from the portfolio analysis process shows that the new global risk of portfolio is 12.01% when resolving the obstacles based on the optimal weight of the available resources.

Resolving the Obstacles: To resolve the *"locality of data"* obstacle, we have catalogued different obstacle resolution tactics. We have explored some potential resolutions to this obstacle. We have listed different resolution in order to guide the selection of the preferred resolution tactic as illustrated in Table 3. Once a resolution tactic has been selected, we probed further for possible obstacles and new resolution tactics for this obstacle. We report on an iteration of this process.

Table 3. Resolving the Compliance Obstacle Data-centre not located in the United Kingdom

Goal: Achieve [Store Personal Data in United Kingdom]	
Obstacles: Data-centre not located in the United Kingdom	
The cloud provider subcontracting to another provider as a backup plan	
Resolution Strategies	
Goal Substitution	None because the obstructed goal is essential
Agent Substitution	Store and process personal data in-house
	Assign the responsibility of obstructed goal to trusted cloud platform
Obstacle Prevention	Avoid the obstacle by negotiating terms and conditions with cloud provider
Obstacle Reduction	Reduce the obstacle by getting a US-EU safe harbor certification that will allow data to be stored in a wider area
Goal Weakening	Relaxing the requirements to include storing of data in the EU as this is covered by the Data Protection Act.
Goal Restoration and Obstacle Mitigation	These include the requirement to alert the organization when that won't be able to store the data in the United Kingdom.
Obstacle Tolerance – Do Nothing	Do nothing

Our objective is to use compliance debt as risk metric for informing the resolution process for this obstacle. We calculate and assign the compliance debt of each alternative, so that the sum of the alternatives is equal 100%. P is the relative cost of the resolution tactics. For this example, we assume that ideal value is the tactic with the least risk value.

Table 4. TD for Resolving the Compliance Obstacle

Resolution Tactic	P	I_P	I_A	Value	Risk Value	Risk %	TD%
Store and process personal data in-house	2	1	2	4	2	7%	4%
Assign the responsibility of obstructed goal to trusted cloud platform	3	1	1	3	1	3%	0%
Avoid the obstacle by negotiating terms and conditions with cloud provider	2	1	3	6	3	10%	13%
Reduce the obstacle by getting a US-EU safe harbour certification that will allow data to be stored in a wider area	2	2	2	8	4	14%	22%
Relaxing the requirements to include storing of data in the EU as this is covered by the Data Protection Act.	2	2	2	8	4	14%	22%
The requirement to alert the organisation when that won't be able to store the data in the United Kingdom.	1	3	2	6	6	21%	13%
Do nothing	1	3	3	9	9	31%	26%

In table 4, we can see that the ideal solution with the lowest risk has the highest principal. If we decide that we only have 2units of resources to spend on resolving this obstacle, the next best resolution tactic will be *tactic 1* has it incurs the lowest compliance debt of 4% for using 2units. Likewise if we decide that we only have 1 unit of resources to spend on resolving this obstacle, the next best resolution tactic will be *tactic 6* has it incurs the lowest compliance debt of 13% for using 1 unit.

We have now applied the technique described in the previous section. The main objective of the approach is to improve compliance by reducing the risks associated with goals obstruction through a diversified portfolio. The compliance debt metric provides better insights on the significance of a tactic in mitigating risks given the resources in hand. This is calculated as the gap between the values of tactic in question relative to the ideal tactic for resolving this obstacle. As investing in the ideal tactic is not always affordable, the metric is an expression for the risks tolerated if *this* tactic is chosen. It also expresses the likely consequences if the risk materialises. This analysis provides analysts and compliance managers with a powerful and objective tool to assess and rethink their investment decisions in elaborating compliance requirements. The use of compliance debt metric had made both the short term and long term risk visible in the selection and allocation process.

5   Discussion and Limitations

Reflecting on the application of the method, we discuss its limitations and threats to validity of what has been observed in section 4. The main objective of the approach is to improve compliance by reducing the risks associated with goals obstruction through a diversified portfolio. The compliance debt metric provides better insights on the significance of a tactic in mitigating risks given the resources in hand. This is calculated as the gap between the values of tactic in question relative to the ideal tactic for resolving this obstacle. As investing in the ideal tactic is not always affordable, the metric is an expression for the risks tolerated if *this* tactic is chosen. It also expresses the likely consequences if the risk materialises. This analysis provides analysts and compliance managers with a powerful and objective tool to assess and rethink their investment decisions in elaborating compliance requirements. The use of compliance debt metric had made both the short term and long term risks visible in the selection and allocation process. Further empirical investigation and application of the method to an extended real case is required to confirm the validity of these claims.

Portfolio theory is a well-accepted concept for diversifying risk; it is well grounded in theory. The framework presented here although useful, has its limitations. Analysing the portfolio depends on identifying threats and estimating their likelihood. This approach assumes sufficient awareness and experience of compliance standards which are related to the case. Furthermore it assumes that stakeholders are confident enough to anticipate the probabilities and the likely risks involved. Nevertheless, anticipating risks is rather a subjective exercise, which can be biased to the perspective and the experience of the stakeholders involved. Consequently, due to the different variables that might be estimated in a subjective way; this approach can only provide a best-case portfolio rather optimal portfolio.

The exemplar has looked at an aspect of security compliance, its goals and sub-goals to illustrate the feasibility of the approach. In the practice, the modelling tends to be complex involving many security goals and inter-dependencies between the goals. Though the goal modelling is inherently scalable to accommodate for such, completeness of the refinements process and the number of iterations tend to vary with the expertise and knowledge of the domain experts involved. Consequently, the mode of application and the quality of the results tends to vary. This is subject for future investigation.

Standards tend to change by time. Though the current exemplar does not explicitly cater for change and evolution of compliance, the prioritisation process assumes the considered requirements provide baseline for realising compliance at that specific time. However, the same process can be reiterated with any incoming requirements and changes in compliance standards.

In this example, the correlation between the obstacles was assumed to be zero. This does not cater for the dependencies and how resolving an obstacle will affect the resolution of other obstacles and the constructed portfolio.

In practice, software like any other system shall be subject to continual review and audit for compliance. Though it is not widely adopted practice for periodically auditing software for compliance, the compliance debt metric and the approach can provide useful input and support to the process. Beyond what we have reported in the exemplar, it would be interesting to see how real life scenarios can leverage on the reported approach to motivate and inform the auditing process.

6   Conclusion

Our working hypothesis is that goal refinement and obstacle resolution for compliance may introduce compliance debt that needs to be managed for mitigating risks. We have explored the link between obstacles and compliance debt when managing compliance. We have proposed a portfolio-based approach to quantify the compliance debt and risk for compliance. The approach can determine the candidate obstacles that need to be managed along with the compliance debt and risks that can be tolerated. Our technique is integrated into existing methods for handling obstacles in goal-oriented requirements engineering with the aim of managing trade-offs and deriving more realistic compliance requirements based on their economics, risks and compliance debt. We have illustrated the approach using an example. The process goal refinement and elaboration through obstacle analysis and handling is iterative and continuous. Our future work will look at how compliance debt can be further estimated and used as a metric to inform stopping criteria and further refinements, elaborations and resolution of obstacles hindering compliance. We will also look at including correlation coefficient as a property to be estimated for the portfolio and determining the correlations between the obstacles through dependency analysis.

References

1. Jansen, W., Grance, T.: Guidelines on Security and Privacy in Public Cloud Computing. In: National Institute of Standards and Technology (2011)
2. Lubars, M., Potts, C., Richter, C.: A Review of the State of the Practice in Requirements Modelling. In: IEEE International Symposium on Requirements Engineering, pp. 2–14 (1993)
3. Nuseibeh, B., Easterbrook, S.: Requirements Engineering: A Roadmap. In: Proceedings of the Conference on the Future of Software Engineering, pp. 4–11 (2000)
4. Saaty, L.: The Analytical Hierarchy Process. McGraw-Hill (1980)
5. Karlsson, J., Olsson, S., Ryan, K.: Improved Practical Support for Large-scale Requirements Prioritising. Requirements Engineering 2(1), 51–60 (1997)
6. Sivzattian, S., Nuseibe, B.: Linking the Selection of Requirements to Market Value: A Portfolio-Based Approach. In: Proceedings of 7th International Workshop on Requirements Engineering: Foundation for Software Quality (2001)
7. Seaman, C., Guo, Y., Izurieta, C., Cai, Y., Zazworka, N., Shull, F., Vetro, A.: Using technical debt data in decision making: Potential decision approaches. In: 2012 Third International Workshop on Managing Technical Debt (MTD), pp. 45–48 (2012)
8. Benbasat, I., Cavusoglu, H., Bulgurcu, B.: Information Security compliance: An empirical study of rationality-based beliefs and information security awareness. MIS Quarterly, 523–548 (2010)

9. Ransbotham, S., Mitra, S.: Choice and Chance: A Conceptual Model of Paths to Information Security Compromise. Information Systems Research 20, 121–139 (2009)
10. Haley, C., Laney, R., Moffett, J., Nuseibeh: Security Requirements Engineering: A Framework for Representation and Analysis. IEEE Transactions on Software Engineering 34, 133–151 (2008)
11. Duboc, L., Letier, E., Rosenblum, D.: Systematic Elaboration of Scalability Requirements through Goal-Obstacle Analysis. IEEE Transactions on Software Engineering 39, 119–140 (2013)
12. van Lamsweerde, A.: Goal-Oriented Requirements Engineering: A Guided Tour. In: Proceedings of 5th IEEE International Symposium on Requirements Engineering, pp. 249–263 (2001)
13. Letier, E., Lamsweerde, A.: Handling Obstacles in Goal-Oriented Requirements Engineering. IEEE Transactions on Software Engineering, Special Issue on Exception Handling 26(10), 978–1005 (2000)
14. Breaux, T., Anton, A., Vail, M.: Towards Compliance: Extracting Rights and Obligations to Align Requirements with Regulations. In: 14th IEEE International Conference on Requirements Engineering, pp. 49–58, 11–15 (2006)
15. Giorgini, P., Mylopoulos, J., Massacci, F.: Modelling Security Requirements through Ownership, Permission and Delegation. In: Proceedings of the 13th IEEE International Conference on Requirements Engineering, pp. 167–176 (2005)
16. Van Lamsweerde, A.: Elaborating security requirements by construction of intentional anti-models. In: Proceedings of 26th International Conference on Software Engineering, pp. 148–157 (2004)
17. May, M., Gunter, C., Lee, I.: Privacy APIs: Access Control Techniques to Analyse and Verify Legal Privacy Policies. In: 19th IEEE Computer Security Foundations Workshop, pp. 13–97 (2006)
18. Burgemeestre, B., Hulstijn, J., Tan, Y.: Value-Based Argumentation for Justifying Compliance. In: Governatori, G., Sartor, G. (eds.) Deontic Logic in Computer Science, pp. 214–228. Guido Governatori (2010)
19. Markowitz, H.M.: Portfolio Selection: Efficient Diversification of Investments. John Wiley & Sons, New York (1957)
20. Guo, Y., Seaman, C.: A Portfolio Approach to Technical Debt Management. In: Proceedings of the 2nd Workshop on Managing Technical Debt, MTD 2011, pp. 31–34 (2011)
21. ALRebeish, F., Bahsoon, R.: Risk-Aware Web Service Allocation in the Cloud Using Portfolio Theory. In: Proceedings of the 2013 IEEE International Conference on Services Computing, pp. 675–682 (2013)
22. Brown, N., Cai, Y., Guo, Y., Kazman, R., Kim, M., Kruchten, P., Lim, E., MacCormack, A., Nord, R., Ozkaya, I., Sangwan, R., Seaman, C., Sullivan, K.: Zazworka. N.: Managing technical debt in software-reliant systems. In: Proceedings of the FSE/SDP Workshop on Future of Software Engineering Research, FoSER 2010, pp. 47–52 (2010)
23. Zardari, S., Faniyi, F., Bahsoon, R.: Using Obstacles for Systematically Modelling, Analysing and Mitigating Risks in Cloud Adoption. In: Aligning Enterprise, System and Software Architectures, pp. 275–296. IGI Global (2013)

Answer-Set Programming in Requirements Engineering

Wenbin Li, David Brown, Jane Huffman Hayes, and Miroslaw Truszczynski

Department of Computer Science, University of Kentucky, Lexington, KY 40506-0633, USA
{wenbin.li,david.b.brown}@uky.edu, {hayes,mirek}@cs.uky.edu

Abstract. [**Context and motivation**] Requirements form the foundation of software systems. The quality of the requirements influences the quality of the developed software. [**Question/problem**] One of the main requirement issues is inconsistency, particularly onerous when the requirements concern temporal constraints. Manual checking whether temporal requirements are consistent is tedious and error prone and may be prohibitively expensive when the number of requirements is large. [**Principal ideas/results**] We show that answer-set programming tools (ASP) can be successfully applied to detect inconsistencies in software and system requirements. Our assumption is that these requirements are given in a formal requirement specification language called Temporal Action Language (*TeAL*). [**Contribution**] We present a translation from *TeAL* to the ASP language format accepted by *clingcon*. We show that *clingcon* can analyze requirements for several real software systems, verifying their consistency or identifying inconsistencies. We also examine the performance of the clingcon translation.

Keywords: temporal requirements, requirement engineering, knowledge representation.

1 Introduction

It is well documented in the software engineering literature that software malfunction can frequently be traced back to problems with software or system requirements [10,6,9]. The analysis of requirements for ambiguity, inconsistency, or incompleteness, if performed manually, is labor intensive, tedious, and error-prone. Indeed, a specification of a system may contain so many requirements that it is simply not feasible to check them manually.

We focus our work on consistency checking of temporal requirements. As many software systems support real-time operations, temporal requirements are common. For instance, a mission-critical financial trading system requires that certain transactions occur within a certain amount of time of other transactions (such as posting the proceeds of a stock sale or logging realized dividend payments); an e-commerce system requires that a payment be received a specified time prior to submitting an order for processing; a safety-critical pacemaker system requires that pacing occur within milliseconds of certain detected events. Moreover, as these examples implicitly suggest, high quality of temporal requirements is essential. Errors in specifying, interpreting, or implementing temporal requirements can lead to disastrous consequences. If one or more requirements

C. Salinesi and I. van de Weerd (Eds.): REFSQ 2014, LNCS 8396, pp. 168–183, 2014.

related to the pacing of the heart are in conflict, a negative heart event might not trigger a necessary lifesaving pacing event.

In this paper we show that answer-set programming (ASP), with its program processing tools, can play an important role in the analysis of temporal requirements. The system we are designing addresses the problem in two main steps. First, textual requirements are analyzed to identify temporal requirements and additional relevant information. These are then translated into a high-level temporal requirement representation language called Temporal Action Language or *TeAL* [15]. *TeAL* extends the action language *AL* [5] with dedicated, intuitive syntax to capture temporal constraints in a way that reflects common linguistic patterns. The language was designed to help requirement engineers build correct *TeAL* representation of the original textual requirements, as well as support partial automation of that step [14]. Second, *TeAL* theory is translated to the ASP language accepted by the ASP solver *clingcon* [12]. This variant ASP language provides syntax for stating integer constraints that are common in temporal constraints present in software requirements, and *clingcon* is a state-of-the-art solver designed specifically for that language.

With the use of *clingcon*, the consistency of the *TeAL* theory (and effectively, of the original textual requirements) is verified. This step is the focus of the present paper. In the main contributions, we provide the details of the translation from *TeAL* to *clingcon* and show its correctness. Practitioners may wonder if formal methods can be applied to non-trivial systems in a timely manner. To address their concerns, we demonstrate the effectiveness of *clingcon* in analyzing several example requirement sets from real software systems and examine the performance of the translation to clingcon.

The paper is organized as follows. In the next section, we present several benchmark requirement documents. They will be used to illustrate our approach. Section 3 provides a brief overview of the language *TeAL* [14] for representing system specifications. Next, we discuss the translation from *TeAL* to *clingcon*. Section 6 discusses *TeAL* representations of benchmark requirement documents and their translations into ASP (*clingcon* input language). That section also presents the results of our benchmark example studies. Our findings are discussed in the last section of the paper, where we also present conclusions and problems for future work.

2   Benchmark Examples of System Requirements

Throughout the paper we will refer to several benchmark examples of requirement documents specifying (fragments of) real software systems. As we are interested in the analysis of temporal requirements, in some cases we modified these examples from their original form by varying durations of actions and including additional temporal constraints. Our objective was to better illustrate both the current functionality of *TeAL* as well as all aspects of the translation from *TeAL* to ASP. We describe one of the examples, **CM1**, in detail. We outline the others and provide just one sample requirement (full descriptions at http://progit.netlab.uky.edu/teal).

CM1. This example is derived from a requirement document produced by NASA for one of its science instruments. The document was "sanitized" (hence the presence of variables rather than specific constants) and released by NASA for use by the software engineering research community [1].

The Control Component shall send the heart beat message to the Interface of Instrument Control Unit at an interval of E milliseconds. The interface will send the message to the Instrument Control Unit. The Control Component shall process commands within F milliseconds of receipt from the Interface of Instrument Control Unit or the Spacecraft Control Unit. The Instrument Control Unit shall send real-time commands to the Interface of Control Component every B milliseconds. Whenever the Interface of Instrument Control Unit receives a message from the Instrument Control Unit, it verifies the message within J milliseconds. If an error is detected, the message is discarded within K milliseconds, then an error report will be sent to the Control Component, and a NAK message transmitted to the Instrument Control Unit within L milliseconds. If the message is correct, the Interface of Instrument Control Unit shall forward real-time commands to the Control Component within C units of receipt from the Instrument Control Unit.

511Phone. This example is derived from a requirement document for the *Regional Real Time Transit Information System*. These requirements focus on the performance of the 511 System and the data transfers with the transit agencies. They are based on the existing procedures and features of the existing real-time system. [4].

If request, then transit agency system sends predictions and vehicle location within var1 seconds after receiving data request from the 511 System.

MODIS. This example is derived from the open source NASA Moderate Resolution Imaging Spectroradiometer (MODIS) documents [2].

Each MODIS standard input data shall be produced every var1 seconds.

UAVTCS. This example is derived from a requirement document for an Unmanned Aerial Vehicle (UAV) Tactical Control System (UAVTCS) of the US Department of Defense for the control of tactical UAVs. [3]

The TCS in the Normal Startup Mode shall initialize the system to the Operation State within 60 seconds from the time power is supplied.

EasyClinic. This dataset describes a variety of artifacts from a small healthcare application. It was developed at the University of Salerno to manage a medical ambulatory [7].

The response time of the service shall be less than A seconds.

iTrust. This dataset is derived from the iTrust project which involves the development of an application through which doctors can obtain and share essential patient information and can view aggregate patient data [7].

An HCP can reassign a previously created lab procedure to a different Lab Technician if the lab procedure is not yet in time.

3   TeAL Overview

TeAL is an extension of the action language *AL* [5] with expressions to represent temporal constraints. One of our goals in this paper is to demonstrate the feasibility of using ASP tools to address the problem of testing temporal constraints for consistency. The choice of *AL* is motivated by the availability of effective translations of *AL* theories into ASP.

The *TeAL* syntax of temporal constraints follows common linguistic patterns to help analysts construct and revise *TeAL* theories representing textual requirements. We provide here a brief overview of *TeAL*'s syntax and semantics to facilitate understanding of the main results of the paper concerning the translation from *TeAL* to ASP. For a detailed description of *TeAL*, we refer to our earlier work [15,14].

Syntax. A *TeAL* theory is a quadruple $\Delta = \langle SI, AD, TC, IC \rangle$, where *SI* is the signature, *AD* is an *action language (AL)* theory [5], *TC* is the set of *temporal constraints*, and *IC* is the set of *initial state constraints*. The signature *SI* contains the names for sorts (for instance, *data* and *agency* in the *TeAL* representation of the 511Phone example discussed below), the constants that are assigned to sorts (*d1* and *a1* in the same example), and the names of *fluents* and *actions*. As usual, fluents represent atomic (boolean) properties of the system. Complete and consistent sets of (possibly negated) fluents describe the state of the system. For example, the fluent *received(p511,d1,a1)* represents the property that the data item *d1* has been received by the phone system *p511*. Actions change fluents and, consequently, the state of the system. Actions are performed by agents. For example, *send(a1,d1,p511)* represents an action performed by the agent *a1* to send the data item *d1* to the phone system *p511*.

The role of an *AL* theory *AD* is to specify the *action domain*, that is, fluents and actions (their preconditions and effects but *not* durations). Namely, *AD* uses *state constraints* (to specify conditions that must hold in every state), *dynamic causal laws* (to describe the effects of an action when performed in a state), and *executability conditions* (to specify preconditions for an action to be executable). The action language is well known and we do not discuss it in any more detail here.

The component *TC* in a *TeAL* theory Δ distinguishes *TeAL* from *AL*. It specifies action durations and *temporal constraints* on actions. To refer to time we use a special term **startTime** that represents the *initial* time moment with respect to which we interpret Δ. We also refer to time indirectly by means of the *prompts* **commence** *a* and **terminate** *a* that stand for the times when action *a* starts and ends, respectively. At present, we assume that once actions are started they terminate successfully. For example, **commence** *update(p511, d1)* gives the time when the action *update(p511, d1)* was initiated. The modifiers **previous** and **next** can be used with prompts to identify the time moments when the previous (next) prompt occurred. For example, to specify the time when the most recent *update(p511, d1)* was initiated we may use the expression **commence previous** *update(p511, d1)*. In the present version of *TeAL*, the keywords **previous** and **next** cannot be nested.

A fluent appearing in a temporal condition represents the time when this fluent has become true. Similarly, the negation of a fluent in a temporal condition represents the time when this fluent has become false [14]. A fluent can change from true to false (or conversely) only because of actions or passage of time. The specification "*a file becomes old if it has not been written to for 10 seconds*" involves the fluent "*old*" (a property of files) that becomes true just because of the passage of time. The passage of time is handled by two special prompts *totrue(fluent)* and *tofalse(fluent)*. We will not discuss this in detail because of space.

Time moments represented by prompts and fluents are connected by temporal relationships *before*, *after*, and *at the same time as* that can also be annotated with specified quantities of time. *TeAL* provides several keyword phrases to allow the user to express these relationships. For example, the temporal constraint

> **commence** *update*($p511, d1$)
>   **noLaterThan** 10 *seconds* **after** *received*($p511, d1, a1$)

encodes the constraint: *the phone system starts to update the data within* 10 *seconds after receiving the data.*

These basic temporal constraints, called *temporal conditions in TeAL*, can be combined by boolean connectives into more complex ones of the form:

$$\text{if } A_1 \& \ldots \& A_k, \text{ then } B_1 \mid \ldots \mid B_m \tag{1}$$

where $A_1, \ldots, A_k$ and $B_1, \ldots, B_m$ are temporal conditions or their negations (represented by **not**) and | stands for "or."

TeAL also provides a dedicated syntax to specify the durations of actions:

$$\text{duration } a \, d \, units$$

where a is an action, d is a positive integer, and *units* is a time unit. *TeAL* allows multiple time units, such as *minutes* and *seconds*, but all time units are converted to the smallest unit during the translation.

The fourth part of Δ, *IC*, defines *constraints* on the initial state. Initial state constraints are of the form:

$$\text{initially } F \tag{2}$$

where F is a list (conjunction) of fluent literals (intuitively, that must hold in any initial state).

Below, we show a *TeAL* representation of the 511Phone requirement document, shortened due to space limitations. It starts with declarations of sorts, constants, agents, fluents, and actions, including action durations. Next, it specifies the initial conditions as well as the effects and preconditions of actions. Lastly, it specifies temporal constraints (each preceded by the textual constraint it represents).

sort *agency*;
sort *p511*;
sort *data*;
constant *agency* a1;
constant *p511 phone*;
constant *data* d1;
agent *agency, p511*;

fluent *received*($p511, data, agency$);
fluent *available*($data$);
action *send*($agency, data, p511$);
action *update*($p511, data$);
duration *send*($a1, d1, p511$) 1 *second*;
duration *update*($p511, d1$) 1 *second*;

initially *available*($d1$);
update($p511, d1$) **causes** *available*($d1$);
impossible *update*($p511, d1$) **if not** *received*($p511, d1, a1$);

Once the data is sent, it will be received in three seconds.
if **terminate** $send(a1, d1, p511)$
        then $received(p511, d1, a1)$ **noLaterThan** 3 *seconds* **after**;
The agency shall send data within 60 *seconds after the system starts.*
commence $send(a1, d1, p511)$ **noLaterThan** 60 *seconds* **after startTime**;
The agency shall send data at least once every 60 *seconds.*
commence $send(a1, d1, p511)$ **noLaterThan** 60 *seconds*
        after terminate previous $send(a1, d1, p511)$;
The phone system shall update the data within 10 *seconds after receiving the data.*
commence $update(p511, d1)$
        noLaterThan 10 *seconds* **after** $received(p511, d1, a1)$;
If a piece of data is not updated for 60 *seconds, it shall become unavailable to users.*
if **not terminate** $update(p511, d1)$
        noEarlierThan 10 *seconds* **before then not** $available(d1)$;

Semantics. We now discuss the semantics of a *TeAL* theory $\Delta = \langle SI, AD, TC, IC \rangle$.
It is largely based on the semantics of AL theories [5]. The key notion is that of a
transition system, which is defined based on the AL theory AD. We will denote it by
T_Δ. Following Baral and Gelfond [5], we define a *path* of Δ to be a sequence

$$\langle s_0, pr_0; s_1, pr_1; \ldots; s_{k-1}, pr_{k-1}; s_k \rangle$$

such that $s_0 \ldots, s_k$ are states; $pr_0, \ldots, pr_{k-1}$ are sets of prompts;[1] for every expression
initially F in IC, the state s_0 satisfies F; and for each $i = 0, \ldots, k-1$, $\langle s_i, pr_i, s_{i+1} \rangle$
is an edge in T_Δ. It should be noted that *TeAL* supports the case that prompts are
performed by "*time*" instead of any entities. This allows the representation of "*system
changes because of the passage of time*", e.g. "*two seconds after receiving the message,
it becomes old.*"

Paths of a *TeAL* theory Δ represent valid evolutions of the system based on actions.
They ignore durations of actions and temporal constraints. To take the temporal aspects
of *TeAL* theories into consideration, we define timed paths. Given a *TeAL* theory Δ, a
timed path with the horizon h (of Δ) is a sequence:

$$\langle s_0, pr_0, t_0; s_1, pr_1, t_1; \ldots s_{k-1}, pr_{k-1}, t_{k-1}; s_k \rangle, \tag{3}$$

where $\langle s_0, pr_0; s_1, pr_1; \ldots; s_{k-1}, pr_{k-1}; s_k \rangle$ is a path and $0 \leq t_0 < t_1 < t_{k-1} < h$.
We assume that all time parameters t_i, $0 \leq i \leq k-1$, and h are scaled to the same time
unit and are integers. Intuitively, t_i represents the time when the prompts in the set pr_i
are executed, causing the system to change to s_{i+1} in the next time moment.

We now present the semantics of a temporal condition $C = \alpha\, T_E\, \beta$, which reads "α
occurs in relation T_E to β." Here α and β are prompts or fluents and T_E is a relation
between time points, for instance, **noLaterThan** x **seconds after**. The relation $p, t \models$
C, which we read as "C holds (or, is satisfied) on p at time t," is defined as follows (we
mention only two representative cases of the definition here and refer to an earlier paper
[14] for details):

---
[1] This is the only difference from the transition system of Baral and Gelfond. In our work,
prompts play the role of actions.

1. If $\alpha = prtSymb\ A$ and $\beta = prtSymb\ B$, the condition C states that the A has to be commenced (or terminated, depending on the prompt $prtSymb$) at the time point that is in the relation T_E to the time point of commencing (or terminating, depending on the prompt) the action B (for instance: "forward message 10 seconds after logging message"). Since there is no connection to t, $p, t \models C$ does not depend on t and holds if for every time s, $0 \leq s \leq h(p)$, such that α holds at time s, there is a time s' such that β holds at time s' and s and s' are in the relation T_E, or if no time point s' in the relation T_E with s falls in the range $[0, h(p)]$.

2. If $\alpha = prtSymb$ **next** A and $\beta = prtSymb$ **next** B, the condition C states that the time of the next occurrence of $prtSymb\ A$ must be in the relation T_E to the next occurrence of of $prtSymb\ B$. Here the concept of "next" is understood with respect to the time t. Thus, we define $p, t \models C$ if (1) there is no occurrence of $prtSymb\ B$ after t; or if (2) there is an occurrence of $prtSymb\ B$ after t, the first one after t takes place at time s, and there are no times s' within the range $(t, h(p)]$ that are in the relation T_E with s'; or if (3) there is an occurrence of $prtSymb\ B$ after t, the next one after t takes place at time s, there are times s' within the range $(t, h(p)]$ that are in the relation T_E with s' and in one of them the first occurrence of $prtSymb\ A$ after t takes place.

All other cases (different combinations of prompts and fluents for α and β), and the case of temporal conditions $C = \alpha\ T_E$, can be handled similarly.

We say that a temporal condition C *holds* on a timed path p (or is *satisfied* on p), written $p \models C$, if for every t, $0 \leq t \leq h(p)$, $p, t \models C$. These definitions extend in an obvious way to arbitrary temporal constraints as they are simply boolean combinations of temporal conditions.

In principle, in order to check that $p \models C$ holds, one has to check that $p, t \models C$ for every t, $0 \leq t \leq h(p)$. However, for each horizon h and temporal condition C there is a finite set of time points $CP(h, C)$, we call them *checkpoints* for C, with the following property: for every timed path p, $p \models C$ if and only if for every $t \in CP(h(p), C)$ $p, t \models C$ holds. This property implies an algorithm to check whether $p \models C$ holds.

We say that a *TeAL* theory is *consistent* if for every h there is a timed path p such that $p \models C$, for every temporal constraint C in the theory. Otherwise, the theory is *inconsistent*.

We note that the choice of the horizon h may have a significant effect on whether constraints are satisfied on timed paths. For instance, given two prompts $pr1$, $pr2$, and a timed path p in which $pr1$ occurs every 4 seconds starting from time 0, and $pr2$ occurs every 5 seconds starting from time 0, it is obvious that the constraint

$$\textbf{if}\ pr1\ \textbf{then}\ pr2\ \textbf{noLaterThan}\ 2\ seconds\ \textbf{after}$$

is satisfied if the horizon is less than 15, but violated on all timed paths with the horizon greater than or equal to 15. The techniques we use later to determine consistency require that the horizon be specified. This example shows that the selection of the right horizon value is important. We comment on this matter later on.

4   From TeAL to *clingcon* Language

We designed a translation from $TeAL$ to clingcon based on two integer parameters: the horizon h (a positive integer) and the number of state changes n (clearly, $n \leq h$), so that each answer set of the translated program represents a valid timed path with the horizon h traversing n states (not counting the initial state) and, conversely, each such path corresponds to an answer set. Given a $TeAL$ theory Δ, we write $\Pi(\Delta)$ for the corresponding clingcon program. $\Pi(\Delta)_{h,n}$ means that the parameters H (horizon) and N (number of states) are evaluated as h and n. Additionally, $\Pi(\Delta)$ can be divided into two parts: $\Pi^{ntemp}(\Delta)$, which corresponds to $\langle SI, AD, IC \rangle$, and $\Pi^{temp}(\Delta)$, which corresponds to $\langle TC \rangle$. Therefore, $\Pi^{ntemp}(\Delta)$ represents the system behavior without the temporal constraints (legal sequences of N states when temporal aspects are disregarded). We write $\Pi^{ntemp}(\Delta)_n$ for that program with the parameter N instantiated to n.

Similarly, $\Pi^{temp}(\Delta)$ represents the temporal constraints of Δ. It involves the parameter H that specifies the time horizon within which the constraints are to be considered. In other words, this time horizon determines the space of timed paths on which the constraints are to be satisfied. We write $\Pi^{temp}(\Delta)_h$ for the program $\Pi^{temp}(\Delta)$ with H instantiated to h.

The program $\Pi^{ntemp}(\Delta)_n$ contains all names in SI and a new sort: *state* with a set of constants $\{0 \ldots n\}$, where n is configurable number. In addition, $\Pi^{ntemp}(\Delta)_n$ contains predicates that specify following relations:

- $holds(F, S)$ (fluent F is true at state S)
- $happen(Pr, S)$ (prompt Pr happens at state S, and changes the system to the next state)
- $agent(Ag)$ (Ag is an agent)
- $act(Act)$ (Act is an action)
- $action(Ag, Act)$ (Agent Ag performs the action Act)
- $dur(action(Ag, Act), Dur)$ (The duration of $action(Ag, Act)$ is Dur)
- $prompt(Pr)$ (pr is a prompt, an event that can change the value of a fluent; the available prompts are $com(action(Ag, Act))$, $ter(action(Ag, Act))$, $totrue(F)$ and $tofalse(F)$, the latter two representing the change caused by passage of time)
- $init(F)$ (fluent F holds in the initial state)
- $engaged(Ag)$ (agent Ag is performing some action)
- $progress(action(Ag, Act), S)$ (agent (Ag) is performing action Act in state S)
- $previous(happen(Pr, S1), S)$ (the latest occurrence of prompt Pr before state S is in state $S1$)
- $next(happen(Pr, S1), S)$ (the earliest occurrence of prompt Pr after state S is in state $S1$)

$\Pi^{ntemp}(\Delta)_n$ contains rules that represent the state constraints, dynamic causal laws and executability conditions from AD, and the constraints on the initial state from IC. The translation is based on the translation from AL to answer set programming [5]. The use of prompts instead of actions introduces additional constraints in $\Pi^{ntemp}(\Delta)_n$ to specify preconditions and effects of the prompts. Intuitively, starting an action a (that is, executing **commence** a) requires that the action is not in "progress." Moreover, an agent starting this action must not be "engaged" in the execution of another. Finally, to terminate an action, the action has to be in progress, and terminating an action makes an agent no longer engaged. To model these constraints, w e use predicates *progress* (*progress(a)* says that action "*a* is in progress") and *engaged* (*engaged(ag)* says that "agent *ag* is engaged"). The following rules show how the constraints pertaining to **commence** can be expressed in ASP. To this end, we recall some elements of the ASP (*clingcon* syntax). A rule of the form :- *cond* expresses a constraint that *cond* must not hold, an expression kS, where S is a set, represents the constraint that at least k elements in S must be true, and finally, a rule of the form a :- $b, c, \ldots$, says that a can be derived as true if $b, c, \ldots$ have been derived as true.

$$:\text{-}\ 2\{happen(com(action(Ag, Ac)), S) : act(Ac)\}, agent(Ag), state(S). \tag{4}$$

$$happen(totrue(progress(action(Ag, Ac))), S)$$
$$\qquad :\text{-}\ happen(com(action(Ag, Ac)), S), state(S), action(Ag, Ac). \tag{5}$$

$$:\text{-}\ happen(totrue(progress(Ac)), S), not\ happen(com(Ac), S), state(S). \tag{6}$$

$$happen(totrue(engaged(Ag)), S)$$
$$\qquad :\text{-}\ happen(com(action(Ag, Ac)), S), state(S), action(Ag, Ac). \tag{7}$$

$$:\text{-}\ happen(totrue(engaged(Ag)), S), agent(Ag), state(S),$$
$$\qquad \{happen(com(action(Ag, Ac)), S) : action(Ag, Ac)\}0. \tag{8}$$

$$:\text{-}\ holds(engaged(Ag), S), happen(com(action(Ag, Ac)), S),$$
$$\qquad action(Ag, Ac). \tag{9}$$

The constraints discussed above are not mentioned explicitly in requirement documents. They represent a common (shared) knowledge and must be made explicit in $\Pi^{ntemp}(\Delta)$. Here is yet another example of an implicit constraint that must be included in $\Pi^{ntemp}(\Delta)$: each state must be associated with at least one prompt, because only prompts can change the states of the system. It can be expressed in ASP as follows:

$$1\{happen(Pr, S) : prompt(Pr)\}:\text{-}\ state(S). \tag{10}$$

Given $\Pi^{ntemp}(\Delta)_n$, the transition diagram T_Δ is constructed according to the rules in Baral and Gelfond's work [5]. We also incorporate prompts and extend the results of *AL* [5] to our theorem.

Theorem 1. *Let Δ be a TeAL theory $\langle SI, AD, IC, TC \rangle$ and n an integer. A sequence $p = \langle s_0, pr_0, \ldots, s_{n-1}, pr_{n-1}, s_n \rangle$ is a valid path in T_Δ if and only if $\Pi^{ntemp}(\Delta)_n$ has an answer set A such that for every i, $1 \leq i \leq n$,*

1. if f is a fluent, then $f \in s_i$ if and only if $holds(f, i) \in A$
2. if pr is a prompt, then $pr \in pr_i$ if and only if $happen(pr, i) \in A$

Moreover, for every answer set A of $\Pi^{ntemp}(\Delta)_n$ there is a valid path $p = \langle s_0, pr_0, \ldots, s_{n-1}, pr_{n-1}, s_n \rangle$ in T_Δ such that A and p satisfy the two conditions above.

This result establishes a correspondence between valid paths in the transition system T_Δ and answer sets of the program $\Pi^{ntemp}(\Delta)_n$. It opens a way to compute valid paths of length n in the transition system T_Δ by applying an ASP solver to the program $\Pi^{ntemp}(\Delta)_n$. This is a stepping stone to computing timed paths for Δ, a key element of our approach to checking consistency of temporal constraints that we are to discuss next.

Next, we outline the structure of the program $\Pi^{temp}(\Delta)$. A valid timed path requires that all temporal constraints are satisfied in every time moment on this timed path. However, checking every time moment is infeasible. As we observed in the previous section, it can be replaced by checking the condition on a finite set of *check points*. Given a temporal condition C, the check points for C are chosen so that if C is satisfied (not satisfied, respectively) at the check point t, it is satisfied (not satisfied, respectively) at all time moments in the interval between t and the next check point (or the horizon). Thus, the task of checking satisfiability along a timed path can be reduced to checking satisfiability at every check point.

For instance, let C be: α **noLaterThan** x seconds **after**. We write $occur(\alpha, t)$ for the statement "α happens at time t." If $p \models occur(\alpha, t_1)$ holds, then for every $t' \in [max(0, t_1 - x), t]$, $p, t' \models C$ holds. Additionally, let us suppose that for some $t_2 > t_1 + x$, we have (i) $p \models occur(\alpha, t_2)$, and (ii) for no t_3 such that $t_2 > t_3 > t_1$, $p \models occur(\alpha, t_3)$ holds. Then, for every $t'' \in [t_1 + 1, t_2 - x - 1]$, $p, t'' \not\models C$. It follows that the check points for C are: $min(t + 1, horizon)$ and $max(t - x, 0)$, for all t such that $p \models occur(\alpha, t)$ holds.

There are two types of check points. The first type comprises the time moments when the system changes, that is, the *last* time moments when the system is still in its present state. These happen to be the time moments when prompts occur. The second type comprises the time moments when nothing changes in the system, but the *satisfaction of temporal conditions* changes as the result of passing time. For instance, given a timed path p, in which a prompt *pr1* only occurs at second 5, the temporal condition

$$pr1 \text{ } \textbf{laterThan} \text{ } 10 \text{ } seconds \text{ } \textbf{before}$$

is satisfied from the 6th to 14th second, and violated at the 15th second.

Each temporal condition is associated with a group of such check points. Each check point has an ID, which is based on its sequence in the timed path, and a value, which is a time moment. Typical answer set solvers will use a relation to represent that *a check point is assigned a time moment*, and the grounding process will generate instances for all possible time moments, which is very inefficient. The key aspect of *clingcon* is that it combines answer set programming with constraint solving. The assignment of time moments to check points, represented as integer variables $time(CP_i)$, where CP_i is a check point, is handled using constraint solving techniques. The rest of the program is constructed according to the standard ASP methodology. This prevents the generation of huge numbers of ground instances of rules.

$\Pi^{temp}(\Delta)_h$ contains rules that set up check points. The following rules are applied to all check points:

$$\$domain(0..horizon). \tag{11}$$

$$1\{map(C, S) : check(C)\}1 :\text{-} state(S). \tag{12}$$

$$:\text{-} map(C1, S1), map(C2, S2), S1 > S2, not \text{ } time(C1) > time(C2). \tag{13}$$

$$:\text{-} check(C1), check(C2), C1 > C2,$$

$$time(C1) < horizon, time(C1) \le time(C2). \tag{14}$$

$$checkhappen(Pr, C) :\text{-} happen(Pr, S), map(C, S). \tag{15}$$

$$checkholds(F, C) :\text{-} holds(F, S), map(C, S). \tag{16}$$

We use the relation $map(C, S)$ to represent that state S is mapped to check point C. Rule (11) states that the range of check points must be within the horizon. Rule (12) states that only one state can be mapped to a check point. Rules (13) and (14) state that the time assignment of states and check points must be based on their sequence in the path. Rules (15) and (16) use two new relations: $checkhappen$ and $checkholds$. They are the "*check point*" version of the $happen$ and $holds$ relations that are used above. These two rules mean that whatever happens or holds in a state must happen or hold in its corresponding check point.

The *Temp* module also contains rules for specifying check points for each temporal condition. Using the temporal condition C above, *Temp* contains the following rules:

$$exist(cp1, C1) :\text{-} check(C2), time(C2)\$ == time(C1) + 1, check(C1),$$

$$checkhappen(\alpha, C1). \tag{17}$$

$$:\text{-} checkhappen(\alpha, C1), not\ exist(cp1, C1),$$

$$horizon >= time(C1) + 1. \tag{18}$$

Rule (17) uses the relation $exist(cp1, C1)$ to define that for any check point $C1$ (when α occurs), there exists another check point immediately after it. Rule (18) means that if α occurs at a check point, and the horizon is large enough, then there must be another check point as defined by $exist(cp1, C1)$. $\Pi^{temp}(\Delta)_h$ also contains similar rules for the check points $t - x - 1$.

$\Pi^{temp}(\Delta)_h$ uses the relation $sat(C, arguments, CP)$ to represent that "*the temporal condition C is satisfied on the check point CP*". The $arguments$ are the actions and fluents involved in C. Let C be the example above, *Temp* contains the following rules:

$$sat(C, \alpha, CP1) :\text{-} checkhappen(\alpha, CP2), CP2 > CP1,$$

$$time(CP2) - time(CP1) <= x. \tag{19}$$

$$\text{-}sat(C, \alpha, CP1) :\text{-} not\ sat(C, \alpha, CP1), horizon >= time(CP1) + x. \tag{20}$$

Rule (19) defines when $p, time(CP1) \models C$, and rule (20) defines when $p, time(CP1) \not\models C$.

Given a temporal constraint of the form (1), $\Pi^{ntemp}(\Delta)_n$ uses the following rule to check that for each check point, the temporal constraint is satisfied.

$$:\text{-} sat(A_1, args, CP), \dots, sat(A_k, args, CP),$$

$$\text{-}sat(B_1, args, CP), \text{-}sat(B_m, args, CP), check(CP). \tag{21}$$

This rule means that for each check point CP, if all the temporal conditions $A_1, \dots, A_k$ are satisfied on CP, then at least one of $B_1, \dots, B_m$ shall be satisfied on CP as well.

Rules of type (21) complete the description of $\Pi^{temp}(\Delta)$ and so, also of $\Pi(\Delta)$. The following result establishes the correspondence between valid timed paths for a *TeAL* theory Δ and answer sets of the program $\Pi^{temp}(\Delta)_{n,h}$.

Theorem 2. *Let Δ be a TeAL theory and h and n integers such that $0 < n \leq h$. A sequence $p = \langle s_0, t_0, pr_0, \ldots, s_{n-1}, t_{n-1}, pr_{n-1}, s_n \rangle$ is a valid timed path of Δ if and only if $\Pi(\Delta)_{h,n}$ has an answer set A such that for every $i, 1 \leq i \leq n$,*

- *if f is a fluent, then $f \in s_i$ if and only if $holds(f, i) \in A$*
- *if pr is a prompt, then $pr \in pr_i$ if and only if $happen(pr, i) \in A$*
- *there is $j, 1 \leq j \leq n$, such that $map(j, i) \in A$ and $time(j) = t_i$.*

Moreover, for every answer set A of $\Pi(\Delta)_{n,h}$ there is a valid timed path $p = \langle s_0, t_0, pr_0, \ldots, s_{n-1}, t_{n-1}, pr_{n-1}, s_n \rangle$ such that A and p satisfy the conditions above.

This theorem shows that timed paths of horizon h and n state changes can be computed by ASP tools such as *clingcon*, thus providing useful information concerning consistency of temporal requirements. We discuss this issue in detail in the next section.

5   Tools Developed for Processing *TeAL* Theories

Theorem 1 suggests an approach to testing consistency of temporal requirements represented by a *TeAL* theory D. First, one constructs the program $\Pi(D)$, as described in the previous section. It involves two integer parameters representing the horizon and the number of states. Instantiating these parameters with specific values h and n of these parameters (we recall that we must have $0 < n \leq h$), yields the program $\Pi(D)_{h,n}$ that we then process with the *clingcon* solver.

If for every $n = 1, \ldots, h$, the program $\Pi(D)_{h,n}$ has no answer sets, then the transition system T_D has no valid timed path of the horizon h. In other words, there is no way to implement the system so that it runs for h time units. This indicates that the requirements are inconsistent.

If, on the other hand, for some $n, 1 \leq n \leq h$, $\Pi(D)_{h,n}$ has answer sets, it means that the requirements are consistent, as long as we only consider running the system for h time units. This is not an absolute guarantee of consistency. It may be that the problem with the requirements shows up only for some larger values of the horizon. For instance, the temporal constraint "*Prompt* **noLaterThan** 10 *second* **after startTime**" is not satisfied by a timed path p if *Prompt* does not occur on p within the first 10 seconds. However, if p has a horizon *less* than *10* then, according to our definition, this temporal constraint is satisfied on p even if *Prompt* does not occur on p. This is because paths of horizon shorter than 10 cannot be used as counterexamples to the constraint — there is always a possibility that should the path be extended, the *Prompt* would occur on it and the constraint would hold. Thus, to demonstrate a problem with this requirement, paths with the horizon of at least 10 must be considered. In general, the larger the horizon for which valid timed paths can be found, the stronger the assurance of consistency.

We built a tool, *TeALTrans* that implements the approach to consistency testing outlined above (full description and the source code at http://progit.netlab.uky.edu/teal). To compute answer sets of programs $\Pi(D)_{h,n}$ the tool uses *clingcon*, an ASP solver integrated with a specialized integer constraint solver *gecode* [16]. Delegating solving linear-integer constraints to *gecode* gives *clingcon* a significant performance advantage over "pure" ASP solvers such as *clasp* [11]. The latter compile all integer constraints into boolean ones, which results in a dramatic blow-up of the theory size.

The lack of the absolute guarantee of consistency is a limitation due to our choice of ASP tools for processing. A more traditional approach to checking consistency of temporal requirements based on LTL [13] and model checking tools such as *Nusmv* [8] in theory does not suffer from these difficulties. We designed a translation from *TeAL* to *Nusmv* and studied the effectiveness of this approach, too.

6   Study Results

We studied the correctness and efficiency of our tool using the six benchmark examples described in Section 2. For each, we created its corresponding *TeAL* representation. We recall that the temporal constraints in our examples involve constants (parameters). Consistency of the constraints depends on specific values one chooses for these parameters. For each benchmark problem, we considered four parameter settings: (1) *underconstrained-relaxed* or *UR*, the temporal constraints leave much room for the system to evolve, they are "easy" to satisfy; (2) *underconstrained-tight* or *UT*, the constraints are still satisfiable but they significantly restrict the ways in which the system can evolve; (3) *overconstrained-barely* or *OB*, the constraints are inconsistent, but a small relaxation of some of them would make them consistent; and (4) *overconstrained-much* or *OM*, the constraints are significantly overconstrained and no small relaxations make them consistent. Finally, we studied three values for the horizon: $h = 50, 100$, and 200 and set the time-out limit at 7200 seconds.

The following table shows the results of our study. For each of the problems, it shows the number of constraints, the parameter settings (UR, UT, OB, and OM), and the running time. For problems that are consistent, the table also shows the number of states, n, for which the constraints were shown to be satisfiable. There were no time-outs when the theories were consistent. For overconstrained cases, the tool timed out several times (for one problem for h=50, for five problems for $h = 100$, and for all problems for $h = 200$). Whenever the tool timed-out, we show in the table the last value of n, for which inconsistency was successfully demonstrated.

As mentioned above, the choice of the horizon h may affect our confidence in the determination that the requirements are consistent, and in general the larger the horizon, the stronger the evidence of consistency. However, there is a flip side to this observation. As the results show, the larger the horizon, the more computationally intensive the computing task becomes. This is because the number of possible values for the number of states grows with h. Estimating a value for the number of states, with which the constraints are consistent, is difficult. So our tool considers all of them in turn starting with $n = 1$. If *clingcon* finds an answer set, we assert that the *TeAL* theory does not contain inconsistency within the horizon and terminate. Otherwise, we proceed to the next value of n or terminate (and declare inconsistency) if $n = h$.

Our results also show that if the *TeAL* theory is consistent, the consistency could be established within the time limit imposed (even for $h = 200$). This is a strong indication of the practical potential of our tool.

Table 1. Results of the study; six problems, 4 parameter settings

Example	# Constraints	Type	Horizon		
			50	100	200
CM1	23	UR	395 sec, 9 states	1139 sec, 17 states	2151 sec, 34 states
		UT	429 sec, 9 states	1353 sec, 17 states	2328 sec, 34 states
		OB	5962 sec	> 2 hours, 40 states	> 2 hours, 37 states
		OM	5913 sec	> 2 hours, 40 states	> 2 hours, 37 states
511Phone	11	UR	564 sec, 9 states	2551 sec, 18 states	3571 sec, 35 states
		UT	572 sec, 9 states	2732 sec, 18 states	3691 sec, 35 states
		OB	> 2 hours, 42 states	> 2 hours, 38 states	> 2 hours, 36 states
		OM	> 2 hours, 42 states	> 2 hours, 38 states	> 2 hours, 36 states
MODIS	10	UR	204 sec, 7 states	589 sec, 12 states	1787 sec, 20 states
		UT	221 sec, 7 states	594 sec, 12 states	1901 sec, 20 states
		OB	4212 sec	7009 sec	> 2 hours, 47 states
		OM	4204 sec	6878 sec	> 2 hours, 47 states
UAVTCS	13	UR	681 sec, 9 states	1677 sec, 17 states	4104 sec, 33 states
		UT	696 sec, 9 states	1783 sec, 17 states	4143 sec, 33 states
		OB	5813 sec	> 2 hours, 42 states	> 2 hours, 35 states
		OM	5771 sec	> 2 hours, 42 states	> 2 hours, 35 states
iTrust	12	UR	606 sec, 7 states	1574 sec, 13 states	3945 sec, 24 states
		UT	601 sec, 7 states	1591 sec, 13 states	4043 sec, 24 states
		OB	6042 sec	> 2 hours, 37 states	> 2 hours, 25 states
		OM	5906 sec	> 2 hours, 37 states	> 2 hours, 25 states
EasyClinic	10	UR	306 sec, 8 states	1025 sec, 14 states	2775 sec, 29 states
		UT	323 sec, 8 states	1236 sec, 14 states	2834 sec, 29 states
		OB	6194 sec	> 2 hours, 38 states	> 2 hours, 31 states
		OM	6275 sec	> 2 hours, 38 states	> 2 hours, 31 states

The situation is different when the theory is inconsistent. It takes a long time for the tool to determine inconsistently. The reason is obvious and related to the discussion above. If the $TeAL$ theory is inconsistent, then for *each* number of states, n, $1 \leq n \leq h$, *clingcon* will attempt to determine consistency (that is, find an answer set) and eventually fail. However, especially when n is large, the grounding bottleneck reappears (variables representing states have to be instantiated). This makes it hard for *clingcon* to handle large values of n.

Our results suggest two practical steps to address the problem. First, for all problems and overconstrained parameter settings (when the constraints are inconsistent), the inconsistency demonstrated itself already when $h = 50$. Thus, if a tool times out with a particular value of h, one might try smaller values of h. If the theory is inconsistent, the tool might now succeed in determining that. Secondly, one might run the tool until it times out. If the last value of n for which the computation succeeded with n is sufficiently large (for instance, at least $h/5$), one might take this as an indication of a *possible* problem with the requirements.

The results also show that changing the parameter combinations from *UR* to *UT* does not affect the time for computing answer sets. Similarly, there seems to be no such effect when we change from *OB* and *OM* (but here we have fewer data points to draw conclusions).

Next, the study shows that the number of constraints in the $TeAL$ theory has much impact on the effectiveness of our tool as does the value of h. The example system with the largest number of constraints, CM1, does not turn out to be more difficult than the others. Finally, the study demonstrates the correctness of our tool. In all cases, the results produced by the tool were consistent with our "manual" analysis of the problems.

We also performed experiments based on LTL, but our translation of the six problems into the input format of *Nusmv* resulted in theories that *Nusmv* could not handle (timed-out in *all* cases).

7   Discussion, Conclusions, and Future Work

We presented an approach for analyzing software requirements using answer-set programming (ASP). We presented a translation from the *TeAL* language for describing temporal requirements to ASP and stated results establishing the correctness of the translation. We used several benchmark examples taken from real software systems to test the correctness and efficiency of our tool.

The results we presented indicate the potential of our approach to assist requirement engineers verify the consistency of temporal requirements. In the six examples that we studied, the tool provided strong evidence of consistency, whenever the requirements were consistent. With one exception, it also was able to detect inconsistency when the theory was inconsistent (with the choice of $h = 50$).

It has to be noted that when we determine consistency, we do not obtain an absolute proof of consistency but only a proof of consistency within the specified horizon. For hard problems, when the tool times out even with smaller values of h, we similarly only obtain support to the claim of inconsistency but not an absolute proof. This is a limitation of our approach.

A more traditional approach to checking consistency of temporal requirements based on LTL [13] and model checking tools such as *Nusmv* [8] in theory does not suffer from these difficulties. However, our paper shows that ASP tools that give rise to an approach based on the parameters h and n are more effective. While the results do not always provide absolute assurances of consistency (inconsistency), by appropriately choosing the parameters we can obtain some balance between the strength of the guarantee we get and the time in which we compute this guarantee.

Our future work involves improving the efficiency of our tool. One possible approach is to estimate the lower bound and upper bound on the number of states n for which it is sufficient to run *clingcon*. Another direction is to study the completeness threshold for the horizon h, that is, find the value of h such that consistency with respect to h gives an absolute guarantee of consistency (for every *TeAL* theory such a threshold exists). Finally, we intend to work on optimizations to our current translation.

At present, when we report inconsistency, we provide no indication which requirements cause the problem. We will develop extensions to the present tool that will suggest to the analyst likely combinations of requirements that might be responsible for the inconsistency.

References

1. CM-1 Dataset PROMISE Website,
   http://promisedata.org/promised/trunk/
   promisedata.org/data/cm1-maintain/cm1-maintain.txt
   (accessed: April 18, 2013)

2. MODIS Science Data Processing Software Requirements Specification Version 2, SDST-089, GSFC SBRS (November 1997),
   http://www.fas.org/irp/program/collect/uav_tcs.htm
3. UAV Tactical Control System (May 2010),
   http://www.fas.org/irp/program/collect/uav_tcs.htm
4. Regional Real-Time Transit Information System System Requirements Version 3.0 (2012),
   http://www.mtc.ca.gov/planning/tcip/
   Real-Time_TransitSystemRequirements_v3.0.pdf
   (accessed: April 18, 2013)
5. Baral, C., Gelfond, M.: Reasoning Agents in Dynamic Domains. In: Minker, J. (ed.) Logic-Based Artificial Intelligence, pp. 257–279. Kluwer Academic Publishers, Norwell (2000)
6. Boehm, B., Papaccio, P.: Understanding and Controlling Software Costs. IEEE Transactions on Software Engineerin 14(10), 1462–1477 (1988)
7. Capobianco, G., De Lucia, A., Oliveto, R., Panichella, A., Panichella, S.: On the Role of the Nouns in IR-based Traceability Recovery. In: IEEE 17th International Conference on Program Comprehension, ICPC 2009, pp. 148–157. IEEE (2009)
8. Cimatti, A., Giunchiglia, E., Pistore, M., Roveri, M., Sebastiani, R., Tacchella, A.: Integrating BDD-based and SAT-based Symbolic Model Checking. In: Armando, A. (ed.) FroCos 2002. LNCS (LNAI), vol. 2309, pp. 49–56. Springer, Heidelberg (2002)
9. Firesmith, D.: Specifying Good Requirements. Journal of Object Technology 2(4), 77–87 (2003)
10. Firesmith, D.: Common Requirements Problems, Their Negative Consequences, and the Industry Best Practices to Help Solve Them. Journal of Object Technology 6(1), 17–33 (2007)
11. Gebser, M., Kaufmann, B., Neumann, A., Schaub, T.: *clasp*: A Conflict-Driven Answer Set Solver. In: Baral, C., Brewka, G., Schlipf, J. (eds.) LPNMR 2007. LNCS (LNAI), vol. 4483, pp. 260–265. Springer, Heidelberg (2007)
12. Gebser, M., Ostrowski, M., Schaub, T.: Constraint Answer Set Solving. In: Hill, P.M., Warren, D.S. (eds.) ICLP 2009. LNCS, vol. 5649, pp. 235–249. Springer, Heidelberg (2009),
    http://dx.doi.org/10.1007/978-3-642-02846-5_22
13. Huth, M., Ryan, M.: Logic in Computer Science: Modelling and Reasoning about Systems. Cambridge University Press (2004)
14. Li, W., Hayes, J.H., Truszczyński, M.: Temporal Action Language (TAL): a Controlled Language for Consistency Checking of Natural Language Temporal Requirements. In: Goodloe, A.E., Person, S. (eds.) NFM 2012. LNCS, vol. 7226, pp. 162–167. Springer, Heidelberg (2012)
15. Li, W., Truszczynski, M., Huffman Hayes, J., Brown, D.B.: Temporal Action Language. University of Kentucky Computer Science Department Technical Report (2012-521-12) (2012)
16. Schulte, C., Lagerkvist, M., Tack, G.: Gecode. Software Download and Online Material at the Website (2006), http://www.gecode.org

Improving the Understandability
of Formal Specifications: An Experience Report

Felix Kossak, Atif Mashkoor, Verena Geist, and Christa Illibauer

Software Competence Center Hagenberg GmbH,
Hagenberg, Austria
`firstname.lastname@scch.at`

Abstract. [**Context and motivation**] The understandability of formal specifications is often considered as one of the main factors that limit the employment of formal methods in industrial applications. [**Question/problem**] Two reasons account for this issue: intricate notations and a coarse style of writing specifications. [**Principal ideas/results**] In this paper, we present our experience of rendering formal specifications understandable yet rigorous. [**Contribution**] The main contribution of the paper is the proposition of intuitive writing style guidelines, based on the ASM method, that enable formal specifications to become understandable.

Keywords: Formal Methods, Software Requirements Specifications, Validation, Understandability, Abstract State Machines.

1 Introduction

In 1995, Bowen et al. [1] proposed several practical guidelines to promote the use of rigorous techniques in software development. Unfortunately, almost two decades, several success stories in high-assurance systems, and numerous appealing notations and tools later, the share of formal techniques in overall software development is still marginal.

One of the major reasons that account for the failure of formal methods to capture a larger market share is associated with the notion of validation. Many stakeholders are still wary of seeing their requirements encrypted behind complex formulas for numerous reasons. For example, domain experts want to validate a specification against their expectations, developers and architects have to transform it into an admissible solution, and managers and customers have to sign off the contracts. The stakeholders cannot approve what they do not fully comprehend.

Validation of a formal model requires an extensive walk-through process. A model is often comprised of formulas and expressions that are even complex for experts. By definition, formal models are sets of mathematical formulas and logical predicates. Furthermore, they are complemented with advanced tactics that can assist (preferably automatic) discharge of proofs. As a result, specifications are written in a counter-intuitive style containing elements enabling automation. The struggle many people already have with mathematics is then multi-fold. In fact, even when each formula in a model can be understood rather easily, the interactions between the formulas and consequences

C. Salinesi and I. van de Weerd (Eds.): REFSQ 2014, LNCS 8396, pp. 184–199, 2014.

induced by the composition of the formulas make it difficult to assess. The problem is not always the specification language but also the style of writing formal specifications.

Commonly used formal validation techniques can be classified into three categories: animations, prototypes, and reviews. Each technique has its own merits and demerits. More importantly, their applicability depends crucially upon the state of the model development.

Model animation is a form of program visualization where fundamental behavior of a specification is displayed, usually graphically and interactively. This is achieved by invoking the operational semantics of the specification language. The advantage of this technique is that the user can directly execute and consequently observe the behavior of the specification. The major difficulty, however, concerns the fidelity of the executional behavior to the original model. Either due to the limitations of the employed tool or due to the specification technique (abstraction, use of non-constructive definitions), specifications often have to undergo a process of transformation [2] that may alter the original behavior of the model. Some of the judgments made on these models then may not be fully trustworthy.

Model prototyping is the process of producing a preliminary version of the final artifact. A prototype is an actual implementation of the model that is often automatically generated. Of course, this can happen only when the model is concrete enough. As an advantage, validation is performed on the real artifact and observations relate directly to the actual model. However, the drawback of this approach is that the development stage where this technique can be applied comes quite late as far as validation is concerned. In an ideal scheme of development, errors must be corrected in earlier phases where they cost less to fix.

The working principle of reviews is to set up readings of the formal description so that all critical issues are raised and examined. Thanks to refinement, this technique of validation can be applied at any stage of development. However, the procedure relies on the assumption that the readers must be able to build a consistent and complete mental image of the model that is sufficiently precise to assess its correctness.

Except for reviews, all other techniques raise a common issue: how to guarantee the fidelity of the executable behavior to the original model? The traditional answers based on semantic preservation are not appropriate: most models are not executable as they are either non-deterministic or contain non-constructive definitions. Resolving the non-executable traits may render the specification incorrect [3].

In such a context, the notation used for describing the model is of crucial importance. Graphical notations, such as UML, are quite effective. Unfortunately, they lack the precise mathematical basis that is required to express and assert critical properties. On the other hand, mathematical-logical based formalisms, such as Z [4] or Event-B [5], are more appropriate for the latter purpose, however, they are difficult to understand.

A specification is considered as *understandable* when the purpose of its elements is clear to the inspector [6]. The understandability issue with formal specifications arises because of two reasons: a complex notation and a counter-intuitive style of writing. We therefore propose certain guidelines, based on the Abstract State Machine (ASM) method [7], that help improve understandability of formal specifications. The ASM method is a formal technique that facilitates the formalization of requirements at the level of abstraction determined by the given application domain while maintaining the *correct-by-construction* paradigm and also keeping specifications easy to understand.

The main objective of this paper is to share the salient points of our experience of writing understandable formal specifications by using a few intuitive specification writing style guidelines based on the ASM method. The paper is organized as follows: Section 2 discusses related work. Section 3 briefly introduces the ASM method. Section 4 details our proposed guidelines followed by their demonstration in Section 5. Section 6 provides the criteria for measuring the understandability of formal specifications and then makes an evaluation of our proposed guidelines. The paper is concluded in Section 7.

2   Related Work

Zimmermann et al. [8] present an investigation about the readability of state-based formal requirements specification languages in which they test the following six factors: the structure of the state machine, the expression of triggering conditions, the usage of macros, the use of internal broadcast events, the transition perspective, and the usage of hierarchies.

In order to discuss the trade-off between legibility and formality in formal specifications, Vinter et al. [9] present a model for predicting human error in reasoning about formal specifications. They stress that "application of the model has strong implications for the ways in which formal specifications are written and for the levels of expertise acquired by those people who work with them."

Similarly, Finney [10] presents an experiment to investigate whether the use of mathematical notations in formal specifications is too complicated for the masses. The study revealed that even participants "already trained in discrete mathematics and the specification notation performed very poorly." This also emphasises the importance to consider the abilities of the "average" domain experts, developers, managers, and customers in order to establish formal specifications in overall software development.

Bidoit and Gaudel [11] offer an experiment in writing an algebraic specification by using Proposition of a Language Useable for Structured Specifications (PLUSS) to evaluate the adequacy of some criteria, mainly the legibility and understandability as well as the reusability of specifications. They state that formal specifications can and should be readable even for someone not so familiar with the underlying formalism and believe that their specification is legible, because most of the axioms can be read as English sentences and because each piece of the specification is quite small.

Choppy [12] presents different, intermingled issues to be addressed in teaching to write formal specifications. One important issue is how to extract the relevant elements to be specified from the corresponding problem description that in turn can be described in a precise, mathematical way. Another important issue is to choose a suitable specification language and to make the best use of it to get a clear and legible specification. The paper focuses on Common Algebraic Specification Language (CASL) and its extensions.

All of these aforementioned approaches address the issues related to the understandability of formal specifications like us, however, choice of the formal notation is the main difference. In addition, [12] focuses on the teaching aspect and approaches like [9,10] state that readability depends on the experience of the related persons. Like [8], we also discuss different factors which influence the readability (e.g., rule and variable names). Just like us, [11] also highlights the importance of using whole sentences in formal specifications.

3 The ASM Method

We base our suggestions for improving understandability of formal specifications on the ASM method, because this method comes with a small set of intuitive core constructs and is very flexible regarding notation. ASMs can be seen as "a rather intuitive form of abstract pseudo-code", though based on a precise yet minimal mathematical theory of algorithms, yet also as "Virtual Machine programs working on abstract data" [7]. Although the ASM language is very intuitive, we give a brief introduction to hint at the formal background.

The ASM method consists of a notation for state-based models (automata) and a method for refinement. Models can be arbitrarily abstract, and abstract models can be stepwise refined towards programming code. Even while compiling and designing a specification, one can start with a very abstract model which is then stepwise refined until it contains all the provisions required (see the demonstration part of this paper).

The main elements of an ASM specification are *rules* and *derived functions*. A rule describes a state transition of the machine. A state is determined by particular values of arbitrary data structures, which are described by *functions*. An example of a simple function would be "emergency", ranging over the standard universe Boolean and indicating whether the system in question is in emergency mode or not. A function can have an arbitrary number of parameters, e.g., a function "floor(lift)" indicating the position of a particular lift. If the value of at least one function for particular parameter values is changed by a rule, the state of the machine changes. Several rules may execute in parallel.

Whether a rule fires or not is typically determined by a *guard* (condition) in the form of an "if ... then ..." statement. This guard will typically query the value of one or more functions. If the query is more complex, or we want to leave it abstract for the time being, we can use *derived functions*, which combine the values of proper (state-defining) functions by arbitrary logical expressions. For instance, "getDirection(currentPosition, target)" may give us the direction from some current position to a given target, where the parameters are the values of proper functions or of other derived functions. Derived functions do not have an effect on the state of the machine.

The "choose" construct, which is part of the core of the ASM language, models an *arbitrary* choice. This can be very helpful in abstract models, including specifications; for instance, we might not want to specify in which order certain objects are processed, leaving more leeway for the developer to come up with an efficient implementation. For the same reason, rules as well as derived functions can be left abstract in a specification if their meaning is obvious.

4 How to Render Specifications Understandable

The issue of understandability and need for training associated with formal notations may be resolved by combining rigor with a way of expression that is closer to natural language. Thereby, both wording (e.g., naming of identifiers but possibly also of keywords) and structure have to be considered.

We will show that we can get relatively close to natural language without actually losing rigor, in particular, such that automated parsing is still possible (albeit sometimes more difficult). But also a language which is strictly regimented yet close to natural language has drawbacks which we will have to consider in their due places. However, the simple insight that there *are* drawbacks suggests that we should not simply propose one rigid guideline for improving readability. We have to stay flexible and be able to adapt to particular sets of stakeholders and to stipulate with them a suitable notation and style in each case.

We will explore how far we can actually get without losing rigor. We discuss drawbacks, in particular of extreme solutions which may, however, still be desirable in individual cases. This shall enable us to adapt our methods and languages for rigorous specifications to the needs and wishes of stakeholders. Most of the examples below are taken from real projects, by the way.

We will discuss the following possibilities for improving the readability of rigorous specifications:

– Naming of identifiers;
– Getting rid of brackets;
– Naming of keywords and respective structuring of expressions; and
– "Defusing" set expressions.

One may wonder how flexibility might be compatible with tool support. Our answer is threefold. First, the choice of identifiers (names for rules, functions, parameters and local variables) is independent of any tool, and identifiers play a very important part in our approach. Secondly, a model-driven approach to the language allows to have a meta-model of the language to which different concrete syntaxes can be mapped. Thereby also keywords can be made configurable in a tool. *Asmeta* provides just such an approach for ASMs with the meta-model *AsmM* (see [26], [27]). And thirdly, we see that tools which allow for, e.g., simulation, model checking, or automated theorem proving always come not only with their custom syntax but also with an amount of overhead which is necessary for the respective task (such as simulation) yet an obstacle to overview and human understandability; thus we think that such a special tool-centric language is not useful for a human-readable specification document, and translations to different concrete languages for different tasks will have to be done anyway.

4.1 Identifiers

The easiest way to improve readability seems to be the naming of identifiers (names of rules, functions, variables, etc.). However, it must be realised that increasing length of names increases the overall bulk of statements, thereby reducing overview.

For instance, consider the following ASM rule:

```
rule ConsumeOneToken(incomingSequenceFlow, instance) =
    choose token in tokensOfSequenceFlowForInstance(
        incomingSequenceFlow, instance) do
        remove token from tokensInSequenceFlow(incomingSequenceFlow)
```

If we choose abbreviations, we can get something like this:

```
rule ConsumeOneToken(inSF, inst) =
    choose t in tokensOfSFForInst(inSF, inst) do
        remove t from tokensInSF(inSF)
```

The algorithm itself is more clearly visible in the second style, and this becomes even clearer with bigger rules. Which style may be preferable will depend on the particular stakeholders, and there is much room for compromise.

Expressive (and thus potentially long) naming is more important for global identifiers than it is for parameters and local variables, because the latter do not have to be remembered beyond the scope of the rule or derived function in question. Thus, abbreviations should be avoided for names of rules and functions, and if possible, also for rule or function parameters. If abbreviations are used for local variables, they should be explained (in natural language) in situ if confusion seems possible.

However, also within longer rules and derived functions, too short abbreviations may cause confusion, and then an "a" suddenly but clandestinely changes its type (e.g. from process to process instance) within a single rule, which can happen even to experienced specifiers, as we noticed. This is particularly dangerous with an untyped language such as that of standard ASMs, of course, but one should not overlook the *advantages* of an untyped language for abstract models.

It is also important to use names consistently throughout the document, even when it comes to local variables in different places. Furthermore, it is important to stick to technical terms of the domain experts in question. For instance, in the context of a business process management system, it is tempting to abbreviate "flow node" with "node", but "node" may be ambiguous for a domain expert. Thus, in the example given above, "SF" is a better choice for abbreviation than, e.g., "arc" because the correct technical term is "sequence flow" while "arc" is never used in the original document.

4.2 Reducing Brackets

Consider the following example (adapted from [13], with identifiers already improved):

```
rule FlowNodeBehavior(flowNode) =
    if eventCondition(flowNode)
            and controlCondition(flowNode)
            and dataCondition(flowNode)
            and resourceCondition(flowNode) then
        DataOperation(flowNode)
        ControlOperation(flowNode)
        EventOperation(flowNode)
        ResourceOperation(flowNode)
```

For someone familiar with the ASM method, it is usual to assume that all the "Operations" can be performed in parallel. However, most people, including developers, will interpret this statement sequentially.

Both strictly sequential processing and possible parallelism should be expressly indicated. On the other hand, people are not good at parsing nested brackets; instead, they are better in interpreting geometric structures as given by the indentations above. Bracketing and indentation can be combined, of course. For instance, for parallel blocks, the tool CoreASM [14] allows to use either set braces or the keywords "par ... endpar".

However, we propose to use keywords which are better understandable by lay people, such as "parallelblock ... endparallelblock". The explicit use of "block" would also fit in more consistently with the keywords "seqblock ... endseqblock", which CoreASM uses for sequential blocks. Set braces may put off lay people while being considered useful by developers, so their use should be discussed in a particular setting.

Still, such brackets (be it set braces or words) use additional lines, and within larger, nested structures, this can reduce overview. A more radical alternative which also gets us closer to natural sentences could look like this:

```
rule FlowNodeBehavior(flowNode) =
  if ... then
  do in parallel
    DataOperation(flowNode)
    ControlOperation(flowNode)
    EventOperation(flowNode)
    ResourceOperation(flowNode)
```

One may wonder whether the latter notation would still be unambiguous within nested "if ... then .. else" structures. But both line breaks and spaces *can* be parsed, albeit considerably harder. So with a *consistent* use of indentation, ambiguity can be avoided.

In any case, people should not be forced to detect nested structures by brackets *alone*, so a *consistent* use of nesting corresponding to semantics is strongly suggested. According to our experience and after some experimentation, we suggest the following guideline:

– To signify semantic dependence (e.g., the scope of "then", "forall", etc.), use a 2-digit indentation with respect to the respective dominant line.
– To continue a long line after a forced line break, use a 4-digit or 6-digit indentation.

There are certainly limits for the capability of human parsing also with indentations. Longer rules or derived functions can easily become hard to overlook. We advise to prevent longer structures through modularization techniques as far as possible.

4.3   Keywords and Structure of Expressions

Some keywords can lead to confusion. Amongst them is "forall", which is typically used for both imperative statements (" forall ... do ...") and within Boolean expressions ("if forall ... then ..."). To keep those two different uses apart, we suggest to consistently use an additional keyword like "holds" (see examples below). To be consistent, we also suggest to use "forsome ... holds" instead of "exists":

> **if forsome** inSet ∈ inputSets(flowNode) **holds** isAvailable(inSet, instance) **then**
>   ...

There is yet another problem with "forall", as can be seen in the following example:

> **forall** vehicles ∈ vehiclesOnBridge **holds** weight(vehicles) ≤ 20t

Here, "weight(vehicles)" is confusing due to the plural form of "vehicles" – it suggests the combined weight of all vehicles, when in fact the weight of each vehicle is to be considered separately. On the other hand, "forall vehicle with ..." sounds unnatural. Therefore, we suggest to use "**foreach**" instead.

Sometimes additional keywords can make statements considerably shorter and simpler, as in this example:

> **do** completionQuantity **times**
>   ProduceToken(outSequenceFlow, instance)

The standard alternative would be to use a "while" or "for" loop (in which the counter variable would actually not be used except for counting iterations). This produces quite a bit of extra bulk which obfuscates the core algorithm. Such keywords can be added *when needed* (and should not be added to the standard set as they will be required relatively rarely). But note that extra keywords or symbols make the whole language more complex.

4.4 Set Expressions

We found expressions concerning sets particularly hard to tackle, because on the one hand, set theory seems to be specially repulsive for relatively many people, and on the other hand, we can hardly do without sets in technical specifications. Consider the following example:

> **derived** occurredGatewayEventNodes(flowNode, instance) =
>   {node | node ∈ eventGateTargetNodes(outgoingSequenceFlows(flowNode))
>   **and** ... }

An alternative expression would be:

> **derived** occurredGatewayEventNodes(flowNode, instance) =
>   **the set containing each** node **for which holds**
>   node **is-in** eventGateTargetNodes(outgoingSequenceFlows(flowNode))
>   **and** ...

This latter version looks not only forced (while still containing the same bits of set theory), but also more bulky, somewhat impeding overview. But some may still prefer it. We could even drop "the set containing", just returning "each node for which holds

..."; but this may bear the danger that people are no longer aware that the result is a *collection* of objects. A compromise can be found in the following demonstration.

In our experience, especially *nested* set expressions have repeatedly led to confusion even with developers, even though they typically yield *much* more concise expressions with a clearer structure (for people used to mathematical notation). Also symbols for union, in particular for a generalized union ($\cup\{...\}$), or for set difference, etc., are prone to confuse. Instead, words like "union" can aid understandability.

We suggest to use the usual set notation if possible, but with care and avoiding complex structures through modularization with informative names for auxiliary functions, even if the result is less concise. However, replacing e.g. a set constructor ($\{x \mid Px\}$) with words (as above) will usually confuse developers while still not be necessarily leading to a *clear* understanding by lay people and should therefore be used with caution; see the compromise in the following demonstration.

5   Demonstration

We now demonstrate what some of our suggestions will look like in practice. We choose the lift example from [15] for its middling complexity, which is just as much as can be handled within the available space (with only a few omissions).

The purpose of this specification is to lay down the requirements for a lift controller such that they are consistent, unambiguous, and complete with respect to the intentions of the customer. The specification must be understandable for the customer's hardware engineers, managers, and maybe also lawyers, as well as for the developers who shall implement the controller. Experience shows that informal specifications tend to be inconsistent, ambiguously worded, and incomplete with respect to gaps between what is "self-evident" for the customer and what is "self-evident" for developers, while classical formal specifications are typically not sufficiently understandable, if at all, for most or even all of the stakeholders named. Our version of a specification aims at meeting all of the given meta-requirements (except from explicit gaps due to lack of space).

The ASM model is accompanied by natural-language text which, in this case, serves one of two purposes. First, we give at least examples of explanatory text for the intended readers *of the specification* to better understand the formal part – which we think cannot be dispensed within a specification. And secondly, we want to draw the attention of the readers *of this paper* to certain points we want to make as well as to problems and possible solutions (which will have to be solved case by case).

We start with the informal specification as stated in [15] (without the properties to be proven):

Design the logic to move n lifts between m floors satisfying the following requirements:

1. Each lift has for each floor 1 button which, if pressed, illuminates and causes the lift to visit (read: move to and stop at) that floor. The illumination is canceled when the floor is visited by the lift.

2. Each floor (except ground and top) has two buttons to request an up-lift and a down-lift. They are canceled when a lift visits the floor and is either traveling in the desired direction, or visits the floor with no requests outstanding. In the latter case, if both floor request buttons are illuminated, only one should be canceled.
3. A lift without requests should remain in its final destination and await further requests.
4. Each lift has an emergency button which, if pressed, causes a warning to be sent to the site manager. The lift is then deemed "out of service". Each lift has a mechanism to cancel its "out of service" status.

In each step, we choose one lift and decide what it shall do. If there is an emergency, however (see point (4) above), we send an emergency warning. (How the latter is done is not specified, i.e., "SendEmergencyWarning" is left abstract.)

```
main rule LiftSystem =
    if emergency = false then
        choose lift in LIFTS do
            NextMove(lift)
    else
        SendEmergencyWarning
```

In rule "LiftSystem", we use "choose" instead of "forall" in order to avoid conflicts when reacting to new requests (two or more lifts might independently choose to react to the same request while other requests are kept waiting).

Note that in this rule, we use several notions – functions and sub-rules – which have not yet been defined. This means we commit *the Sixth Sin of the Specifier* according to Meyer [16]: "The presence in the text of an element that uses features of the problem not defined until later in the text." But while we cannot deny that Meyer has good reasons for declaring this a "sin", we do not think that starting with all the details and ending up with the main rule is really good for human understanding. The problem is that readers are first confronted with notions which they cannot yet fit into the greater picture and for which they sometimes cannot even guess the motivation. Moreover, they have to remember all this until they are able to put the jigsaw puzzle together at the very end.

Instead, we rely on names (of functions and sub-rules) which already convey sufficient (albeit not detailed and formal) meaning for understanding what is supposed to happen. Thereby, we can follow a method of stepwise refinement already in the course of the specification – in the course of requirements analysis as well as in the presentation of the specification. The readers first get the big picture and are then stepwise introduced to the details.

A major factor for deciding what the chosen lift should do is the state which it is in:

```
rule NextMove(lift) =
    if state(lift) = Halt then
        NextMoveInHaltState(lift)
    else if state(lift) = Move then
        NextMoveInMoveState(lift)
```

If the lift had been halting, we first check whether it has a destination, i.e., a request already chosen by the lift to fulfill, for then it shall simply move in the respective direction. Else, we look if there is a pending request which is not yet being dealt with by another lift; if so, we select such a request and make it the lift's new destination. (Note that we cannot move the lift before setting the new destination and direction first.)

```
rule NextMoveInHaltState(lift) =
    if destination(lift) != undefined then
        MoveLift(lift)
    else if pendingRequests(lift) != empty then
        choose request in pendingRequests(lift) do
            if floor(request) = position(lift) then
                CancelRequest(request)
            else
                let newDirection = getDirection(position(lift), floor(request)) in
                do sequentially
                    destination(lift) := request
                    direction(lift) := newDirection
                    MoveLift(lift)
```

The derived function "pendingRequests" will return only requests not yet chosen by some lift as a destination. To simply "choose" some pending request means that we do not prioritize some requests above others, which is not demanded in the original requirements either.

If the lift is currently moving, we check whether the current destination has been reached; if so, the lift halts and the respective request is canceled. Else, we check whether the lift can satisfy a request at its current position, even if this is not the current destination; if so, the lift halts and the respective request is canceled (but the current destination is kept; note, however, that this was not originally specified). Else, the lift simply keeps moving on in its current direction (i.e., towards its current destination):

```
rule NextMoveInMoveState(lift) =
// assert: direction(lift) ≠ undefined and destination(lift) ≠ undefined
    if floor(destination(lift)) = position(lift) then
    do in parallel
        state(lift) := Halt
        destination(lift) := undefined
        direction(lift) := undefined
        CancelRequest(destination(lift))
    else if forsome request in pendingRequests(lift) holds
            floor(request) = position(lift)
            and (direction(request) = undefined
                    or direction(request) = direction(lift)) then
    do in parallel
        state(lift) := Halt
        foreach request in pendingRequests(lift)
                with floor(request) = position(lift)
```

```
            and (direction(request) = undefined
                   or direction(request) = direction(lift)) do
        CancelRequest(request)
    else
        MoveLift(lift)
```

Above, we made an explicit assertion in the form of a comment. Alternatively, the assertion could be conjoined to the guard, or "assert" could be made a keyword with a formal semantics. What we want to express here is, first, that if this expression does not evaluate to true, something has gone wrong already in the calling rule (NextMove) or before; thus, putting it into the guard should actually not be necessary; it would constitute a redundancy with all its formal problems. And secondly, we want to make the reader aware that this condition is supposed to hold in this place in order to aid understanding. For both reasons, a comment (i.e., a non-formal element) suffices.

Also note the lack of indentation of "**do in parallel**" with respect to "**if ... then**". One might feel that this *should* be indented. However, in our experience, too much indentation often leads to extra line breaks to the detriment of a clear structure, and in the case of a "**do in ...**" clause following a **then**, we think that the indenting can be omitted without ambiguity. However, some find this confusion, so this must be left open to discussion.

We omit the rules "MoveLift" and "CancelRequest" for lack of space, and because they do not give much more insight into our proposals. And with that, we are finished with the update rules. Now we need to specify what constitute pending requests as far as they are relevant for a particular lift. These requests correspond to those pressed buttons which are either within the lift in question or on some floor (characterized by lift(button) = undefined). We also exclude those requests which have already been chosen by some (other) lift as its destination.

```
    derived pendingRequests(lift) =
        { every button for which holds
            button is-in BUTTONS
            and pressed(button) = true
            and (lift(button) = lift or lift(button) = undefined)
            and not forsome otherLift in LIFTS holds
                button = destination(otherLift) }
```

The last two lines above state that *there is no lift which has already chosen the given request (button) as its destination*. Thereby, we rule out that two or more lifts are trying to fulfill the same request while other requests are kept waiting.

The last line above is particularly difficult to understand. However, the natural language equivalent given in the previous paragraph would certainly pose tremendous problems to a machine parser. Thus, we have to explain this part to the reader in accompanying natural-language text. (Note that such explanatory text should always stand right next to the formal text to facilitate maintenance.)

Another issue that may be raised in connection with "pendindRequests" is the equation of requests and (pressed) buttons. Typically, one should stick to one consistent name. This example shows that compromises must sometimes be made. An expression like "pendingButtons(lift)" would be just as confusing as "pressed(request)". The equation happens explicitly at one point, which is the derived function "pendingRequests", and we expect it to be intuitively understandable by anyone who is not "indoctrinated" to keep names consistent. Still, consistent names are very important indeed and the respective rule should be flouted with good reasons and great care only.

Note also that the local variable "otherLift" (in "pendingRequests", above), while clearly expressing the intention behind this variable, does not quite fit the respective quantification over LIFTS, which includes the currently considered lift. However, the whole expression is still formally correct as the currently considered lift currently does not have any destination anyway. Replacing "LIFTS" by "LIFTS without lift" would be more confusing than helpful. So this is yet another example of common-sense compromises which can hardly be avoided in practice.

The derived function "getDirection" will be omitted here. It is trivial and *may* be left abstract in such a specification if all stakeholders agree.

Next, it will be necessary to state the signature, including all universes and proper functions. An appendix will have to list and explain the keywords used, auxiliary routines, linguistic conventions (including naming conventions) and font conventions (the use of italics, bold font, typewriter font, etc.), a glossary, etc. We skip this here.

6   Discussion and Evaluation

The demonstration in Section 5 has already shown that the targeted exploitation of the suggested approach can lead to improved understandability. In order to assess the quality of the approach, we propose an initial framework for measuring the understandability of formal specifications and evaluate our approach along the proposed cornerstones.

There are several approaches for applying software metrics to formal specifications, e.g., [9,17,18]. Relevant criteria for practitioners that are closely related to understandability are, for example, complexity, readability, required know-how, usability, modifiability, consistency, and traceability. With respect to most of these criteria, the use of formal methods generally enhances quality considerably, and the ASM method is no exception. Thus, without making claims for completeness, a notation suitable for understandable formal specifications should at least provide support for:

- **conventions and guidelines** – The notation needs to come up with naming conventions as well as structural and lexical guidelines in order to cope with complexity.
- **multilingual specifications** – Different dialects for different audiences to support multilingual specifications, i.e., one abstract model and different concrete syntaxes (cf. *Asmeta*), for example programming-like or natural-language syntaxes, should be offered to tackle the issue of readability and required know-how.
- **graphical representation** – The notation should provide support for graphical representation to enhance usability.
- **integrated tool support** – A set of integrated tools is important to facilitate analysis of formal specifications and to improve further quality criteria, e.g., modifiability, consistency, and traceability.

Complexity of specifications can be significantly reduced by considering an appropriate naming of identifiers (see Section 4.1) and enforcing a cognitive structuring of rules and functions (see Section 4.2). However, a critical factor for reviewing formal specifications – even for experts in formal notations – is the size of the specification. When applying formal validation techniques, users often set up a mental model by walking through the specification. Regarding the capability of human parsing, the ASM method allows for specifying individual parts of the specification and horizontal/vertical additions targeted at the respective stakeholders. Thus, reviewers do not need to have the whole model in mind but are able to work with small, well-designed model fragments. This decreases the overall complexity, which can also be investigated via complexity measures. For example, regarding the Halstead Metrics [19], the difficulty measure is proportional to the number of distinct operators and the ratio between the total number of operands and the number of distinct operands. A further advantage of the suggested approach is that, in contrast to the assumption that "people find formal specifications difficult to read because of the large use of symbols" [10], additional keywords can make statements considerably shorter and simpler, as suggested in Section 4.3.

Of particular importance for enhancing the understandability of formal specifications are factors like the expertise level of the user, the extent to which the specifications are abstract, and the logical constructs used within the specifications [9]. We have already commented on the issue of *readability* in Section 4, which we see as a major advantage of the ASM method in light of the diverse readership a specification may have. ASMs provide a formal way to write specifications and can be adjusted to be "readable" for different target users without losing rigor (see the demonstration in Section 5). Thus, by using multilingual specifications to support different views with different levels of detail for different aspects also tailored to different user groups, the *required know-how* of actual users can be taken into account. For example, applying "user-friendly" naming and keywords (see Sections 4.1 and 4.3) might make it easier to express propositions that most people will understand, whereas using set theory might be challenging for most non-mathematicians (see Section 4.4).

Another way to enhance the understandability is visualization. Graphical representations "provide cognitive support by highlighting the most relevant interactions and aspects of a specification for a particular use" [20]. By using static visualization, parts of the specification that are not of current interest, e.g., precisely defined mathematical-logical expressions describing system properties, can be hidden. Dynamic visualization presents the system behavior as it changes over time (animation). Both kinds of visualization help stakeholders to develop, validate, and understand formal specifications.

Given the notion of ASMs, a combination of the graphical Statecharts notation [21] and a tabular notation would make sense to visualize the textual specifications in a more "user-friendly" notation. Currently, there is no tool support for graphically representing ASMs. However, well-known methods from model checking can be used to generate state-machine diagrams from code. There also exists work in progress for developing a graphical editor for the *Asmeta* tool set [22] by using the Eclipse Graphical Modeling Framework (GMF). In addition, several research approaches provide principles for designing graphical representations of formal specifications, e.g., [23,20,24], from which we can benefit. (Problems may arise due to the fact that states in ASMs are implicitly given by variables/functions. In order to cope with infinite state sets we can define bounds.)

In addition, to scale effectively, formal methods must be supported by powerful and easy-to-use tools. According to our experiences, a set of integrated tools should at least consist of a specification editor, a consistency checker, a graphical visualizer, a simulation component, and a verifier. The availability of such a central tool box for formal specifications can improve quality criteria such as *modifiability*, *consistency*, and *traceability*. A problem of modifiability is rooted in the consistency between the specification and the program code. ASM models can be stepwise refined from the ground model of the specification via design right down to code of any programming language. Provided that changes are introduced on the respective level of abstraction, they can be subsequently propagated to all the lower levels of abstraction. Thereby, the ASM refinement method obviously also helps to make changes traceable.

Unfortunately, tool support for ASMs is limited. However, there do exist interpreters for certain dialects (with respective constraints), such as CoreASM [14]. Such interpreters allow simulation, which is an important tool for validation. General ASM models can typically be refined relatively easily to interpretable models, which is valuable since specifications can be tested from early development phases in order to gain confidence in their correctness. Formal verification of an ASM model with the employment of tools like proof checkers or automated theorem provers will certainly require much more effort than when using methods like Event-B, and Z, where such tool support is already integrated. However, for most practical purposes, manual verification on a high abstraction level is sufficient, and this is easily possible within the ASM method.

7 Conclusion

In this paper, we have proposed several intuitive specification writing style guidelines, based on the ASM method, that improve the understandability of formal specifications. The set of proposed guidelines is based on our experience that has been gathered while working in industrial projects. Though the guidelines have been conceived while working with ASM specifications, yet most of them are generic enough and can be adopted for other formal methods as well. However, more rigorous empirical analysis is required to assess up to what extent that generalization is possible.

As this is an experience report focusing on the understandability issue of formal specifications, we have intentionally omitted the discussion about the possible impacts of our propositions on provability, automated parsing, semantic consistency, and tool support. Of course, proofs can always be discharged manually on papers but their automation would really be a sought-after trait. We have experienced that, despite the appealing notation, the tool support of ASM is a concern. Either already available tools for ASM can be improved in this direction or other successful tool sets, such as Rodin [25], can be extended to support this method.

References

1. Bowen, J.P., Hinchey, M.G.: Ten Commandments of Formal Methods. Computer 28, 56–63 (1995)

2. Mashkoor, A., Jacquot, J.-P., Souquières, J.: Transformation Heuristics for Formal Requirements Validation by Animation. In: SafeCert 2009, York, UK (2009)
3. Mashkoor, A., Jacquot, J.-P.: Stepwise Validation of Formal Specifications. In: APSEC 2011, pp. 57–64 (2011)
4. Spivey, J.M.: The Z Notation: A Reference Manual. Prentice-Hall, Inc. (1989)
5. Abrial, J.-R.: Modeling in Event-B: System and Software Engineering. Cambridge University Press (2010)
6. Boehm, B.W., Brown, J.R., Lipow, M.: Quantitative Evaluation of Software Quality. In: ICSE 1976, pp. 592–605 (1976)
7. Börger, E., Stärk, R.: Abstract State Machines - A Method for High-Level System Design and Analysis. Springer (2003)
8. Zimmerman, M.K., Lundqvist, K., Leveson, N.: Investigating the Readability of State-based Formal Requirements Specification Languages. In: ICSE 2002, pp. 33–43 (2002)
9. Vinter, R., Loomes, M., Kornbrot, D.: Applying Software Metrics to Formal Specifications: A Cognitive Approach. In: METRICS 1998, pp. 216–223 (1998)
10. Finney, K.: Mathematical Notation in Formal Specification: Too Difficult for the Masses? IEEE Trans. Softw. Eng. 22(2), 158–159 (1996)
11. Bidoit, M., Gaudel, M.-C., Mauboussin, A.: How to Make Algebraic Specifications More Understandable? In: Algebraic Methods: Theory, Tools and Applications, pp. 31–67 (1989)
12. Choppy, C.: Teaching Formal Specifications What About Abstraction. In: SEEFM 2007, pp. 188–199 (2007)
13. Börger, E., Sörensen, O.: BPMN Core Modeling Concepts. In: Handbook of Conceptual Modeling: Theory, Practice and Research Challenges. Springer (2011)
14. Farahbod, R., Gervasi, V., Glässer, U.: CoreASM: An Extensible ASM Execution Engine. In: 12th Int. Workshop on Abstract State Machines, pp. 153–165 (2005)
15. Davis, M.: The Universal Computer: The Road from Leibniz to Turing. W.W. Norton (2000)
16. Meyer, B.: On Formalism in Specifications. IEEE Software 2, 6–26 (1985)
17. Briand, L.C., Morasca, S.: Software Measurement and Formal Methods: A Case Study Centered on TRIO+ Specifications. In: ICFEM 1997, pp. 315–325 (1997)
18. Olszewska, M., Sere, K.: Specification Metrics for Event-B Developments. In: CONQUEST 2010, pp. 20–22 (2010)
19. Halstead, M.H.: Elements of Software Science. Operating and Programming Systems Series. Elsevier Science Inc. (1977)
20. Dulac, N., Viguier, T., Leveson, N.G., Storey, M.-A.D.: On the Use of Visualization in Formal Requirements Specification. In: RE 2002, pp. 71–80 (2002)
21. Harel, D.: Statecharts - A Visual Formalism for Complex Systems. Sci. Comput. Program. 8(3), 231–274 (1987)
22. Gargantini, A., Riccobene, E., Scandurra, P.: AsmEE: An Eclipse Plug-in in a Metamodel based Framework for the Abstract State Machines. In: First Int. Conf. on Eclipse Techn. (2007)
23. Moody, D.: The "Physics" of Notations: Toward a Scientific Basis for Constructing Visual Notations in Software Engineering. IEEE Trans. Softw. Eng. 35(6), 756–779 (2009)
24. Kim, S.-K., Carrington, D.: Visualization of Formal Specifications. In: APSEC 1999, pp. 102–109 (1999)
25. Abrial, J.-R., Butler, M., Hallerstede, S., Hoang, T., Mehta, F., Voisin, L.: Rodin: An Open Toolset for Modeling and Reasoning in Event-B. Journal on Software Tools for Technology Transfer 12(6), 447–466 (2010)
26. Asmeta - Overview, http://asmeta.sourceforge.net
27. Gargantini, A., Riccobene, E., Scandurra, P.: Metamodelling a Formal Method: Applying MDE to Abstract State Machines, Tech. Rep. 97, DTI Dept., University of Milan (2006)

Problem-Based Requirements Interaction Analysis*

Azadeh Alebrahim, Stephan Faßbender, Maritta Heisel, and Rene Meis

paluno - The Ruhr Institute for Software Technology – University of Duisburg-Essen
`firstname.lastname@paluno.uni-due.de`

Abstract. **[Context]** The ability to address the diverse interests of different stakeholders in a software project in a coherent way is one fundamental software quality. These diverse and maybe conflicting interests are reflected by the requirements of each stakeholder. **[Problem]** Thus, it is likely that aggregated requirements for a software system contain interactions. To avoid unwanted interactions and improve software quality, we propose a structured method consisting of three phases to find such interactions. **[Principal ideas]** For our method, we use problem diagrams, which describe requirements in a structured way. The information represented in the problem diagrams is translated into a formal Z model. Then we reduce the number of combinations of requirements, which might conflict. **[Contribution]** The reduction of requirements interaction candidates is crucial to lower the effort of the in depth interaction analysis. For validation of our method, we use a real-life example in the domain of smart grid.

Keywords: Requirements interactions, problem frames, feature interaction, Z notation.

1 Introduction

Nowadays, for almost every software system various stakeholders with diverse interests exist. These interests give rise to different sets of requirements. The combination of these sets leads to unwanted *interactions* among the requirements. Such interactions among requirements cannot be detected easily.

In general, the deviation between the intended behavior and structure as formulated by single requirements of a stakeholder and the overall behavior and structure of the resulting system- or software-to-be is called requirement *inconsistency* [1,2]. Such inconsistencies can stem from different sources. The *first source* is the different understanding of terms and different views on the system-to-be of different stakeholders. Missing or misleading information also adds to this class of inconsistencies [1], [3]. A *second source* are inconsistencies which stem from the transformation between different kinds of representations and models [1]. *Another important source* are interactions between requirements which lead to an unexpected behavior. For functional requirements this source is already known as feature interaction for a long time, e.g. in the

---

* Part of this work is funded by the German Research Foundation (DFG) under grant number HE3322/4-2 and the EU project Network of Excellence on Engineering Secure Future Internet Software Services and Systems (NESSoS, ICT-2009.1.4 Trustworthy ICT, Grant No. 256980).

C. Salinesi and I. van de Weerd (Eds.): REFSQ 2014, LNCS 8396, pp. 200–215, 2014.

domain of telecommunication [4,5]. For interactions, one can distinguish between unwanted and desirable interactions. The strongest type of interactions are conflicts in which requirements deny each other, and dependencies where one requirement can be only fulfilled when another requirement is also fulfilled. Between these extrema, there are different shades of negative or positive influences [2], [6]. For this paper, we assume that inconsistencies in terms of the first and second source are solved and we will focus on conflicts. But our method also allows to find other kinds of interactions.

Requirements engineering is concerned with describing the problem that the software has to solve in a precise way [7]. The problem is located in the environment in which the machine will be integrated and not in the computer [8]. Therefore, reasoning about the requirements involves reasoning about the environment and the assumptions made about it [7]. Zave and Jackson define the three terms *requirements (R)*, *domain knowledge (D)*, and *specification (S)* in their extensive work [9]. The requirements describe the desired system after the machine is built. The domain knowledge represents the relevant parts of the problem world. The specifications describe the behavior of the machine in order to meet the requirements. These three descriptions are related through the entailment relationship $D, S \models R$, expressing that the specification within the context of the domain knowledge should satisfy the requirements.

As a basis for requirements analysis, we use the problem frames approach [8] based on the work of Zave and Jackson [9]. It suggests to decompose the overall software problem into simple subproblems. Each subproblem is related to one or more requirements. The solutions of the subproblems will be composed to solve the overall software problem. The composition will only be successful if there is a consistent set of requirements (subproblems). Therefore, the identification of interactions and inconsistencies in the requirements analysis is essential to avoid costly modifications later on in the software development life cycle and to improve the overall software quality.

In this paper, we propose a formal and structured method composed of three phases to identify interactions among functional requirements involving the environment. We start with a full set of requirements representing subproblems. In all three phases, we narrow down the set of combinations of requirements which might interact. The narrowing process is formally defined using the Z notation [10,11] for each step of our method. The formal Z specification is the basis for the tool support of our method. We developed our specifications using the Community Z Tools[1]. After the final phase, the remaining candidates have to be analyzed in detail to choose appropriate measures to avoid the interactions. The analysis of the remaining candidates is out of the scope of this paper, but our method reduces the amount of candidates and thus the effort necessary for further analysis.

The rest of the paper is organized as follows: Section 2 gives a brief overview of the problem frames our method relies on. As running example, we introduce a sun blind control system in Section 3. Our method to detect interacting requirements is described and applied to the sun blind control system in Section 4. We validate our method by using a real-life example of smart grids in Section 5. Section 6 presents related work, while Section 7 concludes the paper and suggests recommendations for future work.

---

[1] http://czt.sourceforge.net/

2   Background

We use the problem frames [8] approach proposed by Jackson to build our requirements interaction method on. Jackson introduces the concept of *problem frames*, which is concerned with describing, analyzing, and structuring software problems. According to Jackson, the computer and the software represent the solution, called *machine*. The requirements and the environment are called *system*.

A problem frame represents a class of software problems. It is described by a *frame diagram*, which consists of domains, interfaces between them, and a requirement. Domains describe entities in the environment. Jackson distinguishes the domain types *biddable domains* that are usually people, *causal domains* that comply with some physical laws, and *lexical domains* that are data representations. *Interfaces* connect domains, and they contain *shared phenomena*. Shared phenomena may be events, operation calls, messages, and the like. They are observable by at least two domains, but controlled by only one domain, as indicated by the name of that domain and "!". For instance, the shared phenomena *openCommand*, *closeCommand*, and *stopCommand* in Fig. 1 are observable by the domains *UserOpenControl* and *User*, but controlled only by the domain *User*. When we state a requirement, we want to change something in the world with the machine (i.e., software) to be developed. Therefore, each requirement constrains at least one domain. Such a constrained domain is the core of any problem description because it has to be controlled according to the requirements. Hence, a constrained domain triggers the need for developing a new machine which provides the desired control. A requirement may refer to several domains in the environment of the machine.

We describe problem frames using UML class diagrams, extended by stereotypes as proposed by Hatebur and Heisel [12]. All elements of a problem frame act as placeholders which must be instantiated to represent concrete problems. In doing so, one obtains a *problem diagram* that belongs to a specific class of problems. Figure 1 shows a problem diagram in UML notation. It describes that the *UserOpenControl* machine pulls up, lowers or stops the sun blind on behalf of user commands *openCommand*, *closeCommand*, or *stopCommand*. The requirement R4 constrains the *SunBlind* domain. This is expressed by a dependency with the stereotype ≪constrains≫. It refers to the *User*, as expressed by a dependency with the stereotype ≪refersTo≫.

3   Running Example

We demonstrate our approach using a sun blind control system. A sun blind is made up of metallic fins which are attached to the outer side of the window. Additionally, we have a sun sensor which measures the sun intensity, a wind sensor which measures the wind speed, and a display which is suitable to display the current sun intensity and wind speed. The sun blind is sensitive to sun and wind. A machine shall be built that lowers the sun blind on sunshine and pulls it up on strong wind. For individual settings it shall be possible to control the sun blind manually, too. The following requirements are given:

(R1) If there is sunshine for more than one minute, the sun blind will be lowered.
(R2) If there is no sunshine for more than 5 minutes, the sun blind will be pulled up.

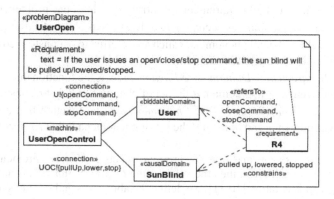

Fig. 1. Problem diagram for the requirement R4

(R3) If there is strong wind for more than 10 seconds, the sun blind will be pulled up, to avoid destruction of the sun blind.

(R4) If the user issues an open/close/stop command, the sun blind will be pulled up/-lowered/stopped.

(R5) If the user interacts with the sun blind, then sunshine and no sunshine are ignored within the next 4 hours.

(R6) If the user deactivates the holiday mode, then the sun blind is turned on.

(R7) If the user activates the holiday mode, the sun blind is pulled up and turned off.

(R8) Sunshine intensity and wind speed shall be displayed on the weather display.

We modeled the requirements as problem diagrams, which are used as input for our method. The problem diagram for the requirement R4 is shown in Fig. 1. The other requirements are modeled in a similar way. Throughout the paper we will refer to this example to describe the proposed method.

4   Interaction Detection Method

Our method starts with a set of problem diagrams. Based on the information provided by these problem diagrams, the structure-based pruning (phase one) takes place and removes all requirements for which the structure of problem diagrams already implies that they will not interact. The result is a first set of interaction candidates. In the second phase, those candidates can be further reduced using the information if requirements have to be satisfiable in parallel (phase two). The sets of requirements that have to be satisfiable in parallel have to be known beforehand and these are an external input to our method. The remaining interaction candidates are finally reduced in the last phase (phase three) by checking whether the conjunction of preconditions of possibly inter-acting requirements is satisfiable. Our formalization is built on the following sets and relations that can be derived from the given problem diagrams.

Requirement is the set of all requirements occurring in at least one problem diagram.

Domain is the set of all domains occurring in at least one problem diagram.

Phenomenon is the set of all phenomena which are referred to or constrained by at least one requirement in a problem diagram.

constrains : *Requirement* × *Domain* → $\mathbb{P}$ *Phenomenon* is the function that assigns to a pair of requirement r and domain d the set of phenomena P that r constrains on d.

refersTo : *Requirement* × *Domain* → $\mathbb{P}$ *Phenomenon* is the function that assigns to a pair of requirement r and domain d the set of phenomena P that r refers to on d.

Please note that *constrains* and *refersTo* are total functions. If a requirement does not constrain or refer to a domain, then the value of the respective function is an empty set of phenomena. In Z notation [10,11], we define the above sets and relations as follows:

[*Requirement*, *Domain*, *Phenomenon*]

$$constrains : Requirement \times Domain \rightarrow \mathbb{P}\,Phenomenon$$
$$refersTo : Requirement \times Domain \rightarrow \mathbb{P}\,Phenomenon$$

4.1   Phase One: Structure-Based Pruning

In phase one, we make use of the structure of the problem diagrams. The steps for selecting the requirements which are candidates of a requirements interaction are described as follows:

Step One: Initial Setup. First, we define a Z schema *Interaction* consisting of three variables, which we will use to describe the actual state of our method. The sets *RelevantDomain* and *RelevantRequirement* contain all domains and requirements which are considered to be relevant for an interaction. The function *MinReqInteraction* returns for each relevant domain the minimal sets of requirements that may interact with each other. A set of requirements is considered as minimal interacting if each strict subset of it does not contain a possible interaction [2].

$$\begin{array}{l} \underline{\quad Interaction \quad\quad\quad\quad\quad\quad\quad\quad\quad\quad\quad\quad\quad\quad\quad\quad\quad\quad\quad} \\ RelevantDomain : \mathbb{P}\,Domain \\ RelevantRequirement : \mathbb{P}\,Requirement \\ MinReqInteraction : Domain \nrightarrow \mathbb{P}\,\mathbb{P}\,Requirement \\ \underline{\quad\quad\quad\quad\quad\quad\quad\quad\quad\quad\quad\quad\quad\quad\quad\quad\quad\quad\quad\quad\quad\quad\quad\quad} \\ \text{dom } MinReqInteraction = RelevantDomain \\ \bigcup(\bigcup(ran\ MinReqInteraction)) = RelevantRequirement \\ \forall d : RelevantDomain \bullet \forall R : MinReqInteraction(d) \bullet \\ \quad \#R \geq 2 \wedge \forall Q : MinReqInteraction(d) \mid R \neq Q \bullet \neg Q \subseteq R \end{array}$$

Initially, we assume that all pairs of requirements which constrain the same domain possibly cause an interaction on it. Formally, we define the initial interaction schema *Init* as follows:

Table 1. Initial requirements interaction table

Requirement / Domain	SunSensor (CausalDomain)	SunBlind (CausalDomain)	WindSensor (CausalDomain)	User (Biddable-Domain)	WeatherDisplay (CausalDomain)
R1	*sunshine*	**lowered**			
R2	*no sunshine*	**pulled up**			
R3		**pulled up**	*heavy wind*		
R4		**pulled up, lowered, stopped**		*openCommand , closeCommand , stopCommand*	
R5		**on, off**		*openCommand, closeCommand, stopCommand*	
R6		**off, pulled up**		*activateHoliday*	
R7		**on**		*deactivate-Holiday*	
R8	*sun intensity*		*wind speed*		**displayed sunshine intensity, displayed wind speed**

```
__Init_____
 Interaction
 _____
 RelevantDomain = Domain
 ∀ d : Domain • MinReqInteraction(d) =
      {r₁, r₂ : Requirement | r₁ ≠ r₂ ∧
           constrains (r₁, d) ≠ ∅ ∧ constrains (r₂, d) ≠ ∅ • {r₁, r₂}}
```

We will visualize our method using so called requirement interaction tables (see Table 1). In these tables, we represent the functions *constrains* and *refersTo* with the restricted domain *RelevantRequirement* × *RelevantDomain*. We highlight the phenomena P of a cell (r, d) in bold font if requirement r constrains phenomena P of the domain d. If r refers to phenomena P, then they are written in italic font. The initial interaction table for our running example is given in Table 1. We start with 21 possible combinations of interacting requirements because we have to assume that each combination of the seven requirements constraining the sun blind causes an interaction.

Step Two: Reducing Relevant Domains. We check for each column, and therefore for each domain, if the domain is constrained at least by two requirements (at least two cells with bold entries). If this is not the case, then the domain is not relevant. The reason is that interactions only occur on domains which are constrained by at least two requirements. Formally, we can define this step with the following Z operation schema.

```
__P1S2_____
 ΔInteraction
 _____
 RelevantDomain' = {d : Domain | ∃ r₁, r₂ : Requirement | r₁ ≠ r₂ •
      constrains (r₁, d) ≠ ∅ ∧ constrains (r₂, d) ≠ ∅}
 MinReqInteraction' = RelevantDomain' ◁ MinReqInteraction
```

Table 2. Requirements interaction table after step 2 of phase 1

Requirement / Domain	SunBlind (CausalDomain)
R1	**lowered**
R2	**pulled up**
R3	**pulled up**
R4	**pulled up, lowered, stopped**
R5	**on, off**
R6	**off, pulled up**
R7	**on**

From Table 1 we can see that no requirements interactions can occur on the sun sensor, wind sensor and user because these domains are only referred to by the requirements in the problem diagrams. Since there is only one requirement constraining the weather display, we also do not expect any requirements interactions on it. On the sun blind domain, we expect requirements interactions from the table because every requirement besides R8 constrains this domain. Hence, after the second step of phase one, we only identify domain *SunBlind* as relevant for interactions. When we apply the operation schema *P1S2* on the initial interaction schema (*Init* ⨾ *P1S2*), we get the interaction table shown in Table 2.

Step Three: Reducing Relevant Requirements. Third, we have to check for each phenomenon of a relevant domain if it is interacting with a combination of phenomena of the interaction table which refer to or constrain the same domain. A set of phenomena is interacting if it is not possible to observe them or different characteristics of them at the same time. Please note that different characteristics of a phenomenon could not be observable at the same time. In such cases, we consider these phenomena as self-conflicting. For each combination, we have to decide whether we can reject the assumption that there is an interaction or not. If we cannot reject this assumption for sure, we have to consider this combination of phenomena as interacting. We are interested in the interactions of phenomena of a domain because these are the source of interactions between requirements that refer to or constrain them. We define the set of the minimal interacting sets of phenomena for each domain using the function *MinPhenInteraction* : *Domain* → $\mathbb{P}\,\mathbb{P}\,Phenomenon$. A set $P \in MinPhenInteraction(d)$ contains a number of interacting phenomena of the domain d - at least two - and each strict subset $Q \subset P$ is free of interactions [2]. This is expressed in the Z notation as follows:

$$
\begin{array}{l}
MinPhenInteraction : Domain \rightarrow \mathbb{P}\,\mathbb{P}\,Phenomenon \\
\hline
\forall d : Domain \bullet \forall P : MinPhenInteraction(d) \bullet \\
\quad P \neq \varnothing \wedge \forall Q : MinPhenInteraction(d) \mid P \neq Q \bullet \neg\, Q \subseteq P
\end{array}
$$

We have to define the function *MinPhenInteraction* manually for the given problem frames model. For this step it is sufficient to define it for the relevant domains of the interaction schema after step two of phase one ((*Init* ⨾ *P1S2*).*RelevantDomain'*). For the precondition analysis in phase three, we also need the interacting requirements on the other domains. For our running example, we identify the following sets of minimal interacting phenomena.

$Sunblind, SunSensor, WindSensor, User : Domain$
$lowered, pulledUp, stopped, on, off, sunshine, noSunshine : Phenomenon$
$strongWind, openCommand, closeCommand, stopCommand : Phenomenon$

$MinPhenInteraction(Sunblind) =$
$\quad \{\{lowered, pulledUp\}, \{lowered, stopped\}, \{pulledUp, stopped\}, \{on, off\}\}$
$MinPhenInteraction(SunSensor) = \{\{sunshine, noSunshine\}\}$
$MinPhenInteraction(WindSensor) = MinPhenInteraction(User) = \varnothing$

Using the minimal interacting sets of phenomena, we can update the function *Min-ReqInteraction* from the interaction schema, which maps a relevant domain to the sets of requirements that possibly interact on the domain. We distinguish two cases. First, two requirements are interacting on a domain if there is a self-conflicting phenomenon where both requirements refer to or constrain. Second, if we can define a bijection between a set of at least two requirements and a set of interacting phenomena, with the property that if the bijection maps a requirement to a phenomenon then the requirement also refers to or constrains it, then these requirements may interact with each other. Formally, we define the following operation schema:

__P1S3__

$\Delta Interaction$

$MinReqInteraction' = \lambda d : RelevantDomain \bullet$
$\quad \{r_1, r_2 : Requirement \mid r_1 \neq r_2 \wedge \exists p : Phenomenon \bullet$
$\quad\quad \{p\} \in MinPhenInteraction(d) \wedge$
$\quad\quad p \in constrains\ (r_1, d) \cup refersTo\ (r_1, d) \wedge$
$\quad\quad p \in constrains\ (r_2, d) \cup refersTo\ (r_2, d) \bullet \{r_1, r_2\}\}\cup$
$\quad \{R : \mathbb{P}\,Requirement \mid \exists P : MinPhenInteraction(d) \bullet \exists F : R \rightarrowtail P \bullet$
$\quad\quad \forall r : R;\ p : P \bullet F(r) = p \Rightarrow p \in constrains\ (r, d) \cup refersTo\ (r, d)\}$
$RelevantDomain' = RelevantDomain \setminus dom(MinReqInteraction' \rhd \{\varnothing\})$

Based on the updated function *MinReqInteraction'*, also the interaction table is reduced by the above operation schema. All requirements that are not in one of the interacting sets can be left out because they are irrelevant. Furthermore, all domains for which no set of possible interacting requirements exists are also irrelevant.

With the above definition of *MinPhenInteraction(Sunblind)*, we get the following sets of possibly interacting requirements for our running example:

$R1, R2, R3, R4, R5, R6, R7 : Requirement$

$(\mu S : Init \,_9^\circ\, P1S2 \,_9^\circ\, P1S3).MinReqInteraction'(Sunblind) =$
$\quad \{\{R1, R3\}, \{R1, R4\}, \{R1, R2\}, \{R1, R6\}, \{R2, R4\}, \{R3, R4\}, \{R4, R6\},$
$\quad \{R5, R6\}, \{R5, R7\}, \{R6, R7\}\}$

In this step, we have reduced the 21 initial combinations of possibly interacting requirements to 10.

4.2   Phase Two: Check for Parallel Requirements

We now investigate whether the possibly interacting requirements have to be satisfiable at the same time. In the case that they do not have to be satisfiable all at the same time, we do not expect interactions among them. Hence, we need a set of sets of requirements *parallelReq* as input for this phase. This set has to be set up manually and shall contain the maximal sets of requirements that have to be satisfiable at the same time, i.e. if we add a new requirement to a set, then there is a requirement in the set that has not to be satisfiable at the same time with the new requirement.

$$parallelReq : \mathbb{P}\,\mathbb{P}\,Requirement$$

$$\bigcup parallelReq \subseteq (\mu\,S : Init \,\overset{\circ}{\scriptstyle 9}\, P1S2 \,\overset{\circ}{\scriptstyle 9}\, P1S3).RelevantRequirement'$$

For our running example, we see that R6 and R7 are exclusive requirements that do not have to be satisfiable at the same time with others. Furthermore, R4 and R5 have not to be satisfiable at the same time because R5 refers to the user interaction of R4 as precondition. The requirements R1, R2, and R3 that are concerned with the observation of the environment have all to be satisfiable at the same time, together with R4 or R5. Hence, we get the following sets of parallel requirements:

$$parallelReq = \{\{R1, R2, R3, R4\}, \{R1, R2, R3, R5\}\}$$

We can now use the set of sets of parallel satisfiable requirements to reduce the sets of minimal interacting requirements. A set of requirements is only interacting if all requirements of it have to be satisfiable at the same time. We get the following operation schema:

P2

$\Delta Interaction$

$MinReqInteraction' = \lambda\,d : RelevantDomain \bullet \{R : MinReqInteraction(d) \mid$
$\qquad \exists\,P : parallelReq \bullet R \subseteq P\}$
$RelevantDomain' = RelevantDomain \setminus \text{dom}(MinReqInteraction' \rhd \{\varnothing\})$

For our running example, we get the following reduced set of sets of minimal interacting requirements.

$$(\mu\,S : Init \,\overset{\circ}{\scriptstyle 9}\, P1S2 \,\overset{\circ}{\scriptstyle 9}\, P1S3 \,\overset{\circ}{\scriptstyle 9}\, P2).MinReqInteraction'(Sunblind) =$$
$$\{\{R1, R3\}, \{R1, R4\}, \{R1, R2\}, \{R2, R4\}, \{R3, R4\}\}$$

Beginning from the 21 combinations of possibly interacting requirements, we have now reduced the number of relevant combinations to 5.

4.3 Phase Three: Precondition-Based Pruning

We now have a reduced set of sets of possibly interacting requirements $(Init \,\overset{\circ}{\scriptstyle 9}\, P1S2 \,\overset{\circ}{\scriptstyle 9}\, P1S3 \,\overset{\circ}{\scriptstyle 9}\, P2).MinReqInteraction'$. For each of these sets, we investigate whether there is a system state that fulfills the preconditions of all requirements of this set. We only consider those parts of the preconditions that are not influenced by the software to be built, i.e. phenomena of domains that are only referred by requirements. We only consider those parts of the precondition because two requirements with contradicting preconditions can interact in the case that one requirement establishes the precondition of the other requirement, such that the postconditions of both requirements could not be satisfied.

As argued in Section 1, requirements have to be expressed in terms of the environment. Therefore, they are normally written according to the general textual pattern: *"If the environment is like this, then it shall be changed like that."* Hence, a requirement has a pre- and a postcondition, both talking about phenomena of the environment [13]. We formalize the textual description of each relevant requirement to a formula *pre* ⇒ *post*. The formula *pre* describes the system state in terms of the referred to and controlled phenomena of the requirement when the requirement has to be fulfilled, and the formula *post* describes the system state to be achieved by the requirement.

For example, the requirement R3 states "If there is strong wind for more than 10 seconds, the sun blind will be pulled up, [...]", and we can express it with the formula *strong wind* ⇒ *pulled up*.

To determine whether a set of requirements is satisfiable, we have to define the function *precondition* : *Requirement* → $\mathbb{P}\,\mathbb{P}\,Phenomenon$ that returns the phenomena of only referred domains (see above) occurring in the precondition of the requirement in disjunctive normal form (DNF). E.g., a precondition $(a \wedge b) \vee c \vee (d \wedge e \wedge f)$ is represented as $\{\{a,b\}, \{c\}, \{d,e,f\}\}$. We assume that the preconditions of all requirements in isolation are free of interaction. Otherwise the requirement is not satisfiable and can be left out.

$precondition : Requirement \rightarrow \mathbb{P}\,\mathbb{P}\,Phenomenon$

$\forall d : Domain;\ r : Requirement \bullet$
   $\forall I : MinPhenInteraction(d);\ P : precondition(r) \mid \#I \geq 2 \bullet \neg I \subseteq P \wedge$
      $\forall p : P \bullet \exists_1 d : ran(dom(constrains \rhd \varnothing)) \bullet p \in refersTo(r,d)$

We define the precondition function as following for our running example.

$precondition(R1) = \{\{sunshine\}\}$
$precondition(R2) = \{\{noSunshine\}\}$
$precondition(R3) = \{\{strongWind\}\}$
$precondition(R4) = \{\{openCommand\}, \{closeCommand\}, \{stopCommand\}\}$

For each relevant domain $d \in (Init \,\mathring{\,}\, P1S2 \,\mathring{\,}\, P1S3 \,\mathring{\,}\, P2).RelevantDomain'$, we now consider each set of possibly interacting requirements $R \in (Init \,\mathring{\,}\, P1S2 \,\mathring{\,}\, P1S3 \,\mathring{\,}\, P2).MinReqInteraction'(d)$ and combine the preconditions of the requirements in R by conjunction and restore the disjunctive normal form using the generic function *dunion*.

$=[X]=$
$dunion : \mathbb{P}\,\mathbb{P}\,\mathbb{P}\,X \rightarrow \mathbb{P}\,\mathbb{P}\,X$

$dunion = \lambda S : \mathbb{P}\,\mathbb{P}\,\mathbb{P}\,X \bullet$
   $\{T : \mathbb{P}\,X \mid \exists f : S \rightarrow \mathbb{P}\,X \mid \forall s : S \bullet f(s) \in s \bullet T = \bigcup(ran f)\}$

For our running example, we get the following combined preconditions in disjunctive normal form.

$dunion(precondition(\!| \{R1, R2\} |\!)) = \{\{sunshine, noSunshine\}\}$
$dunion(precondition(\!| \{R2, R3\} |\!)) = \{\{sunshine, strongWind\}\}$
$dunion(precondition(\!| \{R1, R4\} |\!)) = \{\{sunshine, openCommand\},$
$\quad \{sunshine, closeCommand\}, \{sunshine, stopCommand\}\}$
$dunion(precondition(\!| \{R2, R4\} |\!)) = \{\{noSunshine, openCommand\},$
$\quad \{noSunshine, closeCommand\}, \{noSunshine, stopCommand\}\}$
$dunion(precondition(\!| \{R3, R4\} |\!)) = \{\{strongWind, openCommand\},$
$\quad \{strongWind, closeCommand\}, \{strongWind, stopCommand\}\}$

A set of interacting requirements can now be rejected if all phenomena sets in the combined disjunctive normal form contain a set of interacting phenomena, because then there is no system state that leads to an interaction between the requirements. Formally, we can specify this step using the following operation schema.

_P3_

$\Delta Interaction$

$\forall d : RelevantDomain \bullet MinReqInteraction'(d) =$
$\quad \{R : MinReqInteraction(d) \mid \exists P : dunion(precondition(\!| R |\!)) \bullet$
$\quad\quad \forall I : \bigcup(\text{ran } MinPhenInteraction) \bullet \neg I \subseteq P\}$

From the above equations, we see that R1 and R2 have interacting phenomena in their combined precondition because there cannot be *sunshine* and *noSunshine* at the same time. Hence, we remove $\{R1, R2\}$ from the set of sets of interacting requirements. For all other requirement sets, we can find system states that satisfy the combined preconditions because there can be sunshine and strong wind at the same time and the user can issue commands independently from the actual weather.

The remaining sets of interacting requirements have to be further analyzed to determine if the requirements are interacting and which measures (such as prioritization) shall be chosen to cope with the interactions.

From our running example we see that our method reduced the 21 initial combinations of requirements that may interact to 4 combinations.

5   Validation

The proposed method was used for analyzing requirements of a real-life example in the domain of smart grids. To use energy in an optimal way, smart grids make it possible to couple the generation, distribution, storage, and consumption of energy. Smart grids use information and communication technology, which allows financial, informational, and electrical transactions. The gateway represents the central communication unit between a household and the grid in a smart metering system. It is responsible for collecting, processing, storing, and communicating meter data, and for controlling a household, e.g., energy supply.

As information sources, we considered diverse documents such as "Application Case Study: Smart Grid" and "Smart Grid Concrete Scenario" provided by the industrial partners of the EU project NESSoS[2]. As sources for functional requirements for such a

---
[2] http://www.nessos-project.eu/

Table 3. Effort spent for conducting the method and resulting reduction

		Method Step						
		Modeling of Problem Diagrams	Initial Setup	Reducing Relevant Domains	Set up MinPhen	Reducing Relevant Requirements	Check for Parallel Requirements	Precondition-based Pruning
Effort	∅ Per Item	28 min. per Problem Diagram	2.5 min. per Problem Diagram	0.5 min. per Domain	9.5 min. per Domain	0.5 min. per Requirement	6.85 min. per Problem Diagram	8 min. per Requirement
	Number of Items	27 Problem Diagrams	27 Problem Diagrams	19 Domains	4 Domains	27 Requirements	27 Problem Diagrams	5 Requirements
	Total	*12.5 person hours*	*1.125 person hour*	*0.16 person hour*	*0.6 person hour*	*0.225 person hour*	*3 person hours*	*0.67 person hour*
Potential Interactions	% of Initial	100%	100%	49%	49%	2.8%	2.8%	1.7%
Left	% of Remaining	100%	100%	49%	100%	5.8%	100%	60%

gateway, we considered "Requirements of AMI (Advanced Multi-metering Infrastructure]" [14] provided by the EU project OPEN meter[3]. We refined the 13 minimum uses cases as described by this document to 27 requirements and modeled them as problem diagrams using the UML4PF tool [15].

The general effort of preparing the problem diagrams and executing our method is shown in Table 3. The steps of our method are added as columns. The rows are divided into 2 main parts. First, the effort per item and the total effort regarding the number of items. Second, the reduction of possible interactions within one step with regards to the total number of interactions or with regards to the interaction left by the previous step. This way, Table 3 provides the information about the effort and the resulting reduction for each step.

The problem diagrams modeling the 27 requirements given by the 13 minimum use cases served as an input to Phase 1, Step 1, resulting in 351 possible requirements interactions. The initial requirements interaction table consisted of 19 domains and 27 requirements. A number of 64 phenomena were documented as relevant, because the requirements mentioned them. In the second step, the number of domains on which an interaction could happen was reduced to 4, and 7 requirements were removed from the set of candidates, which could cause an interaction. At this point, the number of possible interactions was already reduced by more than fifty percent to 171 (see Table 3). The involved number of possibly involved phenomena was cut down to 19. Three of the phenomena were identified as possibly interacting phenomena. As a result, only 1 domain and 5 requirements remained after Step 3. Thus, at the end of Phase 1, we already reduced the number of possible interactions to 10, which makes a reduction by more than 95 percent (see Table 3). Since all of the requirements left may have to be fulfilled in parallel, no further reduction was possible in Phase 2. While checking the preconditions in Phase 3, one more requirement could be rejected to be a candidate for an interaction. In the end, 4 requirements, sources for 6 possible interactions, had to be analyzed in depth.

The analysis revealed that the requirements left caused 2 interactions. One of the original use cases in [14] described a process where the energy provider is able to

---

[3] http://www.openmeter.com/

disconnect a household from the grid by ordering the gateway to cut off the electricity supply. One reason could be unpaid bills. On the other hand, the provider can order the gateway to reconnect the household. A second use case describes that the customer is able to define a power consumption threshold. If the threshold is reached by the actual power consumption, the household is also cut off the grid by the gateway. But for this case, the consumer is allowed to override the cut-off manually, reconnecting the household. The two use cases, and therefore also the requirements, did not refer to each other, allowing the customer to override a cut-off ordered by the provider. Or the other way round, the provider could reconnect a household which was taken off the grid on demand of the customer. Hence, we found 2 real interactions.

To sum up, the effort to investigate requirements for interactions in depth was reduced by more than 95 percent. For the interactions left over to the in-depth analysis, the precision was 33 percent (2 real interactions / 6 possible interactions), which is acceptable considering the overall reduction. For calculating the recall, we made a full in depth analysis of all requirements and found no additional interactions which makes a perfect recall of 100 percent. In general, when looking for interactions, it is favorable to have a high recall rather than having a high precision. The reason is that missing one real interaction makes any effort reduction worthless.

For the smart grid case study, especially the effort spent for phase one payed off (see Table 3). Phase 2 and 3 resulted only in a minor reduction of possible interactions. This result should be subject to further research, as it may depend on the special structure of the smart grid case study. But overall, the effort of executing our method is reasonable with regards to the reduction.

6 Related Work

Although the problem of interaction between requirements has been known for a long time, there exist only few approaches dealing with this problem.

Egyed and Grünbacher [16] introduce an approach based on software quality attributes and traces between requirements. They assume that two requirements are conflicting only if their quality attributes are conflicting and there is a dependency between them. The authors do not consider the case of conflicting requirements due to their functionality and not their quality.

The approach proposed by Alférez et al. [17] finds candidate points of interaction. The authors first analyze the dependencies between use cases to identify potential candidates of conflict. Then they determine whether the detected use cases are related to more than one feature. In contrast to our method, it is not formally defined. Furthermore, this approach is based on use cases, whereas we rely on problem frames.

Kim et al. [18] propose a process for detecting and managing conflicts between functional requirements expressed in natural language. After identifying, documenting, and prioritizing requirements using goals and scenarios in the first phase, the requirements are classified through the requirements partitioning criteria in the second step. In the third phase, conflicts are detected using a syntactic method to identify candidate conflicts and a semantic method to identify actual conflicts. Step four manages the detected conflicts according to the priorities. Similar to our method, this process reduces the scope of requirements to be considered by performing a syntactic analysis. The semantic analysis is performed manually by the analyst to check and answer a list of questions. As opposed to our method, this method is not formally specified.

In contrast to our problem-based method, Hausmann et al. [19] introduce a use case-based approach to detect potential inconsistencies between functional requirements. A rule-based specification of pre- and postconditions is proposed to express functional requirements. The requirements are then formalized in terms of graph transformations that enable expressing the dependencies between requirements. Conflict detection is based on the idea of independence of graph transformations. The authors provide tool support to represent the results of the analysis. Similar to our method, the results of the conflict detection method have to be analyzed further manually. Our method detects a set of interaction candidates that need to be analyzed further for real interactions. This approach detects dependencies that represent errors or conflicts to be decided by the modeler. This is due to the incomplete nature of use cases.

Lamsweerde et al. use different formal techniques for detecting conflicts among goals based on KAOS [2]. One technique to detect conflicts is deriving boundary conditions by backward chaining. Boundary conditions refer to combination of circumstances causing inconsistency in among different goals. Every precondition yields a boundary condition. The other technique is selecting a matching generic pattern. Our method for finding conflicts among requirements can be seen as complementary to this approach that provides techniques for detecting goal conflicts and resolving them. However, to use our method in connection with this approach, requirements as refinement of goals have to be modeled as problem diagrams.

Heisel and Souquières [13] developed a formal and heuristic method to detect requirement interactions. Each requirement consists of a pre- and a postcondition. The authors analyze whether the postconditions are contradictory by sharing common preconditions. They also determine postcondition interaction candidates by looking for incompatible postconditions. As opposed to our approach, the authors formalize the whole set of requirements, which is costly and time-consuming. Our approach utilizes the structure of problem diagrams to reduce the effort for the formalization.

An approach to detect feature interactions in the software product line (SPL) is proposed by Classen et al. [20]. The authors link feature diagrams used in the SPL to the problem frames approach by redefining the notions of *feature* and *feature interaction* based on the entailment relationship $D, S \models R$ [8,9]. This enables the authors to consider the environment in addition to the requirements, similar to our method. To detect feature interactions, four algorithms are presented based on a set of consistency rules. This work is complementary to our work. Using our approach, the sets of requirements and domains that have to be considered for interactions can be reduced and therefore the modeling and formalization effort is reduced.

7   Conclusions and Future work

In this paper, we investigated how to identify requirements interaction using a problem-based method. We described a structured method to identify requirements interactions between functional requirements. The method is formalized using Z and this specification serves as basis for the tool support of the proposed method. For the first phase, we explained how to identify candidates for an interaction among a set of requirements modeled as problem diagrams. In the second phase, we showed how to reduce this set of candidates further using the information whether requirements have to be fulfilled in parallel or not. In the third phase we further reduced the possibly parallel requirements by checking their precondition. For the paper, we explained our method using a running example. For validation, we applied the method to a real example in the smart grid domain. The main contributions are:

- A re-usable requirements interaction detection method which provides structured guidance for a software engineer.
- A significant reduction of the initial set of requirements to be analyzed in depth which makes the use of heavy weight analysis methods, such as formal methods, practicable.
- A formal basis which enables tool-support that eases the execution of our method.[4]
- Identifying interactions among more than two requirements.

Considering the scalability of our method, we experienced a less than linear increase in effort for a rising number of requirements regarding the pruning steps. The reason is that the size of the requirements interaction table depends on the number of requirements and the number of domains. Even for a large amount of requirements, in most cases, the number of involved domains remains stable. And even for a large table, each decision can be done based on the information of one entry of the table. The table itself can be generated automatically and tool support is existent or developed right now for each pruning step. Hence, for the pruning the most effort stems from the modeling of the requirements themselves (see Table 3). But this is a necessary and unavoidable step when analyzing requirements in a structured way. By applying our method to a real-life case study in this paper, we showed the feasibility and usefulness of the method.

For the problem frames approach itself, we experienced a linear increase in effort for each additional requirement (see Table 3). Thus, the scalability is acceptable. Note that our method can be applied to any other requirements notation as long as it provides all involved domains in the environment, the constrains or refers relations between functional requirements and domains, and the phenomena for the constrains and refers relations. This also means that we do not use all information given by problem diagrams. But from our point of view the full problem frames approach is a natural solution for collecting this information as it is system centric, considers the environment with its domains, and provides a structured method to deal with functional requirements and refine them in the needed way.

For the future, we plan to add support for considering quality requirements. Additionally, we strive for extending the tool support. For example, we will implement the possibility to express the concurrence of the fulfillment of requirements in graphical way, e.g. using UML interaction overview diagrams. This enables the automatic generation of sets of parallel requirements. Finally, we plan to work on a method which will guide the process of interactions resolving and the according modification of the requirements.

---

[4] Tool-support for generating the initial requirements table is available under http://www.uml4pf.org/rit/rit.html.

References

1. France, R., Rumpe, B.: Model-driven development of complex software: A research roadmap. In: 2007 Future of Software Engineering, FOSE 2007, pp. 37–54. IEEE Computer Society, Washington, DC (2007)
2. van Lamsweerde, A., Letier, E., Darimont, R.: Managing Conflicts in Goal-Driven Requirements Engineering. IEEE Trans. Softw. Eng. 24(11), 908–926 (1998)
3. Sommerville, I., Sawyer, P., Viller, S.: Viewpoints for requirements elicitation: A practical approach. In: Int. Conf. on RE: Putting Requirements Engineering to Practice, pp. 74–81. IEEE Computer Society (1998)
4. Calder, M., Kolberg, M., Magill, E.H., Reiff-Marganiec, S.: Feature interaction: a critical review and considered forecast. Comput. Netw. 41, 115–141 (2003)
5. Cameron, E.J., Velthuijsen, H.: Feature interactions in telecommunications systems. Comm. Mag. 31(8), 18–23 (1993)
6. Robinson, W.N., Pawlowski, S.D., Volkov, V.: Requirements interaction management. ACM Comput. Surv. 35, 132–190 (2003)
7. Cheng, B.H.C., Atlee, J.M.: Research Directions in Requirements Engineering. In: Future of Software Engineering, FOSE 2007, pp. 285–303. IEEE Computer Society (2007)
8. Jackson, M.: Problem Frames. Analyzing and structuring software development problems. Addison-Wesley (2001)
9. Zave, P., Jackson, M.: Four dark corners of requirements engineering. ACM Trans. Softw. Eng. Methodol. 6, 1–30 (1997)
10. Wordsworth, J.: Software development with Z - a practical approach to formal methods in software engineering. International computer science series. Addison-Wesley (1992)
11. Spivey, J.M.: The Z notation: a reference manual. Prentice-Hall, Inc., Upper Saddle River (1989), http://spivey.oriel.ox.ac.uk/mike/zrm/zrm.pdf
12. Hatebur, D., Heisel, M.: A UML profile for requirements analysis of dependable software. In: Schoitsch, E. (ed.) SAFECOMP 2010. LNCS, vol. 6351, pp. 317–331. Springer, Heidelberg (2010)
13. Heisel, M., Souquières, J.: A heuristic algorithm to detect feature interactions in requirements. In: Language Constructs for Describing Features, pp. 143–162. Springer (2000)
14. OPEN meter project: Requirements of AMI. Technical report, OPEN meter project (2009)
15. Côté, I., Hatebur, D., Heisel, M., Schmidt, H.: UML4PF – a tool for problem-oriented requirements analysis. In: Proc. of the Int. Conf. on Requirements Engineering (RE), pp. 349–350. IEEE Computer Society (2011)
16. Egyed, A., Grunbacher, P.: Identifying requirements conflicts and cooperation: How quality attributes and automated traceability can help. IEEE Softw. 21(6), 50–58 (2004)
17. Alférez, M., Moreira, A., Kulesza, U., Araújo, J.A., Mateus, R., Amaral, V.: Detecting feature interactions in SPL requirements analysis models. In: Proc. of the 1st Int. Workshop on Feature-Oriented Software Development, FOSD 2009, pp. 117–123. ACM (2009)
18. Kim, M., Park, S., Sugumaran, V., Yang, H.: Managing requirements conflicts in software product lines: A goal and scenario based approach. Data Knowl. Eng. 61, 417–432 (2007)
19. Hausmann, J.H., Heckel, R., Taentzer, G.: Detection of conflicting functional requirements in a use case-driven approach: a static analysis technique based on graph transformation. In: Proc. of the 24th Int. Conf. on Software Engineering, ICSE 2002, pp. 105–115. ACM (2002)
20. Classen, A., Heymans, P., Schobbens, P.-Y.: What's in a *feature*: A requirements engineering perspective. In: Fiadeiro, J.L., Inverardi, P. (eds.) FASE 2008. LNCS, vol. 4961, pp. 16–30. Springer, Heidelberg (2008)

Analyzing the Effect of the Collaborative Interactions on Performance of Requirements Validation

Nelly Condori-Fernández[1], Sergio España[1], Klaas Sikkel[2], Maya Daneva[2], and Arturo González[1]

[1] Universitat Politècnica de València
Camino de Vera 46022, Valencia, Spain
`{nelly,sergio.espana,agdelrio}@dsic.upv.es`
[2] University of Twente
Drienerlolaan 5,
7522 NB Enschede, The Netherlands
`{m.daneva,k.sikkel}@utwente.nl`

Abstract. [Context] Requirements validation is critical in the pursuit of quality software. It usually demands the collaboration of multiple stakeholders with different perspectives. [Question] Our community has reported scarce experimental studies on the role of collaborative interaction in requirements validation. The goal of this study is to explore the effect of collaborative interactions on the performance of requirements validation. [Principal ideas] We performed a quasi-experiment involving 118 bachelor students to act analysts, and 40 volunteering students from the Social Sciences department to act clients. The requirements were specified using UML activity diagrams. The overall performance is measured in terms of efficiency (missing requirements correctly identified in a time interval), and effectiveness (degree to which the validation yielded the correct result). Moreover, we measured also subjects' satisfaction on collaboration (questionnaire). [Contribution] We found that the teams composed exclusively of analysts showed better efficiency and effectiveness than mixed teams (client and analysts). However, for certain types of requirements, the mixed teams' efficiency was superior. Also, the degree of satisfaction was higher among the clients than among the analysts. We end up with identifying future research topics.

Keywords: activity diagrams, reviews-based validation, validation effectiveness, validation efficiency, requirements process performance, collaboration satisfaction.

1   Introduction

Requirements validation is a key activity in requirements engineering (RE); it aims to ensure that specifications accurately express the stakeholders' needs [1]. Through the requirements validation process, errors in a software requirements specification (SRS) are identified and corrected before it is used in further system development. Usually, a

C. Salinesi and I. van de Weerd (Eds.): REFSQ 2014, LNCS 8396, pp. 216–231, 2014.
© Springer International Publishing Switzerland 2014

requirements validation process demands the collaboration of multiple stakeholders with various needs and perspectives. In environments where stakeholders can freely discuss, share their opinions and resolve conflicts among them, it is often particularly challenging to facilitate the validation of the requirements in an efficient and effective manner.

Evaluation of collaboration interactions in software and non-software projects has been the subject of research in a number of contexts, be it virtual [8], [9], [11] or face-to-face [10], [11]. To evaluate the effectiveness of collaborative interactions, both quantitative and qualitative reasoning approaches have been proposed.

In software engineering, various publications analyze the effect of different human factors, such as personality or communication skills, in pair programming [2], [7], [10]. While these sources have been useful in planning our research, especially in developing awareness of the potential threats experienced by other authors in studies on collaboration and communication, we found few experimental studies focused on requirements validation in collaborative contexts [15, 16, 17]. Also, whatever work has been done, it is conducted from the requirements analysts' perspective. E.g. Gemino [15] carried out an experiment to compare the effect of animation and narration techniques on requirements validation. Furthermore, He et al. [17] report results of a post-task survey on the application of an inspection technique during requirements validation. Both studies were conducted only from the analyst's perspective. We note however that RE textbooks (e.g. [12]) treat requirements validation as a client-focused activity. It is therefore surprising that we as a community lack any in-depth understanding of how collaboration between clients and analysts possibly affects important outcomes of the requirements validation process. This gap of knowledge motivated us to initiate an empirical study in order to collect and analyse evidence to systematically address the gap.

The goal of this paper is to provide better understanding of how collaborative interactions affect the performance of requirements validation. We achieve this by conducting an exploratory experiment that was set up in three different scenarios: i) individual review from a client viewpoint; ii) requirements validation from an analyst viewpoint, working in pairs; and iii) requirements validation from combined client and analyst viewpoints.

The following sections provide a detailed account of our study. Section 2 provides a background on reviews-based requirements validation and positions our exploration within a requirements validation process that relies on reviews. Section 3 describes our experiment plan and Section 4 reports our results. Section 5 discusses the validity threats and Section 6 concludes the paper.

2   Reviews-Based Requirements Validation

There is a wide range of requirements validation techniques [12], [23]. This section briefly describes reviews-based validation. We opted for this class of techniques because it has been widely applied in the software industry [5], [20]. A requirements review process is usually performed by a number of people from different backgrounds, meeting together to detect conflicts, omissions, inconsistencies and errors in specifications.

The steps of the process are the following: 1) Planning of review in terms of participants. 2) Distributing documents to the review team members. 3) Individuals read the relevant documents searching for inconsistencies, conflicts, omissions and other problems before the review meeting (pre-review). 4) Individual comments and problems are discussed; a set of actions to address the problems is agreed upon. 5) Follow-up actions to check if the agreed actions have been performed. 6) Final document is revised and the team members either accept it or plan further review iterations.

As stated in [5], a significant disadvantage of this process is its resource-intensiveness as review meetings span across several sessions and this in turn hinders the involvement of people from different departments at the same time. Hence, resource availability may easily become an issue.

In this empirical study, we, the experimenters, carried out the first two steps of the requirement review process. Steps 3 and 4 were carried out by the experimental subjects. The subjects had to check the completeness of a long SRS, represented by UML activity diagrams. In contrast to previous empirical studies ([15], [17], [21], [22]), we involve the viewpoint of the client, who had to review the SRS both by himself/herself and in collaboration with a team of analysts.

3   Experiment Planning

The goal of our experiment is to analyze the effect of the collaborative interaction on the performance of the requirements validation; in the context of bachelor students majoring in various IT sub-fields at University of Twente (UT), the Netherlands. We set out to answer three research questions (RQ):

RQ1: When teams are validating SRSs, is their efficiency affected by the type of collaborative interaction?

RQ2: Is the validation effectiveness affected by the type of collaborative interaction? We are also interested in assessing whether the type of requirements that are identified as missing in the SRS has an effect on validation effectiveness.

RQ3: Is the efficiency of teams in validating requirements affected by the degree of collaboration satisfaction?

3.1   Variables and Hypotheses

In our attempt to investigate how the collaboration among stakeholders with different background can affect in the performance of requirements validation, we considered the following independent variables:

- The *collaborative interaction type*. Given the lack of prior studies that involve the client viewpoint, we considered two types of collaborative interactions: interaction among participants with a different role (client and analyst), and interaction among participants with the same role (analyst).

- The *type of missing requirement*. Given the exploratory nature of the experiment, we limited the investigation to three types of requirements:
  - Missing *business activities* that are part of the company's work practice.
  - Missing *constraints* that apply to the business activities.
  - Missing *business forms* that are filled in/created/used by company's staff.

Fig. 1 overviews the variables of the experiment and their hypothesised relationships.

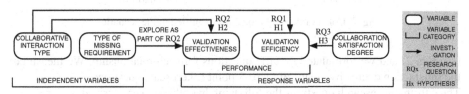

Fig. 1. Overview of the relationships among variables

We identified the following response variables (a.k.a. dependent variables):

Validation efficiency indicates how well a team used time to correctly identify missing requirements. In this study, 12 requirements were removed from the original specification (For more detail, see the description of the experimental object in sub-section 3.2). Also, it is important to note that apart from correctly-identified missing requirements, we considered two types of errors that might be committed by the teams: 1) A functional fragmentation error, which means a functional requirement is correctly identified, yet incompletely specified and therefore appears in the form of two or more fragments (encapsulations). 2) A functional aggregation error, when two or more missing functional requirements were aggregated to a single 'higher-level functional' requirement.

Regarding the validation time, as reviews-based requirements validation usually requires several sessions to be completed, in order to increase control, we limited the time to a single 2-hour session for all teams that participated in the experiment.

Validation effectiveness is the degree to which the teams execute the validation task correctly. The test subjects were given a SRS from which the researchers had removed a set of requirements. Effectiveness is measured as the number of missing requirements correctly identified, divided by the total number of missing requirements.

Collaboration satisfaction degree. A questionnaire was designed for each of the two roles (i.e. client and analyst) that participate in the different interaction scenarios (de-scribed in Sect. 3.4). We consider two key points for the formulation of the questions [4]: (i) the members' satisfaction is the basis of the team satisfaction; (ii) the degree of satisfaction derives from the working relationship. Based on these points, we identified the different collaboration relationships in the Scenarios II and III

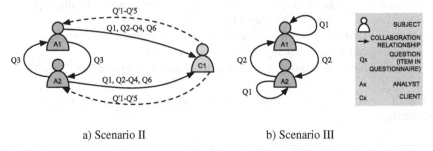

a) Scenario II   b) Scenario III

Fig. 2. Collaboration relationships identified in the scenarios

(see Fig. 2) and we formulated specific questions for each relationship. We measured the satisfaction degree by means of these 5-point Likert scale questions[1].

Thus, from our research questions the following hypotheses were derived.

- **$H1_0$:** The efficiency of teams in validating requirements is the same independently of the collaborative interaction type.
- **$H2_0$:** The requirements validation effectiveness is the same independently of the collaborative interaction type.
- **$H3_0$:** The efficiency of validating requirements is the same independently of the degree of collaboration satisfaction.

3.2   Experimental Context

Experimental Subjects. As we wanted to account for two different viewpoints in requirements validation, we included two different profiles of subjects. 1) Client role: 40 students from the UT Social Sciences Department, without any background in modeling languages, volunteered to be trained in the business domain. Participants were invited by sending them a flyer offering 50€ for participation. 2) Analyst role: 118 first-year bachelor students enrolled in the Information Systems (IS) course at UT were selected by convenience sampling and trained to play the analyst role. The students were majoring in IT sub-fields such as Computer Science, Business Information Technology, and Technical Management Science. The IS course objective is to train the students in UML-based IS requirements specification and is taught by the 3rd author of this paper.

A demographic questionnaire revealed that the group of analysts was quite homogeneous. 93% of the students had not participated in any previous course on dynamic- or static-oriented modelling techniques (also, see their perceived knowledge in Fig. 3, left). Their level of English was good; only 9% of them had obtained a grade 5 or lower out 10 points in English language (see Fig. 3, right).

---

[1] The question numbers refer to the satisfaction questionnaires available at
http://users.dsic.upv.es/~nelly/valid.htm

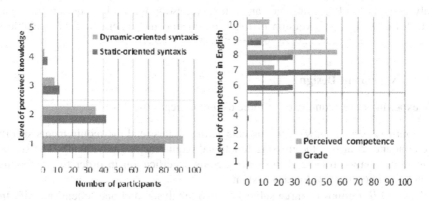

Fig. 3. Demographic results of the participants playing the analyst role

Experimental Objects. The SRS describes the information system needed by a Photography Agency that manages illustrated reports provided by photographers and distributes them to publishing houses. The SRS was created by the 2nd author using UML activity diagrams. We chose this type of diagrams because it is commonly used in industry to interact with clients during review and requirements validation [13]. The other authors checked the appropriateness of the SRS for the experiment. The SRS is 49 pages long. We decided to use the whole specification and remove 12 requirements – the missing requirements that the subjects had to identify. Table 1 (in Sect. 4.1) classifies the requirements in three types: missing business activities, missing constraints, and missing business forms. The explanation of each missing requirement is omitted for the sake of brevity and can be found at http://users.dsic.upv.es/~nelly/valid.htm

3.3   Experimental Instruments

Demographic questionnaires. The demographic questionnaire the students acting analysts aims at assessing the subjects' English language proficiency and their background in RE modelling. The latter is operationalized by means of 7-point Likert-scale questions about their knowledge and experience with 8 IS modelling techniques that deal with static (e.g. Class Diagram) and dynamic aspects (e.g. Activity Diagram) of the system. The results are shown in Fig. 3. The questionnaire distributed to the clients also corroborated that their proficiency in English was very good.

- *Satisfaction questionnaire.* It uses 5-point Likert-scales to elicit the personal satisfaction of both the client and the analysts with their interaction during the collaborative validation; and the interaction between analysts when using a textual description.
- *Post-task survey.* It gathers information about the difficulties encountered during validation with respect to the reviewed SRS.

Moreover, a validation form was implemented to get details on the missing requirements that the subjects identified. For each missing requirement identified, the analysts ought to offer a rationale and a textual description of the requirement identified. A link to the web version of the experimental instruments and is available at http://users.dsic.upv.es/~nelly/valid.htm

3.4   Experiment Design

The experiment was conducted in three different scenarios.

- *Scenario I.* (Pre-review). The subjects acting clients read the requirements specification and identified the missing functional requirements individually. The subject with the analyst role read the requirements specification in order to get familiar with the Photography Agency system.
- *Scenario II.* Groups of three subjects – two 'analysts' and one 'client' identify the missing functional requirements cooperatively.
- *Scenario III.* Pairs of subjects with the analyst role identify missing functional requirements, by using an additional textual description of Photography Agency.

Considering the two types of collaborative interaction (interaction among participants with and without different role), our experiment adopted a between-subjects design (scenarios II and III). Scenario I was also considered as part of the study, because according to the review-based requirements validation process an individual review (Pre-review) is required.

3.5   Experimental Procedure

Training Process. The subjects acting clients received 6 hours of training in the business domain (the Photography Agency). For this, we used the demonstration/practice method [3]. First, slides about the Photography Agency were used to present the Agency and its main activities. Then, in order for the subject to acquire some practice in the agency's domain, they were given three exercises to solve. After a break of 15 min, a test (a questionnaire with 12 closed questions) about the problem domain was completed by the students with the purpose of verifying their acquired knowledge. Using the grade points average ([0-1]), we found that subjects had more difficulty to correctly answer Question 7: *"Who establishes the yearly rates of the agency?"* (mean = 0.26; std dev = 0.44); this question expects the subject to identify the organizational role in charge of a given business activity. The rest of the questions had an acceptable average, which varied between 0,68 and 0,95.

The subjects acting analysts were trained on the UML activity diagrams and requirements validation as a regular part of the course. It took four two-hour sessions spread over multiple days, which consisted of lectures, exercises with multiple choice questions, and supervised exercises in the computer lab. We assessed their competence level (high:[10, 7[; medium:[7, 5[; low:[5,0])[2] in UML activity diagraming and requirements validation. We found that 70 % of the 118 subjects demonstrated a

---

[2] Reverse square brackets are used in (semi-)open intervals. For instance [10, 7[means "any real number with a value ranging from 10 to 7, including the value 10 but excluding the value 7".

medium level to assume their role as analyst. The subjects with a low competence level in modeling and validating (6.5% and 8.6%, respectively) were not considered.

Execution. Afterwards, following a guideline that specified what to do and which forms to use, the subjects, once assigned to one of the three scenarios, proceeded to identify the missing requirements applying the reviews-based requirements validation technique. The pre-review (Scenario I) was carried out individually by the clients (to identify missing requirements) and the analyst (to get familiar with the problem domain). Time expected was about 1 hour. Two days after this session, each client discussed with a team of two analysts his/her individual comments and problems that he/she had during the requirements pre-review (Scenario II). Besides, this requirements review was also carried out by 22 pairs of analysts at the same time, but in a different building of the university (Scenario III). For both scenarios (II and III) the reviews took 2 hours. Subsequently, a questionnaire was distributed with the purpose of eliciting the personal satisfaction of the collaborative validation process.

4   Analysis and Interpretation of Results

Once data collection was over, two evaluators (the first two authors) reviewed the validation forms completed by all the teams. From this review, three possible values were considered for our list of missing requirements: i) identified correctly, ii) identified with error, iii) not identified.

4.1   Analyzing the Effect of Type of Interaction on Efficiency

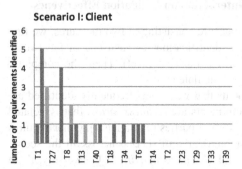

Fig. 4. Missing requirements identified by client

To calculate the efficiency of the requirements validation, first the size of the output of the validation process is calculated, by analyzing the data collected in the evaluation forms. The requirements identified but described with any type of error were grouped and counted separately.

As Fig. 4 shows, during the pre-review, a maximum of 5 out of 12 missing requirements were identified by one of the 'clients'. Most 'clients' found at least 1 missing requirement.

26 out of 40 'clients' were not able to identify any missing requirement (the majority of them invented new requirements). However, when they interacted with the team of analysts (Scenario II), this number was reduced to 17 subjects, meaning an improvement of 22% was observed (see Fig. 5, left). We found that teams of analysts that carried out the validation task without the client support (Scenario III) showed a better efficiency than the teams of analysts supported by a client (see Fig. 5, right).

We applied the Mann-Whitney U test to verify our first hypothesis (H1$_0$), by using the data in Scenario II and III, considering only the requirements correctly identified by the teams. We found that the two groups differed significantly from each other with U(61) = 147.5; Z=-4.536; p = .000. This suggests that the interaction strictly among analysts, using an additional textual description of Photography Agency, had a beneficial effect on efficiency of requirements validation.

Analyzing the post-task survey, we found that the pre-review of the specifications based on activity diagrams was very difficult for the clients, thus the communication does not seem to help when the clients only know their business and the analysts only know the modeling language. Communication and interaction difficulties among 'clients' and 'analysts' ' could have affected in the validation efficiency.

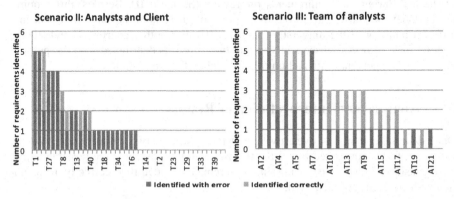

Fig. 5. Number of missing requirements identified in scenarios II and III

4.2   Analyzing the Effect of Type of Interaction on Validation Effectiveness

As validation effectiveness is an indirect measure consisting of two measures, we first discuss the results related to frequency of identification for each one of the twelve expected missing requirements to be identified (success level). Then, the completeness rate by type of missing requirements is calculated.

According to the Table 1, the requirements that were most frequently identified are R4 (36 hits) and R12 (28 hits). Both requirements are *business forms*; that is, related to documents that the company sends to external parties (e.g. a letter). Other requirements were also identified with an acceptable degree of success across all the scenarios, such as R2 and R3 (*constraints*), or R1 (*business activities*). Conversely, there were requirements that were difficult to identify, as the results show. First, for R6, R11, although some teams of analysts in Scenario III (A) were able to completely identify them, the participants of Scenario II (C+A) were completely unable to identify this type of requirements. Similar results were obtained for the second type of requirements, where R3 and R5 could not be correctly identified by any team. However, for requirements R8 and R10 (*business forms*), we observed that analysts of the third scenario score less than analyst from the second scenario (A+C). What makes them different? Both requirements involve processes that do not change any data in the

Table 1. Success level (total of hits) for each one of the twelve missing requirements (MR)

Type	MR	Scenario	Identified w. error	Correctly identified	Total
Business activities	R1	A+C	6	1	7
		A	7	1	8
	R6	A+C	2		2
		A		4	4
	R11	A+C	1		1
		A	2	4	6
Constraints	R2	A+C	6		6
		A	7	1	8
	R3	A+C	6		6
		A	7		7
	R5	A+C	1		1
		A	2		2
Business forms	R4	A+C	11	2	13
		A	5	10	15
	R7	A+C	5	1	6
		A	7	3	10
	R8	A+C	1		1
		A			0
	R9	A+C			0
		A	3	2	5
	R10	A+C	1	1	2
		A			0
	R12	A+C	8	2	10
		A	10	3	13

system. It has to be remarked, however, the scores for teams of this scenario (A+C) are low, so that doesn't say much.

For requirement R9, we observed that no analysts with the client support (A+C) could ever find it, while analysts without clients did score fairly well. R9 is a business requirement related to the acquisition process, but it involves no system interaction. So, the analysts from the second scenario (A+C), who looked primarily at the diagrams, had to rely on the clients (who all missed it) and would not spot this from the diagrams. The analysts' teams without clients did look into the requirements document, saw that R9 was defined as part of the process, and identified it as missing in the specification.

Now, by calculating the completeness rate by type of missing requirements, we found that the second group of requirement (missing constraints) were the less scored by the teams from both scenarios (Scenario II and Scenario III). Applying the Mann-Whitney U test, we corroborated that the collaborative interaction type had a clear effect on validation effectiveness ($H2_0$), but only for the missing requirements of the type *business activities* and *business forms* (see Table 2).

The interaction only among analysts with the support of a textual description had some beneficial effect on the validation effectiveness. This result indicates that requirements validation done by comparing documents is more effective than validation by means of meetings with clients.

Table 2. Mann-Whitney U statistics for completeness rate by type of missing requirements

	Business activities	Constraints	Business forms
Mann-Whitney U	306.500	400.500	180.000
Wilcoxon W	1167.500	1261.500	1041.000
Z	-2.962	-1.724	-4.110
Asymp. Sig. (2-tailed)	.003	.085	.000

A possible reason for this could be that documents comparison can be done systematically by checking if each textual statement in the description is represented in the requirements specification. On the contrary, there is no systematic way of recalling and checking each and every piece of domain knowledge in the mind of the client. Moreover, we consider that the way in which requirements were documented, by using an activity diagramming technique, played an important role in ensuring that analysts-only teams could more easily read and validate them than analyst teams with the participation of clients.

4.3   Analyzing the Effect of Collaboration Satisfaction on Efficiency

As collaboration is fundamentally a social activity relying on interaction between two or more individuals, it is inevitable that some degree of task-related effort remains at the individual level. Although we did not measure the individual performance, we evaluated the personal degree of satisfaction of the respective members in each team. To do this, we analyzed the data collected from the questionnaires that were applied in the Scenarios II and III. First we averaged the answers to the items of the questionnaire to obtain a representative value of the (client's or analyst's) satisfaction of collaborative requirements validation. Then, a 3-points ordinal scale (not at all satisfied, somewhat satisfied, and satisfied) was used in order to interpret better the results obtained (see Fig. 6). The low significance values obtained ($p < 0.05$) throughthe chi-square test suggests that the average rate of the subjects does differ in terms of satisfaction degree. In Fig. 6, (left) we observe that 80% of the clients were satisfied with the analysts' performance. Clients considered the interaction with analysts to be very helpful in identifying missing requirements. However, analyzing the effect of their personal satisfaction with the efficiency of requirements validation ($H3_0$), we observe (Fig. 6, right) that the effect is not significant. A possible explanation is that the clients were unaware of the correctness of the missing requirements identified and their satisfaction did not affect the efficiency in the requirements validation.

Regarding the analysts of Scenario II, Fig. 7 (left) shows the results to questions related to degree of satisfaction about (i) the information provided by the clients to facilitate the understanding of the problem domain (60% not at all satisfied) or the identification of missing requirements (60% not at all satisfied) and (ii) working with their partner (83% satisfied).

On the other hand, when clients were asked about the individual-proactive participation of the analysts, we found that 32% of the clients indicated that only one of the two analysts was proactive. For the purpose of verifying the consistency of the answers given by clients and analysts of scenario II, we carried out a correlation analysis.

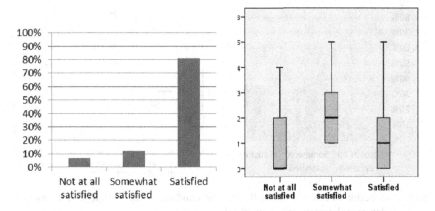

Fig. 6. Distribution of effect of the collaboration satisfaction degree (left) and its effect (right) on the efficiency of clients in Scenario II

Due to lack of space, we show only the box plot for the degree of satisfaction on the client's feedback to understand the problem domain (Fig. 7, right).

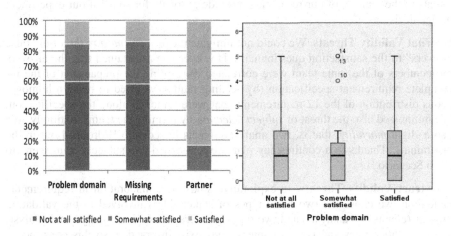

Fig. 7. Distribution of effect of the collaboration satisfaction degree (left) and its effect (right) on the performance of analysts in Scenario II

Regarding the effect of the degree of collaboration satisfaction on the analysts' efficiency in Scenario III ($H3_0$) (Fig. 8, right), we observed that the analysts that were 'somewhat satisfied' showed a greater efficiency than those who were 'satisfied'. However, only 35% of these analysts were satisfied with their partners (Fig. 8, left).

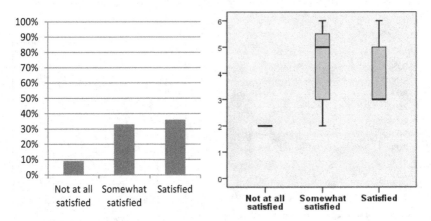

Fig. 8. Distribution of effect of the collaboration satisfaction degree (left) and its effect (right) on the efficiency of the analysts in scenario III

5   Threats and Lines for Further Empirical Research

In this experiment, we have balanced exploration – which offers the chance of gathering new knowledge, and control – which minimizes risks. Below, we discuss the threats to the validity of our results and provide rationale for some of our experiment design decisions.

Internal Validity Threats. We could not mitigate the *instrumentation threat* of "false answers" to the satisfaction questionnaire. However, we ascertained that the answers by members of the same team were correlated. Regarding the preparation of the incomplete requirement specification (by seeding faults), we tried to make a homogeneous distribution of the 12 requirements that were removed along the specification. We minimized also the threat of *subject selection* by forming the teams randomly. We had a slight *mortality*; that is, two analyst subjects in scenario II dropped out in the last minute. Thanks to a contingency plan we reassigned two subjects from scenario III to Scenario II.

Construct Validity Threats. In explorative study on collaboration in requirements validation, we chose the two basic types of stakeholders involved in the validation process (clients and analysts) and two types of interactions (client-analyst and analyst-analyst). Other roles and types of interactions exist in practice, so this construct is under-represented. However, we opted for increasing complexity gradually (see considerations below). The same applies to the types of requirements. We deliberately did not use a complex SRS, to keep the experiment under control, both in terms of time to complete the training and the experimental task. To minimize the threat of an *inadequate preoperational explication of constructs*, the collaboration satisfaction degree was operationalized according to two key issues proposed by Jun et al [4].

External Validity Threats. We think that our sample of subjects was quite representative for real clients because we involved students with no modeling competence to act as clients. In order to guarantee enough knowledge about the problem domain, a training session was conducted with the 40 participants. As for subjects acting analysts, they received intensive training on requirements engineering and UML modeling as part of their education, prior to the experimental task. Additionally, we did tests to assess the competence of both types of subjects: i) clients: domain knowledge test; ii) analysts: UML and validation competence tests.

The use of students as surrogates for real practitioners is common practice ([14], [6]) and, given the exploratory nature of the experiment, we preferred having a large number of subjects (the chances of interesting effects to appear is increased) than using fewer practitioners. Also, the length of the Photography Agency SRS (537 IFPUG functions points) intended to be manageable for experimentation but realistic enough to include some complexity.

Considerations for Further Research. The exploratory experiment provides preliminary results, on top of which further experiments can be designed. To deepen into the mechanisms of the validation process, it may be interesting to consider additional types of stakeholders, not only based on their roles but also in their characteristics.

Similarly, other types of requirements can be included in the SRS. Our experience while trying to classify requirements and compare the way students treated the missing requirements indicates that a requirements taxonomy is needed. We found that in confronting a process-aware information system, it is not enough to distinguish between functional and non-functional requirements. As a starting point, we opted for classifying missing requirements into activities, constraints and business forms. Adopting an existing requirements taxonomy or classification (e.g. [22]) or proposing a suitable one is a recommended line for future research. We expect this to help formulate more precise hypotheses concerning the performance of subjects while validating SRSs.

An advanced experiment would require a detailed requirements classification that has proved to be valuable (even if just in research settings) and a domain case that includes both a greater variety of types of requirements and more requirements of each type. This way, the researchers can remove several requirements of each type and test whether there exist differences in their identification during validation, and whether the collaborative interaction has a significant effect. We expect such results to shed light on the mechanisms of the validation process.

Our results also show that comparing a textual description of the domain with the more technical SRS (activity diagrams) is more productive and effective than validating requirements by reviewing the with clients. However, a textual description is itself an SRS. In an industrial setting, a stakeholder needs to create this document. Also, it is subjected to the same risks as the technical SRS; namely, incompleteness and invalidity. If a textual description is to be used for this purpose, it needs to be validated first. What is the difference in terms of performance between validating a textual specification and a diagram-based one? how does the language of the specification impact the collaborative interaction? To answer these questions, further empirical research needs to be done to better understand the practical use of activity diagrams (and other notations, e.g. BPMN) in validating requirements with different stakeholders. It is also challenging to investigate how the interaction between stakeholders (clients and analysts) actually takes place during the interviews. For instance, time devoted to each task (e.g. phatic communication, answers, responses), disruptions (e.g. misunderstandings and time devoted to solve them), attitudes (e.g. proactivity).

This requires audio recording and transcribing the most relevant information. It would allow comparing the actual interaction with the perception of the subjects.

Last but not least, once more precise hypotheses have been defined for improved experiments, the use of real practitioners can be considered.

6   Conclusions and Future Work

This paper has explored the collaborative interaction effect during requirements validation and has revealed certain relationships that deserve future investigation. We found that clients validating a requirements specification on their own are limited by their knowledge of the technical languages; their performance increases when they work collaboratively with a team of analysts. However, as per our results, the most successful scenario has been a team of analysts checking the specification against a textual description of the domain. Since this scenario entails certain difficulties and risks when applied in industrial settings (e.g. the textual description is a specification itself and may be incomplete or unavailable as one monolithic document but exist in the form of scattered interview proceedings) it is necessary to investigate deeper the collaborative interaction of clients working hand by hand with analysts.

We also found that clients were more satisfied with the collaboration during requirements validation, than analysts, which can be due to the fact that analysts feel more responsible towards to outcome of the interview since they often lead it. Other interesting outcomes have appeared, but they need to be contrasted with an observation of the behavior of subjects during the interview; this is planned as future work.

We are aware of some risks due to removing certain requirements from the full SRS, e.g. too much emphasis on one type of requirements can cause problems of allocating equal time/schedule and resources to other requirements types. We, therefore, plan to propose and evaluate a requirements taxonomy that applies to business information systems in general and aids in requirements validation. On the other hand, as the selected validation technique could have had also an effect on response variables (e.g. satisfaction), we seek to replicate the experiment by including others interesting review-based validation techniques, such as the checklist-based reading technique.

Acknowledgments. We would like to thank the anonymous reviewers for their valuable comments, and the participants of this study for their time and contribution. This work has been supported partially by the EU Marie Curie Fellowship Grant 50911302 PIEF-2010, the Spanish project PROS-Req TIN2010-19130-C02-02, the Generalitat Valenciana project ORCA (PROMETEO/2009/015) and the European FP7 Project CaaS 611351.

References

1. Cheng, B., Atlee, J.M.: Research Directions in Requirements Engineering. In: Future of Software Engineering (FOSE), ICSE 2007, pp. 285–303. IEEE CS Press (2007)
2. Panagiotis, S., Ioannis, S., Lefteris, A., Ignatios, D.: An experimental investigation of personality types impact on pair effectiveness in pair programming. Empirical Softw. Eng. 14(2), 187–226 (2009)

3. DOE Handbook, Alternative Systematic Approaches to Training, 1074-95 (January 1995)
4. Jun, L., Ya-Feng, L.: A Method of Evaluating Collaboration Satisfaction Degree of NPD Team. In: Proc. CSCWD 2010, pp. 156–160 (2010)
5. Saqib, B., Sheraz, A.: Requirements Validation Techniques practiced in industry: Studies of six companies, Blekinge Institute of Technology, Sweden. Master thesis, Software Engineering (Octotber 2008)
6. Condori-Fernandez, N., Daneva, N., Sikkel, K., Herrmann, A.: Practical relevance of experiments in comprehensibility of requirements specifications. In: EMPIRE 2011 Collocated at the RE Conference, Trento-Italy, Italy, pp. 21–28 (August 2011)
7. Walle, T., Hannay, J.E.: Personality and the Nature of Collaboration in Pair Programming. In: Proc. ESEM 2009, pp. 203–213 (2009)
8. Dwyer, P.: An Approach to Quantitatively Measuring Collaborative Performance in Online Conversations. Computers in Human Behavior 27, 1021–1032 (2011)
9. Lin, C.-P., Wang, Y.-J., Tsai, Y.-H., Hsu, Y.-F.: Perceived Job Effectiveness in Cooperation: A Survey of Virtual Teams within Business Organization. Computers in Human Behavior 26 (2010)
10. Choi, K.S., Deek, F., Im, I.: Pair Dynamics in Tem Collaboration. Computers in Human Behavior 25, 833–852 (2009)
11. Patel, H., Pettit, M., Wilson, J.: Factors of Collaborative Working: a Framework for a Collaboration Model. Applied Ergonomics 43, 1–26 (2012)
12. Lauesen, S.: Software Requirements: Styles and Techniques. Addison-Wesley (2002)
13. Dobing, B., Parsons, J.: How UML is Used. Commun. ACM 49(5), 109–113 (2006)
14. Runeson, P.: Using Students as Experiment Subjects - an Analysis on Graduate and Freshmen Student Data. In: 7th Int. Conf on EASE, Staffordshire, UK, pp. 95–102 (2002)
15. Gemino, A.: Empirical comparisons of animation and narration in requirements validation. Requir. Eng. 9(3), 153–168 (2004)
16. Condori-Fernandez, N., Daneva, M., Sikkel, K., Wieringa, R.J., Dieste, O., Pastor, O.: A Systematic Mapping Study on Empirical Evaluation of Software Requirements Specifications Techniques. In: ESEM 2009, pp. 503–505. CS Press (2009)
17. He, L., Carver, J.C., Rayford, B.: Using Inspections to Teach Requirements Validation. CrossTalk: The Journal of Defense Software Engineering 21(1) (2008)
18. Basili, V.R.: The Empirical Investigation of Perspective-Based Reading. J. of Empirical Softw. Eng. 1(2), 133–164 (1996)
19. Leite, J.C.S.P., Freeman, P.A.: Requirements Validation through Viewpoint Resolution. IEEE Transactions on Software Engineering 17, 1253–1269 (1991)
20. Raja, U.A.: Empirical Studies of Requirements Validation Techniques. In: 2nd International Conference on Computer, Control and Communication, vol. 1(9), pp. 17–18 (2009)
21. Albayrak, O.: An Experiment to Observe the Impact of UML Diagrams on the Effectiveness of Software Requirements Inspections. In: ESEM 2009, pp. 506–510 (2009)
22. Walia, G., Carver, J.: Using Error Abstraction and Classification to Improve Requirements Quality: Conclusions from a Family of Four Empirical Studies. J. of Empirical Softw. Eng. 18(4), 625–658 (2013)
23. Aurum, A., Petersson, H., Wohlin, C.: State-of-the-art: Software Inspections after 25 Years. Journal of Software Testing Verification and Reliability 12(3), 133–154 (2002)

Argumentation-Based Discussion
for User Forum: A Research Preview

Itzel Morales-Ramirez[1,2] and Anna Perini[1]

[1] Software Engineering Research Unit, Fondazione Bruno Kessler, Via Sommarive 18,
38123 Trento-Povo, Italy
{imramirez,perini}@fbk.eu
[2] International Doctoral School ICT- University of Trento, Italy

Abstract. [**Context and motivation**] User forums provide a virtual
space in which participants post comments, upon their experience in
using a software, that analysts can eventually redirect to an issue tracking system. Before users post any comment, they should search for a
request that is the closest to the one they are about to submit. In
doing this, they can face with large, unstructured discussions. [**Ques-
tion/problem**] Current user forum discussions are usually developed
as sequential comments that hide an explicit recognition of the attitude
of the participants (i.e. "in favour" or "against") wrt. the initial request.
This poses difficulties to the analysts who should identify worth requests
to be further analysed. [**Principal ideas/results**] The key idea in our
approach is to exploit AI argumentation. The resulting argumentation-
based discussion will allow participants to get an overview of the trend of
such a discussion, and support analysts to identify important requests.
[**Contribution**] In this research preview, we describe how we represent
the forum's discussion management problem in terms of AI argumentation concepts, and a sketched algorithm for supporting the forum's
participants tasks. A research plan for implementing and evaluating the
proposed argumentation-based discussion is also described.

Keywords: Requirements engineering, User forum, Argumentation
framework.

1   Introduction

The role of social media to enable collaboration in software projects has been discussed in recent work [1–6], which point out potential benefits and challenges.
An example of a collaborative platform is, for instance, an online user forum
that provides a virtual space in which participants exchange views on issues
about a software application on the basis of their experience in using it. Forums
are widely exploited by open source software projects where users of such applications post comments and other participants called "volunteer" developers
act as analysts who redirect relevant requests to an issue tracking system (e.g.
Bugzilla). In order to prevent the creation of complex, entangled discussions,
the participants are requested to follow some rules, e.g. *"Do NOT submit a*

C. Salinesi and I. van de Weerd (Eds.): REFSQ 2014, LNCS 8396, pp. 232–238, 2014.
© Springer International Publishing Switzerland 2014

problem report without searching the existing ones first to ensure that the issue you are reporting has not already been addressed", this rule is specified in the issue tracking system of Apache OpenOffice (AOOo) [7]. This implies that users should search for the closest request to the one they are about to submit, by simply making a text searching. Once, they find the request they might read the whole sequence of comments and provide theirs upon the read, but they could get lost if the discussion is large, as reported also in [8]. Only a careful reading of the content of each comment may reveal to which previous comment it refers to, thus inferring participants' attitude (i.e. "in favour" or "against") towards the comment that initiated the discussion. Usually an overview of participants' attitude in the discussion is missing, and this challenges also the task of analysts when evaluating what is worthy to be further analysed, as for instance to identify new candidate requirements.

The goal of our research is to define methods and techniques to support users and analysts of user forums when performing the above mentioned tasks. We structure it along the following research questions:

RQ1. How can the attitude of the participants in user forums be made explicit and recorded within the structure of a discussion?

RQ2. How can a structured discussion support decisions on what comments should be further analyzed?

To answer these questions, we propose to represent an online discussion as a structured set of arguments according to the AI argumentation [9] that describes a theory of logical inference and techniques for deriving conclusions from arguments. Based on this, participants would be able to provide new comments wrt. existing ones in the ongoing discussion, in a straightforward way. Moreover, the overall attitude towards the initial comment will be automatically inferred. This will allow analysts to recognize the relevant requests, and we believe that also the quality of comments will improve.

In this paper we give a preview of our research by stating the forum's discussion management problems in terms of the AI argumentation in Section 2. The related work is mentioned in Section 3. A research plan for implementing and evaluating the proposed approach along with some concluding remarks are presented in Section 4.

2   Argumentation-Based Discussion Forum

We propose an extension to the Dung's abstract argumentation framework [9] to enable a structured discussion in user forums. According to [9] an *abstract argumentation framework* (AF) is a pair $\langle \mathcal{A}, Def \rangle$. $\mathcal{A}$ is a set of arguments and $Def \subseteq \mathcal{A} \times \mathcal{A}$ is a binary relation of *defeat* between arguments. *Defeat* means that an argument y_i *attacks* an argument y_j, therefore $(y_i, y_j) \in Def$. The concepts *conflict-free* and *defence* are defined as follows.

- Let $\mathcal{B} \subseteq \mathcal{A}$.
- A set $\mathcal{B}$ is *conflict-free* iff there exist no y_i, y_j in $\mathcal{B}$ such that y_i defeats y_j.

– A set $\mathcal{B}$ *defends* an argument y_i iff for each argument $y_j \in \mathcal{A}$, if y_j *defeats* y_i, then there exists y_k in $\mathcal{B}$ such that y_k *defeats* y_j.

A full implementation of this framework in terms of a directed graph is given in [10]. We adapt and extend it to represent an *Argumentation-based Discussion Forum* (ADF) as follows. A *comment* is an abstract argument, the *Def* relation is refined into the *support, rejection* and *neutral* relations between pairs of comments[1], and we include the explicit representation of the *participant* with her knowledge confidence (i.e. $know_c$) as a weight associated to her comments. We represent an ADF as a directed acyclic graph (DAG), referred to as $\mathcal{G} = (V, E)$ where:

– $\boldsymbol{V}$ is the set of comments in the discussion, i.e. vertices in $\mathcal{G}$.
– $\boldsymbol{E} = S \cup R \cup N$ is the set of pairs of comments represented as edges in $\mathcal{G}$, where S is the set of support relations, R is the set of rejection relations and N is the set of neutral relations that are defined as follows:
  • $R \subseteq V \times V$ is the set of pairs of comments between which a rejection relation holds, i.e. $Reject(y_i, y_j)$, if y_i rejects (attacks) y_j. This is based on the set *Def* introduced above.
  • $S \subseteq V \times V$ is the set of pairs of comments between which a support relation holds, i.e. $Support(y_i, y_j)$.
  • $N \subseteq V \times V$ is the set of pairs of comments (y_i, y_j), such that y_i adds extra information to y_j.

Currently, we consider that a vertex (comment) contains information such as an identifier (ID), participant's name, description and the $know_c$ parameter. This last is a real number ranging from 0 to 1, which represents participants' perception on their own expertise level. The $know_c$ is asked to the participants using a likert-type scale, e.g. novice=0, initiate=0.25, apprentice=0.50, advanced=0.75, and expert=1, this is adapted from [12] and [13]. This parameter is used for the computation of support and rejection relations between a pair or comments, see Algorithm 1.

To exemplify an ADF let's look at an excerpt of a discussion found in AOOo bugzilla, see Figure 1. As can be observed, the current format of a discussion (top) is sequential and hinders the trend of supporting and rejecting comments wrt. a given comment.

On the other side, the ADF graph (down) makes explicit that comment 3 rejects comment 1, while comment 8 and 11 support the comment 0 and 3, respectively. Comments 0, 3, 8, and 11 define a set of relevant comments for comment 0 (i.e. $RelC_{y_0}$), which is a set of comments where given an initial comment y_0 belonging to the set, there are no comments, included in the set, that reject y_0.

We use DAG search algorithms to define procedures that can help participants and analysts. Example of procedures for participants are: *(i)* finding if a given

---

[1] Analogous works extend *Def* relation with the support relation but not with the neutral one (e.g. [11])

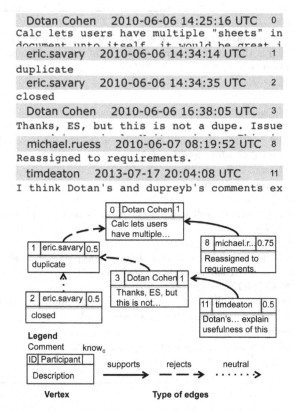

Fig. 1. Excerpt of the discussion #112163 in AOOo bugzilla (top), representation of it as an ADF directed acyclic graph (down)

comment y_0 in the actual discussion is supported or rejected; *(ii)* finding the set of comments that support, reject or are neutral wrt. a selected comment y_0; *(iii)* computing the effect of adding a new comment (either reject or support type) to the actual discussion. To support analysts: *(iv)* finding the most supported request in the discussions that are active in a forum.

To give a flavour of the basic algorithms used, Algorithm 1 sketches how to compute *RelC* for a given ADF. Lines 14 and 16 show how the parameter $know_c$ is used to compute the strength of the support and rejection relations.

To update *RelC* once a discussion is modified, by the addition of a new comment, we can use an incremental search algorithm that considers only the subgraph affected by the change.

3   Related Work

Recent work shows a growing interest within the Requirements Engineering research community towards social media as distributed, collaborative work

---

Algorithm 1. proc_RelC(G, v): pseudocode for computing *RelC* in ADF

Input A DAG G representing an ADF, v is a starting *vertex in $V(G)$*

Output RelC which is the set of relevant comments of v. {//*RelC* is initialized to $\emptyset$}

1: **if** v is a *leaf* **then**
2:    **return** $RelC \leftarrow RelC \cup \{v\}$ {//iif v is *root*}
3: **else**
4:    neutral=0 {//Counts the number of neutral relations}
5:    supportS=0.0 {//Counts the weight $know_c$ of v in the support relation}
6:    rejectionS=0.0 {//Counts the weight $know_c$ of v in the rejection relation}
7:    **for each** edge $e \in G.adjacentEdges(v)$ **do**
8:       $v' \leftarrow G.adjacentVertex(v, e)$
9:       **switch** $v'.outgoingRelation$
10:         **case** NEUTRAL
11:         neutral++ {//Recursive call and addition of neutral comments}
12:         proc_RelC(G, v')
13:         **case** SUPPORT
14:         supportS+=proc_RelC(G, v') + $v'.know_c$/(supportS + rejectionS + neutral){//Recursive call and normalisation of supportS}
15:         **case** REJECTION
16:         rejectionS+=proc_RelC(G, v') + $v'.know_c$/(rejectionS + supportS + neutral){//Recursive call and normalisation of rejectionS}
17:       **end switch**
18:       $RelC \leftarrow RelC \cup \{v'\}$ {//iif $supportS_{v'} > rejectionS_{v'}$}
19:    **end for**
20: **end if**

---

enablers. For instance, the discovery of stakeholder communities by using concept lattices to extract hidden profiles for the set of requirements of a certain project [6], or the StakeRare method described in [2] uses social networks and a collaborative filtering to elicit and prioritise requirements in large projects. Similarly in [14], participants' opinions posted through social networks are analyzed and exploited for requirements prioritisation. In [15] collaborative filtering is used to facilitate online discussions for requirements identification. These three works assume to start with an initial requirements set to be refined through social collaborations, while in our research we see the discussion as the potential source for requirements.

In [4] is presented a software platform, called Requirements Bazaar, that supports gathering and negotiation on user feedback about software applications. Focusing on on-line discussions, the IdeaTracker [8] tool provides a way to support interface design review via discussion, by associating a color-code to comments classified along their affective tone (i.e. negative-red, positive-green, or both-yellow). Both works require users to explicitly express their preference (vote) on the emerging requests, while in our approach we aim at automatically inferring the effects of the developed argumentation on the statement that initiated it.

Concerning the use of argumentation-based approaches in RE, worth mentioning are the work of Jureta et al. [16] that proposes the ACceptability Evaluation Framework (ACE), to support stakeholders when performing requirements validation. This framework was applied in [17] to support validation of law-compliance of software requirements by a team including law experts and software engineers. Analogously in [18] argumentation techniques are proposed to validate requirements and to highlight inconsistencies that may foster the elicitation of missing requirements.

An extension to the Dung's framework [9] is described in [11], this work adds the possibility of assigning a strength to the argument, and use it for inference. We make extensions to Dung's framework to include for instance the participants' knowledge confidence that will be used for the computation of their attitude in the discussion.

4 Concluding Remarks and Research Plan

In this paper we introduced the two research questions that drive our work on argumentation-based discussion for user forum, which rests on an extension of Dung's framework and exploits DAG algorithms to compute the supported and rejected comments, whose participants' knowledge confidence about the topic under discussion is also taken into account. We illustrated on a simple example taken from the Apache OpenOffice bugzilla how participants' attitudes towards the initial statement can be made explicit in a structured discussion ADF. We are implementing the proposed ADF using Neo4j [19] and collecting experimental evidences on the scalability of the ADF management algorithms on artificial dataset containing argumentation with increasing numbers of comments (vertices) and different percentages of support, reject and neutral relations (edges). We plan to use different functions to compute the relevant comments, thus performing a sort of sensitivity analysis. As a longer term objective, we aim at integrating the proposed argumentation-based discussion into an collaborative platform, e.g. [8], thus a further task will be that of selecting an hosting platform and integrating our approach in it. This will allow us to perform an empirical evaluation on the effectiveness of our Argumentation-based Discussion Forum with users and analysts.

References

1. Begel, A., Bosch, J., Storey, M.: Bridging software communities through social networking. IEEE Software 30(1), 26–28 (2013)
2. Lim, S.L., Finkelstein, A.: Stakerare: Using social networks and collaborative filtering for large-scale requirements elicitation. IEEE Trans. Softw. Eng. 38(3), 707–735 (2012)
3. Pagano, D., Maalej, W.: How do open source communities blog? Empirical Software Engineering 18(6), 1090–1124 (2013)

4. Renzel, D., Behrendt, M., Klamma, R., Jarke, M.: Requirements bazaar: Social requirements engineering for community-driven innovation. In: 21st IEEE International Requirements Engineering Conference, RE 2013, pp. 326–327. IEEE (2013)
5. Sutcliffe, A., Sawyer, P.: Requirements elicitation: Towards the unknown unknowns. In: 21st IEEE International Requirements Engineering Conference, RE 2013, pp. 92–104. IEEE (2013)
6. Azmeh, Z., Mirbel, I., Crescenzo, P.: Highlighting stakeholder communities to support requirements decision-making. In: Doerr, J., Opdahl, A.L. (eds.) REFSQ 2013. LNCS, vol. 7830, pp. 190–205. Springer, Heidelberg (2013)
7. Apache: Apache openoffice bugzilla (2010), https://issues.apache.org/ooo/
8. Zilouchian Moghaddam, R., Bailey, B.P., Poon, C.: Ideatracker: An interactive visualization supporting collaboration and consensus building in online interface design discussions. In: Campos, P., Graham, N., Jorge, J., Nunes, N., Palanque, P., Winckler, M. (eds.) INTERACT 2011, Part I. LNCS, vol. 6946, pp. 259–276. Springer, Heidelberg (2011)
9. Dung, P.M.: On the acceptability of arguments and its fundamental role in nonmonotonic reasoning, logic programming and n-person games. Artif. Intell. 77(2), 321–357 (1995)
10. Bex, F., Prakken, H., Reed, C.: A formal analysis of the aif in terms of the aspic framework. In: Proceedings of the 2010 Conference on Computational Models of Argument: Proceedings of COMMA 2010, pp. 99–110. IOS Press, Amsterdam (2010)
11. Leite, J., Martins, J.: Social abstract argumentation. In: Proceedings of the Twenty-Second International Joint Conference on Artificial Intelligence, IJCAI 2011, vol. 3, pp. 2287–2292. AAAI Press (2011)
12. Ericsson, K.A.: The Cambridge handbook of expertise and expert performance. Cambridge University Press (2006)
13. Likert, R.: A technique for the measurement of attitudes. Archives of Psychology (1932)
14. Fitsilis, P., Gerogiannis, V., Anthopoulos, L., Savvas, I.: Supporting the requirements prioritization process using social network analysis techniques. In: 2010 19th IEEE International Workshop on Enabling Technologies: Infrastructures for Collaborative Enterprises (WETICE), pp. 110–115 (2010)
15. Castro-Herrera, C., Cleland-Huang, J., Mobasher, B.: Enhancing stakeholder profiles to improve recommendations in online requirements elicitation. In: 17th IEEE International Requirements Engineering Conference, RE 2009, pp. 37–46 (2009)
16. Jureta, I., Mylopoulos, J., Faulkner, S.: Analysis of multi-party agreement in requirements validation. In: 17th IEEE International Requirements Engineering Conference, RE 2009, pp. 57–66 (2009)
17. Ingolfo, S., Siena, A., Mylopoulos, J., Susi, A., Perini, A.: Arguing regulatory compliance of software requirements. Data & Knowledge Engineering 87, 279–296 (2013)
18. Mirbel, I., Villata, S.: Enhancing goal-based requirements consistency: An argumentation-based approach. In: Fisher, M., van der Torre, L., Dastani, M., Governatori, G. (eds.) CLIMA XIII 2012. LNCS, vol. 7486, pp. 110–127. Springer, Heidelberg (2012)
19. Neo Technology, I.: Neo4j (2013), http://www.neo4j.org/

A Requirements-Led Approach for Specifying QoS-Aware Service Choreographies: An Experience Report

Neil Maiden[1], James Lockerbie[1], Konstantinos Zachos[1], Antonia Bertolino[2], Guglielmo De Angelis[2], and Francesca Lonetti[2]

[1] School of Informatics, City University London, London, UK
[2] Istituto di Scienza e Tecnologie
dell'Informazione "A. Faedo" CNR, Pisa, Italy
{N.A.M.Maiden@,James.Lockerbie.1@,kzachos@soi.}city.ac.uk,
{antonia.bertolino@,guglielmo.deangelis@,francesca.lonetti@}
isti.cnr.it

Abstract. [**Context and motivation**] Choreographies are a form of service composition in which partner services interact in a global scenario without a single point of control. The absence of an explicitly specified orchestration requires changes to requirements practices to recognize the need to optimize software services choreography and monitoring for satisfaction with system requirements. [**Question/problem**] We developed a requirements-led approach that aims to provide tools and processes to transform requirements expressed on service-based systems to QoS-aware choreography specifications. [**Principal ideas/results**] The approach is used by domain experts to specify natural language requirements on a service-based system, and by choreography designers to adapt their models to satisfy requirements more effectively. Non-functional requirements are mapped to BPMN choreography diagrams as quality properties, using the Q4BPMN notation, that support analysis and monitoring facilities. [**Contribution**] We report the new integrated approach and provide lessons learned from applying it to a real-world example of dynamic taxi management

Keywords: service choreographies, requirements monitors, user task models, adaptive systems, quality properties, requirements-led life-cycle.

1   Introduction

Choreographies are a form of service composition in which, unlike orchestration, services interact to achieve a goal without a single point of control [1]. The increased flexibility of architectures based on choreographies can deliver more adaptive service-based systems that satisfy more ambitious requirements of certain types on these systems. However, we still need new techniques to design flexible choreographies that can be argued to satisfy system requirements, and new mechanisms for monitoring services invoked in these choreographies to show continued requirements satisfaction.

The traditional approach to service composition uses orchestration coordinators and arranges services according to a predetermined business logic and execution

C. Salinesi and I. van de Weerd (Eds.): REFSQ 2014, LNCS 8396, pp. 239–253, 2014.
© Springer International Publishing Switzerland 2014

order [2] based on design choices about the type and granularity of available services. This execution order and logic is often expressed as a workflow using notations such as BPEL [2]. Whilst service orchestration is a widely deployed form of system architecture, it can result in a failure to satisfy requirements in increasingly adaptive environments as the predefined execution order and/or business logic can be rendered invalid by changes to a service consumer's context. One advantage of service choreographies is that they impose fewer architecture-level constraints than orchestrations, and as a consequence have greater potential to deliver adaptive systems that continue to satisfy the evolving requirements on them. They make fewer design choices about the granularity of services to be invoked, an execution order for these services does not need to be specified, and business logic is specified independent of the services [3].

Requirements work is needed to specify the required behavior and qualities of choreography activities in a model. Quality of Service (QoS) has been acknowledged as a main concern in service-oriented computing (SOC) and in QoS-aware service composition. Relevant work in SOC includes quality-of-service ontologies and measurement [e.g. 4], however little research or practice traces service qualities back to the originating quality requirements on the systems. These specified behaviors and qualities are needed to guide local enactment of services and to enable the run-time monitoring of each choreography activity for continued requirements satisfaction. Indeed, this alternative paradigm for service technology creates new challenges, including how to:

1. Optimize the specification of choreography diagrams with respect to system requirements;
2. Associate specified system requirements with choreography activities in a choreography diagram;
3. Enhance choreography diagrams with quality properties that trace system requirements, to support analysis and monitoring facilities.

In this paper, we report results from the CHOReOS project (*www.choreos.eu*) to address the three challenges using a real-world dynamic taxi management example. The next section outlines the CHOReOS approach for specifying QoS-aware service choreographies. In sections 3 and 4 we report how this requirements approach uses user task models to generate a first-cut BPMN choreography diagram. Section 5 describes Q4BPMN (*http://labsedc.isti.cnr.it/tools/q4bpmn*) for extending BPMN models with specifications of different types of quality properties [5], and how these extended models can drive the instantiation of corresponding monitors. Section 6 presents lessons learned and the paper ends by looking at related work, reviewing current omissions in the approach, and outlining the next steps.

2   The CHOReOS Approach

Among the various challenges posed by the vision of the Future Internet (FI) [6], is how to provide user-centric processes to support the whole life cycle of SOC systems from their design, to their development, up to their maintenance and governance at run-time [7]. Requirements specification is a fundamental part of dealing with this challenge. A distinctive feature of the FI vision affecting this activity is the active role of domain experts, who are intended to take the place of requirements analysts. The CHOReOS project tackled this challenge by elaborating an approach that considers the user as an active part in the choreography life cycle, and developed it from a business standpoint by leveraging realistic B2B and B2C scenarios provided by the industrial project partners e.g. the dynamic taxi management example in this paper. The result was a domain-expert centric approach supporting non-technical users to specify the desired choreography with respect to their business goals, requirements and quality expectations [8]. An overview of the approach is depicted in Figure 1.

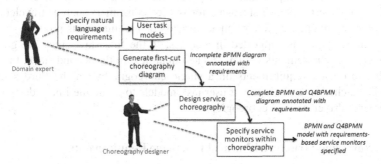

Fig. 1. The key stages of the user-centric requirements-led approach

A domain expert specifies the requirements on a future service-based software system in natural language using the new CHOReOS Requirements Tool. To maximize the uptake of the approach, we decided not to adopt more formal requirements specification techniques that would have necessitated trained analysts. Instead, the primary input to the approach is a small set of natural language requirements that need domain knowledge rather than analytic training to write (see Sections 3.1 and 3.2). To generate a first-cut choreography diagram that satisfies the requirements, the expert uses procedures adapted from previous work to retrieve user tasks models that match the requirements (see Section 3.3). The Requirements Tool then automatically reasons with retrieved models to generate a first-cut model of an under-constrained choreography diagram that can satisfy the matched requirements (Section 4). The choreography designer can select and refine the generated BPMN choreography activities that are the best-fit abstractions of the requirements problem to complete the design of the choreography. Finally, the requirements mapped to the functional BPMN choreography diagram can be used to specify non-functional systems engineering properties using the existing Q4BPMN notation, an extension of BPMN (see Section 5).

If it is applied successfully, the approach will transform functional and quality requirements on a system expressed in natural language into a single service choreography specification that is expressed using BPMN and Q4BPMN, and optimized to satisfy the requirements and the domain constraints extracted from matched user task models. In addition, the specification of such Q4BPMN properties of the choreography activities enables the definition of software modules monitoring the fulfillment of QoS constraints directly traced from the requirements [9].

3   From Natural-Language Requirements to First-Cut Choreography Specifications

An objective of our requirements-based approach was for it to be usable in the largest number of service-oriented projects possible. Natural language continues to be the most used form of requirements expression [e.g. 10], so our approach assumes that functional and quality requirements to be satisfied by the service choreography will be expressed in natural language by domain experts rather than trained analysts. It assumes that a domain expert gathers requirements from the consumers of its services – the domain expert acts as a surrogate for service consumers such as travelers needing a taxi, who are unlikely to participate directly in a requirements process.

The domain expert is supported in 3 stages. In the first stage, they are guided to express system requirements with associated qualities. In the second stage, the expert is guided to cluster requirements on a single choreography. In the third stage, the cluster is matched to a catalogue of user task models to guide the initial design of the requirements-driven service choreography.

3.1   Expressing Structured Natural Language Requirements

Whilst our experiences have shown that domain experts with minimum training can write functional requirements in natural language [e.g. 11], we do not believe that they can express measurable quality requirements such as performance and reliability as effectively. Therefore we developed requirements writing guidelines based on the notion of a qualifier from the anatomy of well-written requirements [10] to transform the functional root of a requirement into one or more quality requirements. These guidelines are built into tool support that guides the domain expert to add one or more qualifiers indicative of different qualities to each specified functional requirement.

The CHOReOS Requirements Tool provides support to the domain expert to define four different qualities considered the most relevant for the project scenarios: accuracy, reliability, performance and security. It tags and parses the functional requirements text written by the domain expert to extract keywords and synonyms, then applies simple rules to infer which of the four qualities, if any, might be associated with the described requirement. The expert is then prompted to consider adding the inferred qualifier to the requirement, which s/he can accept or reject. For example, the functional requirement written by a domain expert in taxi management: *The user shall receive a prompt notification of how long it will take for their taxi to arrive* is parsed to infer a possible performance qualifier based on the keyword *prompt*. Next, to make each quality requirement measurable [12], the expert simply indicates the quality rating on a Likert scale of 1 (very low) to 5 (very high). The expert can then apply additional qualifiers if required, however the tool ensures that only one quality can be selected as the most important, as shown in Figure 2. Each response on the scale for each quality type has been associated with a predefined range of measures to determine satisfaction with the requirement. We describe this in detail in Section 5.2.

The output from this stage is a set of structured natural language requirements on systems that can be implemented as service choreographies.

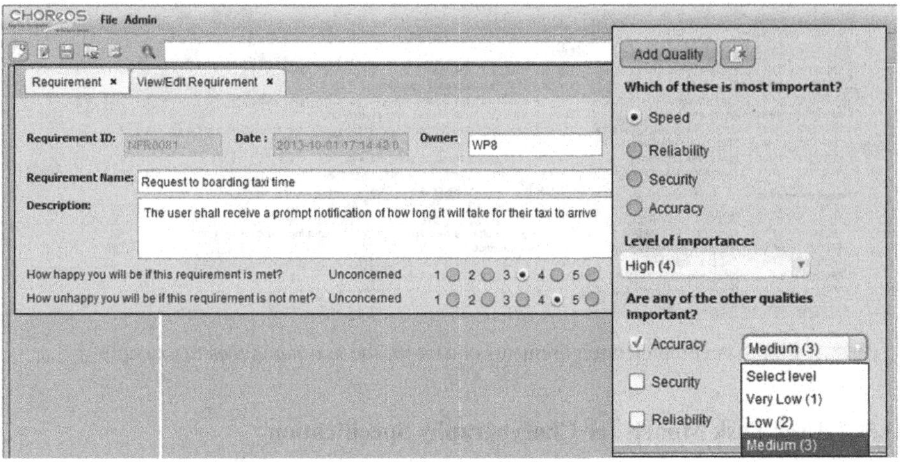

Fig. 2. Expressing quality requirements in the *CHOReOS Requirements Tool*

3.2   Clustering Requirements

Domain experts write requirements on systems rather than service choreographies. However, before these requirements can be mapped onto choreography activities, work is needed to cluster similar requirements that will map onto a single choreography and its elements such as activities and roles. This is because a domain expert acts as the ghost author of requirements from multiple service consumers, and more than one requirement can specify the same or a similar function or quality. Therefore, to optimize the specification of a single choreography, similar and overlapping requirements need to be discovered and handled.

To do this, the Requirements Tool provides the capability to calculate the semantic similarity between any pair of requirements in the set of requirements, similar to a linguistic approach for large-scale requirements management reported in [13]. The algorithm for computing semantic similarity is based on one element of an existing algorithm that computes measures of similarity between natural language requirements and service descriptions during service discovery [14]. The Requirements Tool invokes the algorithm as a third party service, taking the selected requirement and computing a measure of its similarity with every other requirement in the set. A description of the algorithm and an evaluation of its effectiveness are provided in [14].

Figure 3 shows an example of a cluster of requirements on the Request Taxi choreography. The similarity algorithm function reorders the *Requirements List* table according to a match score (the most relevant at the top) and the expert can simply select and add the requirements into the *Requirements Cluster*. Similarly, there is also a keyword search that moves the matched requirements to the top of table.

The output from this stage is a cluster of system requirements that are matched to user task models to inform the design of a first-cut service choreography.

Cluster ID:	C0002		Cluster Name:	CoTaxiing				Owner:	WP8				

Requirements Cluster:

ID	Owner	Name	Description	Sp	A	R	S	
NFR0077	WP8	Efficient Taxi booking	The user shall be able to use the taxi booking system efficiently	4	0	3	0	...
NFR0078	WP8	Reliable Taxi booking	The user shall be able to book a taxi reliably	4	0	5	0	...
NFR0079	WP8	User preferences for booking	The user shall be able to express preferences on their taxi booking	3	3	0	4	...
NFR0080	WP8	Route preferences	The user shall be able to express route preferences	0	3	0	4	...
NFR0081	WP8	Request to boarding taxi time	The user shall receive a prompt notification of how long it will take for their taxi to arr...	4	3	0	0	...
NFR0082	WP8	Booking receipt duration	The user shall receive a taxi booking within an acceptable time	0	4	0	0	...
NFR0083	WP8	Secure taxi booking	The user shall receive the taxi booking securely	0	0	0	4	...
NFR0084	WP8	Secure transmission of data	The transmission of user requests shall be secure	3	0	0	4	...

Requirements List   Add To Cluster   Remove from Cluster

ID	Owner	Name	Description	Sp	A	R	S	
FR0001	WP8	Web check-in via MID	MID shall be able to arrange web-check-in as well as anything that is related to the ch...					...
FR0002	WP8	MID voice and vibration ale...	MID alerts shall be voice and vibration					...
FR0005	WP8	Call prioritization	The service consumer shall be able to request higher prioritization regarding calls or ...					...
FR0007	WP8	Weather forecast on MID	MID shall be able to receive weather forecasts					...
FR0021	WP8	Changed coordinates	MID shall be able to inform navigator about changed coordinates					...

Find Similar requirements

Fig. 3. A completed requirements cluster for the *taxi management* example

3.3   User Task Models for Choreography Specification

A user task model is a description of the structured activities that are often executed by a user during the interaction with a system in its contextual environment to attain goals [15]. Research exploiting user task models to design service-based systems is scarce. For example, Paterno et al. [16] delivered an environment to support tasks and services matching with CTT task models to develop user interfaces but the association between tasks and services was manually established and not cost-effective. Ruiz et al. [17] proposed a method for designing web services that analyzed user task descriptions to identify a web application's required operations. Unlike Paterno's work, this approach was automated but did not include activities such as discovering, selecting and composing software services specific to the design of service-based applications.

Our approach utilizes class-level user task models expressed in the Concur-TaskTrees (CTT) formalism [15] to apply an engineering approach to user task modeling. The precise semantics of CTT enable greater automated guidance with which to specify choreographies, whilst the CTT models can bridge the semantic gap between natural language specifications and formal choreography specifications. For the approach, we built upon the existing library of domain-independent CTT models developed in S-Cube, the EU-funded Network of Excellence for Software Services (*www.s-cube-network.eu/*). We used commonly occurring class-level tasks such as requesting and booking and extended them with knowledge from the applied domains. The CTT models were developed manually in a process reported in [18].

Figure 4 depicts the CTT model *Request taxi*. This CTT model follows a common 3-tier structure we specified. The top-level user goal, *Request taxi*, is decomposed into intermediate level tasks such as *Retrieve data*. In turn, this task is decomposed into the application task level. Application tasks include *detect current location*; *retrieve date and time*; and optional tasks *retrieve preferences* and *retrieve taxi membership*. A description of the full semantics of CTT models can be found in [19].

Important to this design guidance, is a set of mappings between CTT and BPMN semantics that we use to generate a first-cut BPMN choreography diagram. The mapping rules are simple, and we can demonstrate them using the *Request taxi* CTT model. The sub-task *Retrieve Data* occurs concurrently (|[]|) with *Provide taxi request details*. These two tasks enable (>>) the sub-task *Submit query*. CTT semantics define enables (>>) sub-tasks as interleaved, so our rule specifies that both sub-tasks can be undertaken in the same choreography activity. The *Submit query* sub-task enables and passes on information ([] >>) to the *Process query* sub-task. CTT semantics indicate that information is passed between the sub-tasks, so our rule specifies a boundary between choreography activities across which messages are exchanged. Finally, the CTT operator choice ([]) denotes a split in the tasks followed, so our rule specifies a split in the flow of the choreography, represented in BPMN as a gateway or loop.

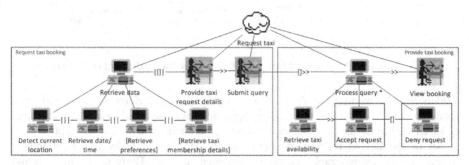

Fig. 4. The CTT specification of the user task *Request Taxi*

Returning to the Requirements Tool, the cluster of requirements is fired at the TEDDiE service, which applies sophisticated information retrieval techniques to identify CTT models relevant to the requirements. Of course, the approach's effectiveness depends upon the accurate automatic retrieval of user task models that match each requirement from the cluster to each CTT model. An evaluation of the retrieval process can be found in [18]. The normal course output from a single invocation of the TEDDIE engine is retrieval of one or more CTT models from the library, and each model is mapped to one or more individual requirement statements in the cluster. First evaluations have revealed that, because the CTT models in the library express class-level tasks rather than more concrete and hence complete business processes, most requirements clusters are likely to match to more than one CTT model.

The output is documented in a XML file that specifies the data with which to generate a first-cut BPMN choreography diagram.

4   Generating a First-Cut Choreography as a BPMN Choreography Diagram with Associated Requirements

Our approach uses the Business Process Model and Notation (*www.bpmn.org*), which is an emerging standard for business process modeling and the specification of service choreographies. The choreography designer designs BPMN choreographies using the MagicDraw visual modeling tool (*www.nomagic.com*), which we configured to accept the XML files output from the Requirements Tool. As a result, the choreography designer receives explicit requirements-based guidance for designing a service choreography based on a first-cut template model annotated with requirements information.

A first-cut BPMN choreography diagram generated for the taxi example is shown in Figure 5. One consequence of the BPMN formalism being more complete than the CTT formalism is that each choreography diagram automatically generated from CTT

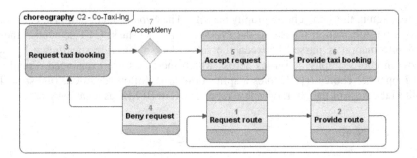

Fig. 5. Automatically generated first-cut BPMN choreography diagram in *MagicDraw*

models will be incomplete. As well as integrating model elements generated from more than one CTT model, the choreography designer may need to add choreography tasks, as well as define the instance-level participant names in the choreography.

All of the design refinement should be directly informed by the requirements linked to each choreography element, presented in MagicDraw as a requirements-choreography task matrix. The matrix maps each original requirement to one or more choreography tasks in the choreography diagram. The designer can use the require-ment traces imported from each matched user task model to refine the specification of the required levels of quality-of-service, and from them support the application of quality properties. An example of a requirements matrix is depicted in Figure 6.

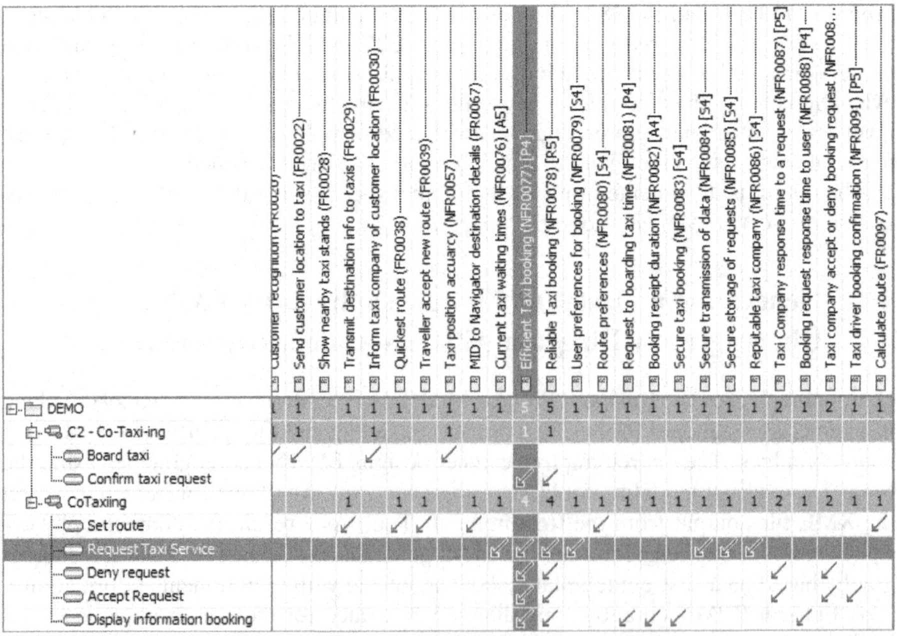

Fig. 6. Completed matrix mapping system requirements to choreography tasks in *MagicDraw*

The output of this stage is a first version of a service choreography diagram specified using the constraints derived from matching user task models, and with each element of the choreography that is annotated with requirements information derived from the original system requirements from domain experts and service consumers. For reference, a final elaborated version of the first-cut choreography diagram shown in Figure 5 can be found at *http://labsedc.isti.cnr.it/tools/q4bpmn/co-taxing*.

5   Monitorable Service Qualities from Requirements

To express qualities on service choreographies we used Q4BPMN (Quality for BPMN), a semi-formal notation for specifying quality annotations at the choreography level [5]. It allows designers to extend BPMN models with quality properties that the services entering the choreography will have to abide by. With Q4BPMN, the choreography designer can state the quality requirements for the choreography and its roles at the same level of abstraction of the tasks' flow without the need for additional models. The explicit introduction of non-functional constraints within a choreography specification supports the verification and validation of their impact on the overall quality requirements. At the same time, prospective participants can use this information to understand the quality level required on their part.

5.1   The Q4BPMN Notation

Q4BPMN is an implementation of the Property Meta-Model (PMM) with which to specify the quality properties, metrics and observable events of a system [20]. Q4BPMN is implemented within MagicDraw as a design tool, and was conceived to support the specification of non-functional properties within a service choreography expressed in the BPMN notation. It provides designers and analysts the means to annotate a choreography diagram with quality requirements [5]. Specifically, Q4BPMN enables the definition of non-functional systems engineering properties that can be directly linked either to a single task (i.e. «Q4Task»), specific participant of a task (i.e. «Q4Participants»), or whole choreography (i.e. «Q4Choreography») [21].

Q4BPMN supports several kinds of properties, which correspond to the class of properties inherited from the PMM meta-model. Specifically, it currently defines four classes of properties: (i) dependability properties concerning the availability of the system and failure rates; (ii) performance properties related to time, mainly from a software and human interaction point of view; (iii) security properties related to encryption of operations and trustworthiness of the business activities; and (iv) accuracy properties that relate to time and space dimensions.

5.2   Mapping Requirements to Q4BPMN

Although Q4BPMN provides the means for expressing quality properties within a BPMN choreography diagram, it does not bind to any specific methodology for defining which values, dimensions or context characterize these properties. In this sense, as commonly happens during their specification, non-functional requirements can conceal underspecified aspects that can allow many different interpretations depending on the context these desired system properties are offered [22]. For example, a user expressed performance requirement such as *NFR0077: The user shall be able to use the taxi booking system efficiently* is useful in the early stages of the requirement elicitation process, as this kind of natural language requirement can be easily understood by non-technical stakeholders (e.g. final users). However, quantifying such a high level user requirement could imply a different interpretation depending on the context and the functionalities intended to impact on it.

To address this, the non-functional requirements and their various potential interpretations were mitigated by quantifying each abstract property in a set of application contexts. From the analysis of our application domains we identified three major concerns representing the different contexts for achieving the quality goals intended by the elicited non-functional requirements. Specifically, such concerns are:

1. *Software System:* the properties specified under this concern represent those quality attributes quantifying either the behavior of software components, or their interactions;
2. *Human–Computer Interaction:* the properties specified under this concern represent those quality attributes quantifying any interactions between a human and any part of the considered software system;
3. *Business Activities:* the properties specified under this concern represents those quality attributes quantifying the admissible constraint used in order to characterize the activities of both the whole system (i.e. software + human related activities), and its actors from a business perspective.

The model shown in Figure 7 shows the requirements to Q4BPMN mapping which includes these concerns, modeled as agent-based quality goals. The left side of the model shows a user expressed systems requirement and the four main qualities that can be associated with it, indicated on scales of 1 to 5 as described in Section 3.1. These user expressed systems requirements correspond directly to four user quality goals on the wider service-based system – accuracy, dependability, performance and security. These goals are then decomposed into the 3 concerns described above: Software System, HCI and Business, and shown as agent-based quality goals. Finally, the model shows the definition of the qualitative properties that could be used by the agent-based goals. In this case, we have instantiated the model for our application to the taxi management scenario. Specifically, for each of the properties we identified: the type and the dimension it addresses; but also its name and the values prescribed for each specific satisfaction level.

In order to define the abstract properties, we drew upon research in disciplines such as software reliability and human-computer interaction to determine prototypical measures of different qualities that the expert uses to refine the requirement measure. For example, we considered the Secure Sockets Layer (SSL) protocol for security encryption-type requirements and Miller's work [23] describing threshold levels of human attention for HCI time performance-type requirements. We then utilised the expert input available to us in our taxi management application domain to review the provided definitions and quantify the predefined ranges.

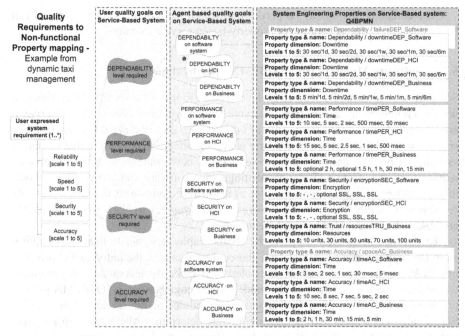

Fig. 7. Non-functional requirements mapping to quality properties in Q4BPMN

Table 1, for example, shows mappings between two original system requirements and the quality properties they relate to. In the first, the traveller details are required to be transmitted with a performance level of 5, which translates to the software time performance property. The required time performance for all software interactions within this choreography task is therefore quantified as 50msec. However, the second requirement is mapped to a participant property limited specifically to the *Taxi Company* operating in the choreography task. It specifies that the taxi company shall be reputable, which maps a onto a trust property related to the business security quality goal. The instantiation of these properties reflect the specification introduced in Figure 7.

Table 1. An example of mapping original system requirements to quality properties

Choreography element, Name	Original requirement Name, ID, description, quality	Quality Property
Task Request Taxi Service	MID send customer details (NFR0012): *MID shall be able to transmit traveller (customer) details to the taxi company* [Performance 5]	timePer_Software_L5 • isHard = true • metrics – DefaultMaxDurationMetric • nature = PRESCRIPTIVE • operator = LESS EQUAL • propertyClass – PERFORMANCE • unit = "msec" • value = "50"
Participant property Taxi Company	Reputable taxi company (NFR0086): *The taxi company shall have an established reputation* [Security 4]	taxiCompanyBusinessTrust • NF Properties = resourcesTRU_Business_L4 • ParticipantRef = Taxi Company

Once complete, the quality properties into which the requirements are mapped can be used to inform the generation of property-based service monitors.

5.3   Software Monitors from Q4BPMN Specifications

Software monitors can be accurately developed to monitor for specified qualities of a service choreography at run-time. A monitor is *a software system that observes a target system's behavior for qualities of interest such as satisfying the target system's requirements* [24]. Effective monitoring is key for adaptation to ensure that the target system can bind to and invoke new services in new contexts to ensure continued requirements satisfaction. Robinson distinguishes software and requirements monitors. He defines a requirements monitor as a software component that *determines the requirements status from a stream of significant input events* [24], where the events are observed and recorded by software monitors.

Our approach explicitly supports the choreography designer to map QoS requirement into monitorable properties on a choreography model, the individual choreography tasks in the model, and on the roles in a task. By leveraging on generative techniques within the context of the model-driven engineering, the Q4BPMN properties support the synthesis of QoS monitoring modules of the service choreography. Specifically, each generated monitoring module determines whether a property associated to a quality requirement is satisfied using observed data and messages. Given the need to map requirements of different types onto different types of event filters, our approach uses a flexible event-based monitoring infrastructure tailored to observe and analyze the behavior of distributed systems and services [25]. The reference implementation of such event-based monitor includes a complex event-processing engine based on Drools Fusion [26]. The details about the model-to-code transformation process of the Q4BPMN properties in presented at length in [27].

Our use of Q4BPMN is related to current requirements metrics such as Planguage, the keyword-driven language for writing measurable quality requirements [12]. Planguage's use of measures and metrics is similar to the Q4BPMN's use of abstract, descriptive or prescriptive properties [27], however we believe that the grounding of these property types in observable data that can be collected using software monitors offers it a distinct advantage for service-based systems.

6   Lessons Learned

We return to the 3 challenges reported earlier to assess whether applying our approach helped to resolve them and report the most important lessons learned:

Optimize the specification of choreography diagrams with respect to system requirements. For the dynamic taxi management scenario, 97 system requirements were successfully specified and used to generate meaningful first-cut choreography diagrams. The simple interface of the requirements tool enabled system requirements to be specified effectively without training, and the similarity algorithm helped the user cluster requirements for specifying a single choreography. However, there was a usability concern with the similarity function, as matching the selected requirement to the other 96 requirements took over 5 minutes using a standard laptop on the City University London network. An option for improving the performance of this function is to store the match results in a requirements matrix to remove the need for invoking the similarity algorithm web service for every requirement pair each time it is run.

The requirements specified retrieved the domain specific *Request taxi* CTT model and the generic *Calculate route* model. Minor refinements were made to the generated choreography tasks, shown in figure 5, and the final choreography tasks listed in Figure 6. Additional tasks included *Confirm taxi request* and *Board taxi* situated at either end of the process flow. While the use of CTT models provided valuable design guidance for the choreography design in this example, varying degrees of success were experienced for other choreographies. For example, in the context-aware traffic management choreography, the first-cut BPMN model elements generated by the retrieved CTT models *Provide traffic information* and *Calculate route* were either discarded or revised beyond recognition. Therefore, further work is needed to expand the catalogue of CTT models and to evaluate the effectiveness of the process in future case studies.

Associate specified system requirements with choreography activities in a choreography diagram. In our example, 38 out of the 40 clustered requirements were automatically mapped to choreography tasks and provided a useful starting point for the user. However, our approach can only match requirements to each retrieved CTT model, therefore matched requirements are automatically allocated to the first choreography task generated from each CTT model. Future work on the TEDDiE service to match the requirements to specific choreography tasks would improve the process and reduce the level of human input required. Also, it was evident that users need to be better supported where requirements are relevant to more than one choreography task in the model. As exemplified by the requirement NFR0077, which is mapped across 5 of the choreography tasks (see Figure 6), high level user requirements could imply different interpretations depending on the context and the functionalities intended to impact on them. One possible way of addressing this would be to use satisfaction arguments, as defined in [29], to provide a means to reason about the relationships between user expressed quality requirements and lower-level system requirements. We have already made an initial attempt to implement satisfaction arguments in the Requirements Tool (see [30]), but we need to explore effective ways of implementing this, or a similar approach, in the MagicDraw modeling environment.

Enhance choreography diagrams with quality properties that trace system requirements, to support analysis and monitoring facilities. Although the Q4BPMN notation already existed, this was the first time that we traced the originating set of system requirements through the choreography specification process. Reconciling the user expressed quality scores with actual values for the quality properties was a challenge. This required a significant level of domain expert input as ultimately context was everything and generic values reported in literature were not necessarily suitable.

Finally, it is worth mentioning the limitation that there is no backwards compatibility between the MagicDraw environment and the CHOReOS Requirements Tool. This restricts the possibility of revising the originating requirements without starting the process again and is an area that needs to be addressed in future.

7   Conclusion and Future Work

In this paper we report an integrated approach for designing service choreographies from system requirements to deliver more adaptive software systems. We integrated new and existing work from different sub-disciplines to develop a pragmatic solution to a pressing problem – how to engineer increasingly adaptive service-based software. We believe the combination of techniques for natural language requirements expression, user task models, quality model extensions to business processes, and transformations of these models to construct requirements-based software monitors, is unique. Not only have we developed an end-to-end approach for generating service-based systems that can be traced to their originating system requirements, but also we have developed an integrated toolkit based on BPMN modeling in MagicDraw.

Of course the approach we presented is not complete – it has some important omissions. One is the lack of discovery techniques to select and bind candidate services to choreographies at run-time. CHOReOS has developed such techniques linked to software service repositories [28]. Another is the lack of support to develop service-level agreements from requirements. Such agreements are needed to manage contractual relationships with the providers of the services invoked in choreographies, and should be derived from requirements. Although the approach provides the foundations for requirements-led development of SLAs, it still has to be extended it to deliver it.

Although we successfully applied the methods and tools in the demonstrated example, the next stage of our work is to evaluate the approach formatively in the development of other service-based systems. We plan to report results from these formative evaluations in future work.

Acknowledgment. The research is supported by CHOReOS project n° 257178 of the FP7 European program: FP7-ICT-2009-5.

References

1. Peltz, C.: Web Services Orchestration and Choreography. IEEE Computer 36(10), 46–52 (2003)
2. Ouyang, C., Verbeek, E., van der Aalst, W.M.P., Breutel, S., Dumas, M., Hofstede, A.H.M.: Formal Semantics and Analysis of Control Flow in WS-BPEL. Science of Computer Programming 2(3), 162–198 (2007)
3. Ben Hamida, A., et al.: An Integrated Development and Runtime Environment for the Future Internet. In: Álvarez, F., et al. (eds.) FIA 2012. LNCS, vol. 7281, pp. 81–92. Springer, Heidelberg (2012)
4. Sawyer, P., Hutchinson, J., Walkerdine, J., Sommerville, I.: Faceted Service Specification. In: Proceedings SOCCER Workshop at RE 2005 Conference, Paris (2005)
5. Bartolini, C., Bertolino, A., Ciancone, A., De Angelis, G., Mirandola, R.: Quality Requirements for Service Choreographies. In: Proceedings WEBIST 2012, pp. 143–148 (2012)
6. ERCIM News. Special Theme: Future Internet Technology. Number 77 (April 2009)
7. Shaw, M.: The Challenge of Pervasive Software to the Conventional Wisdom of Software Engineering. In: Keynote speech at ESEC/FSE (August 2009), http://www.esec-fse-2009.ewi.tudelft.nl/downloads/ESECFSE09-shaw.pdf
8. Autili, M., Di Ruscio, D., Inverardi, P., Lockerbie, J., Tivoli, M.: A Development Process for Requirements Based Service Choreography. In: Proceedings RESS 2011, pp. 59–62 (2011)

9. Bartolini, C., Bertolino, A., Ciancone, A., De Angelis, G., Mirandola, R.: Apprehensive QoS Monitoring of Service Choreographies. In: Proceedings SAC 2013, pp. 1893–1899 (2013)
10. Alexander, I., Stevens, R.: Writing Better Requirements. Addison-Wesley (2002)
11. Maiden, N.A.M., Jones, S.V., Manning, S., Greenwood, J., Renou, L.: Model-Driven Requirements Engineering: Synchronising Models in an Air Traffic Management Case Study. In: Persson, A., Stirna, J. (eds.) CAiSE 2004. LNCS, vol. 3084, pp. 368–383. Springer, Heidelberg (2004)
12. Gilb, T.: Competitive Engineering: A Handbook For Systems Engineering, Requirements Engineering, and Software Engineering Using Planguage. Elsevier (2005)
13. Nattoch Dag, J., Gervasi, V., Brinkkemper, S., Regnell, B.: A linguistic engineering approach to large-scale requirements management. IEEE Software 22(1), 32–39 (2005)
14. Zachos, K., Maiden, N.A.M., Zhu, X., Jones, S.: Discovering Web Services To Specify More Complete System Requirements. In: Krogstie, J., Opdahl, A.L., Sindre, G. (eds.) CAiSE 2007 and WES 2007. LNCS, vol. 4495, pp. 142–157. Springer, Heidelberg (2007)
15. Paterno, F., Santoro, C.: Preventing User Errors by Systematic Analysis of Deviations from the System Task Model. International Journal of Human-Computer Studies 56(2), 225–245 (2002)
16. Paterno, F., Santoro, C., Spano, L.D.: User Task-based Development of Multi-device Service-oriented Applications. In: Proceedings of the International Conference on Advanced Visual Interfaces, Roma, Italy (2010)
17. Ruiz, M., Pelechano, V., Pastor, O.: Designing Web Services for Supporting User Tasks: A Model Driven Approach. In: CoSS International Workshop on Conceptual Modeling of S-oSS, pp. 193–202 (2006)
18. Zachos, K., Kounkou, A., Maiden, N.A.M.: Exploiting Codified User Task Knowledge to Discover Services at Design-Time. IJSSOE 3(2), 30–66 (2012)
19. Paterno, F., Mancini, C., Meniconi, S.: ConcurTaskTrees: A Diagrammatic Notation for Specifying Task Models. In: Proceedings of the IFIP TC13 International Conference on Human-Computer Interaction, pp. 362–369 (1997)
20. Di Marco, A., Pompilio, C., Bertolino, A., Calabrò, A., Lonetti, F., Sabetta, A.: Yet another meta-model to specify non-functional properties. In: Proceedings QASBA 2011, pp. 9–16 (2011)
21. Bartolini, C., Bertolino, A., Ciancone, A., De Angelis, G., Mirandola, R.: Non-functional analysis of service choreographies. In: Proceedings PESOS 2012, pp. 8–14 (2012)
22. Pohl, K.: Requirements Engineering - Fundamentals, Principles, and Techniques. Springer (2010)
23. Miller, R.B.: Response time in man-computer conversational transactions. In: Proceedings of the Joint Computer Conference, pp. 267–277. ACM, New York (1968)
24. Robinson, W.: A Roadmap for Comprehensive Requirements Monitoring. IEEE Computer, 64–72 (May 2010)
25. Bertolino, A., Calabrò, A., Lonetti, F., Sabetta, A.: GLIMPSE: a generic and flexible monitoring infrastructure. In: Proceedings EWDC 2011, pp. 73–78 (2011)
26. Drools Fusion: Complex Event Processor,
    http://www.jboss.org/drools/drools-fusion.html
27. Bertolino, A., Calabrò, A., Lonetti, F., Di Marco, A., Sabetta, A.: Towards a Model-Driven Infrastructure for Runtime Monitoring. In: Troubitsyna, E.A. (ed.) SERENE 2011. LNCS, vol. 6968, pp. 130–144. Springer, Heidelberg (2011)
28. Ali, M., De Angelis, G., Polini, A.: ServicePot – An Extensible Registry for Choreography Governance. In: Proceedings SOSE 2013, pp. 113–124 (2013)
29. Hammond, J., Rawlings, R., Hall, A.: Will it work? In: Proceedings 5th IEEE International Symposium on Requirements Engineering, pp. 102–109. IEEE Computer Society (2001)
30. http://www.choreos.eu/bin/view/Documentation/Requirements_Tool

Experience-Oriented Approaches for Teaching and Training Requirements Engineering: An Experience Report

Andrea Herrmann[1], Anne Hoffmann[2], Dieter Landes[3], and Rüdiger Weißbach[4]

[1] Herrmann & Ehrlich, Stuttgart, Germany
herrmann@herrmann-ehrlich.de
[2] Siemens AG, Erlangen, Germany
anne.hoffmann@siemens.com
[3] University of Applied Sciences, Coburg, Germany
dieter.landes@hs-coburg.de
[4] Hamburg University of Applied Sciences, Hamburg, Germany
ruediger.weissbach@haw-hamburg.de

Abstract. [**Context & motivation**] Experience-oriented learning is known to be more efficient than learning by listening. Small team projects can teach practical issues of applying methods and soft skills. [**Question/problem**] RE is a core qualification for diverse stakeholders, not only for software engineers. In trainings and academic education, people with different professional backgrounds and different experiences, representing different stages in the Dreyfus model of skill acquisition, come together. The teaching's setup should take this into account. [**Principal ideas/results**] This experience report presents examples of various approaches for teaching RE in academia and industry. We discuss findings from interdisciplinary projects and game-oriented approaches, differences of these learning settings and differences which are to be considered when designing didactic settings for different target groups. [**Contribution**] This article presents diverse course concepts and experiences, and shall inspire other instructors to seek for additional learning approaches by taking into account their participants' heterogeneous background.

Keywords: Dreyfus model, experience-based learning, experience-oriented learning, interdisciplinary, learning, requirements engineering, teaching, training

1 Motivation: Why Teaching and Training Requirements Engineering?

Relevance of Requirements Engineering: Requirements Engineering (RE) is known to be critical for the success of software projects [1] and the education of software practitioners [2]. While this is a good motivation for learning and teaching RE, the growth of RE-related conferences and the rising number of RE certifications show that RE training has been recognized and accepted as being important.

C. Salinesi and I. van de Weerd (Eds.): REFSQ 2014, LNCS 8396, pp. 254–267, 2014.
© Springer International Publishing Switzerland 2014 2014

Yet, RE knowledge is not only relevant for the software development team, but also for customers and other stakeholders, especially in the context of agile development. For instance, we see an increasing importance of business departments in decisions on information systems. This is not only caused, but intensified in the context of Cloud Computing, where business departments are able to buy Software as a Service (SaaS) products [3]. This trend is reflected in the authors' "experience" in teaching and training RE not only for IT specialists, but for marketing and engineering staff.

Whilst RE is typically seen as a task in an early stage of a waterfall project, RE is part of agile development, too.

Teaching vs. Training: We distinguish between teaching and training:

"Teaching" means the education that is part of the university curriculum during the studies and that prepares students for diverse work environments and roles. Most of the students have no work experience. Therefore, teaching cannot presuppose specific previous experiences or problem-awareness.

In our understanding, "Training" is defined as commercial training given to professionals. It is typically customized to the "target group's environment", to the role (developer, project manager, etc.), and to the domain (e.g. automotive), and takes company- or domain-specific standards into account. Most participants in trainings have work experience and attend the course with specific questions in their minds which they seek answers for.

In this experience paper, we try to find some answers to the question: "Which approach is appropriate for teaching or training RE to participants on which Dreyfus level?" This paper is founded on the practical experiences and the reflections of the authors compiled in diverse RE teaching and training situations.

2   Related Work

2.1   Four Forms of Experience-Oriented Learning Methods

"According to Lethbridge's survey" [2], software professionals think that their education has been moderately relevant for their job (3.5 points on a scale of 0 to 5). From their point of view, it was more important to learn how to think than to learn specific methods.

It is known that learning by listening is not as efficient as learning by doing [4]. While sitting in a lecture and **listening to the lecturer**, the student learns facts. However, only by **applying a method**, they get experience and learn the soft facts which cannot be transferred easily by lecturing.

For instance, learning the elements of an UML model is only the first step in learning UML. When applying the method to a simple toy example, already many practical questions arise. However, applying UML modeling to more complex systems gives rise to further questions, like the ideal level of granularity or how to check for completeness. When students **run a project** from beginning to end, building on the requirements which they elicited and modeled themselves, they get direct feedback about the quality of their requirements. **Working in a team** additionally allows them to train soft skills they will need in practice. In distributed teams the students learn to work in virtual teams [5]. The most realistic learning effect can be achieved when students work in a **real-life project** with real organizations. A real-life project, compared to a role game, introduces difficulties beyond applying the rules of the RE methods. As the course has a certain duration and speed, it is not always easy to define a real-life project with the suitable scope.

Role games or project simulations are conducted in a protected and controllable university environment. Consequently, for instructors these approaches are often an ideal compromise between applying methods to unrealistically simple examples and complex and barely controllable real-life projects.

We define the difference between "role game" and "project simulation" as follows: Role games are a collection of individual games like an interview or an example where different methods are applied. In project simulations, methods and roles are applied to the same project. The teacher controls the role game or simulation by defining clear rules for the roles´ interactions during each step of the game.

Examples of role games in RE teaching are:

- The agile hour [6] and the extreme hour [7] where within one hour the learners simulate an agile project with three iterations, with the objective to implement a result by drawing it.
- Simulated customer interviews and subsequent development tasks [8], [9], which can be combined with improvisational theatre [10].
- A business game where students create software companies and bid for a large scale development project [11].
- Performing a development project which leads to a user interface design [12] or to a prototype software [13].
- Simulating a software project in the form of a card game [14], [15].

Additional roles games within different types of engineering and natural science courses are discussed by Fadali et al. [16].

Compared to real-life projects, games are shorter interactions within a canonized set of rules and under controlled circumstances. Dawson [17] even recommends to play tricks on the students in order to better prepare them for work life. Such tricks can be: to present an uncertain and naive customer, to change requirements and priorities, and to have conflicting requirements and pressures. In real-life projects, the longer duration increases the possibilities of interventions and disruptions.

Another way of learning is to analyze and discuss case descriptions, either real or invented cases. Cases are derived from realistically large projects in a way to highlight a specific aspect that is to be learned. Thus, students can learn from real projects, without the risks involved in executing them themselves.

Improvisation theatre was invented by Keith Johnstone [18] to support students in acting and drama improving their acting abilities. Johnstone invented so-called games each training certain aspects of communication and self-awareness. The REIM approach utilizes storytelling to map these games to typical Requirements Engineering situations, see [19, 20] for details.

2.2   The Dreyfus Model

The Dreyfus model, introduced by Stuart and Hubert Dreyfus in 1980, describes five stages through which a person passes in order to acquire skills needed in a certain area: novice, competence, proficiency, expertise, and mastery [21]. Most people will only reach the "competence" stage in a certain field ([22], p.28). According to the Dreyfus brothers, while one becomes more skilled he or she "depends less on abstract principles and more on concrete experience".

The main characteristics of the stages are:

- **Novice:** Novices need to be given non-situational tasks and a set of rules to fulfill a certain task ([22], p.18f).
- **Competence:** With a certain experience acquired, comes competence. With competence, one can deviate to a certain degree from prior rules given to the novice ([22], p.20).
- **Proficiency:** With proficiency, one can solve known problems, seek guidance from experts and apply the advice given successfully ([22], p.20f).
- **Expertise:** This is the first stage where one is able to reflect and correct oneself. On this level, one oversees the big picture and can learn from experience others made ([22], p.21ff).
- **Mastery:** On this level, one has a huge fund of experience and works best based on intuition. Interestingly, if forced to use rules, persons on the mastery level have proven to become less successful fulfilling their tasks ([22], p.23f).

The Dreyfus model allows us to align the approaches presented below to the different levels of expertise for which they can be used.

3   Case Descriptions

3.1   Characteristics

In this chapter, we report on several cases that were run at universities in Germany and Switzerland and in industrial settings. These cases focus in particular on bringing some of the complexities of real projects into an academic setting, either in real life projects (Chapter 3.2, Chapter 3.3) or using role games (Chapter 3.4). Another case description shows the usage of improvisation theatre in professional education (Chapter 3.5). Additional aspects of these cases that are not directly related to RE are "also discussed elsewhere, [19, 20, 23, 24, 25, 26]".

The case descriptions emphasize various aspects, such as

- Interdisciplinarity and complexity in social interactions, due to different skills and backgrounds of the participants (Chapter 3.2, Chapter 3.3)
- Approximation to reality (Chapter 3.2, Chapter 3.3)
- Methodical rigor (Chapter 3.4) vs. "real world muddling through" (Chapter 3.2, Chapter 3.3)

These cases can be categorized with respect to Dreyfus' levels of competence as indicated in Table 1. The levels were assigned based on asking the participants about their experiences and our observations during the course. We define a teaching resp. training experience as successful if the training objective is achieved. Empty entries in the table are still open for future research. Table 2 gives a short overview of the cases.

Table 1. Participants´ Dreyfus levels on which the authors applied the training method successfully. The numbers refer to the chapter where the case is presented

	Impro theatre	Role game	Simulation	Real life
Novice	3.5	3.4	3.4	3.2, 3.3
Competence	3.5		3.4	
Proficiency	3.5		3.4	
Expertise	3.5			
Mastery				

Table 2. Overview of the cases presented in this paper

Case	3.2	3.3	3.4	3.5
Learning objective	Elicitation and negotiation of requirements, understanding the roles of other stakeholders, communication across disciplinary boundaries	Methods for elicitation, specification, management, soft skills, understanding of the user's role in the process,	Elicitation methods, specification methods, soft skills	Soft skills and their specific aspects in RE-related situation such as requirements clarification, prioritization
Learning method	Real life projects with internal or external stakeholders	Real life projects with external stakeholders	Project simulation including role games	Interactive games from Improvisation Theatre, storytelling
Course Size	25-30	25-40	4-25	???
Group size	10-25, depending on the number of students and customers	5-12, depends on the number of students	2	8-25, depends on trainer's experience
Success criterion	Customer accepts project outcome. Self-reflection on achievements and failures in a post-mortem review.	Projects are conducted in a real life situation. Customer accepts results. Additional written test with reflections on methods.	Requirements specification and test cases satisfy quality criteria, customer accepts prototype	Tasks per games are solved, anticipated results are achieved

Important dimensions for the description of the cases are the following:

- Controllability: The instructor's ability to control and adapt the initial conditions and the course of the learning experience.
- Co-location: eligibility of the approach to be run with a distributed team or in a co-located fashion.
- Feedback types: moment in time and method used by the instructor to obtain feedback about learning success.
- Supervision need: Need of the learners to be supervised by instructors.
- Requires theoretical / practical knowledge of participants: prerequisite RE knowledge for the course.

These dimensions will be discussed in the chapter 4.

3.2   Joint Project with ICT and Business Students

Description

One approach to gain experiences with some of the complexities of real projects is the students' work in teams on projects that have a realistic goal or even a real customer. In particular if there is a real customer, interdisciplinary aspects come into play since in general the customer is active in a different application domain, i.e. students and customers do not share the same disciplinary background. In the cases that we ran at Coburg, we emphasized this even further since the project teams consisted of ICT and business students who had to establish ways to cooperate even across disciplinary borders in order to succeed in the project. In addition, project teams tended to be fairly large, giving rise to unexpected social interactions and coordination problems [24, 25]. Participants are in the final year of their bachelor's studies. Each of them already passed one semester of compulsory internship.

So far, we ran three iterations of such a project. Project I dealt with developing a software system in order to support claims handling in a (fictitious) insurance company. Business students played the role of the customer, expressing requirements and being involved in acceptance testing, while ICT students were in charge of building the system after figuring out what the system was supposed to do. In contrast to project I, there was a real customer in projects II and III (CEO of a medium-sized factory). Each of the projects ran over a complete term, i.e. roughly four months, calling for a weekly effort of approximately four hours for each participant. Each project was concluded by a post-mortem review which focusses on achievements and failures in the project. Furthermore, instructor observed the participants' behavior during the project.

As learning goals, participants should be capable of eliciting and negotiating requirements across disciplinary boundaries in a co-operative manner. Furthermore, participants should get a deep understanding of the roles of all the involved stakeholders. Learning goals are assumed to be achieved if the project outcome could be happily accepted by the customer and participants appropriately reflect their work in the post-mortem review.

Experiences

Each project fostered a much deeper understanding of the importance of requirements and the difficulties in handling them properly. Although both ICT and business students had been introduced to RE, they still did not really believe that there is a problem. In particular, in project I business students (in the role of customers) initially thought that quite a few things simply go without saying (for example the log on process). They assumed that ICT students would fill in the gaps that, from their point of view, were so evident that they would not bother addressing them explicitly. Conversely, ICT students had not expected that their customers, consciously or not, would tell them only part of the story. This experience for both sides was reinforced during acceptance testing: business students first complained about missing important functionalities of the delivered software product, but had to accept that they never expressed a requirement that mentioned these features. For the ICT students, it was a new experience that there were still hidden requirements, even after having asked their customers several times if there were additional issues that the solution should cover. Similarly, students initially tend to believe that requirements never change. Furthermore, projects can help to understand that other stakeholders may have a different perspective on particular things.

But there are quite a few issues that are hard to handle in projects. First of all, the supervision of projects is difficult for larger numbers of students. As a second difficulty, it is hard to foresee what will happen in a specific project, especially when an external customer is involved. Therefore, it is hard to force particular phenomena, e.g. misunderstandings or requirements changes. Consequently, the learning outcome is to some extent left to chance, namely that a particular phenomenon actually happens in a project setting. If the focus of the learning arrangement is on a particular set of phenomena, other formats, such as role games, are more appropriate than projects simply as they are easier to control, yet at the expense of realism.

3.3   Teaching Requirements Engineering to Business Students

Description

At Hamburg University of Applied Sciences [UAS], we continuously conduct a joint course for marketing bachelor students with marketing and RE content since winter 2009/10 [26]. About 30 marketing students are working every semester in 4-6 real life projects which last 7 weeks. The course is in the last semester, so that all students have business experience of at least 6 months. The aim of the task is to solve a marketing problem with ICT support. The students have to define the requirements and then to decide about a software solution, to improve the usability of a web site, to implement a small solution etc. Participating organizations are commercial organizations as well as departments of the university or non-profit organizations.

One professor for marketing and one for business informatics teach and coach the student groups in project management and RE. In some lessons, both professors stand together in front of the class and demonstrate different professional and individual points of view. For special tasks (usability tests), other departments of the university are co-operating. The students organize this co-operation process themselves.

Intended learning outcomes are (a) methodological knowledge for project management and requirements engineering and (b) "soft skills" from the experience of real life projects.

Experiences

At Hamburg UAS, a periodical evaluation of the courses is implemented. The students' feedback is generally positive; they state learning success a well as fun. The different professional cultures of marketing and business informatics are perceived as a confusing, but realistic impression.

For the participating organizations, these projects are important and the students' expertise is accepted as a professional expertise. This is important for the self-confidence of the students and for their role change as future professionals at the end of their university years. Some organizations conduct several projects consecutively with us, so that a student group will continue the work of a former team. In reality, this is a normal situation, but it is not common in teaching project management.

Students criticize the expenditure of time (which correlates to the number of credit points), but first of all the organizational problems. Most of them are caused by the real life situation: Stakeholders have to react on a shift in priorities etc.

The success rate regarding the students' point of view is 100% - no project work deliverable was rejected by the co-operating organizations. The implementation rate of the projects is > 80%, only few of the projects have not been implemented due to changes in the co-operating organization or in their environment.

Problems of the real life situation are:

- Students have a pressure to succeed – therefore the projects have no "gaming" or "exploring" character.
- Due to the required skills and the current curriculum, it is only possible to run such a course at the end of the BA curriculum.
- Due to the different aims in the projects – from implementing only changes on a web site to developing algorithms fur customer clustering -, the focus on methods is different. This is challenging for the students and the teachers, but demonstrates the context-sensitivity.
- Project work can only indirectly reflect students' success. To guarantee a common basic "body of knowledge", a written exam is the base for the grade. The project work can affect the grade positively.

3.4   Requirements Engineering for Engineers

Description

The following format for a role game project simulation worked well for computer science students as well as for business informatics and electrical engineering students, and also for experienced practitioners: Each student plays the role of a customer who wants to get custom-made software and is the provider/ contractor for "another students' project". They work in pairs and change roles. They choose a project which they have implemented themselves before, a problem they have met or something they will implement soon. The most frequently chosen (and most simple) example was the design of a web site or web shop. But also more complex projects were chosen like steering a manufacturing system or the watering of a system of tennis courts. The objective of the project is to write a requirement specification, test cases and to develop a graphical user interface prototype. No software implementation is needed. However, students who are very experienced in web programming volunteered to "develop the customer's website as a prototype".

This role game has successfully been applied four times:

- In a lecture for computer science and business informatics students at the Technical University of Braunschweig, Germany (three groups),
- In a lecture for business informatics students at the University of Bern, Switzerland,
- In a summer school for engineering students and practitioners at the University of Stuttgart, Germany, and
- In a summer school for computer science students and practitioners, at the University of Applied Sciences in Furtwangen, Germany.

In the university context, the project simulation took the whole semester and the exercises were partly done as homework and partly during the course. The summer school courses took two whole days and no (or few) homework was possible to be done. So, the exercises were all done during the course and took more than half of the course time. Therefore, a shortened version of the project was executed then, with less software artifacts to be written.

The students were led step by step through the process of requirements elicitation (using interviews, but also creativity techniques), UML specification, prioritization, and the implementation of a prototype and its acceptance test by the customer. Before each activity, the instructor provided theoretical knowledge about how to execute a method and standards of notations. As several teams work in parallel, the trainer cannot supervise all interactions but gets feedback about the learning progress when reviewing intermediate results.

The teaching objective was that the requirements specification satisfies the typical quality criteria (completeness, consistency, etc.) and the customer accepts the prototype.

Experiences

The role games make the course a lively and interactive experience. As the same example project is used consistently from beginning to end of the course, the participants see how different RE methods for elicitation, specification and prioritization work together. Errors made in earlier steps are felt in later steps. However, the learning experience is less easily controllable by the trainer than when executing separate role games.

The participants are highly motivated to do the specification well because they have a customer who is interested in the project, and sometimes the product is even planned to be built. This is more motivating than to describe the same library system as the other students in the same course and in the years before.

The project simulation worked well with novices as well as with advanced participants who have work experience. The novices need more support and direct feedback during the exercises. Different participants learn different lessons from the same experience: Novices learn the RE methods and modeling notations, while advanced participants discuss with the lecturer more advanced questions like the ideal level of granularity or questions from their practical experience.

For the teacher, it is an advantage that the projects are all different. This makes the correction and grading of the specification documents an interesting task. And when working in homework, students ``cannot copy other students´ results''.

The role play in this form makes only sense with a maximum of 20 participants. Students are working in two person teams (with one three person team, if the number is odd).

The projects always are very different in complexity. It is important to tell the students that it is more important to apply the methods correctly than to end up with a complete specification. This is the difference between this exercise and a real project.

When the course includes homework, it is important that all homework can be done alone and those exercises which must be done in pairs, take place during the course times to guarantee meetings.

So, all in all, this form of the course demands a constant and individual steering by the trainer, who must be able to understand all projects in the course and help with their specification. This demands more than understanding just one sample solution.

3.5   Using Improvisation Theater to Create Interaction

Description

The REIM format (Requirements Engineering and Improvisation) has been developed to train both factual knowledge and soft skills related to RE [19]. REIM follows a typical Improvisation Theater training session but utilizes Storytelling elements to adjust to the participants' background (see [20] for details).

Each REIM workshop session consists of the three phases: warm-up, training and feedback. During each phase different types of improvisation games are played. Only the training games focus on the training of factual knowledge and soft skill competences [20]. Each training game addresses several related soft skill competences. As REIM is quite flexible in this aspect, the trainer prepares upfront which competences shall be addressed. On the other hand, given sufficient experience, games can be adjusted to the participants' needs as the workshop goes along. (This seems to be quite common in industrial trainings)

For instance, RE prioritization is mainly taught and trained fact-oriented. One learns which methods exist and how to apply them, but the participant is left alone to realize this experience. REIM creates this experience by utilizing the "Requirements Game", which – among other aspects – demonstrates priority setting and its difficulties. This is addressed by bringing the participants into a situation where they are so busy fulfilling the (factual-oriented) task given, that they forget to obey other rules which implicitly undermine the priority setting.

The workshop has proven to work well for novices as well as experts in the field of RE. The Improvisation games being used are the same for both parties. Yet, the stories being told differ. Interestingly, the reported personal learning outcomes differ depending on the degree of experience starting from the creation of numerous aha-effects for novices reaching to intense discussions among participants for experts.

Experiences

REIM is an interactive format which activates each and every single participant. This is in fact what the warm-up games are used for: They are creating the atmosphere. There is no option of participating by observing.

REIM very quickly connects factual knowledge to soft skills and creates experience for each and every participant.

REIM has been applied to numerous groups and was always well perceived. The level of experience in these groups differed from novice to experts, maybe even mastery. During feedback, it became clear that different participants report on different issues that were most valuable in their learning. This seems to be related to the different stages of the Dreyfus model [21], but has not yet been validated. In addition, each participant rates his personal learning-to-having-fun ratio. Interestingly, more experienced groups tend to report a higher learning experience whereas beginners emphasize on the aspect of having had fun.

REIM can be used for up to 40 participants, working best with 15-25. More participants could be (and have been trained) by splitting up the group into two and using a second trainer or repeating the session. This might however result into different non-comparable learning.

From a trainer's perspective, the REIM format appears to be quite complex. In order to utilize the format, the trainer needs some knowledge in improvisation theater games as well as storytelling. It is the trainer who dominates and steers the approach (and thus the success of the workshop) quite significantly.

Even though a Train-the-Trainer description has been formulated as a pattern and a trial session with other trainers was run [23], this complexity might still prevent the workshop format from becoming more widely spread in the community. This might be particularly true for the university area where trainers are often not trained prior to teaching but rather thrown in at the deep end.

REIM appears to be an interesting workshop format to combine factual knowledge and soft skill training into one. It has however not yet been formally validated, nor has the correlation to the Dreyfus model been proven to be valid. This is part of a current investigation of one of the authors and shall result in a sophisticated understanding who REIM works within different group set-ups.

4   Discussion

The above case descriptions provide only a part of the four authors' teaching and training experiences. Based on the experiences described in this paper and on additional experience, Table 3 describes the different preconditions for four forms of experience-oriented learning methods.

The table indicates that there is no "silver bullet" and that methods could be and have to be adapted to special circumstances. It must be noted that the positive definition "the x-way of teaching fits to the situation y" does not automatically imply that x will not fit to any other situation. To evaluate this could be an important task in future research.

We suppose that not only the level in the Dreyfus model but also the concrete situation of the learner will influence the selection of the effective type of teaching.

Table 3. Different preconditions under which four different types of teaching/ training have been used successfully

	Improvisation theatre	Role games	Project simulation, toy project	Real-life project with real customer
Group size	Some games are possible with small groups only and others with large groups	When group size is large, then need to form sub-groups	When group size is large, then need to form sub-groups	Only for small groups, because of limited availability of customer
Controllability	High	High	Average	Low
Distributed team	No	Possible	Possible	Possible
Equipment	Room without chairs	Depends, usually seminar room with chairs	Room with tables, chairs and computers	Work places and meeting room
Supervision need	Active supervision for the whole time	Active supervision for the whole time	Initial explanations, answering questions, solving problems	Regular supervision
Theoretical knowledge of participants	None needed	Must be provided	Must be provided	Must be provided
Practical knowledge of participants	None needed	None needed	None needed, but desirable	Essential for success
Feedback to trainer about learning success	Immediate	Immediate	When reviewing intermediate results	When reviewing intermediate results
Dreyfuss level of participants	All levels	Novice, competence	Novice, competence	All levels. For the levels of expertise and mastery, the character will be more a coaching than a training

5   Conclusion and Future Work

This experience report presents four approaches for teaching RE in academia and training in industry. In particular, we presented findings from four interdisciplinary, game-oriented courses. We analyzed these approaches with respect to different settings in which we applied them successfully and in which they also might be applicable, as well as additional issues that need to be considered when designing didactic settings for different target groups. In particular, we found that each of the techniques we employed is suitable for an audience on the novice level of the Dreyfus model, both for teaching and training. On the higher levels of the Dreyfus model, training on specific topics becomes more relevant. Consequently, methods like role games, project simulation and improvisation theatre are appropriate on these levels, primarily due to their good controllability. It should be noted, however, that our findings are derived after the fact from the specific cases that we explored. It is a matter of future work to analyze to what extent our findings are generalizable.

Our discussion about our experiences led to some further research questions, like: How can we assess the level of expertise of the participants ex ante? And which level does the trainer need to have? How can trainers be trained? Further empirical substantiation of experiences as summarized in Tables 1 and 2 would test whether the training methods can be useful for participants on other Dreyfus levels, too.

References

1. Standish Group: Extreme CHAOS (2001)
2. Lethbridge, T.: A survey of the relevance of computer science and software engineering education. In: llth International Conference on Software Engineering (1998)
3. Cap Gemini: IT-Trends 2013, Berlin (October 2013),
   http://www.de.capgemini.com/ressourcen/it-trends-studie-2013
4. Foppa, K.: Lernen, Gedächtnis, Verhalten: Ergebnisse und Probleme der Lernpsychologie, 9th edn. Kiepenheuer & Witsch, Cologne (1975)
5. Damian, D., Hadwin, A., Al-Ani, B.: Instructional Design and Assessment Strategies for Teaching Global Software Development: A Framework. In: 28th International Conference on Software Engineering, Shanghai, China, pp. 685–690 (2006)
6. Lübke, D., Schneider, K.: Agile Hour: Teaching XP Skills to Students and IT Professionals. In: Bomarius, F., Komi-Sirviö, S. (eds.) PROFES 2005. LNCS, vol. 3547, pp. 517–529. Springer, Heidelberg (2005)
7. http://c2.com/cgi/wiki?ExtremeHour
8. Yusop, N., Mehboob, Z., Zowghi, D.: The Role of Conducting Stakeholder Meetings in Requirements Engineering Training. In: REET International Workshop on Requirements Engineering Education and Training, pp. 133–139 (2007)
9. Regev, G., Gause, D.C., Wegmann, A.: Requirements Engineering Education in the 21st Century, An Experiential Learning Approach. In: 16th IEEE International Requirements Engineering Conference (2008)
10. Mahaux, M.: Improvisational Theatre: an Approach to Soft Skills for Requirements Engineers. In: REET International Workshop on Requirements Engineering Education and Training, pp. 133–139 (2007)

11. Neville, K., Adam, F.: Integrating Theory and Practice in Education with Business Games. Informing Science, Special Series: Informing Each Other 6 (2003)
12. Zapata, C.M., Awad-Aubad, J.G.: Requirements Game: Teaching Software Project Management. CLEI Electronic Journal 10(1), PAPER 3 (June 2007)
13. Favela, J., Peña-Mora, F.: An experience in collaborative software engineering education. IEEE Software 18(2), 47–53 (2001)
14. Baker, A., Oh Navarro, E., van der Hoek, A.: Problems and Programmers: an educational software engineering card game. In: ICSE 2003 Proceedings of the 25th International Conference on Software Engineering (2003)
15. Carrington, D., Baker, A., van der Hoek, A.: It's All in the Game: Teaching Software Process Concepts. In: 34th ASEE/IEEE Frontiers in Education Conference, Savannah, GA, October 20-23 (2004)
16. Fadali, M.S., Robinson, M., Mcnichols, K.: Teaching Engineering to K-12 Students Using Role Playing Games. In: ASEE Annual Conf., American Society for Engineering Education, Washington, DC (2000)
17. Dawson, R.: Twenty Dirty Tricks to Train Software Engineers. In: 22nd International Conference on Software Engineering (ICSE 2000), Limerick, Ireland (2000)
18. Johnstone, K.: Improvisation und Theater. Alexander Verlag (2010)
19. Hoffmann, A.: REIM - An Improvisation Workshop Format to Train Soft Skill Awareness. In: 5th International Workshop on Cooperative and Human Aspects of Software Engineering (CHASE). IEEE (2012)
20. Hoffmann, A.: Game Language. In: EuroPLoP 2012: 17th European Conference on Pattern Languages of Programs, Hillside (2012)
21. Dreyfus, S., Dreyfus, H.: A five-stage model of the mental activities involved in direct skill acquisition, No. ORC-80-2. Univ. Berkeley Operations Research Center (1980)
22. Hunt, A.: Pragmatisches Denken und Lernen – Refactor your wetware! Carl Hanser Verlag GmbH & Co. KG (2009)
23. Hoffmann, A.: A Trainer's Guideline to Teaching Soft Skills Using Improvisation Theater - A Workshop Format Exemplified on a Requirements Engineering Game. In: EuroPLoP 2011: 16th European Conference on Pattern Languages of Programs (2011)
24. Landes, D., Pfeiffer, V., Sedelmaier, Y., Mottok, J., Hagel, G.: Learning and Teaching Software Process Models. In: IEEE Global Engineering Education (EDUCON), Marrakesh, Morocco, pp. 1153–1160 (2012)
25. Rausch, P., Landes, D.: "Ihr könnt nur zusammen gewinnen" – Interdisziplinäre Praxisprojekte in der Hochschulausbildung. In: Dorn, K.-H., et al. (eds.) Projekte als Kulturerlebnis, pp. 63–74. Dpunkt Verlag, Heidelberg (2009)
26. Weißbach, R.: Bridging the Communication Gap in Information System Projects. Enabling Non-IT Professionals for the Requirements Engineering Process. In: Kettunen, J., et al. (eds.) Applied Research and Professional Education. First CARPE Networking Conference, p. 259. Turku UAS, Turku (2012), http://julkaisut.turkuamk.fi/isbn9789522162519.pdf

An Analysis of Priority-Based Decision Heuristics for Optimizing Elicitation Efficiency

Norman Riegel and Joerg Doerr

Fraunhofer IESE, Fraunhofer Platz 1, 67663 Kaiserslautern, Germany
{norman.riegel,joerg.doerr}@iese.fraunhofer.de

Abstract. **[Context & motivation]** Requirements are often elicited in hierarchies, with more fine-grained requirements being derived from abstract ones. This approach is typically used in business-process-driven requirements engineering (BPRE) where fine-grained system functions are derived from business activities contained in business processes. **[Question/problem]** Especially in large requirements hierarchies, requirements engineers are faced with the challenge of having to identify the best elicitation order that maximizes business value. This is an essential activity for incremental development projects, where the most valuable functionality should be released as early as possible to achieve the highest return on investment. **[Principal ideas/results]** We developed and analyzed a set of priority-based decision heuristics in order to support requirements engineers in deciding which requirements should be elaborated next at a certain point during elicitation. **[Contribution]** We simulated the heuristics on different business-process-based requirements trees and compared them with regard to efficiency measures. We were able to identify significant differences between these heuristics.

Keywords: Requirements Prioritization, Decision Heuristic, Requirements Elicitation, Business-Process-Driven Requirements Engineering, BPRE.

1   Introduction

In many information systems (IS) development projects, requirements are elicited and structured in hierarchies with several abstraction levels. Such a hierarchy is also created in business-process-driven requirements engineering (BPRE) projects, where the requirements elicitation starts at the level of business processes and successively derives more fine-grained software requirements from these [1][2] (see Fig. 1). Especially in incremental development projects, where functionality is delivered in several releases, the most valuable functionality should be released as early as possible to achieve the highest return on investment [3]. Thus, requirements engineers are faced with the challenge of having to identify the best requirements elicitation order that maximizes business value. This means that elicitation effort should be spent on the most promising requirements in terms of business value while at the same time minimizing elicitation effort for less important requirements.

Imagine the following scenario in a BPRE setting, where several business processes should be analyzed: The flow of one of the processes has been elicited; the

C. Salinesi and I. van de Weerd (Eds.): REFSQ 2014, LNCS 8396, pp. 268–284, 2014.

activities included in the process have been identified and prioritized; some (but not all) have been analyzed in detail to derive the system functions. Is it now beneficial to continue specifying the remaining activities (and resulting system functions) until the requirements for this specific process are complete, or is it more beneficial to focus the elicitation effort on analyzing another business process from the processes in scope? The remaining requirements of the already (incompletely) analyzed process might not bring as much business value as the requirements from the new process.

Thus, focusing on requirements of minor importance can lead to (1) wasted effort for unnecessary (RE) activities; (2) postponed elicitation of more valuable requirements to a later point in time (which might ultimately lead to a loss of revenue because important functionality is released too late).

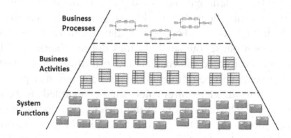

Fig. 1. Business-process-based Requirements Hierarchy

In order to determine the most valuable requirements in a project, prioritization techniques are typically applied. In the literature, numerous prioritization approaches can be found, differing, e.g., in terms of procedure and complexity of the calculations (cf., e.g., [4]). Also, several approaches exist to prioritize requirements structured in hierarchies [5]. However, these approaches lack an important aspect: they do not support decision making during requirements elicitation, which is an essential issue especially in large requirements hierarchies.

To overcome this problem, we developed a set of priority-based decision heuristics in order to support requirements engineers in deciding which requirements should be elaborated next at a certain point during elicitation. In a controlled experiment, we simulated the different heuristics on different data sets, i.e., different business-process-based requirements hierarchies. By utilizing simulation, decision heuristics can be investigated on many different data sets, which would not be possible in a real-world setting. Our main research question to be answered was whether *requirements elicitation efficiency in BPRE differs between these decision heuristics*. Thus, the focus of this paper is not on the prioritization of the requirements in such a hierarchy (as discussed in [2]), but rather on the decision heuristics, based on priorities that lead to a certain elicitation order within the requirements hierarchy.

The remainder of this paper is structured as follows: Section 2 describes the context and problem in more detail, section 3 discusses related work in the area, section 4 presents our controlled experiment (using simulation) including descriptions of the compared heuristics as well as our findings, and section 5 finally concludes the paper and gives an outlook on future work.

2   Problem Definition

The decision heuristics to be evaluated in this study are applied to a typical BPRE requirements hierarchy (Fig.1) [2] consisting of three requirements layers: (1) business processes, (2) business activities, and (3) system functions. Business processes consist of business activities, which in turn consist of several system functions. An example of a business process could be "Travel Management", a process that is performed if an employee wants to request approval for a business trip. A business activity in this process could be "Create Travel Request", describing the activity of an employee of filling out and forwarding a travel request form to his / her boss. A system function to support this activity could be "Show Travel Request Form", a function of the system that shows the user a form on the screen.

The focus of the decision heuristics in this paper is on the requirements selection decisions made during elicitation. This means that prioritization is not only done at the end of the elicitation phase, but several times during elicitation. Thus, elicitation and prioritization are performed alternately and prioritization is used to determine which of the requirements will be refined in the next elicitation step.

The elicited and prioritized requirements can be regarded as being stored in a requirements backlog. Each requirement in the backlog is a candidate for refinement in the next elicitation step. The requirements backlog therefore consists of requirements on different levels of abstraction, with the requirements on the lowest abstraction level serving as input for the realization phase, i.e., development. This concept is based on the idea of agile approaches such as Scrum [3], where requirements are stored in a product backlog for further refinement.

It is assumed that at the beginning of a project, the requirements tree is unknown, except for the list of (black-box) business processes in scope. "Black box" means that these processes have been identified but have not been analyzed yet, i.e., the workflow and the included activities are unknown. These business processes form the initial requirements backlog. The processes are then prioritized and the first decision to be made is which business process should be analyzed first. This decision is provided by the decision heuristic.

After the decision has been made, the chosen business process is elicited (e.g., in an elicitation workshop), becomes "white box", and the contained business activities are revealed (again as black boxes). These business activities are then prioritized. At this point in time, the requirements backlog consists of the prioritized remaining black-box business processes as well as the newly revealed prioritized black-box business activities. Again, a second decision is needed as to which of these requirements in the backlog shall be refined further. Depending on the rule of the decision heuristic (e.g., depth-first or breadth-first search [6]), one of the business activities or one of the processes will be analyzed next.

This alternating procedure between prioritization, selection decision, and resulting elicitation is repeated until the project ends, i.e., until the requirements tree is complete or until the resources for elicitation are exhausted. The goal of a decision heuristic is to guide the requirements engineer in such a way that the most valuable functionality is elicited first while at the same time using as little elicitation effort as possible. Thus, we have two relevant parameters in our study: the business value of a requirement (represented by its priority) as well as the elicitation effort that is incurred when eliciting this requirement. An important point to mention is that it is assumed that the priority of a requirement already includes an estimation of its realization effort (e.g., development costs, risks etc.), as otherwise it would be meaningless to optimize the elicitation order. The assumptions about the different parameters are described in section 4.1.

3   Related Work

Several prioritization approaches that can be applied in requirements hierarchies have already been described in the literature, e.g., Hierarchy AHP, Hierarchical Cumulative Voting [7] (and deviations like Value-oriented HCV) or Quantitative WinWin, which we already assessed with regard to their suitability for the BPRE context in our previous work [5]. One important outcome of this assessment was the lack of guidance for the order of elicitation, i.e., the prioritization approaches typically take as input a set of already finalized requirements (e.g., for release planning as in [8] or [9]). This means they are intended to be used after the elicitation process has finished (in order to determine the ranking of requirements or features for development) but not during elicitation. In other words, they do not provide any heuristic on how to decide which requirements shall be refined next at a certain point in time in the elicitation process. Closing this gap is the goal of this study.

The decision heuristics and the resulting elicitation order within the requirements hierarchy in this paper are similar to well-known algorithms for traversing trees, e.g. depth-first search or breadth-first search [6]. To be more precise, best-first search [6] makes use of heuristics to determine which node (in a graph or tree) to visit next. However, best-first search algorithms are mostly designed to be applied on trees where the size and structure are known in advance. In our problem, we have a tree of requirements whose size is unknown at the beginning of a project. Most approaches dealing with such problems stem from the domain of (shortest) path finding, especially the robot movement [10][11][12][13][14]. At each node of an unknown graph or tree, the robot follows a certain edge along the graph based on a proposed heuristic. In our case, the edge weights are the combination of the business value (priority) of a requirement and its elicitation effort, whereas in path-finding problems, the edge weights represent the distance between nodes.

In contrast to these problems, the edge weights are not fixed during traversal of the requirements tree: if, for example, two business processes are elicited, the costs for traversing over these nodes of the tree are incurred only once. After that, traversing over these nodes (for example jumping between the activities of these processes) does not re-incur any elicitation effort for the business processes. A similar kind of problem can be found in [10], where the robot is allowed to jump between already revealed nodes. However, our problem is not to find the shortest path between nodes in the tree but to optimize the business value compared to the elicitation effort.

Simulation of prioritization strategies has been applied before in the work of Port et al. [15]. In this work, simulation was used to investigate agile and plan-based prioritization approaches. The simulations are done on base sets of (independent) requirements where new requirements emerge during runtime and are allocated to development iterations by utilizing prioritization. Dynamism is an important part of this study. The performance of the strategies is compared by analyzing different measures, e.g., total value and total costs. In contrast to that, our work is based on requirements hierarchies where priorities are influenced by these dependencies. Furthermore, our focus is on elicitation effort, not on development costs. What the decision heuristics we investigated (section 4.2.2.) have in common with the prioritization strategies in [15] is that they utilize the priorities of the requirements to make a decision. However, the goal of the decision heuristics is to determine which requirements to refine further, whereas the prioritization strategies in [15] aim at ranking the requirements and allocating them to development iterations with respect to effort constraints. Thus, they have some parts in common, but are not directly comparable as the purpose is different.

In our study we use a representative measure (the net present value, see section 4.1), which is able to express that early value generation is more profitable than late value generation while at the same time regarding elicitation effort. This means that, for example, heuristic A could be better than heuristic B if the tree is traversed completely but not if the tree is traversed only partly (for example, if the budget has been exhausted). As the requirements tree is unknown in advance, an optimal solution cannot be pre-calculated. Thus, we are interested in decision heuristics that will lead the requirements engineer to a good solution in most of the cases, even if information about the tree is unavailable. To the best of our knowledge, no such study has been performed before in the area of requirements prioritization and elicitation.

4   Controlled Experiment

This section will describe our controlled experiment and our findings based on two different simulations and tests.

4.1   Goal, Questions, Hypotheses and Metrics

We used the GQM approach [16] as a basis for defining the measurements in our experiment. The evaluation goal was to *analyze nine priority-based decision heuristics for the purpose of comparison with regard to elicitation efficiency from the viewpoint of requirements engineers in the context of a controlled experiment of simulations.*
The following research questions were to be answered:

RQ$_1$: *"Is there a difference in elicitation efficiency when applying different decision heuristics in BPRE?"*
Thus, the hypothesis is: **H$_{1,1}$** *There is a difference in elicitation efficiency in BPRE when applying the decision heuristics*[1].
RQ$_2$: *"Is there a difference in elicitation efficiency when applying different decision heuristics in BPRE compared at different control points during project runtime?"*
Thus, the hypothesis is: **H$_{2,1}$** *There is a difference in elicitation efficiency when applying the decision heuristics compared at different points during project runtime.*

---

[1] For reasons of brevity, we omit the corresponding null hypotheses here.

To compare elicitation efficiency between different heuristics, we performed tool-based simulation on different BPRE requirements hierarchies (see section 4.2.4).

To express elicitation efficiency, we utilize the concept of net present value (NPV), which allows expressing that (1) early value generation is more profitable than late value generation, and (2) lower elicitation effort is better than higher elicitation effort. The NPV is a business administration measure for dynamic investment calculations. In [17], this measure was already utilized to determine the return of investment of packaged software releases. By discounting to the beginning of an investment, payments occurring at an arbitrary point in time can be compared. The net present value NPV is given by:

$$NPV(i,N) = \sum_{t=0}^{N} \frac{Z_t}{(1+i)^t}$$

- t: the period of the cash flow, typically in years
- i: the discount rate, i.e., the rate of return that could be earned on an investment in the financial markets with similar risk
- Z_t: the net cash flow, i.e., (cash inflow – cash outflow) at period t
- N: the total number of periods

In our case, we needed to adapt the NPV (because we did not compare payments) and assume the following for its parameters:

Cash inflow & cash outflow:

- Cash inflow is generated during the period when the elicitation of a requirement on the lowest abstraction level (i.e., *system function*) is finished. Thus, the assumption is that this system function is directly developed, released, and produces business value (e.g., revenues) without any delay. It also generates a constant cash inflow during each period after completion of its elicitation.
- Cash inflow corresponds to the priority of the system function.
- Cash outflow corresponds to the elicitation effort for a requirement during a period. We did not investigate development effort here.
- Each requirement in the hierarchy needs a certain amount of time to be elicited (= # *of periods*), as well as a certain amount of resources (persons) that are needed for elicitation; thus, the total elicitation effort for a requirement is described by (# *of periods needed for elicitation*) * (# *of resources needed for elicitation per period*)
  - o   The time length of a period is defined as one hour.

Net Cash Flow (Z_t): Because we do not deal with monetary values, we normalize business value and elicitation effort to make them comparable. Net cash flow thus describes the difference between the relative business value created and the relative elicitation effort required in the period. This corresponds to the assumption that the sum of the business values of all system functions is equal to the total elicitation effort of all requirements.

Interest Rate (i): The interest rate is assumed to be

$$i = 1.1^{\frac{1}{360*8}} - 1$$

which is the conformant interest rate for periods of less than a year, i.e., in our case for one hour (assuming 360 days per year and 8 hours per day) if the interest rate for a year is 10%. As the interest rate and periods are set to hours, the effect of time in each period is rather small. The above definitions imply that elicitation efficiency is described by the business value that is generated by the elicited system functions compared to the required elicitation effort, and that it is additionally influenced by time. Furthermore, business value is only generated by system functions, i.e., the elicitation of business processes and business activities is assumed to be not generating any value. Their business value is only realized by their system functions. We calculate the NPV for each heuristic at five control points until the requirements hierarchy is completely traversed. The control points are at 20%, 40%, 60%, 80%, and 100% of the number of periods needed to traverse the whole hierarchy (i.e., they are determined based on the number of the requirements and the number of periods needed for elicitation of these elements).

4.2 Experimental Design and Setup

Based on the study goals, the hypotheses, and the related metrics, the experiment was designed and prepared. Below, we describe the details of the experiment setup.

4.2.1 Model Parameters of the Requirements Hierarchies

In order to run our experiment, we created several requirements hierarchies (i.e., the subjects) where the different decision heuristics were applied. Each hierarchy consists of a certain number of business processes (BPs), business activities (BAs), and system functions (SFs). The root node can be considered as a "project". The hierarchies (trees) were created according to the following properties:

Requirements Numbers

Business processes: The number of BPs for each tree is normally distributed in the whole population of the trees with a mean value of 30 and a standard deviation of 25%, i.e., 7.5 BPs.

Rationale: The number of business processes in scope is based on our past experiences in BPRE projects, as well as on some interviews with business process management (BPM) solution providers. In the interviews it was reported that the automation of around 30 business processes can be achieved within a time frame of two to six years by most of their customers (depending on company size). Furthermore, we decided to determine the number of BPs in our own institute and assessed how many of them could potentially be software supported by an IS, which finally resulted in the mean value of 30. To have a roughly homogenous group, the standard deviation should not be too high, so we set it to 7.5.

Business activities: The number of BAs for each BP is normally distributed with a mean of 20 and a standard deviation of 25%, i.e., five business activities.

Rationale: Again, from our past projects and the interviews we determined that most BPs have an average of 10-30 business activities. As we do not have any quantitative data here, we set the mean to 20 based on these previous experiences.

System functions: The number of SFs for each BA is normally distributed with a mean of 5 and a standard deviation of 25%, i.e., 1.25 SFs.

Rationale: Based on our past experience, a typical BA description (e.g., a use case) normally contains 2-10 steps and around five SFs are refined from that.

Priority Values

As we are not interested in the actual prioritization of the requirements (this is a topic in [2]) but only in the decisions based on the priorities, the tree is prefilled with priorities for our simulations. This is done by randomly (equally distributed) assigning a value between 1 and 100 to the requirements and then normalizing and weighting them (see Fig. 2). This procedure is adopted from the hierarchical cumulative voting (HCV) method in [7].

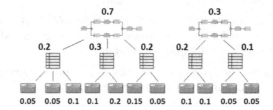

Fig. 2. Relative Priorities in a Requirements Hierarchy

Elicitation Effort:

As described above, the elicitation effort for a requirement is described by *# of periods* and *# of resources*. The configuration is as follows:

Business processes: The *# of periods* for BP is based on the number of the BAs that are contained in the BP. This means that larger BPs will have a larger number for *# of periods*. We utilize a ratio with a base of ten BAs (i.e., where this ratio calculates to 1). The mean of the elicitation effort is determined based on the following formula:

$$(\# subBAs / 10) * baseMeanBP, \text{ where } baseMeanBP = 3$$

Briefly this means that the elicitation periods base for BPs (*baseMeanBP*) will be adapted by a factor based on the process size. After that, a randomly generated normally distributed number around this mean is generated with a standard deviation of 0.75. The *# of resources* is determined by

$$Log_3(\# subBAs) * resourceMutliplierBP, \text{ where } resourceMutliplierBP = 4$$

resourceMutliplierBP is the resource number base (i.e., the number of persons needed for eliciting a BP in an elicitation session) we assume for BPs.

Rationale: As we recorded the elicitation effort in our past projects, we were able to derive the base numbers (e.g., a 3-hour elicitation workshop for a BP containing ten BAs) from this data (but only from a small data set). By using a normally distributed number we express that the elicitation time needed for BPs with the same size actually differs in reality. The *resourceMutliplierBP* of 4 (one requirements engineer and three stakeholders in a business process elicitation workshop) is also derived from our past data and the log_3 is used to adapt it to different BP sizes. The log helps to raise the number of resources only slowly for larger BPs (because the number of stakeholders participating in a workshop does not increase linearly with the process size). This adaptation also matches the data derived from our past projects.

Business activities: The *# of periods* for BAs is also based on the number of its sub-elements (i.e., SFs). We utilize a ratio that is 1.5 times as high if the number of SFs is doubled and 0.5 times as high if the number of SFs is halved. The base is eight SFs (i.e., where this ratio calculates to 1). After that, the ratio is multiplied with the *baseMeanBA* of 2 to generate a mean value. A randomly generated, normally distributed number around this mean is generated with a standard deviation of 0.5. The *resourceMutliplierBA* is set to 2.

Rationale: We assume a base effort of two hours for the elicitation for BAs, which is slightly adapted based on the sub-elements and also randomly generated and normally distributed. The *resourceMutliplierBA* assumes a one-to-one interview (one stakeholder, one requirements engineer) for eliciting a BA.

System functions: The *baseMeanSF* for *# of periods* for SFs is set to 1. Based on this, a normally distributed random number around this mean is generated with a standard deviation of 0.5.The *resourceMutliplierSF* is set to 2.

Rationale: We assume the base effort for SFs as a 1-hour interview between two resources (one stakeholder and one requirements engineer).

4.2.2 Compared Decision Heuristics

In search algorithms, a heuristic is a function that ranks alternatives at each branching step based on available information to decide which branch to follow [6]. In order to run our experiment, we defined and implemented several decision heuristics (i.e., the *treatments*). The heuristics are based on the literature as well as on our own ideas: Heuristics DH1 and DH2 are based on the most common heuristics found in the literature (depth-first [6] and highest value first [15]). Based on that, we created further heuristics in a derivation process: DH3 was created as a combination of DH1 and DH2. A more sophisticated idea led to DH4-DH7 (see description of DH4). DH8 is based on the idea of comparing values and costs to make a decision, which is also often discussed in the literature [4][15] (the difference here is that the costs are not development costs, but elicitation effort). Finally, we created DH9 as a kind of reference heuristic. DH9 has information about non-revealed requirements on lower levels. Thus, heuristics DH1-DH7 are only based on the priority values that are available at a certain point during traversal of the requirements tree, whereas DH8 and DH9 also utilize the costs incurred by refinement. We included them in order to check if this information advantage leads to a significant difference in performance. We do not deem this list of heuristics to be complete. Additional heuristics might emerge due to adaptation and further research. In the following, we will describe the decision rules of the heuristics. Due to space limitations, we omit pseudo code. The heuristics take as input a set (*backlog*) of already prioritized business processes.

DH1. Highest Value (HV) First: *At each decision point in the hierarchy, always refine the requirement with the highest priority next.* This heuristic represents the typical intuitive, "straightforward" approach if requirements are chosen by priorities, as already applied in [15], for example.

DH2: System Functions (SF) First: *Refine the requirements in depth-first order according to priority, i.e., refine the highest-valued business process, the highest-valued business activity, and then all system functions of this business activity in order of their value; go to the second-highest business activity and refine all system functions in order of their value; repeat this procedure until the business process has been completely traversed and go to the next process.* This heuristic represents a typical waterfall-like approach (depth-first search like [6]; steered by highest priority).

DH3: SF First-HV First: *Proceed as in DH2, but whenever there are no system functions in the backlog, refine the requirement with the highest priority.* This is a combination of DH1 & DH2; we combined them in order to see if it is more valuable to "jump" to the highest prioritized element after refining all system functions.

DH4: Remaining Value Global: *Get the sum of the priorities of the most detailed requirements available in the backlog; check if this sum is greater than the highest priority of the requirement on the hierarchy level above; if it is, refine the low-level requirement with the highest priority; otherwise, go to the higher hierarchy level and repeat the procedure.* This is one of our newly created heuristics. To the best of our knowledge, it has not been applied before in requirements prioritization and elicitation. It is based on the idea that if, for example, the highest-valued business activity in the backlog has lower priority than the sum of the available system functions, the system functions that can be revealed by refining this business activity (children of this business activity) will still have lower priority in sum. Thus, the system functions are refined until the sum is lower than the highest-valued business activity.

DH5: Remaining Value Global All: *Proceed as in DH4, but compare the sum on the system function level to the business activity level and the process level at the same time (instead of only checking against the business activity level).* This is a variation of DH4, which we created because it might happen in DH4 that a business process with a high value is not refined as long as the system functions together have a higher value than the available business activities. This is prevented here.

DH6: Remaining Value: Same as DH4, but only the elements in the same branch are summed up and compared.

DH7: Remaining Value All: Same as DH6, but the sum of the system function values in the branch is compared to the highest-valued business activity in the backlog (instead of the branch).

DH8 (informed heuristic): Value-Cost Optimal: *Always refine the requirement with the highest value-effort relation.* Basically, this is a combination of DH1 with the effort that is needed for elicitation. Please keep in mind that we assume that the priorities already include cost estimations for development.

DH9 (informed heuristic): Optimal Solution: *Calculate the best path (based on values and costs) to each system function in the hierarchy. Refine all requirements on the best path. Repeat.* This heuristic is based on DH8, but instead of looking at the available requirements in the backlog, this heuristic "knows" the priority and the effort values of all requirements beforehand. Thus it is even better informed than DH8.

4.2.3 Experimental Design

The experiment was designed as a two-way repeated measures ANOVA [18]. In this way we were able to identify possible differences between the heuristics over several control points (CP). Thus, one factor are the heuristics with nine levels, while the second factor are the control points with five levels. Each heuristic was applied to each requirement tree (within-design). The dependent variable is the elicitation efficiency represented by the NPV (see section 4.1), which is measured for each heuristic at each control point (5x9).

4.2.4 Experiment Procedure and Data Collection

Simulation 1 for testing $H_{1.1}$: We configured our decision heuristics tool (developed for this purpose) with the aforementioned parameters for the requirements hierarchies. The sample size was pre-calculated with G*Power 3^2 for a repeated measures ANOVA (within-factors) with nine groups and five measurements. To test the first hypothesis, we assumed a small effect size f = 0.1 (as we are dealing with normalized values to calculate the NPV), which we adapted based on the description in [19] to f' = 0.2236 for five measurements, an alpha error probability of 0.05, and a power of 0.95. Based on our experience from test runs, we recognized a high correlation among the repeated measures, which made nonsphericity correction necessary. Correlation was set to 0.9 and nonsphericity correction to 0.2. The proposed sample size of G*Power was n = 18. As mentioned in [19], for more than two groups the adapted f' leads to slight overestimation of the power and underestimation of the required sample size, so we corrected the sample size to n = 25. Thus, we generated 25 trees and stored them in a database. The trees contained a total of 813 business processes, 16,267 business activities and 81,700 system functions in total, i.e., 32.52 business processes, 650.68 business activities and 3,268 system functions on average per tree. After that we simulated each heuristic on each of the generated requirements trees. The tool automatically calculates the NPV and at each control point, the data is saved to the database for later analyses accompanied by meta data such as configuration parameters, runtime, etc. Thus, we had 45 measurements for each requirement tree in total, resulting in 1,125 data points for the whole simulation. The total runtime of the simulation (including the generation of the requirements trees) was 01h:15m:40s on a standard PC, with an average of 03m:02s for each tree.

Simulation 2 for testing $H_{2.1}$: After the first simulation, we adapted the parameters of G*Power to test our second hypothesis. As we are interested in the performance of the heuristics at each control point, we decided to create an own sample to test each control point separately. In contrast to the first simulation (and based on the experience from that), we set f = 0.1 (in this case we only have one measurement, so it is not adapted to f'), and nonsphericity correction = 0.24 to determine the sample size. The proposed sample size of G*Power was n = 73. We rounded up to n = 75 and generated 375 trees to test each heuristic at each control point separately. The trees contained a total of 11,472 business processes, 229,373 business activities, and 1,150,227 system functions in total, i.e., 30.59 business processes, 611.66 business

---

^{2} http://www.psycho.uni-duesseldorf.de/abteilungen/aap/gpower3

activities and 3,067.27 system functions on average per tree. The total runtime of the second simulation was 22h:16m:16s, with an average of 03m:34s for each tree.

4.3   Experiment Analysis and Results

The data gathered from the simulation was imported into the statistical tool PASW 19. First, the collected data was checked for normal distribution using the Kolmogorov-Smirnov and the Shapiro-Wilk tests. Both tests were not significant, meaning that there was no significance for non-normal distribution. We cross-checked this result by creating histograms and Q-Q plots for each of the 45 measurement variables. No violation of non-normality could be identified by visual inspection, which confirmed the results of the other tests. After that we applied the two-way repeated measures ANOVA on the data of the first simulation. As we did not have any hypotheses about the performance of the heuristics, no contrasts were defined in advance. In the second analysis, we applied one-way repeated measures ANOVA on the data of the second simulation. This means that we applied it five times in total, on 75 trees (of the 375) at a time for testing each control point. We did not use the data of the first simulation for these tests because of two reasons: 1) we estimated the sample size for a two-way ANONVA, so the sample size for the other tests would be too low; 2) statisticians do not universally approve the use of tests of simple main effects due to concerns regarding the conceptual error rate [20]. Thus, we decided to create samples to run our own one-way ANOVA for each control point.

Simulation 1: The two-way repeated measures ANOVA with a Greenhouse-Geisser correction determined that mean elicitation efficiency differed statistically significantly between all heuristics over all control points ($F(1.943, 46.620) = 471.860, p < 0.001$). Thus, the corresponding hypothesis $H_{1,1}$ *"There is a difference in elicitation efficiency in BPRE when applying decision heuristics"* can be accepted (see Table 1 for descriptive statistics). Fig. 3 shows the mean NPV for control points 1-3 (we omitted the others in favor of readability). There is almost no interaction between the heuristics, i.e., the refinement decisions at the beginning of the tree traversal (before CP1) seem to have the greatest influence on the outcome. Also, the interaction between control points and heuristic differed significantly ($F(1.888, 45.324) = 299.149, p < 0.001$). We do not investigate this interaction here because we analyzed the control points separately in our second simulation. Post-hoc tests using the Bonferroni correction revealed the statistically significant differences between the heuristics shown in Table 2. It can be seen that the two heuristics DH5 and DH9 have a significantly higher mean NPV than all other heuristics. DH9 even has a slightly (though not significantly) higher mean than DH5. Also noticeable is that DH1 has a significantly lower mean than all other heuristics. A ranking would look like this:

DH9 ~ DH5 > DH4 ~ DH8 > DH3 > DH6 > DH2 ~ DH7 > DH1

The two informed heuristics DH9 and DH8 share the first places with the non-informed heuristics DH5 and DH4 in this ranking. The "simple" heuristics DH1 and DH2 are ranked in the last places.

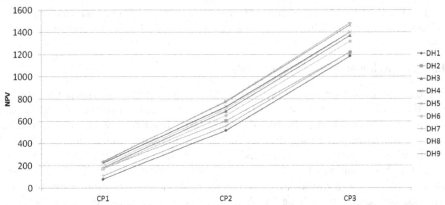

Fig. 3. Mean NPVs of the Heuristics over Control Points CP1-CP3

Table 1. Descriptive Statistics (Simulation 1)

	CP1		CP2		CP3		CP4		CP5	
	Mean	*SD*	*Mean*	*SD*	*Mean*	*SD*	*Mean*	*SD*	*Mean*	*SD*
DH1	78.822	25.90	518.21	107.72	1185.45	220.23	1940.53	342.1	2709.98	462.87
DH2	172.97	38.52	605.15	120.23	1219.84	225.59	1939.56	343.85	2701.28	463.32
DH3	179.93	38.48	692.25	131.77	1371.53	249.33	2124.6	372.99	2893.08	494.5
DH4	224.54	46.13	730.41	136	1400.88	249.06	2150.74	370.29	2919.51	490.51
DH5	237.96	49.07	773.70	143.95	1465.82	261.18	2225.69	384.57	2995.44	505.82
DH6	173.28	36.02	652.07	121.24	1320.01	233.31	2071.71	356.93	2839.96	478.66
DH7	110.97	25.18	558.53	101.61	1223.57	213.17	1976.92	336.13	2746.01	457.60
DH8	199.99	44.51	712.01	141.54	1398.7	259.18	2158.01	382.57	2927.76	503.66
DH9	233.26	49.09	782.07	148.59	1483.88	268.97	2245.92	393.91	3014.25	515.58

Table 2. Pairwise Comparisons (i-j) of the Heuristics (Simulation 1)

	DH1	DH2	DH3	DH4	DH5	DH6	DH7	DH8	DH9
DH2	41.16*	-							
DH3	165.68*	124.52*	-						
DH4	198.62*	157.46*	32.94*	-					
DH5	253.13*	211.96*	87.45*	54.51*	-				
DH6	124.81*	83.65*	-40.87*	-73.81*	-128.32*	-			
DH7	36.60*	-4.56	-129.08*	-162.02*	-216.52*	-88.21*	-		
DH8	192.70*	151.53*	27.02*	-5.92	-60.43*	67.89*	156.09*	-	
DH9	265.28*	224.12*	99.60*	66.66*	12.15	140.47*	228.67*	72.58*	-

=statistically significant with p < 0.001

Simulation 2: The one-way repeated measures ANOVA (applied separately at each control point) with a Greenhouse-Geisser correction determined that mean elicitation efficiency differed significantly between all heuristics for CP1 ($F(1.766, 130.694) = 1126.961$, $p < 0.001$), CP2 ($F(1.604, 118.686) = 792.293$, $p < 0.001$), CP3 ($F(1.648, 121.982) = 935.815$, $p < 0.001$), CP4 ($F(1.940, 143.575) = 827.989$, $p < 0.001$), and CP5 ($F(1.861, 137.714) = 819.073$, $p < 0.001$). Again, post-hoc tests using the Bonferroni correction revealed statistically significant differences between the heuristics. For the sake of brevity, we omit the descriptive statistics here and only present the results in a ranking notation:

CP 1: DH5 > DH9 ~ DH4 > DH8 > DH3 ~ DH2 ~ DH6 > DH7 > DH1
CP 2: DH9 > DH5 > DH4 > DH8 > DH3 > DH6 > DH2 > DH7 > DH1
CP 3: DH9 > DH5 > DH4 ~ DH8 > DH3 > DH6 > DH7 ~ DH2 > DH1
CP 4: DH9 > DH5 > DH8 ~ DH4 > DH3 > DH6 > DH7 > DH1 ~ DH2
CP 5: DH9 > DH5 > DH8 ~ DH4 > DH3 > DH6 > DH7 > DH1 > DH2

Thus, the corresponding hypothesis $H_{2,1}$ *"There is a difference in elicitation efficiency when applying decision heuristics compared at different points during project runtime"* can be accepted. The results for the single control points differ only slightly from the results of the first simulation over all control points, e.g., DH9 and DH5 are still ranked in the first places and DH1 and DH2 mostly in the last.

4.4   Threats to Validity

Concerning the validity of the experiment, some threats typically occurring when humans are used as subjects can be excluded here (e.g., evaluation apprehension, learning effects). Still, there exist some threats to validity that shall be discussed.

Concerning *construct validity*, one possible threat is the use of the NPV as a measure for elicitation efficiency. We assume that value and effort can be directly compared, even if the value of a system function might not directly create monetary benefits that are comparable to effort. To cope with this threat, we only used normalized values in the calculations, which in turn make it hard to interpret the actually measured numbers of the NPV. Furthermore, there are possible threats regarding the requirements trees and their model parameters. We assume a three-level hierarchy in our simulations. In practice, this might be common, but hierarchies with only two levels or with even more than three levels are also conceivable. Further simulations are needed to assess the heuristics on these kinds of trees. To minimize the threat concerning the model parameters, we tried to set them up as realistically as possible; however, most of them are only based on our experience in past projects (and thus may be biased) and have not been further validated. Even though the detected differences in elicitation efficiency are significantly valid within this setting, the actual results could differ when replicating the experiment using requirements trees with different parameters. This refers to tree sizes and structure, to elicitation effort for requirements, as well as to priorities. However, we ran further simulations with different tree sizes (very small and large process numbers; not reported here) and it appears that these results are at least not sensitive to different process numbers.

Besides the already described model parameters, *internal validity* should not be affected by further inferences. Concerning *external validity*, there are also possible threats regarding the content of the requirements trees. We only focused on requirements directly derived from the processes. Other requirements types (e.g., non-functional requirements for the whole system) are not regarded here. Also, reuse of requirements is not regarded (e.g., system functions that can be utilized in different business activities). Furthermore, we assume that the business value is generated directly after the elicitation of a system function is finished. In reality, implementation takes time, produces additional effort, and the actual releases might differ from the elicitation order produced by the heuristics. Further simulations are needed to investigate this issue. This is not represented in our model or formulas.

Concerning *conclusion validity*, we assured that all requirements for the statistical tests that we applied (repeated measures ANOVA) were fulfilled.

4.5   Interpretation and Possible Implications for Practice

The results of this controlled experiment have shown that the usage of the right decision heuristic has the potential to make the requirements elicitation process more efficient. Noticeably, intuitive decision heuristics (e.g., DH1, DH2) seem to perform very low in contrast to more sophisticated ones. This also confirms the results in [15], even if the simulations there were different. It might be that the simple heuristics either "jump" too much between the different processes without generating value (refining too few system functions at the beginning of a project); or, on the other hand, "jump" too little, refining too many system functions of the same process and thus not exploiting the higher value of other processes. Another interesting insight is that informed heuristics that take into account elicitation effort are even outperformed (esp. DH8) by heuristics based only on priorities (DH4, DH5). This implies that if no elicitation effort judgment is at hand, it is still good advice to base decisions on reasonably defined priorities. This is certainly a remarkable result for practitioners working in the areas of BPRE and business process improvement and further strengthens the need for effective prioritization as stated in [2]. In further simulations with smaller (mean value of 8 and standard deviation of 2) and larger (mean value of 70 and standard deviation of 8) tree sizes, which are not reported here, we already got the impression that the results (which have not been analyzed statistically yet) are similar.

As we were dealing only with relative numbers in the calculations of the NPV, we want to conclude with an example using monetary numbers: given the parameters of our model, suppose we could save 3 minutes of time for each activity in a process with 20 activities. Suppose we have 14 processes with 60 instances per month for each process and labor costs of $100 per person-hour: this would result in $84,000 of savings a month (=$350 an hour). If we simulate this setting, the output in the first line of Table 3 is produced. The second line is the output produced when using normalized numbers as in our experiment.

Table 3. Example: NPV for Specific Setting of 14 Processes

| DH5 | DH9 | DH4 | DH8 | DH3 | DH6 | DH2 | DH7 | DH1 |
NPV	NPV	NPV	NPV	NPV	NPV	NPV	NPV	NPV
$58,276	$54,930	$53,016	$42,919	$36,047	$27,469	$20,731	$19,144	$10,171
(1447)	(1439)	(1432)	(1404)	(1387)	(1362)	(1339)	(1339)	(1314)

As can be seen, the highest NPV of DH5 ($58,276) is 5.7 times as high as the one of DH1 ($10,171), and still 6% higher than the second one of DH9. Therefore, the application of a suitable decision heuristic during elicitation affects the value of the overall project outcome significantly. Of course, this is only an example with static numbers for each process, but these numbers indicate significant savings when using the top-rated heuristics.

5   Conclusion and Future Work

This paper reported on an experiment with different decision heuristics applied in business-process-driven requirements hierarchies. These heuristics aim at supporting the requirements engineer in his / her decision-making to optimize the order of elicitation in terms of elicitation efficiency during the requirements elicitation process. The results have shown that elicitation efficiency significantly differs when applying different decision heuristics during traversal of the requirements hierarchy. Surprisingly, well-known heuristics such as highest value first performed very low and were outperformed by newly proposed ones, which is an interesting finding for practice.

For the future, it will be interesting to see if the heuristics perform in the same way when applied to requirements hierarchies with different parameters, e.g., smaller or higher numbers of requirements. Furthermore, it would be interesting to extend our model of the requirements hierarchies to include different monetary values that can be used in the calculation of elicitation efficiency. We plan to investigate the influence of development effort and extend the simulation tool for use in industrial case studies. Last but not least, the results of this study will be integrated into our BPRE prioritization framework as proposed in [2] to support requirements engineers during prioritization and elicitation in BPRE.

References

1. De La Vara, J.S., Díaz, J.S.: Business process-driven requirements engineering: a goal-based approach. In: CAiSE 2007 Workshop Proceedings. Tapir Academic Press (2007)
2. Riegel, N.: Guiding Requirements Elicitation using a Prioritization Framework. In: REFSQ 2013 Workshop Proceedings, pp. 133–144 (2013)
3. Racheva, Z., Daneva, M.: How Do Real Options Concepts Fit in Agile Requirements Engineering? In: 8th ACIS International Conference on SERA (2010)
4. Daneva, M., Herrmann, A.: Requirements Prioritization Based on Benefit and Cost Prediction: An Agenda for Future Research. In: Proc. of RE 2009, pp. 125–134 (2009)
5. Riegel, N., Doerr, J., Hummel, O.: Tackling Prioritization in Business-Process-Driven Software Development. In: REFSQ 2012 Workshop Proceedings, pp. 175–180 (2012)
6. Russell, S., Norvig, P.: Artificial Intelligence: A Modern Approach, 3rd edn. Prentice Hall, Upper Saddle River (2009)
7. Berander, P., Jönsson, P.: Hierarchical Cumulative Voting (HCV) - Prioritization of Requirements in Hierarchies. International Journal of Software Engineering and Knowledge Engineering 16(6), 819–849 (2006)
8. Saliu, O., Ruhe, G.: Supporting Software Release Planning Decisions for Evolving Systems. In: Proc. 29th Annual IEEE/NASA SEW, Washington, DC, pp. 14–26 (2005)
9. Dong, X., Yang, Q., Wang, Q., Zhai, J., Ruhe, G.: Value-Risk Trade-off Analysis for Iteration Planning in eXtreme Programming. In: 18th Asia Pacific APSEC, pp. 397–404 (2011)
10. Albers, S., Henzinger, M.R.: Exploring Unknown Environments. In: STOC 1997 Proc. of the 29th Annual ACM Symposium on Theory of Computing, pp. 416–425 (1997)
11. Duncan, C.A., Kobourov, S.G., Kumar, V.S.A.: Optimal Constrained Graph Exploration. ACM TALG 2(3), 380–402 (2006)

12. Panaite, P., Pelc, A.: Exploring Unknown Undirected Graphs. Journal of Algorithms 33, 281–295 (1999)

13. Papadimitriou, C.H., Yannakakis, M.: Shortest path without a map. Theoretical Computer Science 84(1), 127–150 (1991)

14. Deng, X., Papadimitriou, H.: Exploring an unknown Graph. In: FOCS 1990, vol. 1, pp. 355–361 (1990)

15. Port, D., Olkov, A., Menzies, T.: Using Simulation to Investigate Requirements Prioritization Strategies. In: 23rd IEEE/ACM International Conference on Automated Software Engineering (ASE), pp. 268–277 (2008)

16. Basili, V.R., Caldiera, G., Rombach, H.D.: Goal Question Metric Paradigm. Encyclopedia of Software Engineering 1, 528–532 (1994)

17. Denne, M., Cleland-Huang, J.: Software by Numbers: Low-Risk, High-Return Development. Prentice Hall (2003)

18. Stevens, J.: Applied Multivariate Statistics for the Social Sciences, 3rd edn. Lawrence Earlbaum Associates, Mahwah (1996)

19. Rasch, B., Hofmann, W., Friese, M., Nauman, E.: G*Power Ergänzungen. Quantitative Methoden. Band 2, 3. Auflage. Springer, Heidelberg (2010), http://www.quantitative-methoden.de/dlcounter/count.php?id=gpower7_A3 (October 22, 2013).

20. How can I do tests of simple main effects in SPSS? UCLA: Statistical Consulting Group, http://www.ats.ucla.edu/stat/spss/faq/sme.htm (October 22, 2013)

The Effects of Requirements Elicitation Issues on Software Project Performance: An Empirical Analysis

Neetu Kumari Sethia and Anitha S. Pillai

Department of Computer Applications, Hindustan University, Tamil Nadu, India
neetu_sethia@yahoo.com,
mca@hindustanuniv.ac.in

Abstract. [**Context and motivation**] Studies have emphasized the need for effective requirements elicitation owing to its significant impacts on software quality and overall project outcomes to meet system objectives. The empirical studies in literature present the relationships between the specific characteristics that affect elicitation and project performance that focus on process control and product flexibility. There is, however, no substantial research on the empirical relationship between the generalized problems in requirements elicitation and project performance. [**Question/problem**]The issues encountered in requirements elicitation generalized through categories of problems of scope, problems of volatility and problems of understanding. This study aims in establishing an empirical model to study the behavior between the requirements elicitation issues and project performance. This study also validates the model for its consistency with practitioner's views and earlier studies. [**Principal ideas/ results**] Researchers and practitioners have focused on developing tools and techniques that will enhance the requirements elicitation and analysis phases. However, the effectiveness of the tool usage is dependent on skills and behaviors of people and organization using them. The aspects of behavior are best modeled using techniques adopted in social research, viz. confirmatory factor analysis; the technique is adopted for this study. [**Contribution**] This study deduced a causal relationship between the requirements elicitation issues and project performance. This study also attempted to establish a priority-setting and decision-making to address elicitation issues that can control and manage residual performance risks.

Keywords: Requirements elicitation issues, Confirmatory factor analysis, Causal model.

1 Introduction

Studies have determined that requirements engineering activities have an increasing impact on the overall project outcomes. This means that poor requirements engineering activities is one of the major causes for project failure. Requirements elicitation (RE) is an essential and foremost activity of the project. This activity, in itself, has a significant influence on the overall project performance. The importance of RE is also

C. Salinesi and I. van de Weerd (Eds.): REFSQ 2014, LNCS 8396, pp. 285–300, 2014.
© Springer International Publishing Switzerland 2014

driven from the fact that attracts a number of issues, as information systems (IS) development shifts more towards adoption of global software development (GSD) frameworks [18].

Christel & Kang [1] categorize RE problems into three groups, namely, problems of scope, problems of volatility and problems of understanding. In their technical report [1], they describe these categories as follows: *Problems of scope* are those in which the requirements may address too little or too much information. This means that the boundaries of the system to be development may be ill-defined. *Problems of volatility* are related to the changing nature of requirements. This implies that requirements evolve over time. *Problems of understanding* are related to the poor understanding of requirements, within groups as well as between groups such as users and developers. These are related to incomplete or poor understanding of requirements, lack of appropriate verbal and written communication, lack of domain knowledge, conflicting views amongst users amongst other critical pre-requisites for a good RE.

Nidumolu [3] focus on uncertainty regarding user requirements because of its central importance in software development. Adopting the theories of Nidumolu [3], requirements uncertainty encompasses three dimensions such as requirements instability, requirements diversity and requirements analyzability. Requirements instability and requirements diversity are dimensions that reflect elicitation issues. The definitions are adopted from [3]. *Requirements instability* is the extent of changes in user environment over the course of the project; this is derived from the concept of environmental instability in organization theory, which describes the extent of changes in the task environment. *Requirements diversity* is the extent to which the users differ amongst themselves in their requirements; this is derived from the concept of organizational heterogeneity in organization theory, which describes the degree of variety or heterogeneity in the task environment.

The survey conducted for this study shows that RE consumes a relatively small percentage of the overall effort required for IS development (Table 1). The impacts of poor RE are severe, though. Researchers have identified several critical causes of poor RE [19, 21]. Prior studies have also established relationships between project performance and specific causes of poor RE such as change [9, 10], knowledge [11], quality [14], stakeholder [12, 13], human factors [14, 15], etc. There is, however, little or no empirical knowledge on how the summarized (say, summarized view of problems of scope, problems of volatility and problems of understanding) effect of issues in RE actually impact the overall performance of the project. There is a need to address this gap, as knowledge on how this summarized view of issues in RE impacts the project performance, is of practical interest.

This study integrates two theories described above to address the gap. One is related to the three categories of RE challenges by [1]; this theory forms the core framework for the rest of this work. The other is related to the dimensions of requirements uncertainty as described by [2, 3]. Based on explanation of these dimensions in Nidumolu's theory, we captured the contextual equivalence between problems of volatility and requirements instability which enabled us to leverage the requirements instability constructs [3]. We also leveraged the construct for requirements diversity owing to similar contextual equivalence between the problems of scope and requirements diversity. We deduced a construct for problems of understanding to capture a summarized view of the challenges in RE. We use the term *elicitation issues* to describe this summarized view of problems of volatility, problems of scope and problems of understanding, for the rest of the discussion.

To summarize, this study empirically confirms the general understanding of the relationship between elicitation issues and project performance. This is accomplished through the adoption of confirmatory factor analysis and causal models.

2   Background

2.1   Theoritical Model

The primary objective is to comprehend RE issues as categorized by [1] into an empirical model. We attempt to construct the causality between RE issues, viz., problems of scope, problems of volatility and problems of understanding and overall project performance. This is done by defining measures that are attributable to behavior and skills required for RE.

Extensive studies have been done in identifying the causes for poor RE, especially in GSD environments [18, 19]. Literature has evidences that theoretically confirm the inability to elicit requirements, which lead to significant gaps; these gaps adversely affect the project execution and the project success. According to Nidumolu [3], these gaps are called *requirements uncertainty*. Adapting Nidumolu's theory of requirements uncertainty, the constructs that play a critical role in this study are requirements instability and requirements diversity. The construct parameters were carefully examined for this study. We have leveraged constructs for elicitation issues needed for this study from Nidumolu's work. Existing constructs have been modified and new constructs have been developed to ensure that the model captures all the dimensions of elicitation issues and meets the required objectives of this study.

Studies have attempted to maximize project performance through implementation of contingency models. The work of Nidumolu [2] discusses the generalized model (figure 1) that establishes links between the following constructs: requirements uncertainty, uncertainty coping mechanisms, residual performance risks and project performance. The objective of the study is to construct causality between elicitation issues and project performance. Therefore, we re-design the existing requirements uncertainty model from [2] as shown in figure 2.

The elicitation issues in the proposed model is expected to influence the residual performance risk in a manner similar to requirements uncertainty, as proven in prior studies. Horizontal and vertical co-ordination has been retained in the model as we experience similar arrangements in practice. The details of the constructs are discussed further in section 3.2.

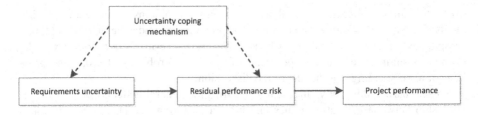

Fig. 1. Generalized uncertainty framework [2]

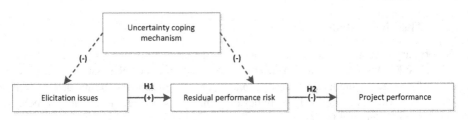

Fig. 2. Proposed requirements elicitation issues model

2.2   Hypotheses

The causal relationship between the constructs is depicted in Figure 2. Based on this, the study proposes two hypotheses that are discussed below. The elicitation issues reported in literature can be broadly characterized as change, communication, human-factors, knowledge, scope, requirements, social and organizational, stakeholder and tools, techniques and methods. Theoretical and empirical studies present the individual impacts of some of these characteristics to the overall project success. There is extensive focus in literature on the adoption of improved processes to enhance the quality of these characteristics so that the overall project quality and outcomes can be improved. Residual performance risk is the amount of risk remaining after the completion of the requirements analysis phases [3]. The characteristics of elicitation issues are critical since they contribute to the residual performance risk, which in turn influences the overall project performance. This means that the degree of successful execution of these characteristics directly or indirectly determines project performance. Based on the above discussion, the study formulates the first hypothesis, as described below:

H1: *Higher levels of elicitation issues will lead to higher levels of residual performance risk. This means that an increase in the effects of elicitation issues will increase the effects of residual performance risks.*

A successful project outcome is characterized by the controlled project cost, adherence to schedules and system benefits, amongst others. The amount of performance risk gradually decreases as performance becomes more evident [3]. Fall-outs due to elicitation issues are carried to the other phases of the project. These in turn contribute to the residual performance risk, impacting the system quality and project outcomes. For example, a common issue is about users not documenting requirements that seem "obvious". This implies the existence of requirements that are overlooked and not documented contributes to the requirements uncertainty. If this issue is not handled or fixed in the project's requirements engineering phase, this issue will increase the risk of the final system not meeting the required objectives. Based on this discussion, the study formulates the second hypothesis, which is described below:

H2: *Higher levels of residual performance risk will lead to lower levels of project performance. This means that a decrease (increase) in the effects of residual performance risk will increase (decrease) the effects of project performance.*

3   Research Method

3.1   Sampling

A total of 203 online survey responses were obtained resulting in a response rate of 92.27%. The sample included individuals extensively involved in RE and have been engaged in that project until closure. This approach was necessary to gather appropriate data for effective analysis.   Purposive sampling was adopted for the purpose of this study. Table 1 represents the demographics features of the survey population.

Table 1. Demographic features (*N=203*)

Characteristics	Value	%/ Mean
Project status	Success	90.15%
	Failure	9.85%
Location of Organization	India	84.73%
	U.K.	1.48%
	U.S.A	13.79%
Project domain	Healthcare/ Insurance	52.71%
	Banking, Financial Services & Capital Market/ Communications/ Consure goods & services/ Defence/ Energy & utilities/ Life sciences/ Manufacturing/ Mining/ Retail/ Technology/ Transportation & logistics/ Travel & hospitality	42.86%
	Others	4.43%
Team strength of the project		43.28
*Overall duration of the project*Note: 186 cases		1.95 years

Table 1. (*continued*)		
Characteristics	Value	%/ Mean
Position of respondents in the elicitation process	Management	58.62%
	Technical	29.06%
	Coaching/ Auditing	2.96%
	Business/ Requirements analysts	21.18%
	Others	1.97%
*Number of [requirements/ business] analysts taking part in the elicitation process	*Note : 198 cases*	7.17
*Number of end-users participating in the elicitation process	*Note : 194 cases*	9.79
*% Proposition of overall system developement effort devoted to RE processes	*Note : 182 cases*	25.27%
*% Proposition of overall RE effort devoted to elicitation process	*Note: 171 cases*	29.35%

*Not all cases were considered since either the questions remained un-answered or they were considered outliers.

3.2 Constructs

Elicitation Issues. Elicitation issues represent the categorization of problems in RE as described by Christel & Kang [1]. Three dimensions describe elicitation issues and are discussed below:

- The *Problems of scope (PoS)* are those in which the requirements may address too little or too much information [1]. This conceptually maps to the *requirements diversity* that describes the extent to which the users differ amongst themselves in the final requirements [3], Three items (PoS1, PoS2, PoS3) adapted from [3] that describe this scale (table 2).
- The *Problems of volatility (PoV)* is the extent of changes that the requirements undergo during the project life cycle [1]. This conceptually maps to the *requirements instability* that describes the extent of changes in user environment over the course if the project [3]. A new item was introduced to capture a complete view based on the description provided by [1]. Five items (PoV1, PoV2, PoV3, PoV4, PoV5) of which top four items adapted from [3] describe this scale (table 2).
- The *Problems of understanding (PoU)* is the degree of requirements understanding absorbed as part of the elicitation process. This describes the extent of ambiguity and communication challenges that can result in poor elicitation. Six items (PoU1, PoU2, PoU3, PoU4, PoU5, PoU6) based on the descriptions provided by [1] describe this scale (table 2).

*.****Project Performance.*** Project performance is a multi-dimensional construct that describes the performance outcomes [3]. Two dimensions are selected to describe this construct:

- The *Process control (PC)* is the extent to which the development process is under control [3]. Four items (PC1, PC2, PC3, PC4) of this construct (table 2) adapted from [3].
- The *Product flexibility (PF)* is the degree of scalability exhibited by the final product. This means the extent to which final product can distinctly support new features and functionalities, according to [3]. Four items (PF1, PF2, PF3, PF4) of this construct (table 2) are adapted from [3].

Uncertainty Coping Mechanisms. Multiple groups are involved in a software-development project. A better coordination is always required for the project development activities to be executed effectively. For this reason, there are two constructs identified that provide a comprehensive view of such coordination [3]. These coordination constructs collectively determine the uncertainty coping mechanism.

- The *horizontal co-ordination (HC)* is the extent to which the co-ordination between users and project staff is undertaken through mutual adjustments and communication [3]. Four items (HC1, HC2, HC3, HC4) of this construct (table 2) are adapted from the work of [3].
- The *vertical coordination (VC)* construct is the extent to which the coordination between the users and project teams is undertaken through decisions by authorized entities such as project managers and steering committees [3]. Three items (VC1, VC2, VC3) of this construct (table 2) are adapted from the work of [3].

Residual Performance Risk. *Residual performance risk (RPR)* is the extent of difficulty in estimating the performance-related outcomes of the project, regardless of a specific estimation technique used. The amount of performance risks present in the later stages of the project after project planning and requirements analysis phases have been completed [2]. Five items (RPR1, RPR2, RPR3, RPR4, RPR5) of this construct adapted from the work of [2] are shown in table 2.

All the above constructs were measured on a 5-point Likert-type scale with 1= strongly agree and 5= strongly disagree.

3.3 Confirmatory Factor Analysis

Confirmatory factor analysis (CFA) is a type of structural equation modeling that deals with measurement models, that is, the relationship between the observed variables and the latent variables [4]; this is used to establish or verify dimensionality of scales [6]. In this study, we have adopted second-order CFA using SPSS AMOS 21 to test the hypotheses. This dimensions described in table 2 are the observed variables whose measures are captured through survey responses. The model is designed (figure 3) based on eight first-order latent construct represented collectively through three second-order latent constructs such as elicitation issues (problems of scope, problems of volatility, problems of understanding), uncertainty coping mechanisms (horizontal coordination, vertical coordination) and project performance (process control, product flexibility).

The estimation technique used to derive factor loadings is maximum likelihood. This technique has shown to be robust [6]. Multiple iterations executed to obtain an

Table 2. Dimension Characteristics

ID**	Dimension charateristics	Factor loading	Mean	S.D
PC1	Significant control over project costs	.913	3.74	1.031
PC2	Significant control over project schedule	.870	3.67	1.114
PC3	Project's adherence to auditability and control standards was high	.519	3.77	.901
PC4	Overall control exercised over the project was high	.783	3.75	.911
PF1	Cost of adapting the software to changes in business was low	.659	3.41	.936
PF2	Speed of adapting software to changes in business was high	.744	3.62	.878
PF3	Cost of maintaining software over its lifetime was low	.746	3.47	.875
PF4	Overall long-term flexibility of software was high	.813	3.66	.878
PoV1	Requirements fluctuated quite a bit in earlier phases*	-		
PoV2	Requirements fluctuated quite a bit in later phases	.850	3.49	1.078
PoV3	Requirements identified at the beginning of the project were quite different from those existing at the end	.561	3.02	1.167
PoV4	Requirements will fluctuate quite a bit in future	.666	3.12	1.008
PoV5	Analyst's interpretation of technical details of requirements significantly low	.409	2.96	1.107
PoS1	Users of this software differed a great deal among themselves in the requirements to be met	.917	3.29	1.085
PoS2	Lot of effort had to be spent in reconciling requirements of various users of this software	.917	3.38	1.108
PoS3	It was difficult to customize software to one set of users without reducing support to other users	.740	3.07	1.103
PoU1	Users not completely sure of what is needed	.707	3.03	1.108
PoU2	Users had low understanding of capabilities and limitations of their computing environment	.655	3.19	1.057
PoU3	Users had low understanding of problem domain	.676	2.83	1.065
PoU4	Users had significant challenges in communicating requirements	.881	2.97	1.087
PoU5	Users omit information that seemed "obvious"	.885	3.33	1.105
PoU6	Users specified requirements which were ambiguous/ un-testable	.826	3.15	1.063
HC1	Oral communication (e.g., face-to-face, telephone, etc) between users and project teams was high	.880	4.02	.965
HC2	Written communication (e.g., memos, notes, etc) between users and project teams was high	.757	4.04	.892
HC3	Scheduled group meetings between users and project teams were high	.799	3.96	.908
HC4	Unscheduled group meetings between users and project teams were high*	-		
VC1	Individual (e.g., a project manager) influence or authority was high*	-		

*removed from subsequent analysis
** PC- Process Control; PF – Product Flexibility; PoV – Problems of Volatility; PoS - Problems of Scope; PoU – Problems of understanding; HC – Horizontal coordination; VC - Vertical co-ordination; RPR – Residual Performance Risk

appropriate model fit resulted in the removal of three items, HC4, PoV1 and VC1 owing to poor factor loadings.

Validity and Reliability. The Cronbach's coefficient α-value determines the internal consistency (reliability) and a value > .70 is acceptable. All factors (table 3) except for vertical coordination computed the α-value > .70 which is found acceptable [6]. Though the inclusion of vertical coordination might pose a problem, we continue to retain this factor in the model, owing to its importance in practice.

Table 3. Internal consistency: Cronbach's coefficient alpha test

Dimensions	PoS	PoV	PoU	PC	PF	HC	VC	RPR
α –value	.862	.726	.883	.862	.769	.740	.553	.886
Overall α-value for 34-items = .795								

It is necessary to establish convergent validity, discriminant validity and composite reliability, when doing a CFA [7, 8]. Convergent validity [7] describes the extent to which the latent factors are explained by the observed variables. Discriminant validity [7] explains the degree to which the latent factor is explained by other variables than its own observed variables. The thresholds for the convergent and discriminant validity and reliability are depicted in table 4.

Table 4. Thresholds for model reliability and validity (adapted from [7, 8])

Measures	Composite Reliability (CR)	Relia-Convergent Validity	Discriminant Validity
Thresholds	CR > 0.7	CR > AVE* AVE > 0.5	MSV** > AVE ASV*** < AVE

*Average Variance Extracted **Maximum Shared Variance***Average Shared Variance*

An excel-based tool, StatsToolPackage.xls [7] aided in the computation of the validation and reliability measures. The results are shown in table 5. The values computed confirm that the model adheres to the validity and reliability measures.

Table 5. CFA model: reliability and validity

					Correlations*			
	CR	AVE	MSV	ASV	PP	RPR	EI	UCM
PP	0.729	0.576	0.404	0.348	**0.759**			
RPR	0.872	0.580	0.514	0.301	-0.554	**0.762**		
EI	0.857	0.669	0.514	0.336	-0.636	0.717	**0.818**	
UCM	0.728	0.604	0.332	0.168	0.576	-0.285	-0.300	**0.777**

The diagonal in the correlation matrix contains the square-root of the AVE (bold)

PP – Project Performance; RPR – Residual Performance Risk; EI – Elicitation Issues; UCM – Uncertainty Coping Mechanism; CR – Composite Reliability; AVE – Average Variance Extracted; MSV – Maximum Shared Variance; ASV – Average Shared Variance

The factor loadings and the computed mean and standard deviations are depicted in table 2. The measurement model (figure 3) produced the following fit indices: $N=$ 203, $\chi2/d.f. = 1.424$, $GFI=.848$, $CFI=.945$, $RMSEA=.046$, $PCLOSE=.790$, $NFI=.839$, $SRMR=.0663$. The fit indices were within the acceptable thresholds [5, 6] of a model fit as depicted in table 6. The fit indices resulted in a good model fit and enabled us to proceed with a causal model.

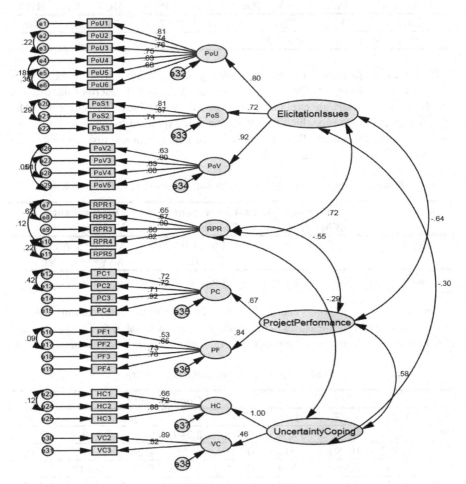

Fig. 3. Measurement model

3.4   "Causal" Model

According to Bagozzi and Yi [6], "SEMs have applicability to testing causal hypotheses yet are relevant to testing functional relationships, generalizations and cross-validations." Figure 4 depicts the final causal model deduced from the measurement

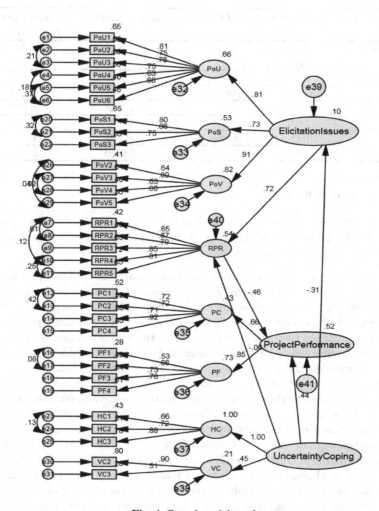

Fig. 4. Causal model results

model. The values in each of the arrow depict the standard coefficients that reflect the degree of the causal relationship.

The causal model produced the following fit indices: *(N=203, χ2/d.f. =1.442, GFI=.846, CFI=.943, RMSEA=.047, PCLOSE=.733, NFI=.837, SRMR=.0700)*. The computed fit indices were within the acceptable thresholds (table 6).

Table 6. Goodness-of-Fit : Comparitive measures

GOF measure	Recommended GOF level [5, 6]	CFA measures	Causal model measures
Chi-square/ d.f.	Recommended level between 1 and 3	1.424	1.442
GFI	0 (No fit) to 1(perfect fit)	0.848	0.846
CFI	0 (No fit) to 1(perfect fit)	0.945	0.943
RMSEA	<0.060	0.046	0.047
PCLOSE	>0.050	0.790	0.733
NFI	0 (No fit) to 1(perfect fit)	0.839	0.837
SRMR	<0.090	0.0663	0.0700

3.5   Discussion of Results

H1: Higher levels of elicitation issues will lead to higher levels of residual performance risk. This means that an increase in the effects of elicitation issues will increase the effects of residual performance risks.

The standardized co-efficient between elicitation issues and residual performance risk is 0.72 (p <.001), which determines a positive link between the latent factors. This proves that increased levels of elicitation issues will lead to increased levels of performance risk. This empirical finding supports H1. This also validates the theoretical view that elicitation issues impacts project performance; in this case is through the residual performance risk. The impacts of elicitation issues to residual performance risk will determine the strength of its association with project performance.

Which problem contributes most to elicitation issues? This computed coefficients provide an interesting insight into the impacts of elicitation issues on residual performance risk. Problems of volatility (coefficient=.91, p< .001) determine a higher impact on elicitation issues, followed by problems of understanding (coefficient=.81, p<.001) and problems of scope (coefficient=.73, p< .001). This shows that the change in the user environment creates comparatively larger impacts. Change has been proven to be a critical characteristic of elicitation issues in theory impacting project outcomes. Based on this empirical result, we conclude the volatile nature of requirements to be the top contributing factor increasing residual performance risk; thereby impacting project performance. This analysis presents a focus on the prioritization on the category of elicitation issues that need to be addressed.

What contributes most within the problem category? This above conclusion can be further detailed to determine the measurement variables contribute to the increased effects of problems of volatility. For example, in this case, the standard coefficient between problems of volatility and POV3 is .80 (p < .001) depicts the strongest factor loading when compared to other parameters. This empirical evidence validates the theory on this observation and confirms that the final requirements drawn are different from those identified during the requirements engineering phases of the project. Similarly degree of impacts of other measures can be drawn.

This discussion can be extended to problems of understanding and problems of scope. The top contributing factor in problems of understanding is POU1 (coefficient=.81, p<.001). POU1 describes that the users are not completely sure of what is needed. The top contributing factor in problems of scope is POS1 (coefficient=.80, p<.001). POS1 describes that the users of this software greatly differed amongst themselves in the requirements to be met. This empirical result validates the related theory that contributes to elicitation issues.

H2: Higher levels of residual performance risk will lead to lower levels of project performance. This means that a decrease (increase) in the effects of residual performance risk will increase (decrease) the effects of project performance.

The standardized coefficient between residual performance risk and project performance is -0.46 (p < .001), which determines a negative link between the factors. This finding supports H2. Similar conclusions have been drawn in past studies [2, 17]. The characteristics of elicitation are discussed in section 2.2. If activities that comprehend these characteristics are not executed according to the project's expectation, the drawback will certainly influence the residual risk, thereby impacting project performance. If the activities in elicitation are executed well, the level of risk that is carried to the other phases of the project is comparatively reduced and performance will improve. Hence, there is a need to execute the requirements phase in a controlled manner so that the residual risks are also controlled and managed effectively through the course of project execution.

Though not explicitly hypothesized, the discussion of uncertainty coping mechanism is important. Horizontal and vertical coordination are important dimensions in any project execution. They influence the overall project performance through their impacts on the residual performance risks. Nidumolu [3] empirically proves this association. His work [3] discusses the negative association of horizontal and vertical coordination with residual performance risk. In this study, we make two critical observations pertaining to uncertainty coping mechanism:

- Firstly, higher levels of uncertainty coping mechanism lead to lower levels of performance risk (coefficient = -.06, p < .001). This means that increased level of interactions between users and project managers, both internally or through the involvement of authorities or steering committee, reduces the residual performance risk and improves project performance.
- Secondly, higher levels of uncertainty coping mechanism leads to lower levels of elicitation issues (coefficient =-.31, p < .001). Given the uncertainty coping mechanism is negatively associated with elicitation issues, increased levels of interactions between users and project staff, either internally or through authorities can reduce elicitation issues and thereby, reduce the related performance risk. These observations support the importance of uncertainty coping mechanism in any project execution for improved project performance.

4   Threats to Validity

This section discusses relevant validity threats based on the categories described under pragmatist view in [20].

Theoretical Validity. The constructs used in this study are generalized categorization of elicitation issues, namely the problems of scope, volatility and understanding.

Detailed factors such as scope, human factors, quality, requirements, etc. that contribute to elicitation issues are not explictly considered to be part of the causal relationship. This generalized view can cause potential deficit in the considering key factors, thereby posing a threat to theoretical validity.

External Validity. 84.73% of participants are from India and mostly associated with projects in the context of offshoring; 52.71% associated with healthcare/ insurance domain. Given the dynamic nature of the domain as well as challenges associated with global software development, the generalizability of outcomes may be challenged. The factor loadings may potentially represent context-dependent results and possibly vary for other domains and/or projects executed in-house, posing a threat to external validity.

Construct Validity. As described in [3], factor analysis is a powerful technique in assessing construct validity. Table 2 describes the factor loadings across the relevant dimensions. Loading < 0.4 were excluded from the study and the remaining were carefully examined and retained for subsequent analysis. This statistically elevates any threat to this validity in this study.

Internal Generalizability. This is concerned with the degree to which conclusions/ inferences are drawn about relationships between variables [20]. The conclusions are drawn based on 203 survey responses over 34 dimensions [table 2]. Practitioners confirm that the correlations drawn based on the causal model lead to accurate conclusions based on the good sample size. This statistically elevates the threat to this generalizability and confirms the conclusions to be reasonable with respect to the collected data.

5   Implications for Research and Practice

This study demonstrates the influence of the general categories of elicitation issues to project performance. Future research could extend this study to address the influence of detailed elicitation issues such as those identified in [19] to project performance. This will be a critical research area to understand and realize the influence of the core factors that contribute to poor elicitation and their influence on overall project performance. Given the dynamic nature of business requirements and applicable mandates and a good percentage of projects being executed in the global software development framework, this enhanced study will be of importance to conduct elicitation effectively.

For practitioners, this study has important implications. In practice, challenges pertaining to lack of knowledge or experience in conducting effective elicitation have been recorded as leading to failures in capturing relevant requirements and in turn potential project failures. The model provides an empirical perspective on the impacts of elicitation issues along with priority-setting of elicitation issues. These priority-setting of parameters can support business analyst and requirements engineers to be prepared to realize and address relevant risks that may potentially surface during elicitation. These findings will support in the *continuous* refinement of elicitation process guidelines that can draw practitioner's attention to determining action on specific areas of focus during elicitation. This is also expected to aid in the decision making processes during the early planning phases of software development.

6   Limitations

Like any research, this study has certain limitations too. Firstly, the study focuses only on requirements elicitation and not any other activities of the project's requirements engineering phase. Secondly, the constructs reflect elicitation issues categorized as problems of scope, problems of volatility and problems of understanding. While the constructs provide an overall view of the impacts on elicitation, they may not best capture detailed factors of elicitation issues [19, 21] and their impacts to project outcomes. Thirdly, the assumption in this study is that project success is governed largely by effective requirements gathering and hence, any other measure that might have contributed to the overall project success (thought elicitation as an activity may not been effective) is not considered or validated in this context. Lastly, Cronbach co-efficient α-value for internal consistency for vertical coordination is $< .70$ can be regarded as a limitation in this study.

7   Conclusion

This study deduced the causal relationship and level of influence amongst 13 elicitation issue characteristics categorized as problems of scope, problems of volatility and problems of understanding with 8 characteristics of project performance categorized as product flexibility and process control. While empirical outcomes support the hypotheses, this study also deduced a priority-setting for categories in elicitation issues that can be addressed appropriately to keep residual performance risks in control throughout the project execution. In this case, the study suggests the factor that contributes significantly to residual performance risk to be problems of volatility followed by problems of understanding and problems of scope. The standard coefficient in the model provides in-depth view on the causes for poor elicitation by further studying the parameters within problems of volatility, problems of scope and problems of understanding. These empirical findings can support practitioners and researchers to strengthen their execution of the RE activities. This can aid in decision-making and project planning processes for improved project performance and reduced risks.

References

1. Christel, M.G., Kang, K.C.: Issues in Requirements Elicitation. Technical Report, Software Engineering Institute (1992)
2. Nidumolu, S.: The effect of coordination and uncertainty on software project performance: residual performance risk as an intervening variable. Information Systems Research, 191–219 (1995)
3. Nidumolu, S.: A comparison of the structural contingency and risk-based perspectives on coordination in software-development projects. Journal of Management Information Systems, 77–113 (1996)

4. Brown, T.A.: Confirmatory factor analysis for applied research. Guilford Press (2006)
5. Cho, K., TaeHoon, H., ChangTaek, H.: Effect of project characteristics on project performance in construction projects based on structural equation model. Expert Systems with Applications, 10461–10470 (2009)
6. Bagozzi, R.P., Youjae, Y.: Specification, evaluation, and interpretation of structural equation models. Journal of the Academy of Marketing Science, 8–34 (2012)
7. Gaskin, J.: Stats Tools Package, http://statwiki.kolobkreations.com
8. Hair, J., Black, W., Babin, B., Anderson, R.: Multivariate data analysis. Prentice-Hall, Inc. (2010)
9. Wang, E.T.G., Pei-Hung, J., James, J.J., Klein, G.: The effects of change control and management review on software flexibility and project performance. Information & Management, 438–443 (2008)
10. Zowghi, D., Nur, N.: A study of the impact of requirements volatility on software project performance. In: Software Engineering Conference, pp. 3–11. IEEE (2002)
11. Al-Zayyat, N.A., Firas, A., Ibrahem, T., Ghassan, A.: The Effect of Knowledge Management Processes on project Management. IBIMA Business Review (2009)
12. Kujala, S., Marjo, K., Laura, L., Tero, K.: The role of user involvement in requirements quality and project success. In: 13th IEEE International Conference on, pp. 75–84 (2005)
13. Lin, W.T., Benjamin, S.: The relationship between user participation and system success: a simultaneous contingency approach. Information & Management, 283–295 (2000)
14. Liu, J., Hun-Gee, C., Charlie, C.C., Tsong, S.S.: Relationships among interpersonal conflict, requirements uncertainty, and software project performance. International Journal of Project Management, 547–556 (2011)
15. Aronson, Z.H., Richard, R.R., Gary, S.L.: The impact of leader personality on new product development teamwork and performance: The moderating role of uncertainty. Journal of Engineering and Technology Management, 221–247 (2006)
16. Sundararaman, A.: Information Quality Strategy - An Empirical Investigation of the Relationship Between Information Quality Improvements and Organizational Outcomes, Ph.D. dissertation (2012)
17. Jiang, J.J., Klein, G., Wu, S.P.J., Liang, T.P.: The relation of requirements uncertainty and stakeholder perception gaps to project management performance. Journal of Systems and Software, 801–808 (2009)
18. Nosheen, S., Faiza, I., Farooque, A., Muhammad, Y.J.: An Iterative Approach for Global Requirements Elicitation: A Case Study Analysis. Electronics and Information Engineering, 361–366 (2010)
19. Sethia, N., Pillai, A.S.: A survey on global requirements elicitation issues and proposed research framework. In: 2013 4th IEEE International Conference on Software Engineering and Service Science (ICSESS), pp. 554–557 (2013)
20. Petersen, K., Gencel, C.: Worldviews, Research Methods, and their Relationship to Validity in Empirical Software Engineering Research. In: Proceedings of the Joint Conference of the 23rd International Workshop on Software Measurement and the 8th International Conference on Software Process and Product Measurement (2013)
21. Sethia, N., Pillai, A.S.: A study on the software requirements elicitation issues – its causes and effects. In: World Congress on Information and Communication Technologies (2013)

Requirements Reuse and Patterns: A Survey

Cristina Palomares, Xavier Franch, and Carme Quer

GESSI Research Group, Universitat Politècnica de Catalunya (UPC), Barcelona, Spain
{cpalomares,cquer,franch}@essi.upc.edu

Abstract. *Context and motivation:* Multiple proposals exist that propose the adoption of reuse practices during requirements engineering processes. *Question/problem:* Which is the current level of adoption of these practices in organizations? *Principal ideas/results:* In this paper we present the preliminary results of a survey initiated at REFSQ'13 that addresses this question. The survey first investigates requirements reuse in general, and then goes in depth asking about a specific technique, software requirement patterns (SRP), which is the backbone of our PABRE framework. *Contribution*: The survey results show that requirements reuse is not a widespread practice in IT projects, being the most common techniques those based on the copy and later modification by hand of requirements coming from previous projects. Regarding the use of SRP, the results seem to support our hypothesis that SRP could help to ameliorate some common problems related to requirements specifications like lack of uniformity and incompleteness.

Keywords: Requirement engineering, Requirement reuse, Requirement Patterns.

1   Introduction

The PABRE (PAttern-Based Requirements Elicitation) framework is the result of the collaboration between the GESSI research group at the UPC and the SSI department at the Public Research Centre Henri Tudor (TUDOR) in Luxembourg to adopt software requirement patterns (SRP) as an approach to reuse. PABRE includes a metamodel for SRP [1], a catalogue of 45 Functional SRP (for the content management system domain) [2], 29 Non-Functional SRP [3] and 37 Non-Technical SRP [4] (best suited for business information systems like customer relationship management, supply chain management and by the like), and several tools for SRP management and use [5].

The formulation of the framework heavily relies on empirical work. The collaboration with TUDOR made it possible to analyze requirement specification documents used in industrial projects, which at its turn required a thorough systematic literature review on requirements reuse in general, and SRP in particular. As part of this empirical approach, we decided to investigate the current perception of requirements reuse by practitioners and academics and that's why we designed and conducted a survey (http://www.upc.edu/gessi/PABRE/Survey.html). The goal of the paper is to report preliminary results on the current use of requirements engineering reuse practices in organizations and their benefits and drawbacks and, taking into account our

C. Salinesi and I. van de Weerd (Eds.): REFSQ 2014, LNCS 8396, pp. 301–308, 2014.

specific approach to requirements reuse, to know the opinion of participants about SRP as reuse artifact. It is worth to remark that the current paper focuses then in the state of the practice, not considering the responses that come from researchers without industrial experience which remains subject of later analysis.

2   Research Method

Research Questions

- *RQ1: Is requirements reuse a usual practice in current RE processes?* Here we investigate the current situation of requirements reuse practices in organizations, i.e. the level of requirements reuse, the type of requirements that are more prone to be reused and the techniques used to achieve it.
- *RQ2: Which benefits and drawbacks can appear from the use of a catalogue of SRP?* Taking into account our specific field of research, we are especially interested in SRP as reuse artefact. This is the reason for asking to the participants in which degree requirements engineering problems can be ameliorated by the existence of an SRP catalogue and about critical aspects and barriers for its introduction in an organization.

Data Points. The data points considered are practitioners and academics with either "significant" or "some" level of experience on requirement engineering. We adapted the questions to each level of experience in order to obtain more accurate responses.

Channel. The survey is implemented as an online questionnaire. Firstly, it was offered to REFSQ 2013 assistants (as part of the Empirical Track) who could answer it during the conference. Afterwards it was also offered to the requirements engineering community through other channels as LinkedIn requirement engineering groups, related tutorials attendees in conferences as RE 2013 and ICSE 2013, and online communities.

Data Analysis. The results presented in this paper are based in descriptive statistics and content analysis (the last one only for questions with results in free text). In case of the questions using Likert scales, their results have been analyzed following the good practices presented in [6]. We are waiting to increase the number of data points before performing correlation and cluster analysis.

Questionnaire Design. In order to avoid typical design errors in online surveys, we accompanied critical questions with a glossary of terms; we added whenever necessary text fields for clarification or for allowing the respondent adding missing values; and we conducted pilots of the questionnaire to ensure its correct understanding and its possible display effects. An excerpt of the online survey containing the questions necessary to answer the research questions analyzed in this paper can be found in [7].

Validity. On the one hand, in order to have a random sampling, aside from proposing the survey in several conferences, we introduced it as discussion topic in the main LinkedIn requirement engineering groups, and we introduced it as an open discussion in the groups to engage not only people that are already using requirement reuse practices. On the other hand, in order to mitigate the problem of coverage of the requirements engineering population and the low response-rate common in online surveys, we proposed the survey through the LinkedIn and community groups with around 12000 members altogether.

3   Results and Discussion

At the moment of writing the paper, we had 50 completed responses from practitioners and researchers with industrial experience, from 19 countries around the world (mostly from North America and Europe). From them, 27 (54%) were requirement engineers in industry, 10 (20%) researchers with significant experience as requirement engineers, and 13 (26%) researchers with some limited experience as requirement engineers.

RQ1: Is Requirements Reuse a Usual Practice in Current RE Processes?

We asked participants about three different aspects (see *About Reuse during Requirements Engineering* and *About Observations on Requirements* sections in [7]):

- *What is the level of requirements reuse they had in their projects* (see Table 1).
- *Which are the types of non-functional and non-technical requirements (NFR, NTR respectively) that were more similar from project to project.* A list of NFR and NTR types was provided so the similarity of each type among projects could be measured (see Table 2). It was possible to add other NFR or NTR types that could be relevant and not stated by the survey.
- *What are the techniques they implemented to achieve requirements reuse* (multiresponse question). This last question was asked only to those participants that implemented some kind of requirements reuse in their projects, i.e. being the requirements reuse level in the first question marked at least as *2-Low* (see Table 3).

Table 1. Requirements reuse level

	#Participants (%Participants)
Not able to answer	1 (2%)
Inexistent or Very Low	11 (22%)
Low	18 (36%)
Medium	9 (18%)
High	9 (18%)
Very High	2 (4%)
TOTAL	*50 (100%)*

Table 3. Requirements reuse techniques

	#Participants (%Participants)
Copy & Paste of Individual reqs.	23 (60%)
Copy & Paste of Groups of reqs.	21 (55%)
Duplicate of a full reqs. specification	19 (50%)
Fill in predefined templates	15 (39%)
Use of a req. patterns catalogue	5 (13%)

Table 2. Requirement types more similar between projects (1 – Totally disagree, 5 – Totally agree)

	Likert Scale Average
4. Usability	3,60
5. Reliability	3,48
6. Security	3,44
7. Maintainability	3,44
2. Performance Efficiency	3,24
11. Business Suitability	3,20
12. Project Suitability	3,16
3. Compatibility	3,08
8. Portability	3,08
1. Functionality Suitability	3,04
10. Product Non-Technical Suitability	2,94
9. Supplier Suitability	2,92

Regarding the first question (Table 1), we got 38 participants (76%) that stated the requirements reuse level as equal or greater than *2-Low*. However, reuse seems not to be an established practice in IT projects since only 22% of the participants marked it as equal or greater than *4-High*.

The results of the second question about the types of NFR and NTR that were more similar from project to project (Table 2) do not highlight a big difference in the level of recurrence of the types, being most of them around 3 (equivalent to *Neutral* value). One of the possible reasons for this neutrality is that most of the people that took part in the survey did not carry out requirements reuse. The four requirement types that were ranked with a higher reuse rate were: Usability, Reliability, Security, and Maintainability.

Regarding the techniques used to implement requirements reuse, the current results of the survey (Table 3) show that the most common techniques, used by more than 50% of the participants, are those based on the textual copy and later modification by hand of requirements coming from previous projects, i.e. *Copy and paste of individual existing requirements* or *Copy and paste of groups of requirements* in the requirements specification under construction and *Duplicate of a full existing requirements specification* and work in its parts as needed. Less common techniques seem to be *Fill in of predefined templates* and *Use of a requirement patterns catalogue*.

Discussion

IT practitioners include reuse in their daily practices, although the reuse process is probably most of the times simple Copy & Paste with its corresponding problems. The rationale behind is simple: during elicitation and definition of requirements, whenever the IT professional remembers some previous project where requirements looked close to the ones of the current project, copying and using them as a starting point seems natural. We think this is the reason why we found that 76% of participants declare to carry out some level of reuse in their projects. Thus our interpretation of the results is that requirements reuse is present in IT projects, but well-defined and mature reuse methods and processes have still to emerge and be integrated into the practice of organizations.

Concerning the type of requirements more similar among projects, non-functional requirements (types numbered from 2 to 8) are considered as more similar among projects than functional ones (numbered as 1), which is corroborated by the fact that non-functional requirements is the main focus of requirements reuse proposals [8][9][10]. In case of non-technical requirements (numbered from 9 to 12 most), the results are not the ones we expected. For instance, in case of the *Supplier Suitability,* which was defined in the questionnaire as corresponding to those requirements on the organization that supplies the software product, it was considered less recurrent than functional requirements. Our interpretation is that non-technical requirements were not well understood by participants, since according to our experience, this kind of requirement is in fact quite recurrent, if we think for instance on requirements about the positioning and strength of the supplier organization, the certifications that this organization has on software processes development, the services it offers or its maintenance and development procedures. This misunderstanding could be caused by the fact that these kinds of requirements are not always included in requirement specifications unless projects are call-for-tenders projects.

Chernak conducted an online survey on requirements reuse during 2010 [11] (henceforth *CheS*). One of its questions can be directly related to the first aspect addressed in RQ1. Its results were that 59% of respondents reused requirements in their latest projects. If we compare this magnitude with ours, in our survey the percentage is higher: considering the respondents with a level of reuse equal or above Low, we observe that 76% of interviewees do some reuse in their projects (Table 1). This difference may be caused by the different population of the surveys: CheS involved software engineers in general, whilst in our case we addressed requirements engineering practitioners. In addition, CheS survey's results indicate that practitioners that adopt reuse practices do not usually follow well-defined reuse processes, sustaining also our results.

RQ2: Which Benefits and Drawbacks Can Appear from the Use of a SRP Catalogue?

To answer this research question we asked the participants to evaluate, using Likert Scales, a list of problems that could be ameliorated by the use of a SRP catalogue, and two lists of critical factors and barriers respectively that could affect the successful adoption of an SRP catalogue (see *About Reuse through Patterns* section in [7]). In the three lists, the participants had the opportunity to add new items not appearing in the lists.

Regarding the problems that could be ameliorated by the use of an SRP catalogue (see Table 4), the four most mentioned problems in the survey are: *Lack of requirements uniformity, Incompleteness of requirements specification, Ambiguity of requirements* and *Having too little time to spend in requirements elicitation.*

Regarding the factors that could be critical for the introduction of a SRP catalogue (see Table 5), all the listed factors were considered critical except the existence of *Help Desk*. Participants added other critical factors, being the most mentioned ones *The existence of a ready-to-use SRP catalogue, The possibility of having free trials periods,* and *The existence of success cases using SRPs.*

Table 4. Problems ameliorated by the use of a SRP catalogue (1 – At all, 3 - A lot)

	Likert Scale Average
Lack of requirements uniformity	2,43
Incompleteness of requirements specification	2,37
Requirements ambiguity	2,32
Too little time invested in requirements elicitation	2,31
Requirements non-verifiable	2,21
Too much time spent in requirements elicitation	2,20
Stakeholders do not know exactly their needs	2,18
Stakeholders needs' change during the requirements elicitation process	2,18
Requirements inconsistency	2,16
Lack of requirements. traceability	2,12
Lack of requirements quantification	2,12
Lack of requirements prioritization	2,04
Conflicts among needs stated by stakeholders	2,00

Table 5. Critical factors for introducing a SRP catalogue (1 – Totally disagree, 5 – Totally agree)

	Likert Scale Average
Well-defined use method	4,22
Tool support	4,12
Community of users existence	3,94
Training courses	3,92
Help desk	3,37

Table 6. Barriers to adopt successfully a SRP catalogue (1 – Totally disagree, 5 – Totally agree)

	Likert Scale Average
Resistance of req. engineers to change	4,10
Integration of the catalogue with the existing req. engineering processes	3,96
Risk of converting requirements elicitation in a stiff process	3,63
Amount of reusable knowledge necessary to create and maintain	3,59

Finally, for the list of factors that may represent a barrier to the successful adoption of an SRP catalogue (see Table 6), all of its items were considered as important barriers that should be taken into account, being the highest rated ones: *The resistance of requirements engineers to change*, and *The integration of the catalogue with the existing requirements engineering process*. Another barrier not included in the list but considered as very important by some participants was *The lack of management support.*

Discussion

The results of the first question are very important because the three problems identified by the survey participants corroborate the aim of our PABRE framework: to increase the uniformity and completeness of requirement specifications and to reduce ambiguity among requirements in these specifications.

The critical factors obtained as more relevant also support our interpretation of the RQ1 results. The importance given to the existence of a reuse method and tool support is probably caused by the absence of a well-defined and mature method to guide the reuse processes undertaken by the participants. Regarding the barriers, it is not surprising that the ones that depend on people involvement are considered the most important: when we talk about processes in organizations, the implication of involved people become a key factor for the adoption and its success [12].

In the CheS survey [11] there are two questions that can be considered indirectly related to RQ2, which ask about benefits and obstacles. In our case, we ask about similar aspects but specifically for reuse through patterns. The main benefit reported by the CheS survey participants was "faster-time-to-market", mentioned by 50% of their respondents. We also had this response (*Too much time spent in requirements elicitation* in Table 4) as a possible answer of problems that could be ameliorated by the use of a SRP catalogue. Although in our case it was not ranked as the most important benefit, it was still considered as relevant by the participants. This "faster-time-to-market" benefit has been proved to be true in real processes, such as Goldin et al. case study [13] conducted in an organization that was incorporating requirements reuse to their requirements engineering processes. On the other hand, CheS' obstacles can be assimilated to barriers in our survey. Both surveys include as barriers the creation and maintenance of reusable artifacts, and the resistance of project managers and requirement engineers (see Table 6). It is difficult to compare both surveys because in CheS, the answers to these questions were open, and in ours a list was provided with an open field to extend it if needed; however, we still may observe that CheS' results are included in ours.

In Hoffmann et al. [14], the result of 5 semi-structured interviews (henceforth *HKHL*) with experienced requirements analysts is presented. They were asked on their opinions on the advantages and success factors they could perceive on the use of SRP approaches. In the case of advantages, 7 out of the 8 most important problems identified as potentially ameliorated by the use of SRP in our survey (Table 4) were also stated in the HKHL interviews. The only one that did not appear in HKHL was *Too little time invested in requirements elicitation*. In the case of success factors and barriers, all of those identified in our survey were also found in HKHL, and the ones in HKHL that were not in our survey are more related to the quality of the SRP catalogue, which we did not considered as an option because we gave it for granted.

4   Conclusions and Further Work

In this paper, we presented the preliminary results of a survey to study the state of the practice on requirements reuse, and on the possible advantages, success factors and barriers of using SRP as reuse artifact. The survey results show that requirements reuse, although is not a widespread practice in IT projects, is used in a certain level in the projects were survey participants participated, but probably there is a lack of well-defined and mature reuse methods and processes. Regarding the use of SRP, the results seem to support our hypothesis that SRP could help to ameliorate some common problems related to requirements specifications like lack of uniformity, incompleteness and ambiguity. The aspects more critical in the application are the implication of requirement engineers and project managers and also the existence of a well-defined method of use and the existence of tool support.

Future work includes the extension of this study by gathering more responses, to include also responses given by researchers without practical experience and conducting correlation analysis and cluster analysis of responses considering also other general questions included in the questionnaire.

Acknowledgements. This work has been supported by the Spanish project TIN2010-19130-C02-01. We would also like to thank all participants of the surveys for their kindly cooperation.

References

1. Franch, X., Palomares, C., Quer, C., Renault, S., De Lazzer, F.: A Metamodel for Software Requirement Patterns. In: Wieringa, R., Persson, A. (eds.) REFSQ 2010. LNCS, vol. 6182, pp. 85–90. Springer, Heidelberg (2010)
2. Palomares, C., Quer, C., Franch, X., Guerlain, C., Renault, S.: A Catalogue of Functional Software Requirement Patterns for the Domain of Content Management Systems. In: Requirements Engineering Track at 28th ACM SAC (RE-SAC), pp. 1260–1265. ACM (2013)
3. Renault, S., Mendez, O., Franch, X., Quer, C.: A Pattern-based Method for building Requirements Documents in Call-for-tender Processes. Int. J. of Computer Science & Applications 6(5), 175–202 (2009)
4. Franch, X., Quer, C., Renault, S., Guerlain, C., Palomares, C.: Constructing and Using Software Requirements Patterns. In: Maalej, W., Thurimella, A.K. (eds.) Managing Requirements Knowledge, pp. 95–116. Springer (2013)
5. Palomares, C., Quer, C., Franch, X.: PABRE-Proj: Applying Patterns in Requirements Elicitation. In: IEEE International Requirement Engineering Conference (RE), pp. 332–333 (2013)
6. Jamieson, S.: Likert Scales: How to (Ab)use Them. Medical Education 38(12), 1217–1218 (2004)

7. Report of the Requirements Reuse and Patterns survey - excerpt,
   `http://www.upc.edu/gessi/PABRE/Survey_Questions.pdf`

8. Jaramillo, A.F.: Non-functional requirements elicitation from business process models. In: 5th International Conference on Research Challenges in Information Science (RCIS). IEEE CS Press (2011)

9. Hoffmann, A., Schulz, T., Hoffmann, H., Jandt, S., Roßnagel, A., Leimeister, J.M.: Towards the Use of Software Requirement Patterns for Legal Requirements. In: 2nd International Requirements Engineering Efficiency Workshop (REEW) at REFSQ (2012)

10. Toval, A., Carrillo-de-Gea, J.M., Fernandez-Aleman, J.L., Toval, R.: Learning systems development using reusable standard-based requirements catalogs. In: Global Engineering Education Conference (EDUCON). IEEE CS Press (2011)

11. Chernak, Y.: Requirements Reuse: The State of the Practice. In: Software Science, Technology and Engineering (SWSTE), pp. 46–53. IEEE CS Press (2012)

12. Dyba, T.: An empirical investigation of the key factors for success in software process improvement. IEEE Transactions on Software Engineering 31(5) (2005)

13. Goldin, L., Berry, D.M.: Reuse of requirements reduced time to market at one industrial shop: a case study. In: Requirements Engineering Journal 18 (2013)

14. Hoffmann, A., Janzen, A., Hoffmann, H., Leimeister, J.M.: Success Factors for Requirement Patterns Approaches. In: Sozio-technisches Systemdesign im Zeitalter des Ubiquitous Computing (SUBICO) im Rahmen der Informatik, Koblenz (2013)

Safety Evidence Traceability:
Problem Analysis and Model

Sunil Nair[1], Jose Luis de la Vara[1], Alberto Melzi[2], Giorgio Tagliaferri[3],
Laurent de-la-Beaujardiere[4], and Fabien Belmonte[4]

[1] Simula Research Laboratory, Norway
[2] Centro Ricerche Fiat S.C.p.A., Italy
[3] Rina Services S.p.A., Italy
[4] Alstom Transport, France
{sunil,jdelavara}@simula.no, alberto.melzi@crf.it,
giorgio.tagliaferri@rina.org,
{laurent.de-la-eaujardiere,fabien.belmonte}
@transport.alstom.com

Abstract. [**Context and motivation**] Safety evidence plays an important role in gaining confidence in the safe operation of a system in a given context. For a large system, it is necessary to provide information about thousands of artefacts that might be used as evidence and about the relationships among themselves and also with other safety assurance assets. [**Question/problem**] Past research has only addressed some needs of traceability in safety-critical systems and thus has not provided a complete picture of safety evidence traceability. Lack of knowledge and awareness of these needs can result in poor evidence management and lead to certification risks. [**Principal ideas/results**] This paper aims to provide a broad overview of safety evidence traceability needs for practice and its associated challenges. We also propose a safety evidence traceability model, which has been validated with data from real-world critical systems. [**Contribution**] We discuss the motivation and challenges for safety evidence traceability, and present the various traces that need to be captured and maintained. This information can help researchers to shape future research based on industry needs and can help practitioners to gain a deeper understanding and a wider knowledge of safety evidence traceability, thereby facilitating safety assurance and certification.

Keywords: Safety evidence, Traceability, Safety assurance, Safety certification, Safety Standard, SafeTIM.

1 Introduction

Critical systems in many domains are subject to a rigorous assessment or assurance process through which the system is deemed safe for a particular context. Such assessment process is usually based on the fulfilment of the requirements of some safety standard. To comply with a standard, system suppliers have to gather and present evidence information supporting their claims about system safety. We define

C. Salinesi and I. van de Weerd (Eds.): REFSQ 2014, LNCS 8396, pp. 309–324, 2014.
© Springer International Publishing Switzerland 2014

safety evidence as *"artefacts that contribute to developing confidence in the safe operation of a system in a given environment"* [1]. Some generic examples of safety evidence are test results, system specifications, and personnel competence. Such artefacts are used to support claims about system safety, and to show compliance with a standard.

For a realistically large system, a system supplier needs to collect and manage a large quantity of safety evidence throughout the analysis, development, verification, maintenance, operation, and evolution of a system. The system supplier must also capture and maintain traces between pieces of evidence information and also from and to evidence and other safety assurance assets (claims, arguments, etc.) in order to be able to demonstrate system safety.

In software engineering, traceability can be defined as the degree to which a relationship can be established between two or more products of the development process (aka artefacts), especially products having a predecessor-successor or master-subordinate relationship to one another [2]. With the above definition in mind, we define safety evidence traceability as *"the degree to which a relationship can be established to and from artefacts that are used as safety evidence"*.

Lack of knowledge and understanding of safety evidence traceability needs can result in improper evidence management, which may indirectly result in certification risks [3]. A system supplier might not be able to demonstrate system safety if the evidence is not well managed and traced. Consequently, a third party certification authority would not gain enough confidence in the safe operation of the system.

Although traceability for safety-critical systems and more concretely safety evidence traceability have been addressed in past research, no study has yet provided a broad and complete picture of safety evidence traceability needs. Most of the research has only focused on the relationships between the artefacts used as evidence (e.g., [4]). The studies that have explicitly or implicitly studied other aspects of safety evidence traceability have not paid much attention to many necessary relationships for evidence traceability. For example, works that have dealt with the relationship between safety evidence and the argument that justifies evidence validity for a claim (e.g., [5]) have usually not paid attention to other traces such as to artefact versions.

This paper aims to present an in-depth analysis of safety evidence traceability needs and its challenges that would be helpful for both researchers and practitioners. Based on others' past work, on our knowledge about the state of the art and practice (e.g., [6][1]), and on own experience in safety assurance and certification projects, we discuss the motivation for safety evidence traceability and its challenges. We also present the traces that must be created and maintained from and to evidence information. As a result, we have created a <u>Saf</u>ety <u>E</u>vidence <u>T</u>raceability <u>I</u>nformation <u>M</u>odel for safety evidence - SafeTIM.

The results presented in this paper are part of the on-going work in OPENCOSS (www.opencoss-project.eu), a large-scale European research project on safety assurance and certification in the automotive, avionics, and railway domains. Beyond the usefulness of the results for the project, we consider that the contribution of the paper is twofold. Firstly, the problem analysis presented and SafeTIM can help researchers to better understand safety evidence traceability needs in industry and thus to identify aspects that might require further study. Secondly, practitioners can benefit by gaining awareness of important aspects related to safety evidence traceability whose management can be essential for safety assurance and certification, thereby improving project management and reducing cost.

The rest of the paper is organised as follows. Section 2 presents the background of the paper. Section 3 discusses the motivation for safety evidence traceability. Section 4 describes the safety evidence traces, and presents SafeTIM and its validation. Section 5 compares SafeTIM with other models and discusses the challenges for safety evidence traceability. Finally, Section 6 presents our conclusions.

2   Background

This section introduces a common certification framework that is being developed in the OPENCOSS project and reviews related work.

2.1   Common Certification Framework

The main technical objectives of OPENCOSS are to (1) devise a common certification framework for railway, avionics, and automotive industries, and (2) establish an open-source safety certification infrastructure.

The common certification framework will consist of several, linked metamodels, each aimed at modelling different aspects of compliance [7]: (1) the safety standards followed; (2) project-specific aspects such as the actual process executed, the artefacts managed, and the argumentation used to justify the key decisions made; (3) the terms used in different safety standards and projects, and; (4) mappings between different standards and projects, in order to support cross-standard/domain certification.

Some of these models have been already published (for e.g., [7]), while others are accessible only for the project members. However, SafeTIM corresponds to a fragment of the large framework. The model presented in this paper contains the set of fundamental concepts and relationships for safety evidence. It must be noted that more information might be necessary in a safety assurance and certification project for other purposes (e.g., for assessment of process-based compliance). We believe that SafeTIM is an underlying model that lies behind the common certification framework and needs to be explicitly modelled to deal specifically with safety evidence traceability.

2.2   Related Work

Traceability has been an important research topic in software engineering during the last two decades. Despite the acknowledged higher importance of traceability for safety-critical systems [8], literature reviews [9][10] have shown that the ratio of papers on the subject is low.

Publications presenting and discussing the motivation (e.g. [11]), challenges (e.g., [12]), and open issues (e.g., [13]) for traceability are available in the literature. Studies on traces (e.g., [14]) and types of traces (e.g., [15]) can also be found, mainly in relation to traceability to and from requirements. Past work have also focused on strategic traceability needs and challenges specific to safety-critical projects [8].

What differentiates this paper from most of the past research on traceability is its focus on safety evidence. The number of publications addressing safety evidence traceability in isolation is limited, and there are few studies that discuss the needs and motivation of such traces [16][17]. For example, the literature on safety evidence traceability needs for evidence reuse is very limited. Given its importance for cost reduction in the development and assurance of new safety critical systems, we considered that it is an area that needs to be further investigated. Furthermore, these pieces of work have a very narrow scope (e.g., specific to a domain or safety standard) and do not provide a complete overview of the motivation and challenges regarding evidence traceability.

Most of the existing studies on traceability for safety-critical systems have focused on traceability between the artefacts resulting from their analysis and development, such as requirements and hazards [18], requirements and components [16], requirements and design [19], or requirements and code [17]. These artefacts and the traces between them can themselves be used as safety evidence. Models including a larger number of artefacts to trace have also been proposed [4][20]. Some papers have focused on traceability for specific safety standards (e.g., DO-178B [21] and ISO26262 [22]) or have modelled entities and relationships that abstract concepts common to different safety standards [7]. However these studies have not dealt with some specific traces to and from safety evidence that will be discussed in Section 4.1. With regard to safety evidence as an element of an assurance or safety case, the traces most frequently studied are with arguments and claims (e.g., [23]).

Some recent works have broadened the scope of safety evidence traceability. SACM (Structured Assurance Case Metamodel; [24]) includes an evidence metamodel that specifies relationships between evidence items and between evidence items and other assurance assets. The link between evidence and the process from which it results is addressed in [5]. An evidence-related conceptual model for IEC61508 with relationships beyond those between artefacts used as evidence [25] and a generic evidence model for safety cases [26] have also been proposed. Although these works have provided valuable insights, they still lack details about safety evidence traceability and their results do not meet all the needs presented in the next section (e.g., the purpose of the traces beyond safety assurance and certification).

Despite the limitations identified in the past research and the fact that no single study that has yet provided enough insights into safety evidence traceability in specific, our review of related work has helped us to better understand safety evidence traceability. As a result, we aimed to build and present in this paper SafeTIM - a holistic safety evidence traceability information model that synthesises traces indicated in the past work on evidence traceability and also deal with aspects that have not addressed in depth yet (e.g., evidence reuse).

3   Motivation for Safety Evidence Traceability

This section presents what we regard as the main reasons for safety evidence traceability: safety assurance, compliance with safety standards, change impact analysis, evidence reuse, and project management. Although some authors [11] have suggested that safety assurance and compliance with safety standards are the main reasons for traceability in safety-critical systems, empirical evidence indicates that other motivations exist too [6].

Some of these motivations such as safety assurance and compliance with safety standards are specific to safety evidence or for safety-critical systems, while the others might be motivated from generic traceability needs. Nonetheless, these generic traceability needs are especially important for safety critical systems because of their rigorous and stringent certification context and the high costs associated to them.

It must be noted that the aspects discussed below are not exclusively independent, but rather related to one another (e.g., evidence reuse and change impact analysis). This also applies to the challenges discussed in Section 5.2.

M1: Safety assurance. A fundamental criterion for any safety-critical system, regardless of having to comply with some specific safety standard, is to ensure that its hazards have been avoided or mitigated. This allows gaining confidence in the overall safety of the system. Maintaining traceability of the evidence information involved is essential for this purpose so as to show that hazard mitigations have been properly developed and validated. For example, safety requirements can be specified from hazard identification and for their mitigation, and their satisfaction can be later verified with techniques such as formal methods.

M2: Compliance with safety standards. In domains such as avionics and railway, safety-critical systems must comply with safety standards for certification purposes. Therefore, system suppliers have to show fulfilment of the requirements of the standards. Traceability can be a means for this activity. In addition, system suppliers might have to explicitly provide traceability specifications as a part of the information that constitutes evidence of compliance [6]. Indeed, some standards mandate this information (e.g., DO-178C [27]).

M3: Change impact analysis. Changes in a safety-critical system and thus in its safety evidence are practically inevitable [28]. Practitioners must ensure that such changes in the system will not have any undesired effect in system safety and in the body of safety evidence. Therefore, such changes have to be managed adequately. For example, it is necessary to assess how a change in a piece of evidence might affect others [6]. Safety evidence traceability is necessary to perform such an impact analysis in order to identify the potential consequences of a change or to estimate what needs to be modified to accomplish a change.

M4: Evidence reuse. Reuse of a safety-critical component (or system) and thus of its evidence is important in industry [6], mainly in order to increase the return on investment in component development and to decrease system cost. However, it must be ensured that evidence reuse is adequate [28], or that a change in a reused piece of evidence is propagated to other uses when considered necessary. Maintaining safety evidence traceability supports evidence reuse and the execution of the associated required activities.

M5. Project management. Project management information such as that related to cost, effort, or degree of compliance is essential to make informed decisions during safety-critical system lifecycle. These decisions can be hard to make without adequate safety evidence traceability. For example, it allows the estimation of the cost of a possible change, and helps practitioners decide whether the change should be implemented or not.

4   Safety Evidence Traces

This section introduces the various traces necessary to create and maintain for safety evidence traceability. We represent these traces graphically in SafeTIM, the traceability information model for safety evidence that we propose.

4.1   Traces to Create and Maintain

Based on (1) the analysis of the motivation for safety evidence traceability in the previous section, (2) the traces that we have identified in previous work, and (3) our knowledge and experience, we present the set of traces that we regard as necessary for safety evidence. Nonetheless, we acknowledge that, depending on their purpose, some practitioners might not need all of the traces for a specific project, or would require other specific traces that are not mentioned below. The overall motivation that drives each trace is mentioned in brackets.

Between Artefacts (M1, M2, M3 & M5). Traces must be created between the artefacts managed during system lifecycle such as a requirements specification and test cases. For those artefacts used as safety evidence, the traces between them can result in a chain of evidence [27]: a series of related pieces of safety evidence. However, traces could also be maintained to and from artefacts for purposes different to safety assurance or compliance [6]. For example, one might need to trace artefacts for change impact analysis. Traces between artefacts can also be used for project management. For example, requirements that have not been tested can be determined.

Between Safety Evidence and Claims (M1-M5). Safety evidence is inherently targeted at supporting claims about system safety and thus at gaining confidence in it. When evidence changes, the confidence in the related claims can vary. Confidence in safety evidence can also vary if a claim changes. Traceability between evidence and claims support evidence reuse when similar or the same claims are made, for instance, in different projects. Analysis of the claims for which safety evidence exists is also part of project management. When a claim refers to requirements of a safety standard, the related evidence aims to show compliance.

Between Safety Evidence and Arguments (M1-M5). Safety evidence alone might not be sufficient to gain confidence in a claim [26], and a justification might be necessary. Such a justification can take the form of an argument [23], which can clarify and substantiate claims based on safety evidence. When safety evidence changes, an argument might be affected, and likewise evidence might have to be revalidated when an argument changes.

Between Artefacts and Reference Artefacts (M2 & M5). Safety standards usually prescribe types of artefacts (i.e., reference artefacts) that have to be produced to show compliance. Practitioners must show how the concrete artefacts produced in a project materialise the reference artefacts. For example, DO-178C requires the creation of a reference artefact called Software Verification Results. Such a type could be materialised in a project by means of, for instance, a specific review (of requirements, code, etc.).

Between Pieces of Safety Evidence in Relation to a Claim (M1 & M3). Safety evidence traced to a claim could not only help gain confidence in its satisfaction, but could also make one lose confidence in the claim [24]. For example, a review could be used as a piece of evidence to support a claim about requirements accuracy, but other pieces of evidence (e.g., reviewer competence) could be used to show that not enough confidence exists in the accuracy. A relationship between two pieces of evidence can be created in order to specify that one supports or challenges the other in relation to a same claim.

Between versions of an Artefact (M1 & M2). An artefact can be modified, making a new version of a previous one. Maintenance of traces between the versions of an artefact can be necessary for safety assurance and even mandated by a safety standard. For example, it might be necessary that the versions of two related artefacts are consistent (e.g., because of temporal constraints), and configuration management practices can be required [6].

Between (re)uses of an Artefact (M3 & M4). An artefact used in a project (e.g., as evidence) can be reused to support different claims in the same or in a different project. Maintaining traces between these uses is necessary mainly for change impact analysis. Modification of an artefact in some of its uses might affect the others. For example, a new fault could be identified in a component used in one project and the same component might have been used in different projects. This trace would help to identify all the projects in which the component has been used and would allow the system supplier to change the required artefacts accordingly. It is also especially important to keep these traces when the artefacts reused are duplicated.

Between Artefacts and Activities (M2, M3 & M5). Artefacts are the result of the execution of some activity [25]. For example, test results can be produced in some validation activity. It is necessary to trace artefacts and activities so that practitioners can (1) identify the activities that might have to be re-executed due to artefact modification, and (2) show that they have executed the activities mandated in a standard. At the same time, this trace can also act as a measure to keep track of activities that have not yet been executed in a project.

Between Artefacts and Techniques used to Create Them (M1, M2 & M5). For safety assurance, an essential aspect of the artefacts managed in a project is to know how the artefacts have been created. More concretely, it is necessary to know the means (i.e., the techniques) used. Safety standards sometimes specify the techniques that should or must be used to create some artefacts. In many regulatory contexts, system suppliers are not completely free to use a given technique unless they justify the suitability of their selection.

Between Artefacts/Pieces of Evidence and Provenance (M1, M3 & M5). Traces between artefacts and the information about their management (who created it, when it was created, artefact evaluations, etc.) can be very important for safety assurance [24]. This information can also help practitioners to decide on who should deal with changes in an artefact. Pieces of evidence can also have provenance information (e.g., who approved it).

4.2   SafeTIM: A Traceability Information Model for Safety Evidence

Based on the traces identified, we propose a traceability information model for safety evidence called SafeTIM. The model is shown in Fig. 1 in the form of a class diagram. The importance of explicitly creating a traceability information model for safety critical projects has already been highlighted in past research [8].

The definition of each class is based on past work. Every class has a unique identification attribute (ID) for implementation purposes [4][8]. SafeTIM classes are defined as follows.

- *Artefact*: Individual, identifiable units of data managed (used, modified, and/or produced) throughout system lifecycle [8][24].
- *Piece of Evidence*: The use of an artefact as evidence for a claim [24].
- *Claim*: Propositions being asserted in relation to system safety (or other safety-related system properties) [24][29].
- *Artefact/Evidence Provenance*: Characteristics of artefacts (or pieces of evidence) that correspond to information related to their lifecycle and the responsibility for their management [24].
- *Project*: An individual or collaborative enterprise [29] for system assurance or certification and in which artefacts are managed [24].
- *Version*: A particular form of an artefact differing in certain respects from an earlier form or other forms [24][29].
- *Argument*: A body of information (or reasons [29]) presented with the intention to establish one or more claims about system safety through the presentation of related supporting claims, pieces of evidence, and contextual information [24]. In essence, an argument aims to justify the validity of a piece of evidence for a claim.
- *Participant*: A party involved in the management of an artefact or piece of evidence [29].
- *Artefact Relationship*: This class represents the existence of a relationship and thus of a trace between two artefacts [30][12]. A relationship can be recorded in an artefact if the relationship itself is used as evidence (e.g., DO-178C explicitly requests the provision traceability information). Examples of types of relationships between artefacts (e.g., with regard to the content, abstraction, or evolution of an artefact) can be found in [24][12][14].

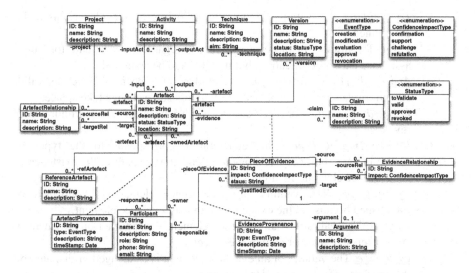

Fig. 1. SafeTIM – A Safety Evidence Traceability Information Model

- **Evidence Relationship:** This class represents the existence of a relationship and thus of a trace between two pieces of evidence in relation to the confidence in the validity of one of the pieces according to the other [30][24][12].
- **Reference Artefact:** Types of unit of data that a safety standard prescribes to be created and maintained during system lifecycle. Reference artefacts are materialised in assurance projects by means of (concrete) artefacts [30]. This means that these artefacts have the same or a similar structure (syntax) and/or purpose (semantics) [4].
- **Activity:** A unit of work that requires, modifies and/or produces artefacts [24] and corresponds to something being performed in system lifecycle [29]. Activities can be defined at different degrees of granularity (process, phase, task, etc.).
- **Technique:** A specific procedure through which a particular way of creating an artefact is accomplished [29].

    There are also three enumerations in SafeTIM.

- **Event Type:** This enumeration corresponds to types of events that can occur in the lifecycle of an artefact or piece of evidence [24][29]. Its literals are:
    - *Creation:* When an artefact or piece of evidence is brought into existence.
    - *Modification:* When a change is made in some characteristic of an artefact or piece of evidence.
    - *Evaluation:* When an element is assessed or evaluated.
    - *Approval:* When an element is accepted as satisfactory or as valid.
    - *Revocation:* When an element is cancelled or withdrawn.
- **Status Type:** This enumeration corresponds to the status of an artefact or piece of evidence, for instance, after a change in some related information. Its literals are:

- *To Validate*: The validity of the artefact or piece of evidence has to be determined.
- *Valid*: The artefact or piece of evidence is regarded as adequate for safety assurance and/or certification, but it still has to be approved.
- *Approved*: The artefact or piece of evidence has been evaluated as valid, and not further evaluation is necessary unless some change takes place.
- *Revoked*: the artefact or piece of evidence has been cancelled, withdrawn or revoked.
- **Confidence Impact Type**: This enumeration corresponds to the types of confidence in the validity of one evidence element as a result of the existence of another evidence element. Its literals are:
  - *Confirmation*: The validity of an evidence element is confirmed or established because of the existence of another evidence element.
  - *Support*: The validity of an evidence element is supported or provided by the existence of another evidence element.
  - *Challenge*: The validity of an evidence element is challenged or disputed by the existence of another evidence element.
  - *Refutation*: The validity of an evidence element is proven to be wrong because of the existence of another evidence element.

4.3   Model Validation

We developed SafeTIM with close reference to the results obtained from two large previous studies: a systematic literature review (on 216 publication) on the state of the art [1] and a survey (with 52 participants) on the state of the practice [6] concerning safety evidence management. In addition, most of the authors of this paper have extensive experience in safety assurance and certification in industry. Although the creation of the model based on our own knowledge and experience could be regarded as an implicit validation, we have performed further explicit validation.

The validation presented in this paper corresponds to the review of documentation (and artefacts) from real safety assurance and certification projects. These reviews were aimed to identify information in the documentation that map to the structure of SafeTIM. This way, we could explicitly validate that SafeTIM concepts and relationship have been used in real projects.

For the validation, we reviewed the following documentations:

- A synopsis of several safety studies and system specifications (e.g., safety requirements) of a sub-system targeted at complying with ISO26262 [31] in the automotive domain.
- The system safety case from a railway project that was certified against CENELEC standards [32].
- The system safety case, the safety plan, two sub-system safety cases, two hazard logs, several safety studies (e.g., the preliminary hazard analysis), several system specifications (e.g., requirements and design specifications), several V&V (verification and validation) plan reports (e.g., test procedures), several V&V results reports (e.g., testing results), and several safety certificates

(which correspond to the approval for executing some activity) from another railway project that was also certified against CENELEC standards.

We provide the following information about the documentation reviewed in order to show the size of the projects. For the sub-system of the automotive domain, the safety studies had a number of hazards that were mitigated and traced back to around 50 specific safety requirements. For the first railway project, the safety case consisted of almost 200 pages. For the second railway project, the safety plan consisted of over 35 pages. One of the hazard logs contained over 500 entries and over 2,500 traces from safety requirements to other six different types of artefacts. A typical example of the type of the railway projects has around 10000 requirements. More specific details cannot be provided for confidentiality reasons.

The main findings from reviewing these projects are as follows:

- All the classes and relationships of SafeTIM could be identified in several artefacts.
- In some cases, SafeTIM information was not explicit in the artefacts. For example, the safety cases did not explicitly contain information regarding arguments. However, arguments for justifying the use of an artefact as evidence could be extracted from the safety cases.
- We did not find any examples of counter-evidence (i.e., confidence impact corresponding to *Challenge* or *Refutation*). The reason could be that the documentation we reviewed corresponded to the final artefacts used to show system safety for the projects. However, we believe that practitioners should consider counter-evidence for their claims for reasons such as avoiding confirmation bias [33]. We neither found artefacts or pieces of evidence that were revoked, probably for the same reason.
- The companies had their own defined event types, but they can be mapped to those proposed in SafeTIM.

It must also be noted that the terminology used in SafeTIM is not exactly the same as the terminology used in some domains or safety standards. For example, the concepts of work product in ISO26262 or data item in DO-178C correspond to *Artefact* in SafeTIM.

In addition to the above documentation, we have also reviewed examples of safety evidence information in related work (e.g., [26]) and in OPENCOSS deliverables (e.g., [34]) to validate SafeTIM. We have also checked different safety standards (e.g., [27][31][32]).

Fig. 2 shows an illustration of the use of SafeTIM based on the information of one of the railway projects. The figure corresponds to an instance of SafeTIM. The information presented in the figure is generic and corresponds to the sanitised version of real data for publication purposes due to intellectual property constraints. Nonetheless, we believe that the illustration is sufficient to show one example of how the elements and relationships of SafeTIM correspond to the information of a real safety assurance and certification project.

In the example, the *Artefact* safety plan has a relationship to the *Claim* made about the description of the methods used to ensure that the safety goals are met. The artefact therefore is used as *evidence* for the particular claim with a confidence impact

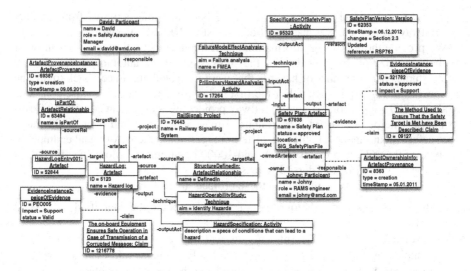

Fig. 2. Instance of SafeTIM concepts and relationships from a railway project

type *Support*. The safety plan is produced as a result of the *Activity* specification of the safety plan. The safety plan is used as input in the *Activity* preliminary hazard analysis. Apart from the activity, specific *Techniques* such as failure mode and effect analysis are employed in the project to give create artefacts. The model also shows some relationships between several artefacts. For example, a specific *Artefact* namely hazard log entry is part of the hazard log. The structure of the hazard log is defined in the safety plan. Since the example illustrates the information reviewed from one railway project, all the artefacts are managed by the same *Project*. Every artefact has *Provenance* information such as who created it and when, who owns it, and what is the role of the person involved along with contact details. Some artefact had versions in this example, as shown in the figure.

5   Discussion

In this section, we compare SafeTIM with other similar models. We also discuss the various challenges of safety evidence traceability and its application.

5.1   Comparison with Other Models

An important difference between SafeTIM and other evidence models (e.g., [24]) is the explicit distinction between artefacts and their use as evidence. In our notion, a piece of evidence cannot exist on its own. An artefact only represents information used, modified, or produced in some activity. An artefact can be used as evidence when associated to a claim. Furthermore, an artefact can be used as evidence for several claims. As a result, emergent evidence properties arise that do not exist in an artefact per se. Such properties depend on a claim. For example, an artefact can support some claims and challenge others. The need of defining new concepts in a conceptual model in such cases has been acknowledged in the literature (e.g., [30]).

When compared to the models reviewed in Section 2.2, SafeTIM can be regarded as a combination of some models. For example, SafeTIM includes process-related and artefact-related information as in [25], and evidence-specific information as in [26]. On the other hand, some models (e.g., [4][25]) correspond to instances of SafeTIM. This is logical given the fact that these models are specific to some projects or safety standards and SafeTIM provides a more abstract picture. In this sense, we have benefited from the past work while trying to mitigate and address possible gaps and limitations. One of such limitation, and as explained above, is the need for differentiating artefacts and pieces of evidence in the model.

One aspect that must be noted in SafeTIM is that it only includes direct relationships to and from safety evidence (i.e., to and from the *Artefact* and *Piece of Evidence* classes). More relationships can be maintained to and from the other classes, and thus indirect relationships with evidence can exist. For example, an activity in a project can correspond to the materialisation of a reference activity of a safety standard. Likewise, relationships can be established between *Activity* and *Technique* in order to specify the techniques used to perform some activity. In addition, more classes can be included for modelling the possible attributes of an *Artefact* (e.g., the result of the execution of a test case, which could be passed or failed) to extend SafeTIM.

Although SafeTIM tries to provide a global picture, we understand and acknowledge that it cannot be regarded as a fully finished model. Firstly, and as we have mentioned, it only deals with the direct relationships to and from evidence. Secondly, the model will be integrated in a common certification framework (Section 2.1). This framework will consist of more concepts and relationships. Thirdly, the model has only been validated in a static way [35]. We plan to conduct case studies to analyse how practitioners can benefit from using SafeTIM. Finally, tool support must be developed to facilitate the adoption of SafeTIM in the industry.

Last but not least, and as acknowledged by several authors (e.g., [4][36][37]), defining a traceability information model at the earliest is essential so that traceability activities succeed in industry. Therefore, we believe that SafeTIM can definitely enable and improve safety evidence traceability practice.

5.2   Challenges for Safety Evidence Traceability

We regard the following list as the major challenges for safety evidence traceability in practice nowadays. Some of these challenges are specific to safety evidence, while others are generic challenges to traceability that has significant effect on safety-critical systems.

Vast Amount of Artefacts and Evidence to Trace. Management of vast amounts of data has always been a challenge for information systems [30], but it becomes even more demanding in the safety-critical domain due to strict regulatory compliance and the vast amount of evidence to create, maintain and trace. For example, we identified a set of 49 basic, generic types of safety evidence from the literature [1], which can correspond to over 100 types for some standards (e.g., [31]). In addition to the challenges inherent to traceability, practitioners can have problems to ensure the consistency of evidence traces. Guidance and tool support are necessary.

Artefacts and Evidence Can be Located in Many Different Locations. Building a critical-system in parts simultaneously in different locations around the world can cause problems in traceability since artefacts used as evidence are in locations different to where the final certification documentation (e.g., a safety case) is developed. This causes problems, such as the coordination of work among distributed development teams and difficulties to ensure that the results are consistent and will not pose any certification risk.

Artefacts and Evidence are Created with and Stored in Different Tools. System suppliers usually have a tool-chain for development, and seamless integration of these tools for safety evidence collection can be difficult. Evidence combination can also be hindered because of the heterogeneity in the formats of the artefacts [24].

Confidence in the Traces Maintained. One of the main challenges that both system suppliers and certifiers face is in gaining confidence in the traces maintained. Providing traces to and from safety evidence are far from enough, as practitioners must aim to be sure that the traces presented are consistent and correct [8].

High Effort and Cost. Although better traceability practices can reduce development effort and costs [9], reality is that it is still a time-consuming activity. As a result, practitioners can end up only dealing with a limited set of traces, usually those mandatory for compliance. However, this might pose certification risks later, or make change management very expensive. Again, adequate guidance and tool support are very important to face this challenge.

Need for Purpose, Value-Based Traceability. In relation to the previous challenge, it is essential that the need for and purpose of safety evidence traceability is clear to those involved in the activity [8]. Otherwise, traceability might not be managed as well as it should be, or its importance might be underestimated. Practitioners must define and be aware of the value of tracing beyond the scope of a single project. For example, adequate safety evidence traceability can facilitate system reuse and change impact analysis in the future, and thus reduce costs.

Some of the above challenges such as the *vast amount of artefacts and evidence to trace, artefacts and evidence located in many different locations,* and *artefacts are created with and stored in different tools* can be tackled by employing a good traceability strategy such as the one proposed in this paper.

6   Conclusion

This paper has presented an analysis of safety evidence traceability based on our knowledge of the state of the art and practice on safety evidence management. The paper presents what we consider as the major motivations that drive the need for evidence traceability. The paper also identifies the traces that need to be created and maintained between safety evidence information items and between evidence and other assurance assets such as claims. As a result of this analysis, we have proposed SafeTIM, a traceability information model for safety evidence.

SafeTIM provides the set of fundamental concepts and relationships necessary to enact evidence traceability in real industrial settings. In addition to making a clear distinction between the artefacts managed during system lifecycle and their use as evidence for a claim, SafeTIM tries to provide a global picture of evidence traceability. We have validated the model with documentation from three different real safety assurance and certification projects. The validation showed that all the classes and relationships of SafeTIM were present in the documentation. In some cases, the presence of the classes and relationships was implicit.

The paper has also compared SafeTIM with other related models and presented what we regard as the major challenges for evidence traceability. In general, we consider that new guidance and tool support can significantly facilitate evidence traceability in industry.

As future work, we plan to extend SafeTIM within the context of the common certification framework to be developed in OPENCOSS, and further validate and evaluate the model in industrial case studies. We also aim to find solutions to some of the challenges presented in the paper.

Acknowledgments. The research leading to this paper has received funding from the FP7 programme under the grant agreement n° 289011 (OPENCOSS) and from the Research Council of Norway under the project Certus-SFI. We also thank the OPENCOSS partners and the colleagues who have provided input and feedback.

References

1. Nair, S., et al.: Classification, Structuring, and Assessment of Evidence For Safety: A Systematic Literature Review. In: ICST, pp. 94–103 (2013)
2. IEEE: IEEE Standard Glossary of Software Engineering Terminology, Std. 610.12-1990
3. Alexander, R., Kelly, T., Gorry, B.: Safety Lifecycle Activities for Autonomous Systems Development. In: SEAS/TR/2009/2 (2009)
4. Cleland-Huang, J., Heimdahl, M., Huffman Hayes, J., Lutz, R., Maeder, P.: Trace queries for safety requirements in high assurance systems. In: Regnell, B., Damian, D. (eds.) REFSQ 2011. LNCS, vol. 7195, pp. 179–193. Springer, Heidelberg (2012)
5. Habli, I., Kelly, T.: A model-driven approach to assuring process reliability. In: ISSRE 2008, pp. 7–16 (2008)
6. Nair, S., et al.: The State of the Practice on Evidence Management for Compliance with Safety Standards. Simula Research Lab. Technical Report (2013)
7. de la Vara, J.L., Panesar-Walawege, R.K.: SafetyMet: A metamodel for safety standards. In: Moreira, A., Schätz, B., Gray, J., Vallecillo, A., Clarke, P. (eds.) MODELS 2013. LNCS, vol. 8107, pp. 69–86. Springer, Heidelberg (2013)
8. Cleland-Huang, J., et al.: Software and systems traceability. Springer-Verlag New York Incorporated (2012)
9. Nair, S., De la Vara, J.L., Sen, S.: A Review of Traceability Research at the Requirements Engineering Conference. In: RE (2013)
10. Torkar, R., et al.: Requirements traceability: a systematic literature review and industry case study. IJSEKE 22(3), 1–49 (2012)
11. Regan, G., et al.: Traceability-Why do it? In: SPICE 2012, pp. 161–172 (2012)
12. Regan, G., et al.: The Barriers to Traceability and their Potential Solutions: Towards a Reference Framework. In: SEAA 2012, pp. 319–322 (2012)

13. Gotel, O., Cleland-Huang, J., Hayes, H., Zisman, A., Egyed, A., Grunbacher, P., Antoniol, G.: The quest for Ubiquity: A roadmap for software and systems traceability research. In: 2012 20th IEEE International Requirements Engineering Conference (RE), pp. 71–80. IEEE (2012)
14. Spanoudakis, G., Zisman, A.: Software traceability: a roadmap. Handbook of Software Engineering and Knowledge Engineering 3, 395–428 (2005)
15. Pohl, K.: Requirements engineering: fundamentals, principles, and techniques. Springer Publishing Company, Incorporated (2010)
16. Lee, J.S., et al.: Means-ends and whole-part traceability analysis of safety requirements. Journal of Systems and Software 83, 1612–1621 (2010)
17. Mason, P.A.J., Saeed, A., Riddle, S.: On the role of traceability for standards compliance: Tracking requirements to code. In: Anderson, S., Felici, M., Littlewood, B. (eds.) SAFECOMP 2003. LNCS, vol. 2788, pp. 303–316. Springer, Heidelberg (2003)
18. Ridderhof, W., Gross, H.-G., Doerr, H.: Establishing evidence for safety cases in automotive systems–A case study. In: Saglietti, F., Oster, N. (eds.) SAFECOMP 2007. LNCS, vol. 4680, pp. 1–13. Springer, Heidelberg (2007)
19. Nejati, S., et al.: A SysML-based approach to traceability management and design slicing in support of safety certification: Framework, tool support, and case studies. Information and Software Technology 54, 569–590 (2012)
20. Katta, V., Stalhane, T.: A conceptual model of traceability for safety systems. In: CSDM-Poster Presentation (2010)
21. Zoughbi, G., Briand, L., Labiche, Y.: Modeling safety and airworthiness (RTCA DO-178B) information: conceptual model and UML profile. Software & Systems Modeling 10, 337–367 (2011)
22. Born, M., et al.: Application of ISO DIS 26262 in practice. In: CARS 2010, pp. 3–6 (2010)
23. Graydon, P., Habli, I., Hawkins, R., Kelly, T., Knight, J.: Arguing Conformance. IEEE Software 29, 50–57 (2012)
24. OMG: Structured Assurance Case Metamodel (SACM) (2013)
25. Panesar-Walawege, R.K., et al.: Supporting the Verification of Compliance to Safety Standards via Model-Driven Engineering: Approach, Tool-Support and Empirical Validation. Information and Software Technology 55(5), 836–864 (2012)
26. Sun, L., Kelly, T.: Elaborating the Concept of Evidence in Safety Cases. In: SCSC 2013 (2013)
27. RTCA: DO-178C - Software Considerations in Airborne Systems and Equipment (2012)
28. De la Vara, J.L., et al.: Towards a model-based evolutionary chain of evidence for compliance with safety standards. In: SAFECOMP 2012 Workshops, pp. 64–78 (2012)
29. Oxford Dictionaries (online), http://oxforddictionaries.com
30. Olivé, A.: Conceptual Modeling of Information Systems. Springer (2007)
31. ISO: International Standard Road vehicles - Functional safety - ISO/DIS 26262 (2011)
32. CENELEC: Railway applications - Communications, signalling and processing systems - Software for railway control and protection systems - EN 50128 (2011)
33. Leveson, N.: The Use of Safety Cases in Certification and Regulation. Journal of System Safety 47 (2011)
34. OPENCOSS: D1.2 – Use case description and business impact (2012)
35. Gorschek, T., et al.: A model for technology transfer in practice. IEEE Software 23, 88–95 (2006)
36. Gotel, O., et al.: The quest for Ubiquity: A roadmap for software and systems traceability research. In: RE 2012, pp. 71–80 (2012)
37. Mäder, P., Jones, P., Zhang, Y., Cleland-Huang, J.: Strategic Traceability for Safety-Critical Projects. IEEE Software 30(3), 58–66 (2013)

Author Index